Making the European Polity

Reflexive integration in the EU

Edited by Erik Oddvar Eriksen

Routledge
Taylor & Francis Group

LONDON AND NEW YORK

First published 2005
by Routledge
2 Park Square, Milton Park, Abingdon, Oxon OX14 4RN

Simultaneously published in the USA and Canada
by Routledge
270 Madison Ave, New York, NY 10016

Routledge is an imprint of the Taylor & Francis Group

Typeset in Baskerville by Wearset Ltd, Boldon, Tyne and Wear
Printed and bound in Great Britain by MPG Books Ltd, Bodmin

British Library Cataloguing in Publication Data
A catalogue record for this book is available from the British Library

Library of Congress Cataloging in Publication Data
A catalog record for this book has been requested

ISBN 0–415–36301–2

Making the European Polity

The EU has developed beyond a mere market and is more than an international organization. But is it becoming a state, something less or something different? This book asks whether the EU is developing into a regulatory entity, a value-based polity or a rights-based post-national union. On the basis of in-depth analyses of social and tax policy, foreign and security policy, identity formation, the reform process and the constitutional effects of enlargement, the authors find that the Union has moved in the direction of a post-national union.

Making the European Polity sets out a reflexive approach to integration. It conceives of the EU as a law-based supranational polity lacking the identity of a people as well as the coercive means of a state. It seeks to compensate for this lack through extensive processes of deliberation. The EU is a polity with no sole apex of authority, but with an organized (limited) capacity to act. It has no sovereign demos – no people – but is involved in reflexive processes of constitutionalizing itself. It is a polity premised on a thin kind of statehood – a supranational polity with a deliberative imprint.

This book will appeal to social theorists and political scientists and particularly to students of European Politics.

Erik Oddvar Eriksen is Professor of Political Science at ARENA, Centre for European Studies at the University of Oslo, Norway. He heads the Commission-funded project on Citizenship and Democratic Legitimacy in the European Union (CIDEL). His main research fields are political theory, democratic governance, public policy and European integration.

Routledge studies on democratizing Europe
Edited by Erik Oddvar Eriksen and John Erik Fossum
ARENA, University of Oslo

Routledge Studies on Democratizing Europe focuses on the prospects for a citizens' Europe by analysing the kind of order that is emerging in Europe. The books in the series take stock of the EU as an entity that has progressed beyond intergovernmentalism and consider how to account for this process and whether it is democratic. The emphasis is on citizenship, constitution-making, public sphere, enlargement, common foreign and security policy and social and tax policy.

1 **Developing a Constitution for Europe**
   Edited by Erik Oddvar Eriksen, John Erik Fossum and Agustín José Menéndez

2 **Making the European Polity**
   Reflexive integration in the EU
   Edited by Erik Oddvar Eriksen

Contents

Illustrations

Contributors

James Francis Bohman is Danforth Professor of Philosophy at Saint Louis University, Missouri. He has published books and articles on political philosophy (including issues of transnational and deliberative democracy), philosophy of social science and German philosophy, including *Public Deliberation: Pluralism, Complexity, and Democracy* (1996), *Deliberative Democracy* (co-edited with William Rehg) (1997), *Perpetual Peace: Essays on Kant's Cosmopolitan Ideal* (co-edited with Matthias Lutz-Bachmann) (1997), *Pluralism and the Pragmatic Turn* (co-edited with William Rehg) (2001) and the forthcoming *Democracy across Borders*.

Gerard Delanty is Professor of Sociology and Head of the Department of Sociology at the University of Liverpool. He has written on various issues in social theory and general sociology, and is Chief Editor of the *European Journal of Social Theory*. A brief selection of his books includes *Inventing Europe: Idea, Identity, Reality* (1995), *Citizenship in the Global Age* (2000), *Nationalism and Social Theory* (with Patrick O'Mahony) (2002) and *Community* (2003).

Erik Oddvar Eriksen is Professor of Political Science at ARENA, University of Oslo. His main fields of interest are political theory, democratic governance, public policy and European integration. Recent publications include *Democracy in the European Union* (co-edited with John Erik Fossum) (2000), *Understanding Habermas* (co-authored with Jarle Weigård) (2003), *The Chartering of Europe* (co-edited with John Erik Fossum and Agustín José Menéndez) (2003) and *Developing a Constitution for Europe* (co-edited with John Erik Fossum and Agustín José Menéndez) (2004).

John Erik Fossum is Senior Researcher at ARENA, University of Oslo and Associate Professor at the University of Bergen. His research is focused on constitutionalism and democratic legitimacy in the EU and Canada. Among his publications are *Oil, the State, and Federalism* (1997) and 'The European Union in Search of an Identity' in *European Journal of Political Theory* (2003). He is also co-editor of *Democracy in the European Union*

(2000), *The Chartering of Europe* (2003) and *Developing a Constitution for Europe* (2004).

Kerstin Jacobsson is Senior Lecturer of Sociology at Södertörn University College and Research Fellow at the Stockholm Centre for Organizational Research (SCORE). Her recent publications include *Mot en europeisk välfärdspolitik? Ny politik och nya samarbetsformer i EU* (with Karl Magnus Johansson and Magnus Ekengren) (2001) and *Learning to Be Employable: New Agendas on Work, Responsibility and Learning in a Globalizing World* (co-edited with Christina Garsten) (2004).

Agustín José Menéndez is Ramón y Cajal Researcher at the University of León and part-time Senior Researcher at ARENA, University of Oslo. Recent publications include *Justifying Taxes: Some Elements of a General Theory of Democratic Tax Law* (2001). He is also co-editor of *The Chartering of Europe* (2003) and *Developing a Constitution for Europe* (2004).

Bernhard Peters is Professor and Executive Director at the Institute for International and Intercultural Studies (InIIS) at Bremen University. His fields of interest include social and political theory, public culture and public discourse and the integration of modern societies. Among his publications are *Rationalität, Recht und Gesellschaft* (1991), *Die Integration moderner Gesellschaften* (1993), 'Deliberative Öffentlichkeit' in Lutz Wingert and Klaus Günther (eds) *Die Öffentlichkeit der Vernunft und die Vernunft der Öffentlichkeit* (2001) and *Identity and Integration: Migrants in Western Europe* (co-edited with Rosemarie Sackmann and Thomas Faist) (2003).

Rainer Schmalz-Bruns is Professor at the Institute for Political Science at the University of Hannover. His current research focuses among other themes on democratic legitimacy in multilevel systems, transnational constitutionalism, supranational and transnational institutions. Publications include *Reflexive Demokratie* (1995), 'Deliberativer Supranationalismus' in *Zeitschrift für Internationale Beziehungen* (1999), 'The Postnational Constellation: Democratic Governance in the Era of Globalization' in *Constellations* (2001) and 'The Normative Desirability of Participatory Governance' in Hubert Heinelt *et al.* (eds) *Participatory Governance in Multilevel Context* (2002).

Helene Sjursen is Senior Researcher at ARENA, University of Oslo. Her fields of interest encompass EU enlargement and the European Foreign and Security Policy. Her publications include *A Common Foreign Policy of Europe?* (co-edited with John Peterson) (1998), *The United States, Western Europe and the Polish Crisis, International Relations in the Second Cold War* (2003) and *Contemporary European Foreign Policy* (co-edited with Walter Carlsneas and Brian White) (2004).

Åsa Vifell is Ph.D. Candidate in Political Science at Stockholm University and Stockholm Centre for Organizational Research (SCORE). Her research project is on the internationalization of the Swedish public administration; and she has published 'Samtal bakom lyckta dörrar' (with Kerstin Jacobsson) in Rune Premfors and Klas Roth (eds) *Deliberativ Demokrati* (2004).

Acknowledgements

This book started with a conference on *Democratic Governance and Institutional Dynamics in the EU* at ARENA (Centre for European Studies) in Oslo, 3–4 October 2003. In addition to contributions from the participants of this conference, I have profited greatly from discussions within the CIDEL consortium. CIDEL – Citizenship and Democratic Legitimacy in the European Union – is a joint research project between ten partners in six European countries. The project is coordinated by ARENA at the University of Oslo and financed by the Fifth Framework Programme of the European Commission. CIDEL involves about 20 researchers within political science, law, media research and sociology. The many workshops on different sub-themes of European integration that this project has hosted, have made it abundantly clear to me how intriguing, in empirical as well as in normative terms, the EU experiment really is. It is very much a theoretical challenge. European integration is unique and multi-dimensional and challenges the established frames of reference of political analysis as well as the building blocks of political science. In this book we set out a reflexive approach to integration based on the assumption that, whenever there is conflict and power mechanisms are lacking, actors have to make out their differences through deliberation. The EU is seen to have developed beyond intergovernmentalism and the question is how to conceptualize the new entity. Is the EU becoming a state, something less or something different?

I am very grateful for the support provided by ARENA both economically and intellectually. I am deeply indebted to the participants of the CIDEL group for critical input as well as for splendid chocolate. Finally, I would like to thank Marit Eldholm and Geir Ove Kværk for excellent support in putting this book together.

Erik O. Eriksen
Oslo, 30 September 2004

Introduction

Erik O. Eriksen

The EU is the first grand-scale project of integration to be driven by peace rather than force. Hostility and conflict in Europe have been replaced by peaceful cooperation. We are witnessing the reorganization of political power in Europe and the transformation of government structures. These transformations are part of a process through which the European nation states transcend the Westphalian order. This order, which prioritized state sovereignty, is being transformed by legal developments that constrain the will power of the state on the basis of the rights of the citizens. Has the EU emerged beyond the status of an international regime or international organization based on the sovereignty of the state? It is a *large-scale experiment* searching for binding constitutional principles and institutional arrangements beyond the mode of rule entrenched in the nation state. It testifies to the fact that societies learn, not only individuals, to talk with Klaus Eder.

There is, however, confusion and disagreement about the core characteristics of the EU as well as about its future design. Currently, there are different notions of the EU as well as different theories of how to explain the integration process. The point of departure of this book is that, while interstate relations of the Westphalian phase were conducted through diplomacy and intergovernmental bargaining, we are now increasingly witnessing problem-solving, goal attainment and conflict resolution in policy networks and transnational institutions as well as in supranational organizations such as the European Parliament, the European Court of Justice and the Commission. What are the main characteristics of this political order and how can we explain its emergence and sustainability?

Both positive political science and political theory are struggling to comprehend the nature of this creature. Whilst positive political science searches for new ways of conceptualizing political orders 'above' intergovernmentalism and 'below' statism, normative theory is struggling with the yardsticks of democracy when assessing a polity which is more than an international regime but less than a state. Deliberative theory, which underpins the reflexive approach, is interesting because it attempts to bridge the gap between normative and positive theory. Deliberationists hold that integration is conducted through intelligent problem-solving and arguing in relation to shared norms and not solely according to the interests of the contracting partners. In this book a particular variant of this perspective is thought of as a theoretical alternative both to (neo)functionalism and liberal intergovernmentalism, which sees integration driven by 'unreflexive' spillover processes and 'non-deliberated' interest maximation respectively.

What does the reflexive approach contribute to in conceiving of the European integration process? This is the first question of this book. The second is how far the EU has moved beyond an international organization, a mere market regime in the hands of the member states, towards a polity in its own right, capable of collective action. What kind of order do the constitutive norms and values of the Union reflect and in what direction are present developments pointing? In addition to the option of a *market regime*, three alternatives are presented: a *regulatory entity* based on transnational structures of governance, a *value-based polity* premised on a common European identity and a *rights-based post-national union* – a federation – based on a full-fledged political citizenship.

The reason for asking such questions is that the Union is currently involved in a process of reforming itself by forging a constitution. Does this mean that the EU is moving towards becoming a sovereign government, a full-blown political polity based on:

- a fixed, contiguous and clearly delimited territory;
- a legitimate authority and entrenched hierarchical principles of law;
- a collective identity derived from a common history, tradition or fate;
- a cultural substrate associated with the nation; and/or
- a public sphere that performs catalytic functions for identity-formation;

or are we witnessing something less than a state, namely, a transnational regime based on a set of explicit principles established and sanctioned by international law?

The first part of the book lays out the reflexive approach to the integration processes and spells out its ramifications. The task is to explicate post-national integration and the ongoing constitutionalizing process. However, the authors disagree about how much 'statehood' a post-national democracy requires. In the first chapter I launch the reflexive approach to integration and underline the role of law and political institutions. James Bohman in Chapter 2 reconstructs the EU as a transnational regime based on multiperspectival deliberative inquiry. Compared to this, Rainer Schmalz-Bruns' take on reflexive integration, in Chapter 3, puts a stronger onus on hierarchical elements. In Chapter 4, Bernhard Peters conceives of the resources for integration much in line with the statehood model and is hence pessimistic with regard to post-national integration.

Can there be a legitimate system of rule when there is no European demos – no European people based on a common identity?

As the EU is a complex organization, and processes are multifaceted and different areas of integration proceed by their own logic and speed – the institutional dynamics are diverse – it is important to conduct issue-specific studies. We therefore in Part II undertake analyses of the steps towards a common social and tax policy and a common foreign policy (Chapters 7, 8 and 9). Together with studies of identity formation, constitution-making reforms, and the constitutional effects of enlargement (Chapters 5, 6 and 10), these make up the second part of the book. Chapter 11 synthesizes the findings.

In Chapter 1, I give a brief account of the deliberative, reflexive perspective on the European integration process. Integration may occur through coercion and intergovernmental bargaining – through blackmail, path-dependency, functional adaptation, copying, diffusion or exit – but it may also occur through reflexive reason-giving and entrenched commitments. I examine integration from a deliberative perspective. Deliberation has to be supplemented with law and trust in order to explain integration. Moreover, in a full-blown polity problem-solving must be complemented with mechanisms of collective goal attainment and impartial conflict resolution. This constitutes the basis for delineating the four stylized analytical models of the EU – a market regime, a regulatory entity, a value-based polity and a rights-based post-national union.

In Chapter 2, Bohman outlines a reflexive approach to integration focused on the constitution-making process of the Union. He conceives of the EU as a *polycentric system of transnational governance* – a regulatory entity. As this system is presently tormented by legal domination it is in need of democratization. The basic normative category is non-domination according to the dictum of 'interdependence without subordination'. The insufficiency of the rule of law for non-domination at the transnational scale, suggests a deliberative framework and reflexive testing of the normative legal framework. Bohman sees the EU as a diverse polity, with multiple overlapping demoi and no apex of authority, where sovereignty is pooled and competencies shared. The solution to the problem of legal domination is that the constitution institute a reflexive legal order best realized in spontaneous and horizontally dispersed polyarchies. This requires a process of practical testing, which is possible only if deliberation can be properly organized. But can such an approach be sustained in normative terms?

Based on a desubstantialized notion of a sovereign demos, Schmalz-Bruns in the next chapter sets out to establish a conceptual alternative that is based on internally linking the idea of people's sovereignty, the principle of public and inclusive justification, with the idea of a demos. This is a normative model of *a transnational polity* of internally deliberative institutions, which is sufficiently reflexive so as to make it democratic, in the sense that political issues, rights and duties, can be passed through the public deliberation of citizens. It is, on the basis of a constitution and the capacity to act that meaning and content can be given to the idea of reflexive integration. Thus a democratic polity must have a hierarchical element, it cannot be just a multiperspectival and horizontally dispersed structure of governance as Bohman contends. In Part II of the book we return to the question of whether the EU is actually becoming more than a polycentric transnational polity. But first we need to know more about the connection between deliberation, identity and a democratic polity.

Peters addresses, in Chapter 4, the relationship between the concepts in the *magic quadrangle* of political theory: discourse, democracy, identity and legitimacy. They represent the conceptual constellation of any political order that aspires to democratic self-government. On the basis of such a model it is hard to see how the EU could establish the necessary conditions, not to say replicate the conditions of nation-state democracy. Is post-national democracy really viable and on what basis should assessments and predictions be made? The answer to what kind of political order is required to ensure basic rights and collective goal attainment beyond the nation state depends to a large degree on empirical facts that we do not possess sufficient knowledge of. Due to the present state of affairs in the media, where the dramatization of conflict and disagreement prevails over the search for consensus, Peters is cautious on the extent to which public deliberation on its own can bear the burden of legitimation. In Europe the public debate is also constrained by the lack of an imagined collective 'we' beyond national borders – *a common European identity*.

These chapters make up the first part of the book. A concept of reflexive integration based on the mechanisms of public deliberation has been established, with the necessary complements in the form of *law* – the requirements of legal rules and sanctions, and *trust* – the requirements of common values and identity. In the second part of the book we apply the four stylized notions of the EU that were fleshed out in Chapter 1 to different policy areas of the Union and ask whether we see a rights-based union in the making. This is undertaken with regard to the constitutional reform process, foreign and security policy, tax and social policy and the constitutional implications of enlargement. But first we ask how we should conceive of a European identity?

Gerard Delanty in Chapter 5 explores what kind of a collective identity a poly-ethnic society such as the EU can possibly have. On the basis of current research on post-national identifications he contends that a European identity should be conceived of in cosmopolitan terms, as embodied in the everyday life of Europeans and not in a supranational European identity. Rather than an official EU identity in tension with national identities, the core characteristic of European identities is found in the pluralized cultural models of a societal identity. One of the striking features of European identities is that they arise in discursive contexts – they are highly diverse and are often *reflexively* articulated – but as identities, they all unavoidably have a familiar European dimension. This amounts to a kind of *cosmopolitan societal identity*, which speaks to the option of the EU as a post-national rights-based polity. The European identity is a form of post-national self-understanding that expresses itself within, as much as beyond, national identities.

John Erik Fossum assesses, in Chapter 6, the question of the EU's legitimacy on the basis of the practice and the results of the Constitutional Convention. Contemporary European constitution-making is made more reflexive. The Convention came up with a draft Constitutional Treaty and represents an exercise that has moved the Union closer to a rights-based polity. On the one hand, in terms of overarching principles, the EU draws on those that mark the *common* constitutional traditions of the member states, and then on already justified norms. But the Convention continued the Union's unique mix of the common constitutional traditions of the member states and treaty law with the effort to distil a constitution from the *acquis*. The draft reduced the polycentricity and enhanced the legal unity and democratic character of the Union. It depicts the EU as a bi-cephalous entity and represents a new blend of intergovernmental and supranational structures.

In Chapter 7, Helene Sjursen analyses the trends towards a post-national foreign and security policy. Discussions about forging a common foreign and security policy have been a central part of the agenda of European integration from its very inception. Since the early 1970s a gradual building of common institutions, positions and policies has taken place. Sjursen questions the predominant perception of the foreign-policy field within the EU that speaks to the EU as a 'problem-solving entity', with little onus on collective tasks and obligations beyond the interests and preferences of the member states. The output is not limited when taking into consideration the institutions and procedures in the making in this field. But as the EU lacks military capability of its own, it is more of an instrument for human security – peacekeeping and rescue tasks.

Agustín José Menéndez, in Chapter 8, reviews the actual powers of the European Union with regard to taxation. The power to tax is one major indicator of a state-like polity, but the EU has very limited legislative tax competencies. However, on the basis of a proper unpacking of the treaty provisions, seeing that it has to do both with 'ordinary' and constitutional politics, Menéndez finds that the legislative power to tax is shared between the Union and the member states. The EU has power to tax, although limited, and has obtained a tax base of its own. In order to establish what this tells us concerning the political nature of the Union, he tests out three models of a taxing EU. The tax base is all too limited for the Union to grasp with its task portfolio, which however also pertains to the lack of effective instruments of policy-making.

In the wake of the Lisbon summit in 2000 the Open Method of

Coordination (OMC) has developed into an important action-coordinating strategy of the EU. In Chapter 9, Kerstin Jacobsson and Åsa Vifell examine the integration potential of this method from a deliberative perspective. OMC makes possible concerted European action in policy areas which are under member-state jurisdiction, such as social and employment policies. Focusing on employment-policy coordination, the authors analyse preparatory committees placed between the Commission and the Council. In spite of the elitist and economic character of deliberation in these committees, where agreements are reached because competing views are excluded, the OMC includes a wide circle of actors and has allowed a *functional expansion* of cooperation into new – and sensitive – welfare areas. While hardly able in itself to balance the problematic aspects of European economic integration, this soft coordination at least serves to complement it by raising other types of concerns and by institutionalizing discourse on them.

In Chapter 10, John Erik Fossum, Helene Sjursen and I address the constitutional effects of enlargement. Does enlargement merely mean the widening of the present Union or does it have further polity implications? The European Union requires that the applicant countries comply with normative principles such as the rule of law, human rights and democracy. However, the Union does not itself comply with these. Due to reason-giving and critical scrutiny promoted through public debate and institutionalized deliberation, living by double standards becomes problematic. But the EU is in the process of reforming itself; and the Constitutional Treaty includes a Charter of Fundamental Rights containing provisions on civil, political, social and economic rights generally associated with constitutional provisions. This analysis not only shows that the EU has moved beyond the principles laid down in the Treaty of Westphalia, it also shows that this transformation is conducted according to the criteria of legitimate government. The EU has left the fate of the new constitution in the hands of states that are still not formally members. What kind of polity is the EU then?

On the basis of preceding chapters, in Chapter 11, I find that the EU has proceeded towards a polity in its own right capable of collective action. Even though the EU is a complex organization where concerted action varies across levels and policy fields, it has amended its competences in most areas and has moved into a quasi-democratic, supranational legal system based on the precepts of higher-law constitutionalism. The pillar structure has been weakened; the allocation of competencies of the decision-making bodies has been circumscribed; the European Parliament empowered. The EU is a law-based supranational polity lacking the identity as well as the coercive means of a state, a lack it attempts to compensate for through extensive processes of deliberation. Hence the concept of *deliberative supranationalism*, which depicts the Euro-polity as a law-based government premised on a particular mode of interaction generating allegiance and making for collective decision-making.

Part I

Reflexive polity-building and post-national integration

1 Reflexive integration in Europe

Erik O. Eriksen

Today's Europe is marked by a remarkable pace of integration. Major changes have taken place within a short period of time. The integration is deepening – a wide range of new policy fields have been subjected to integrated action and collective decision-making – as well as widening.[1] The European Union (EU) now consists of 25 member states. However, there is confusion and disagreement about its future design among experts as well as laymen. But despite disagreement the EU is currently about to transform itself and establish itself as an autonomous polity. It is about to proclaim itself as a political union with extended competencies. Since the late 1980s, European cooperation has progressed and changed the cooperative scheme of an international organization whose legitimacy derived solely from the member states – the Masters of the Treaties – to an organization in its own right. Increasingly, majority vote has replaced unanimity as a decision rule in several policy fields. Progressively the Union has obtained a resource basis of its own. It has become a polity which allocates and reallocates values throughout Europe. In fact, the EU, which is a creature of the member states, has contributed to transform them, either directly or by unleashing processes of mutual learning and adaptation.

These transformations are part of a process through which the European nation states transcend the Westphalian order. Integration in Europe, then, not only testifies to the Europeanization of the nation states but also to new forms of political governance emerging beyond the system of interstate relations. It constitutes a new type of political order that does not fit into the traditional dichotomy of intergovernmental versus nation-state regulation. What is the EU then? Integrated European cooperation has moved it beyond the status of a market regime, but does the EU simply represent transnational risk regulation and problem-solving, or is it reflective of a supranational move based on common values – a value-based community – and/or reflective of a development towards a rights-based post-national union, based on a full-fledged political citizenship?

In this book we explore the possibility of deliberation as an analytical category to explain integration beyond the nation state. Deliberation designates the rule of reasons, namely, that actors coordinate their actions by

giving and responding to reasons (Habermas 1981; Forst 2001). Deliberative theory based on communicative rationality constitutes the reflexive
approach. The actors reflexively monitor the circumstances of their activities and base their interventions on intersubjectively accessible reasons.
The usefulness of this approach to transnational and supranational
systems of governance stems from the fact that such systems to a large
degree lack forceful compliance mechanisms. The EU is a non-hierarchical
system based on voluntary cooperation. The reflexive approach is seen as
an alternative to the rational choice perspective underpinning 'liberal
intergovernmentalism', which sees integration as driven by the interest
maximation of the contracting parties (Moravcsik 1998). It is also an
alternative to neo-functionalism's perspective on 'unreflective' spillover
processes from 'low' to 'high politics' (Haas 1961).

In this chapter I outline the reflexive approach to the European
integration process with regard to the basic analytical categories, *deliberation* and *problem-solving*. First, I address some developments of the EU
integration process and the dynamics that have pushed it in a supranational direction. Second, I point to deliberation as the medium of
problem-solving, which, however, requires *trust* and *law* as complementary
resources for collective action. In a third move I see polity-building as a
problem-solving procedure based on experimental inquiry, but one that
needs to be supplemented with mechanisms for *collective goal attainment*
and *impartial conflict resolution*. After this I outline four analytical models of
the EU which represent ideal-typical polity options. They are premised on
different merits of deliberation – epistemic, transformative and moral.

A heterarchical order?

The EU is not a federation nor is it a confederation. While the latter
depicts a union of states – with indirect and delegated powers – a federal
system is *a union of citizens* based on an institutional arrangement like that
of a sovereign state albeit more complex. The European polity has clear
supranational elements such as the European Court of Justice (ECJ),
which guarantees supremacy of EU law within its field of competence, and
a directly elected Parliament which has obtained the power of co-decision
with the intergovernmental Council in a wide range of policy fields. The
term polity in the present use does not imply a full-fledged state, but a
system in which a central polity coexists with local units. In Europe the
member states and the EU have both shared and independent powers
with neither having supreme authority over the other. The EU has got
supranational political institutions, a Central Bank, a single currency and
a material constitution. It is now also aspiring to be a polity with competencies on foreign and security policy. The EU has supranational dimensions but does not fit the customary concept of state, as it does not possess
the required means, such as monopoly of violence and taxation, or a well-

developed collective identity necessary for majority vote, to enforce its will. It is not sovereign within a fixed, contiguous and clearly delimited territory.[2] There are no European jails, army or police force.

The EU is a polity without a nation and a state. The supranationality marking it is non-hierarchical and a consequence of its peculiar 'separation of powers', which is due to the role of the Commission and the Council, which combine representative and executive functions. This kind of supranationality ensures the member states a strong and consistent say in collective decision-making processes, in particular through the Council of the European Union. The institutional structure of the EU embodies a complex mixture of supranational, transnational and intergovernmental elements. There is disagreement among scholars with regard to how this order should be portrayed.

Some analysts see the EU as a *system of multilevel and multi-centric governance.* Decision-making and implementation are diffused to networks, partnerships and private actors in transnational structures of governance. Common problems requiring common solutions are coordinated by joint problem-solving in agencies and committees.[3] The exercise of political authority is no longer exclusively statal – the relationship between state and non-state actors is non-hierarchical. Such a regime is based on shared authority, and the major task is not 'redistribution', but 'regulation' of social and political risks. Hence the prevalence of *governance* and not political rule through responsible institutions such as parliament and bureaucracy – generally thought of as *government* based on one single (mono-cephalous) line of accountability anchored in the rights of the citizens. Governance represents innovative practices of networks and horizontal forms of interaction. It is based on a private-law framework where the production of norms is seen as the result of a spontaneous coordination process. It is a method for dealing with political controversies in which actors, political and non-political, arrive at mutually acceptable decisions by deliberating and negotiating with each other on the basis of 'soft law'. In this view the EU comes close to a *heterarchy:* political authority is not centralized as in the hierarchical order of the state model nor is it decentralized as in an anarchical order. Rather the units of the system pool their sovereignties. There is:

> a shift from a hierarchical substantive orientation, to be found in given rules and aims, to a horizontal heterarchical and procedural approach, operating with the localised and linked potential generated from private and public action and the linkages inherent to them.
>
> (Ladeur 1999: 156)

Heterarchy is, however, deficient in empirical terms because a supranational structure endowed with a *dispute-resolution mechanism* is in place, namely, a court that bases its rulings on recognition of the primacy of

Union law and on the principle of rule of (hard) law. The integration process has moved the EU beyond an international organization as well as beyond a heterarchy. Due to this fact, democracy needs to be brought to bear on the EU. Its actions have consequences for the citizens' interests and values, for their freedom and welfare. The acts of the Union are thus not merely regulative as they allocate resources throughout Europe and affect EU citizens in most walks of life, even if only by means of impeding other levels' ability to act. Heterarchy is deficient with regard to democracy in that there is little chance of equal access and public accountability. Egalitarian structures of law-making are lacking. An order exercising power in the form of conflict resolution and resource allocation is in need of popular control according to the dictum that all legislative power stems from the people. 'Whatever a people cannot impose upon itself cannot be imposed upon it by the legislator either' (Kant 1797: 85). I return to the democratic problem of the Union in Chapter 11. The question now is how to explain the making of a supranational order.

The dynamics of integration

European cooperation started out as a pragmatic form of collaboration on coal and steel, underpinned by the peace motive. World Wars I and II profoundly affected the states and citizens all over Europe; and all depended on each other for a peaceful restoration of Europe after the war. Cooperation was initially problem-solving for the members due to their interdependence. Solving common problems led to more cooperation, the building of trust relationships and to the discovery of new areas of common concern. Increasingly, supranational polity formation took place with conflict-resolution and goal-attainment institutions of its own, which, however, spurred new questions about the legitimacy basis of such a polity.

> In the beginning, [the European Union] was more of an economic and technical collaboration. [...] At long last, Europe is on its way to becoming one big family, without bloodshed, a real transformation clearly calling for a different approach from fifty years ago, when six countries first took the lead.
>
> (European Council 2001b)

The reflexive approach sees cooperation as a response to societal problems, and institution formation as a response to the indirect consequences of such cooperation, which increasingly catches on and has polity consequences. Polity-building is the result of deepened integration driven by intelligent problem-solving, but problem-solving leads to juridification, to more legal regulation, which again triggers claims to democracy and *reflexive juridification*, as James Bohman puts it in the present volume. It is 'legalization without democratic politics' (Brunkhorst 2004: 100). Hence the integration process is not a linear mono-causal process driven by unintended feedback loops as analytical functionalism suggests, neither by the federalist ideas of constitutionalists like Altiero Spinelli (1966) and Ernesto Rossi, nor by 'the hidden hand' of Jean Monnet who foresaw a federation as the necessary outcome of closer cooperation (Monnet 1978: 392f). Rather, the integration process is to a large degree driven by contestation and opposition as it came to be seen as a technocratic, elite-driven project conducted in isolation from the people. The obvious answer to such allegations comprised democratic reforms, which, however implied more integration and supranationalism.

Integration is a process where actors shift their loyalties and activities towards a new centre with the authoritative right to regulate interests and allocate resources (Schmitter 1969: 166). Integration thus entails solving the problem of collective action – the free-rider problem. In causal terms, we may conceive of integration beyond the nation state as a process where states and non-state actors cooperate in joint problem-solving sites across national borders in Europe, thereby creating a *transnational society*. As the activities increase, common standards, rules and dispute-resolution mechanisms – regulation and coordinating mechanisms – become necessary, which, in turn, trigger reflexive and self-reflexive processes conducive to the establishment of authoritative institutions that can control and command obedience in the name of all. Hence the European institutions develop into something more than agents of the member states (Stone Sweet 2004: 236). The EU becomes a polity in its own right.

The supranational character of the Union's legal structure started with the constitutionalization of the treaty system, which transformed the EC from an international regime into a quasi-federal legal system based on the precepts of higher-law constitutionalism. All legal persons and not just states, have judicially enforceable rights. Furthermore, Article 177 of the Treaty of Rome (EEC) states that, whenever Community law is needed for the resolution of a dispute before a national court, the presiding judge may (sometimes must) request the ECJ for an adequate and authoritative interpretation. Due to case law, the *Doctrine of Supremacy* (1964) states that, in cases of disputes between a national norm and an EC legal norm, the national norm must give way; and the *Doctrine of Direct Effect* (1962, 1974) says that, under certain conditions, EC norms – Treaty law and secondary legislation – grant the citizens rights that must be protected in national courts. In the Treaty establishing a Constitution for Europe, recognition of the primacy of Union law is now stated (European Council 2004c: Articles I-6 and I-12). Further, the progressive strengthening of the doctrines of supremacy and direct effect is coupled with the growth of the number of EU provisions and Court rulings, where the Court acts as a trustee of the treaty and not as an agent of the member states. The net upshot is that:

The constitutionalization of the Treaty of Rome constitutes an 'unintended consequence' of monumental proportions. The member states, after all, had designed an enforcement system that one can characterize as 'international law plus', being (a) the compulsory nature of the Court's jurisdiction, and (b) the obligatory participation of the Commission in various proceedings.

(Stone Sweet 2003: 27)[4]

The present state of affairs is due to a protracted process of integration since its inception with the Paris Treaty. The basis for cooperation deepened and broadened: from the Paris (1951) and Rome (1957) Treaties, through the Single European Act (1986), Maastricht (1992), Amsterdam (1997), Nice (2000), to the Laeken Declaration (2001) and the present-day work on forging a constitution. The EU is clearly something less than a federation but more than a club, a 'Zweckbundnis' (Verband), regime or a confederation. The latter cannot be democratic as it is the states not the citizens that are the masters; states are the sole sources of legitimacy and they act internationally on indirect and delegated powers on governance functions. The member states are the contracting parties in an intergovernmental organization. However, at least from the early 1990s, the EU has proclaimed its commitment to democracy, and to the principle of *direct legitimacy*: the power-wielding institutions should be authorized by the people and be accountable to the affected parties. The Charter of Fundamental Rights (2000) included now as part II of the Constitutional Treaty is the most explicit commitment as yet to a full-blown political union founded on democracy and human rights – a rights-based citizens' Union (Eriksen *et al.* 2003a).

In order to understand the dynamics of such a development, we need to explore the concept of problem-solving which is at the heart of the European integration project. It is a vital issue in explaining the integration process but what does its coordinative power consist of?

Problem-solving, voting and bargaining

In political science *problem-solving* is a mode of decision-making distinguished from *bargaining* and *confrontation*. Confrontation denotes the appeal to the will (volition) or preference of a dominant actor (or coalition of actors) who has the means to compel compliance if necessary. In formalized political systems majority *vote* is the basic mechanism of sanction in the confrontational mode. It is those who control the most votes that win. Bargaining may be depicted as the strategic employment of threats and warnings in order to achieve given ends.[5] Control over vital resources outside the negotiation site – such as the threats of exit, strike and lockout – is the action-coordinating mechanism of bargaining. In bargaining sites it is the resources not the votes that decide (Rokkan 1966).

In both cases external-sanction mechanisms are employed – the number of votes and the resources at disposal – in order to reach a decision. Voting and bargaining both sanction action and terminate the decision-making process solely on the basis of quantitative vectors. When it comes to problem-solving there need not be such external sanction mechanism in play to ensure compliance with a plan of action. Rather its coordinative power may stem from the cooperation process itself, or so I shall argue.

Fritz Scharpf (1988: 258) contends that problem-solving is premised on the 'appeal to common ("solidaristic") values' and 'resort to ostracism and exclusion as the ultimate collective sanction'. The capacity to coordinate action is in this case dependent upon the prevailing habits, customs, conventions and then on the ultimate threat of exclusion of non-compliers. However, problem-solving also takes place when such preconditions do not exist. The coordinative force of problem-solving – its ability to harmonize action – should therefore be sought for in the process itself, in the process of finding efficient or right solutions.[6] Scharpf's conception of problem-solving seems to: 1) overestimate the pool of collective values required; and 2) underestimate the force of reasons in the coordination of actions.

1   Agreement on values, on the common good, may be more or less present, may be diffuse and may even be non-existent as a resource for joint problem-solving. Further, given the social and cultural complexity of modern societies, such a 'collectivistic substrate' can not merely be taken for granted. The presence of *a value consensus* based on common virtues and a collective we-feeling may not be counted on in a pluralistic context. On the other hand, a common value base required for collective action can be created through enduring social interaction and communicative practices. It can result from intensified cooperation.

2   Problem-solving refers to the use of knowledge in a given situation. It has a cognitive dimension and is thus accessible for rational appraisal. Critical interlocutors may query whether the knowledge base is adequate for the choice of action. Is sufficient information collected for cogent decision-making? Problem-solving has to do with the finding of answers to posed questions and with solutions that may or may not be rational, namely, well grounded. It is a cooperative effort in order to overcome exigencies and obstacles in a manner that can be deemed successful or not successful, good or bad, right or wrong.

The logic underpinning problem-solving thus differs from that of the other two modes of decision-making – bargaining and voting – in that it does not contain a clear-cut external sanction mechanism, but is dependent on the *process*. That is, on the manner in which the participants define problems and suggest solutions and on the nature and quality of the process in which they assess and justify proposals and solutions. This means that the resource base and the potential for effective sanctioning are not at the same level of formalization as that of the former two, making calculation and prediction of the results of the interaction process more difficult. Problem-solving is inherently linked to reflection, reason-giving and reaching common understanding. The medium for this is *deliberation* as it compels actors to verbalize and justify their plans of action in case of conflict. This may change someone's attitudes or beliefs, which is necessary in order for actors to harmonize action plans voluntarily.

Deliberation and will formation

When identities and values are involved, when actors do not know who they are or what they want, they cannot bargain or vote; when opinions differ and consensus on a common metric is missing, actors must argue. In this way deliberation reaches deeper than bargaining and voting. One cannot hold a vote or bargain unless alternatives are clarified and conflicts resolved so that a common understanding, at least as to what one disagrees about, is established. One must also *argue for* choosing the bargaining and voting procedures. The deliberative process of arguing and counter-arguing is a process 'that shapes *the identity and interests* of citizens in ways that contribute to the formation of a public conception of the public good' (Cohen 1989: 19). Deliberation designates the process of reaching agreement through reason-giving. Such a process may end in consensus with regard to a particular decision, or in conflict. In the latter case, deliberation needs to be succeeded by bargaining and/or voting.

In theoretical terms, deliberation is an action-coordinating mechanism suited to explaining the level of agreement and consensus reached in committees, conventions and networks. Its explanatory power is based on the motivational *force of reasons*, namely, that the insights into good reasons have behavioural consequences. Deliberation denotes an actor's attempt to come to an *agreement* about the definition of a situation, i.e. to reach a common *understanding* of how a given situation should be described. The ability to reach consensus on empirical and normative questions is due to the obligation to provide reasons, which is forced upon every participant in real discourses. In a well-performed deliberative process the participants will find out which reasons are good enough. Deliberation increases legitimacy as it includes affected parties and gives them a chance to argue their case. It also makes for qualitatively good and fair decisions as far as the members put forward arguments and respond to counter-arguments in a rational manner. Rational deliberation has a number of merits, including:

1   Deliberation leads to improvements in information and judgment: it is a cognitive process for the assessment of reasons in order to reach

just decisions and establish conceptions of the common good. This *epistemic value* of deliberation by implication also increases the likelihood that losers comply with majoritarian decisions.

2   Deliberation has the capacity of shaping preferences and transforming opinions conducive to collective will formation, namely, the *transformative value* of deliberation. This is due to the 'world-disclosing effect' of deliberation changing empirical and normative outlooks as well as collective self-interpretations.

3   It also has *moral value* as it is a constraint upon political power-holders. Only by justifying collective decisions towards the ones affected can one know whether or not they are right. Deliberation is a principle that sets the conditions for how to reach correct decisions, hence the concept of deliberative democracy.

Thus, deliberation does not merely constitute the medium of rational problem-solving and a coordinative mechanism, it also provides a democratic standard. One should, however, keep in mind that the epistemic dimension is vital to all theories of deliberation as far as they are premised on the acquisition and employment of knowledge and hence the force of reasons.

Reflexive polity-building

In this perspective deliberative politics is seen as a *reflexively organized learning process* – as a problem-solving procedure that brings in knowledge and relevant normative perspectives and qualifies (or validates) them in order to establish mutual understanding and agreement. 'Politics has the function of coordinating the learning process of the whole society' (Deutsch and Markovits 1980: 38). Deliberative politics, when institutionalized correctly, contributes to resolve conflicts impartially and achieve common aims legitimately. Consequently, we may conceive of societies as problem-solving entities in which success can be measured according to *collective rationality* – that is, according to standards of justice and the common good (Peters 1991: 204ff; Habermas 1996: 319).

The democratic procedure is a special variant of the idea of societal problem-solving as it represents the institutionalization of communicative processes for the selection of problems and solutions for a community. Reflexivity is here taken to depict the actor's rational monitoring of the circumstances of their activities. Deliberation is, then, not solely an instrument for reaching better decisions but also for learning through the testing of arguments. That agents can provide self-reflexive interpretations of, as well as provide intelligible, intersubjective reasons for, their behaviour is procedurally entrenched. The democratic procedure makes voice possible, challenges arguments and compels actors to justify their claims by institutionalizing critical opposition and choice opportunities. It spurs reflection over the process. Hence, we may speak of *institutional reflexivity*, which Giddens (1991: 20) defines as '[t]he regularized use of knowledge about circumstances of social life as a constitutive element in its organization and transformation'. Such *procedural self-reference* entails communication over communication and reflection over the selection of selections, to talk with Niklas Luhmann.[7] Of course, selections may be perverse and communication may fail,[8] but can, due to the epistemic value of public deliberation, be corrected. This value then not only increases the probability for compliance but also grounds the assumption of collective rationality as the outcome of well-conducted deliberative processes.

Such a perspective sits very well with the pragmatist theory of John Dewey (1927), to whom successful problem-solving depends on the degree to which actors manage to collaborate and engage in deliberation on a free and equal basis. Voluntary cooperation on practical questions, based on the free access to information and mutual deliberation, constitutes an 'intelligent' problem-solving method. The more free the participants are to suggest proposals and to assess information and assumptions, the more rational the problem-solving. It is this model of societal cooperation that Dewey applies to democracy, as he sees it as the political form of organization based on conscious deliberation and experimentation in which human intelligence can be fully realized. The growth of democratic communication is a requirement for *experimental inquiry* – for problem-solving within most fields of action in modern societies (Putnam 1991).

Dewey reconstructs polity-building stemming from simple forms of cooperation on solving common problems, namely, the collective inquiry of the citizens. There is no postulation of a collective identity or common interest at the outset – the society is not conceived of as an ethical society – but commonality is established during the process of attending to and solving the problems facing the actors:

> Recognition of evil consequences brought about a common interest which required for its maintenance certain measures and rules, together with the selection of certain persons as their guardians, interpreters, and, if need be, their executors.
>
> (Dewey 1927: 17)

The combined, unintended consequences of problem-solving lead to the formation of public spheres because it is in the affected parties' interest to control such consequences but also because there is an obligation to provide reasons to the ones affected.[9] A public sphere and subsequently a polity come about and become organized as far as the indirect consequences are discovered and the affected ones succeed in establishing regulative schemes of action by 'internalizing the externalities'.

Those indirectly and seriously affected for good or for evil form a group distinctive enough to require recognition and a name. The name selected is the Public. This public is organized and made effective by means of representatives who as guardians of custom, as legislators, as executives, judges, etc., care for its especial interest by methods intended to regulate the conjoint actions of individuals and groups. Then, and in so far association adds to itself political organization, and something which may be government comes into being: the public is a political state.

(Dewey 1927: 35)

However, in this theory of polity-building there is a true danger of scientism and technocracy.[10] Consequentialism bears the burden of justification. The rights that protect the integrity and autonomy of the individual, independent of their interests and problems, are missing. The principle of democratic justification in a deontological sense can hardly be compensated for by the inquiry of the citizens coming together to solve common problems. We are faced with the risk of forfeiting the individual for the collective good. The Deweyan perspective has to be supplemented because practical problem-solving according to the standards of efficiency and the collective good, involves burden-sharing and the allocation of costs, hence bringing about questions of rights and justice. There is a hierarchical dimension to the idea of reflexive self-constitutionalization, according to Schmalz-Bruns (Chapter 3), as reflexivity entails the public use of reason that establishes the *moral point of view* according to which moral reasons can appear as what they are – hierarchically superior. Democracy conceived of as self-government constituted by the unintended consequences of action must be supplemented with a rights-based perspective. Moreover, we should distinguish between the case when actors face the same challenge in a situation and wish to overcome it cooperatively, and when they run into a conflict which they want to solve consensually (Habermas 1989b). The former refers to what goals or what 'good society' we would like to realize – *goal attainment*, the latter to the rules for *conflict resolution*. The general problem of political integration on democratic terms, which has to do with the relationship between deliberation, law and trust, can be reconstructed in three steps.

Law, trust and deliberation

First, as integration has to do with shifting the bounds of loyalty and with the solving of the free-rider problem, it requires surrender or delegation of sovereignty. For integration to come about there is a need to overcome the problem of collective action, which arises as soon as a common good cannot be restricted for the ones bringing it about. For such, moral, deontic norms that tell what is obligatory, right and just are required to stabilize social relations. Interests and pragmatic concerns shift according to the problems to be solved and establish no stable basis for a polity. They do not guard against defection. The problem here is that, even though deliberative theory explicates the ability of actors to abide by the better argument, by standards of truth and justice, it does not explain collective action or the delegation of sovereignty. There may be reasons to oppose even a rational agreement; and nobody is obliged to comply with social norms unless all others also comply. Pure virtues and unsanctioned norms are too weak to integrate activities in larger collectivities; as instruments they are not strong enough to harness individual behaviour. Social norms need to be supplemented with legal statutes connecting breaches and defection with sanctions. Moreover, deliberation does not determine the necessary scope of participation in the deliberative process itself. These are the reasons why law based on subjective rights entitlements is such a conspicuous feature of modern societies.

Second, there is an unsettled issue with regard to the social or cultural substrate required for action coordination by means of communicative rationality. A minimum level of trust and confidence, a *modicum of non-egoistic commitment,* is necessary for cooperative goal attainment and conflict resolution to come about, for fair play and promise-keeping. Informal modes of social coordination are needed to solve numerous collective-action problems. Absence of trust paralyses collective action (Offe 1999). A common value base entrusts actors to engage in communicative relations, to enter the deliberative circle, allowing themselves to be swayed by the force of the better argument. Trust functions to absorb the risk of social disintegration that may arise when political orders are reproduced only through the mechanisms of law and deliberation. This condition refers to the pertinent question of the value base of Europe, the commonality, the shared we-feelings, belongings and aspirations that make for integration. These can range from a common spiritual basis, via the legacy of the Enlightenment to the postwar peace motive and the idea of a united Europe, which all points to a motivational substrate for integration engendering trust and confidence.[11] The research problem has to do with squaring the following circle: how much legal institutionalization is needed for cooperation to come about, how much deliberation is required before common commitments become obligatory commitments?

Third, cultural values are context-bound and possess only relative validity. Rights derived from universal moral norms are called for in order to stabilize a wide and composite polity. But rights may be given by non-democratic entities. Even non-enfranchised citizens – even children, slaves and illegal immigrants – enjoy rights. Rights may be decided and allocated autocratically. Courts and administrative agencies adjudicate conflicts autonomously according to established rights but only the democratic enactment can validate them. The legal medium is not merely a system of sanctions, it is also one of presumably rational principles. When law is rational and legitimate, people may obey out of *insight*, not merely

because of its attendant sanctions. What then is needed is to bring democracy, the principle of popular self-rule, to bear upon the integration
process, because only by including those affected can one know whether a
law is legitimate.

The deliberative perspective alerts us to the fact that political integration starts when actors face problems and seek to solve them cooperatively; when the consequences and by-products of this cooperation affect
third parties and become visible and problematic in legitimacy terms.
That is when one has to answer questions like: Who are responsible for
inflicted harms? Who should pay for negative by-products? Who should be
held to account when third parties suffer? The proposition here is that
when a *value consensus* is no longer there to handle questions of this kind
automatically, reflexive processes come about. Critique and opposition
trigger reflection and justificatory discourses in post-traditional contexts.
In the EU the value-based 'permissive consensus' has come to an end
(Abromeit 1998). The EU is contested and opposed by large groups in
many countries.

Law is a reflexive mechanism for solving conflicts in modern societies. It
is also through legal procedures that legitimation problems can be allevi-
ated. Of the long-established authorities, religion, law, state and tradition,
it is only law that has survived the corrosion process of modernity
(Frankenberg 2003). But under modern conditions there is, as mentioned,
a split between problem-solving within the domain of politics and within
the domain of law. Both are specialized on reaching collectively binding
decisions, but while politics has to do with the will formation necessary for
efficient *goal attainment,* law pertains to the stabilization of behavioural
expectations necessary for peaceful *interest regulation–conflict resolution.*

Beyond problem-solving

The dynamic and multifaceted character of the EU means that the development of cooperation in Europe may take different directions: it may
become more tightly integrated; it may become more complex and multifaceted; or the integration may unravel. The open-ended nature of the
present situation can be illustrated by the challenge of enlargement.
Enlargement can be handled either through scaling down the ambitions
of the polity-makers in the EU (reduce or roll back integration), or
through increasing the capabilities of the EU (further deepen and widen
integration).

A distinction is needed between a problem-solving, derivative entity
(from the member states), performing governance and risk-regulation
functions, and a full-fledged polity able to mediate conflicts and (re)allo-
cate resources through collectively binding decisions. The former treats
problems of a mundane, technical-economic nature and preferences that
do not invoke strong evaluations: in cases of conflicts of interest, disputes

can be resolved with reference to *justice as mutual advantage* (Barry 1989). This concept of justice pertains to the benefits of mutual cooperation and stems from the constraints self-interested parties may rationally install on themselves in order to realize their long-term interests (cp. Gauthier 1986). Problem-solving for mutual benefits will not do in normative terms when the questions to be answered and the problems to be solved involve conflicts over norms, over values and identities – when actions have distributional costs. Then authoritative institutions for impartial conflict resolution and collective goal attainment are required, which speaks to another concept of justice – *justice as mutual recognition* (cp. Scanlon 1998: 162; Forst 2001: 362; Habermas 1993: 32).

This concept rests on the insight that actor-neutral reasons are needed to justify a norm. Reasons based on self-interest do not fulfil the requirement of impartiality: morality entails upholding norms simply because they are right and because violating them is wrong, hence some disputes cannot be settled with reference to mutual advantage. Simply establishing an equilibrium outcome does not imply that it is right. When cooperation affects the interests and identities of the members, when it has distributive effects, conflicts have to be resolved with reference to higher-ranking principles and moral norms revolving on *what is equally just for all*. In a deonto-logical, Kantian perspective, norms are valid when they can be justified from every affected party's perspective, namely, when everybody's interests and values are taken into consideration and given a due hearing. According to the discourse theory, the test of the validity of norms is not whether they are profitable for one or the other but whether it can reasonably be expected that all would agree – for identical reasons – in a rational discourse. However, all would not agree unless non-compliers face sanctions – hence the prevalence of law.

When integration catches on and brings about public institutions for regulating interpersonal conflicts and for realizing collective goals authoritatively and legitimately, consistent with the rule of law and the principle of popular sovereignty, we may talk about a democratic polity capable of collective action. The more proper procedures and institutions that are in place to regulate conflicts impartially and allocate collective resources according to conceptions of the collective good, the more the polity becomes a polity in its own right. It obtains the authoritative power to solve problems and command in the name of all the members.

What kind of entity is the EU then? Is it a regulatory regime, a value-based polity or a fledgling post-national federation (Eriksen and Fossum 2004)?

Four polity options

As mentioned, the EU faces pressures both in terms of efficiency and in terms of democratic legitimacy. With ten new member states (25 in total), its ability to live up to expectations of efficient problem-solving will now be put to the test. In present (and future) debates about forging a citizens' Europe, the EU faces the challenge of finding an appropriate balance between the competing requirements of efficiency and legitimacy. However, democratic legitimacy may be obtained in two ways. It may be obtained indirectly via national democracy or directly on the basis of the polity's own actions and procedures. As long as, or to the degree that, the EU is an intergovernmental organization in the hands of the member states, when it is merely a means for them to solve their perceived problems, its legitimacy basis can be derived from the democratic processes of opinion formation and decision-making at the national level. But when this is no longer the case, when the EU's actions profoundly influence the identities and interests of the member states and their citizens, when the EU becomes a supranational entity, democratic theory requires it to establish a legitimacy basis of its own. Hence, we talk about *direct legitimacy* obtained through the processes and procedures of the Union itself.

Legitimacy is one thing, efficient problem-solving another. They are, however, interrelated because capability – an organized capacity to act – is part and parcel of democracy, understood as citizens' self-rule through politics and law, as the citizens have to be able to influence their cooperative conditions to be autonomous in a public sense. Thus, legitimacy without capability is futile. But capability bereft of legitimacy is unstable and inefficient. The EU faces a tension between efficiency and legitimacy as it is torn between solving the immediate problems of the member states and gaining popular support. While efficient problem-solving requires capability to achieve goals, legitimacy has to do with shaping policies in a democratic manner and gaining approval for actions undertaken.

How able is the Union to undertake collective measures and to solve problems rationally? There are, as mentioned, two forms of collective will formation which become necessary in the absence of a value consensus and when the issues raise more than pragmatic questions: *goal attainment* and *conflict resolution*. The first one is the prototypical political mode of collective decision-making based on the mobilization of support for collective goal realization. The authoritative allocation of resources is forged on the basis of the collective mobilization of resources for goal attainment subsequently decided on and implemented by political and administrative institutions (Easton 1953). Conflict resolution is prototypically the domain of law as it involves the settling of disputes through adjudication. The decision-making standard here is justice: impartial assessment of all the interests and values of the affected parties. The basic action-coordinating problems of a social order then have to do with impartial conflict resolution and the pursuit of collective goals according to standards of the common good.[12]

When we cross-tabulate the legitimacy dimension and the collective decision-making dimension and apply them to the integration process, four possibilities appear (see Figure 1.1). One option is to conceive of the

DECISION-MAKING

	Collective goal attainment	Interpersonal conflict resolution
Indirect	MARKET-BASED COOPERATION	REGULATORY RISK REGULATION
Direct	VALUE-BASED REDISTRIBUTION	DEMOCRATIC RIGHTS-ASSIGNMENTS

(Left axis label: DEMOCRATIC LEGITIMACY)

Figure 1.1 Functions of the ideal-typical polity options.

Union as an international organization performing market functions. Onus is then on *efficient problem-solving* and the four freedoms of market integration. The second option arises when one takes the *regulation of risks* into consideration and the complex arrangements in place in the Union to deal with these problems. But this activity is not merely regulative – it has market-correcting and redistributive effects, and as legitimacy here is derived (from the member states) as in the first model, it is deficient in democratic terms. However, some argue that, due to the epistemic value of deliberation, this kind of network governance constitutes a viable alternative to government.[13] The third option is to deepen the collective self-understanding, so as to make the EU into a value-based *community*, founded on a common European identity. In this way, a people or a demos emerges so as to enable the EU to cope with its integration problems. However, legitimation through collective identity need not comply with the criteria of democratic self-government; and democracy is the one remaining legitimating principle of government in post-conventional societies (cp. Dryzek 2000). Hence the fourth polity option which envisions a constitutional-democratic entity, namely, one based on entrenched *political* citizenship – a set of common civil and political rights – to empower the citizens to be and see themselves as the 'co-authors' of the law.

A market-based regime

The EU may be conceived of as an interest-based entity as from the very start it was held to be an instrument for solving the perceived problems of the original few member states. From this stems the free-trade conception of European integration. This type of organization comes close to the notion of the EU as a 'special purpose association of functional integration' (Ipsen 1972). The legitimacy of the EU depends on its discernible benefits for the members. In this economic conception, the EU is based on the notion of a legally regulated market with a common currency and a common set of rules regulating the movement of goods, services, capital and people (Moravcsik 1998). Cooperation is restricted to the realm of economics. The role of the institutions at the EU level is to sustain the Single Market. They are entirely dependent on the member states for their funding and to a large extent also for the implementation and functioning of the market. Member states are directly represented in the core decision-making bodies as an additional means of ensuring that the entity does not expand beyond the economic realm and encroach upon state prerogatives pertaining to security, welfare and identity. This system is, thus, premised on the notion of indirect legitimacy, i.e. the EU is legitimate in so far as it sustains an efficient market and respects the preferences of the member states in non-economic matters (Scharpf 1999a). Preferences are respected and aggregated, not shaped, amended or tested in deliberative sites. However, as integration has grown deeper and more demanding, as the realms of common action and policy-making have increased and as institution-building has continued, this notion of the entity has been challenged.

A regulatory entity

More recently the EU has come to be seen as a regulatory entity made up of a wide range of politically independent institutions such as specialist agencies, Central Banks, judicial review boards, and delegation of policy-making powers to independent regulatory commissions (Majone 1996a). This entity is more comprehensive than a Single Market, in that its foremost role is to resolve the problems of the member states in an increasingly globalized world on the basis of approved knowledge bases. Globalization entails a range of additional problems pertaining to environmental degradation, social dislocation, international crime, terrorism and migration. Hence the *risk scenario* of modern society: the unforeseen and unknown consequences – the negative by-products – of human activities that cannot be rationally calculated nor safeguarded against (cp. Beck 1986: 386ff; Luhmann 1991). Participation in epistemic communities enhances knowledge and reduces the information problem with regard to choice under conditions of risk. In the EU many boundary-crossing problems are addressed by cross-national regulatory agencies. As with the Market model, the member states bar the structure at the EU level from affecting core state interests and preferences. This, together with well-developed systems for accountability and surveillance, is held to suffice in ensuring legitimacy. In transnational structures of governance the epistemic value of deliberation bears the burden of democratic legitimation (Cohen and Sabel 1997, 2003; Gerstenberg 2002a).

Proponents of the regulatory model contend that the existing institutional complex of the EU does, in fact, also produce a more transparent and accountable policy process than the domestic policy processes of the member states actually do. The argument is that this structure provides for a constant presence of national officials in the Council and in comitology. The oversight of 15 (now 25) national governments, the tradition of publicizing Council decisions, the complex and multilevel stages of decision-making, and the extensive publicity and interest intermediation and the role of the NGOs, etc., keep the EU in close contact with the constituencies. From the limited perspective of the EU as a regulatory entity, dealing with regulation, not redistribution, this, it is contended, will suffice. But as already hinted, regulatory politics within the Union is not merely pragmatic problem-solving, as it has costs, allocates values and is deeply involved in issues of a moral and ethical-political nature.

A value-based community

The third notion of the EU is that of a value-based community. The EU is here seen as a geographically delimited entity whose states share a common identity, which can serve as the basis for developing stable goals and visions, based on the revitalization of traditions, mores and memories of the common European values and affiliations. Because of a sense of common destiny, a common fate induced by common vulnerabilities, people are turned into compatriots willing to take on new collective obligations to provide for each other's wellbeing. This is seen to be the solidaristic basis of the nation state as well as of the welfare state, and the EU also needs such a symbolized collective 'we' if it is to be authoritative and legitimate. To sustain an ability to make collective decisions over time, a European identity is required (Grimm 1995b; Miller 1995; Offe 1998). Such a search for a common European identity can make the EU into a value-based community, which does provide a sound basis for citizenship, for specifying rights and duties of its members and to set the terms for inclusion/exclusion. It is a means of drawing bounds, by defining who are Europeans and who are not. This entity is premised on achieving a *value consensus* founded on a given and shared set of cultural identifications. Enlarging such an entity is a major challenge as it will proceed in the direction of and according to value-based similarity between the EU and the applicant states. However, Europe exhibits pluralistic value patterns and, since there is no European nation – no identity of a 'Staatsvolk' – that a polity can be based on, a value-based community is obsolete, at least for the foreseeable future. That is as long as the intermediate structures of civil society such as Europeanized party systems, NGOs, social movements, media and a common language, factors which enable transnational discourse on the same topics at the same time, are lacking. At present, there is no European people that can govern itself democratically and give itself a constitution (Grimm 2004). The question of a viable Union is seen to depend on the ability to shape a common identity through a collective process of self-interpretation among Europeans, hence speaking to the transformative value of deliberation.

However, there is yet another alternative, as European law has already acquired *supranational normativity* and is thus binding on the member states and the citizens. It has changed the boundaries and the logic of cooperation between the states in Europe in such a way that a legitimacy basis has to be derived from the entrenched rights and procedures at the supranational level.

A post-national union

In the age of globalization the subject of democracy is multinational, resting on a plurality of demoi rather than on one people conceived of as a macro-subject. But only a polity that has obtained legitimate power to act on the common action norms is sovereign. A federation is a composite state constituted by diversity, which, however, exhibits one identifiable seat of authority complying with the basic democratic doctrine that 'all power stems from the people'. In the EU the legitimizing principle of a sovereign authority in the form of a people or a properly elected assembly symbolizing the people is not in place. But what may be counted on as a legitimizing principle is a system of rule emanating from a constitution-making process. The fourth and final conception of the EU is that of a federal-type entity stemming from the fusion of European constitutional traditions and horizons (Bogdandy and Nettesheim 1996). This entity needs to be equipped with a democratic constitution, with citizenship based on entrenched political rights and delineated competencies along vertical and horizontal lines (i.e. between the institutions at the EU-level and the member states, and among the institutions at the EU-level, respectively). This polity is premised on the democratic constitutional state and represents an extension of this model to the European level (Habermas 1996; Mancini 1998). The standards of democratic government are brought to the fore through the principles and values adopted by the EU as well as through its institutional and constitutional developments, in particular from the making of the Charter of Fundamental Rights in 2000 and onwards.

This model is premised on direct legitimacy: the citizens are included directly or via their representatives in the decision-making process of the EU. Key words are a bill of rights and a competence catalogue, a Parliament based on direct representation of European citizens and a Council of States as a second chamber. The institutional complex of the Union, the rights, the procedures, the policy-making processes and sites it embodies, make for participation in and accountability of the law-making process. In this conception a European demos and a collective will are also shaped, but the approach is quite different from that associated with the EU as a value-based community set out above. This conception is premised on the reconciliation and the transformations of the member states' identities due to the public use of reason, with regard to justice as mutual recognition, and not merely through the hermeneutical interpretation of who we are. Deliberation on the basis of rights and norms shapes collective interests and is a constraint upon the power-holders, hence the moral merit of deliberation. The challenge of enlargement is to ensure that new member states are willing and able to uphold the democratic values entrenched in this conception of the EU.

Notes

1 See e.g. Caporaso 1996; Tsoukalis 2003; Stone Sweet 2003, 2004; De Búrca 2003.
2 Sovereignty may take different forms, but the classical doctrine states that 'first, no one can be the subject of more than one sovereign, second, only one sovereign power can prevail within a territory, third, all citizens possess the same status and rights, and fourth, the bond between citizen and sovereign excludes the alien' (Linklater 1996: 95).
3 There is a large body of literature on this; see e.g. Marks 1993; Marks *et al.* 1996; Majone 1996a; Hix 1998; Jachtenfuchs 1996; Jachtenfuchs and Kohler-Koch 1996; Joerges and Vos 1999; Ladeur 1999; Kohler-Koch and Eising 1999; Eriksen *et al.* 2003b; Neyer 2003, 2004; Olsen 2004.
4 Now it is contested whether this is merely an 'unintended consequence', as 'l'idée européenne' had been around for several centuries when, on 9 May 1950, Robert Schuman, French minister of foreign affairs proposed the plan for Europe, a plan that 'a représenté une étape capitale dans la construction européenne: il a marqué le début du rapprochement franco-allemand, condition préalable à toute organisation de l'Europe de l'Ouest, et il a crée la première institution supranationale européenne' (Gerbet 1983: 101).
5 Or in Jon Elster's formulation: 'To bargain is to engage in communication for the purpose of *forcing* or *inducing* the opponent to accept one's claim. To achieve this end, bargainers rely on threats and promises that will have to be executed outside of the assembly itself' (Elster 1992: 15).
6 It may also be seen as merely a question of rational choice: 'The underlying process involves choosing among alternatives by using some decision rule that compares alternatives in terms of their expected consequences for antecedent goals. The model is one of intendedly rational choice under conditions of risk and is familiar in statistical decision theory, as well as in microeconomic and behavioral theories of choice' (March and Olsen 1989: 59; cp. March and Simon 1958).
7 'Von Reflexivität soll immer dann die Rede sein, wenn ein Prozess als das Selbst fungiert, auf das die ihm zugehörige Operation der Referenz sich bezieht' (Luhmann 1987: 601, see also 610, cp. Maus 1986: 391).
8 On perverse selectivity see Brunkhorst 1999: 378; Luhmann 1997: Chapter VII.
9 'The public consists of all those who are affected by the indirect consequences of transactions to such an extent that it is deemed necessary to have those consequences systematically attended to' (Dewey 1927: 15–16). On this, see Honneth 1998; Putnam 1991; Schmalz-Bruns 1995: 214ff; Kettner 1998: 60; Joas 1996; Brunkhorst 1998.
10 And we should also note, as another pragmatist does, that '[a]s democracy now exists, there is not this development of communication so that individuals can put themselves into the attitudes of those whom they affect' (Mead 1934: 328).

11 Consult note 4 on this point.
12 'Collective will-formation refers to the stabilization of mutual behavioral expectations in the case of conflict or the choice and effective realization of collective goals in the case of cooperation' (Habermas 1989b: 145). Cp. the AGIL scheme of Parsons (1951).
13 See e.g. Bohman's contribution to this volume; Dryzek 2000; Cohen and Sabel 1997, 2003; Gerstenberg 2002a.

2 Reflexive constitution-making and transnational governance

James Bohman

The construction of the European Union has been an ongoing project, now more than ever with the prospect of a new constitution. As the debate nears its conclusion, the possibility of a new constitution for Europe inspires fear and hope: fear in those who worry that the integrative achievements of the Union will somehow be compromised and its structure made more cumbersome by standard representative institutions and traditional constitutional checks and balances; hope in those who seek to overcome the 'democratic deficit' by defining and broadening the scope of European citizenship and its schedule of rights. For still others, the current constitutional debate is an historical oddity, since it does not in any way mark a 'founding moment'. In this regard, Neil MacCormick is surely right in arguing that the European Union *already* has a constitution in every respect but the name implicit in its Treaties and in its well-articulated (if overly complex) functional, organizational and decision-making structures. He sees the debate caught in a 'conceptual straightjacket' imposed by too much talk about democracy: 'the assumption that law belongs either paradigmatically or only within the framework of a sovereign state or a sovereign federal union' (MacCormick 1997: 331). An adequate conception of democracy that avoids this assumption must clearly be structurally different from these alternatives.

Current debates have led some revisionists to reject the very idea of a democratic deficit (Moravcsik 2003), and still others to deny the need for a new constitution (Bellamy and Castiglione 2000). At the same time, those who advocate theories of deliberative democracy have generally favoured some form of a European constitution, arguing that it would provide the basis for a distinctly deliberative form of democracy that is applicable at a variety of different levels (Eriksen and Fossum 2000; Habermas 2004a). Such deliberative arguments often appeal to an emerging 'European public sphere', the organization of which could be aided by the construction of more robust parliamentary democratic institutions that are open to influence through citizens' public deliberation. If deliberative democracy is to make any contribution to these debates, however, its generally rather conventional understandings of constitutionalism and institutional design will have to be rethought.

Instead of thinking of every convention as a founding or refounding upon the basis of a new constitution, the European Convention is properly a 'constitutional moment' in the broadest sense. It is clearly not a constitutional moment that has been initiated by 'the People'; it is a case, when the very idea of the 'People' is at stake. Can the European Union be a People of Peoples, a demoi rather than a demos? This issue is not unique to the European Union; a similar constitutional moment was at stake when the Supreme Court of Canada ruled concerning the admissibility of tribal stories as evidence in land claims or in the Reconstruction amendments to the American constitution or *Brown v Board of Education*, that created a multiracial polity. After the decision, however, Canada is a different, more multiperspectival polity, just as after *Brown* the United States became a multiracial polity that it was not before. Both decisions shift the reflective equilibrium of the practical understanding of its complex democratic ideal and expand the range of possible reasons and legitimate claimants, instituting something closer to what Frank Michelman calls the 'full blast condition' for deliberation (Michelman 1999: 59). In other respects, the current moment is also an institutional learning process that is rather like the case of the New Deal, motivated by both democratic and functional failures of its existing, not fully constitutionalized use of administrative and political power (Ackerman 1991: 3–33).[1] Thus, it is a moment made more pressing as a result of the very success of European integration, especially judicial integration, that has gone on without much public deliberation or broad civic participation.

The democratic possibilities of this moment remain open: its emerging constitutionalism may promote further innovation, but only to the extent that it does not 'merely replicate on a larger scale the typical modern political form' (Ruggie 1996: 195), the unified nation state in which democracy is exercised through liberal constitutional and representative institutions. On the one hand, there are indeed many new and effective problem-solving methods and innovative democratic processes in the European Union which may with further development provide a model for governance at the transnational or cosmopolitan scale. On the other hand, the European Union, such as it is, still falls well short of the achievements of the democratic nation state, making it more difficult to motivate the transfer of power from a known form of democracy to an uncertain and seemingly less democratic form of organization. My purpose here is to try to provide an answer to both sides of the debates about European constitutionalism. The European Union has good reason to make its constitutionalism more explicit, and by doing so to more successfully employ its political innovations without the legitimation problems it currently faces. It can do so only by creating the first explicit transnational constitutional form.

My argument for such a *transnational constitutionalism* has three steps, which can be summarized through three questions:

1 What sort of polity is the EU becoming?

- What sort of democracy is suggested by some of the more novel aspects of the European integration?
- How can its deliberation be organized?

2   What sort of domination is it that remains a problem for the European Union?

- Is it that of *juridification*, or the possibility of legal domination in the face of institutions that cannot organize a singular and unified popular sovereignty?

3   How is it possible to solve the problem of legal domination?

First, constitutionalism introduces reflexivity into the basis of political order: that is, democracy becomes recursive and self-referential. Second, I defend a form of deliberative, polyarchical federalism as the best way to implement democratic non-domination in a polycentric and diverse polity. Third, the institutions of this federalism ought to be characterized through their 'multiperspectival' form of inquiry.

Democracy and constitutionalism: reconstructing the goal of a constitution

To ask whether Europe needs a constitution is to make a judgment about what it is or should become. The European Union has been described politically in any number of ways: as an intergovernmental body, as a federation, a problem-solving body without solidarity, a 'commonwealth', an 'extended civic nation', a supranational state, a 'mixed polity', a 'deliberative supranationalism' governed by committees, a 'condomino', a combination of several of these features, and so on. As Phillipe Schmitter (1998: 32) notes, the Union clearly does not have many of the most basic characteristics of the nation state, such as exclusive monopoly over the legitimate means of coercion, a fixed territory, a clearly defined supreme authority, an overarching and shared collective identity, and a unique capacity to direct implementation of its decisions, and so on. At the same time, it does possess legal supremacy over national laws and courts, the capacity to integrate the common market, legislative and diplomatic powers, its own currency, and so on. No longer reducible to intergovernmental agreements, these powers and practices exercised through the Community Method have made it a distinctive and unprecedented political arrangement with elements of a post-sovereign and non-hierarchical order. It also seems still to face a democratic dilemma. If it is to be a more standard democracy, it must become more recognizably like the modern state or federation, in which case it gives up its polycentricity and post-sovereignty; or, if it is to be a novel form of democracy without sovereignty and hierarchy, then it must also give up the standard requirement that its polity constitute a determinate and sovereign demos. The current constitutional debate puts the Union precisely at these crossroads, even if a clear resolution one way or another is not yet to be expected. Neither fish nor fowl, the European Union is not easily categorized as a polity.

Accordingly, the best way to put this question is not 'What sort of polity is the European Union?' but rather 'What sort of polity is it *becoming*?' Can it become more democratic? Here it is wrong to suggest, with Robert Dahl (1999), that the essential issue is a 'reasonable threshold' of size. Once we think of participation as mediated though various public spheres, the deliberative advantages of diversity and numerosity outweigh the loss of direct influence (Waldron 1999: 49–68). The objection is more telling, however, if the emergence of the EU and its acquisition of greater powers are traceable to the need for a larger political unit in order to solve problems. On this account, the purpose for going to a larger size polity is primarily to solve problems that are not solvable at lower levels. In this case, the following dilemma results: in order to handle problems effectively, the democratic unit may then be enlarged while the capacity of citizens to influence and 'to participate effectively in governing is diminished' (Dahl 1999: 22).

However compelling as a practical difficulty, this way of formulating the dilemma is problematic in that it sees higher-level political integration solely in problem-solving terms. Such an account is empirically implausible: in order to solve problems with the increased burden of coordination, some sort of normative framework is necessarily presupposed in order to get deliberative problem-solving off the ground. Once actors who then appeal to its norms to solve problems employ such a framework, the norms themselves can become the subject of deliberation, especially when they are themselves the source of conflicts. Dahl's dilemma thus ignores the pervasive appeal to norms that is evident in the various stages of modifying the treaty basis of integration, including the introduction of new principles such as subsidiarity, which can then be used in implementing the Community Method and tested by the European Court of Justice. According to this reconstruction then, every increase in problem-solving would entail the construction of new norms and principles, which in turn become the object of reflexive deliberation. It is in this sense that the European Union already has a constitution: it is a legal order that not only demands the fusion of the horizons of the various constitutional traditions; this order is also based upon explicit norms built into its treaties that can be used by various actors in processes of deliberation, adjudication, legislation and policy-making. Any constitutional reform or constitutional moment poses the question of whether or not such a framework is sufficient for the purposes to which it is put in the polity.

Transnational constitutionalism: reflexivity

The current constitutional debate in the EU is not about whether there should be a new constitution as such, but rather about whether the current treaty-based material constitution is sufficient for a democratically legitimate legal order (cp. Menéndez 2004b). The current material constitution acts as a normative framework for a legal order and represents a stable reflective equilibrium among various norms that enable problem-solving to occur. In this context a *constitutional moment* would entail the emergence of a new framework and thus of an ever wider reflective equilibrium that is the result of a long-term learning process. The European Union is still undergoing this learning process, so that its constitutional moment may not be exhausted by the recent Convention and the normative disequilibrium about rights and powers may continue without some further innovation at the level of the normative framework itself. This innovation in the case of the European Union would be a transnational constitution.

Certainly, innovative institutions and policy formation and implementation have developed that significantly revise and re-elaborate the treaty basis of the non-hierarchical Community Method; and with the emergence of civil society, regions and other new actors, the public now deliberating and influencing policies is no longer the public for whom the intergovernmental treaties were formulated. Dewey sees a similar process in the constitutional state in which the normal, problem-solving functioning of democratic institutions is based on robust interaction between publics and institutions within a set of constrained alternatives. When the institutional alternatives implicitly address a different public than is currently constituted by evolving institutional practice and its consequences, the public may act indirectly and self-referentially by forming a new public with which the institutions must interact. Such interaction initiates a process of democratic *renewal* in which publics organize and are organized by new emerging institutions with a different alternative set of political possibilities as a new political form. This is a difficult process: 'to form itself the public has to break existing political forms; this is hard to do because these forms are themselves the regular means for instituting political change' (Dewey 1927: 81).

The inevitability of such a normative framework for successful political processes of problem-solving explains other features of the current juncture in European politics. The reflexive appeal to norms is essential to accountability and contestability. Cast in terms of the accountability of dispersed authority rather than in terms of the self-governance of the demos, the scale of a polity has no intrinsic relation to the ineffectiveness of participation or its potential for domination. Dahl and others who make this objection have assumed a particular relation between *polity and regime* in democracy, between polity as the scope and membership in the political community and the particular regime with its institutions and decision-making procedures. The polity here is not understood in terms of the self-governance of citizens as members of a single demos, but rather in multiple and overlapping demoi; the regime is then not such that all must participate in the same set of institutions or suffer the consequences of a uniform policy; as a unit of other units, it is difficult to square the nature of the Euro-polity with the idea of a single demos operating behind a multilayered common regime. More than simply adding a layer of authority, creating a multilevel polity is rather a matter of redefining the interactive relationships among the local, the national and the supranational levels of scale.

Given the requirements of democracy as an entry condition, the European Union is a polity of demoi. If it is to become a democracy, it seems it must be decentred: it is not in the process of becoming a demos simply by acquiring some supranational features. As a 'people of others', in Weiler's terms, the demos whose boundaries are constituted once and for all has to be replaced by a more porous conception with some of the same core normative content. The obvious candidate is a more open-ended and indefinite structure, such as a public, tied to a multilevel and dispersed institutional regime. Whatever the supranational successes of political integration that pushes the EU towards a new moment, they do not do away with the diverse and dispersed character of the polity. If this reconstruction of the process of European political integration is correct, then a more unitary democratic structure is certainly not desirable. Nor could it be accomplished simply by the move from a treaty to a constitution. While constitutions make the framework more explicit and regularize the process of change, their reflective equilibrium may also become sufficiently unsettled to lead to a moment of transformation. In these transformations, the polity is 'reformed' in both senses of the word. In an emerging transnational polity, the very idea of the relation between the constitution and a people is reflexively at stake. The same is true of the distinction between treaties and constitutions; once a polity consists of demoi rather than a demos, the differences fall on a continuum, especially when citizens see the institutions of representative government as adequate to their circumstances of politics. Indeed, as the example of the constitutional crisis in Canada shows, any diverse and dispersed polity may undergo an iterated and reflexive dialectic between the treaty and constitutional aspects of the normative framework of the polity (Ackerman 1997: 770–9).

From demos to demoi

Theorists who take up opposite horns of this dilemma generally contrast complex polycentric 'governance' with the formal and constitutional institutions of democratic 'government' (Stoker 1998). While this dichotomy is easily overdrawn, it is unlikely that the European Union will acquire sufficient powers through constitutional reform to become a supranational federal government. Nor does it seem likely that, short of the widespread victory of the far right in Europe, the Union will give up those regulatory powers that it has for a pure market-like governance structure. So it would seem that the EU constitutional debate is stuck in the double negation common to discussions of international organizations: the Union will neither be a federation or federal government with all direct powers nor will it be a confederation with merely indirect and delegated powers and governance functions, but something '*in-between*' (Held 1995: 230; Archibugi 1998: 212). Held fills in this in-between status in terms of broadly representative institutions (particularly a bicameral legislature or parliament), which enact 'the broad framework' for policies of common, global concern. This parliamentary body would set such a framework for the common concerns of Europe and be organized in such a way as to give a fair hearing to relevant points of view.

On Habermas' version of this account, the development of the European Union itself ought to be a matter for the European Parliament, opening the structure of the EU to debates among European parties within a European public sphere and an internal domestic policy necessary for redistributive politics (Habermas 2001a: 77). This 'domestic' model is insufficiently dispersed to avoid the problems of hierarchy. Even if adequate schemes of representation could be developed without reliance on national polities as constituent units, it would still be an open question at which level any particular decision should be made and in which representative body. Whatever weaknesses there may be in such current institutions, the goal of their reform according to the cosmopolitan approach is always to construct a potentially European demos whose post-national political culture becomes the basis for Habermas' 'constitutional patriotism' at the European level.

What accounts for the appeal of this conception of cosmopolitan patriotism, even given the lack of evidence that such representative institutions and a European-wide public sphere can be effectively organized? Its appeal lies in holding the norms of democracy constant, while varying them only in strength and scale. Held and others admit that participation may be both more extensive and intensive at lower levels. If this is the case, is democracy at the various levels based on the same set of principles, such as collective self-determination? Once we abandon the assumption that the justification of democracy is univocal across levels, democracy is no longer a question of degree. One level is not *more* or *less* democratic, but rather is to be judged as democratic according to different criteria of adequacy. MacCormick puts it this way in considering the legitimacy of the European Union: 'The issue about Europe ought not to be whether it is totally or completely democratic, but whether it is adequately democratic given the kind of entity we take it to be' (MacCormick 1997: 345). Even if the purpose of this question is to weaken expectations about democracy in the EU, the point can be used for a rather different and more democratic purpose. If democracy has no univocal measure across levels, then the basic issue of the realizability of democratic ideals should be stated differently. Certainly, one of the original reasons for establishing the European Community after the destruction wrought by the World Wars was a widespread belief in the crisis of democracy within the nation state.[2]

The difference between the nation state and the EU is a difference in *kind* and thus not merely a question of size or scale, problems that representative institutions putatively solve. Given the diversity of peoples within the territories, national democracies are currently facing problems that begin to make their constitutions resemble treaties, as when the Quebecois ask to opt out of the order entirely. Similarly, the political space that the EU occupies is not empty, but rather one that is already politically structured by democratic institutions of various kinds, each with their own distinctive properties and norms of adequacy for their type. Given the plurality of competing democratic claims by different polities at different levels, there is no institutional grammar or distinct political identity that solves the recurrent problems of composition and constituency once and for all. Thus, a constitution provides the basis for an *ongoing conversation* about the nature of democracy in the European Union, not a binding contract that obligates its members to surrender their objections to a particular institutional arrangement or to acquire some particular post-national political identity (Tully 2002; Chambers 1998).

Different understandings of constitutionalism suggest different possible purposes for an explicit written constitution in a democratic polity. The understanding of the EU constitution as a self-binding contract has a particular purpose: to constitute a European demos as a solution to the problem of its democratic legitimacy. Here the two issues intertwine, since this proposal and the sort of constitution that fulfils it entail a particular understanding of democratic legitimacy for political entities of this type. The European Union is the result of 'pooling of sovereignty' in its creation, not of the attempt to create a unitary sovereignty that stands in a hierarchical relation to other forms of authority. The problem is then that there are multiple forms of authority that are the result of such pooling so that none of the authorities are sovereign in the sense that they were prior to the formation of the EU. In other words, the categories of modern democratic theory revolve around the state and 'typically presuppose the existence of a demos' (Weiler 1999: 268). This assumption is also built into more cosmopolitan and supranational understandings of the European Union, especially those whose primary institutional goal is to expand the role of representative institutions such as the European Parliament so that they become more genuinely representative. Indeed, the ultimate goal is grander: to constitute the EP as the self-legislating author and addressee of laws of the European demos.

A defender of the assumption of a sovereign European demos could find it expressed in the weakened form of a legal hierarchy, whereby the European Union is a legal order of legal orders. According to this objection to an overly strong version of the multiple demoi thesis, Community law and treaties function as a metalegal order, establishing the conditions by which to judge the legal validity and limit the diversity of such legal orders and constitutional traditions.[3] Such a reflexive application of legal norms does not establish anything like the public autonomy of the common European will; it rather suggests, as Weiler argues, only that there is a common and *revisable framework* for testing legitimacy and diversity within the European polity of polities. Given the absence of uniformity among legal orders at lower levels and the endorsement of second-order norms for a variety of reasons, such testing does not suggest anything like a common will expressed in a fixed social contract. Rather than see the constitution as a contract, the analogy to an ongoing conversation among various traditions is more proper in the case of multiple demoi and suggests that each can remain true to its democratic and constitutional commitments reflexively only by submitting itself to those judgements of others; in this way, they can each remain diverse even while together they fulfil their broad commitments to democracy and non-domination.

In the type of polity that is the European Union, each act of acceptance of constitutional discipline is not the subordination to the higher sovereignty of the demos, but its deliberative acceptance that is constantly tested and 'endlessly renewed on each occasion' as expression of many different wills and political commitments (Weiler 2002: 568).[4] In case they cannot obey (not on each revisable occasion but in the long run), in a constitutional order they also have the normative power to amend the framework. Such testing once again seems to be a matter of the reflexive application of norms within a reflexive equilibrium of mutually responsive demoi. In a transnational polity of polities the dialectic between the framework and particular laws is unavoidable. Actors can appeal to the possibility of changing the framework in order to undermine local domination; and they may jointly with others attempt to widen legitimate diversity in order to undermine hierarchy and legal domination.

The alternative is simply to accept that the EU cannot fulfil two of the most basic assumptions of standard democratic theory: that there is a demos whose collective will should be the outcome of democratic decisions; and that the purpose of representative institutions is to give expression to that collective will. We should with Weiler then accept that there is 'no demos' for the European Union, and the EU constitution cannot by itself perform the task of founding one. The European Union is an entity that has multiple demoi and its constitution will have to be constructed with just this sort of dispersal of democratic authority. All such democracies must exercise 'constitutional toleration' in Weiler's sense, in that they accept that they are 'bound by precepts articulated not by "my people" but by a community composed of distinct political communities: a people, if you wish, of others' (Weiler 2002: 568). The European Union is then a model for international democracy for this reason: it is unprecedented to the extent that the pooling of sovereignty has helped to develop institutions whose *democratic* structure cannot resemble the unified structure of the nation state that organizes the will of a 'people'. In this sense, the EU is both diverse and dispersed. It is diverse since there are at any location many different peoples; and it is dispersed since political authority is exercised at many different sites and at many different levels. More precisely, it is a political structure that does not attempt to construct democratic decisions in a single unified political will. Its lack of territoriality and a unified sovereign will means that it is not a 'single perspective' political structure, but a new political form, a shift to a 'multiperspectival polity' (Ruggie 1996: 199).

Juridification solved: constitutional reflexivity

Before developing this descriptive and normative claim about the EU's implicit constitutionalism further into a criterion of democratic adequacy, there is still the issue of the purpose of the constitution at this historical juncture in the development of the appropriate form of democracy. What are the problems that the constitution is supposed to solve, if not the political identity of the demos? The problem is much more concrete and related to a more specific problem of legitimacy, produced by the EU's prodigious success in achieving political integration. The problem is endogenous to its novel, yet incomplete political form: it is the problem of *juridification*, its effective use of law as an integrating and regulatory instrument for market integration. Under these conditions constitutionalism has a different object than the elimination of tyranny, that is, domination as the subordination to the arbitrary will of an individual or group. Its object is to eliminate legal domination, the use of law to impose a cooperative scheme upon others without their being able to influence its terms. Democracy is the solution to the problem of juridification precisely because it permits the authorization and amendment of a cooperative scheme from within.

Juridification denotes the tendency toward the increasing expansion of law and law-like methods of formal rules and adjudication to new domains of social life. As Habermas argues, this has the consequence that many social relations and informally regulated domains of social life are 'formally organized', with the consequence that they are increasingly opened up to the state and the market (Habermas 1987: 356). As a long-term trend in modern societies, juridification has until recently taken place by means of the territorial state. More and more areas of economic life and transactions are being juridified in various ways. With the emergence of institutions that regulate global trade and capital such as the WTO, NAFTA and certain aspects of the European Union, juridification has now become a global phenomenon. Certainly, the EU is quite advanced in the replacement of state forms of juridification, given that an increasingly larger portion of legal policy in the EU derives from Community directives and intergovernmental proceedings (Habermas 2004a: 19–20). This supranational form of juridification is based on the doctrines of direct effect and the legal supremacy of EU law over national law, and other

such regulatory institutions such as the WTO have the same effect of creating a system of obligations for individuals, states and corporations, all the
while imposing a scheme of global economic cooperation that bypasses
the democratic mechanisms of the representative constitutional state
(Tully 2001: 5; Bohman 1996: 151–96). In this sense, the EU constitutional debate is paradigmatic for *transnational democracy* because it is part
of a larger trend of global juridification: the more directly it interacts with
democratic state organizations, the more explicit become the debates
about re-democratization as a response to such hierarchical and administrative juridification. In order to solve the problem of legal domination
successfully, this process requires more than mere 'reparliamentarization'
by itself. Whatever the laudatory consequences of giving the European
Parliament (EP) more powers, this constitutional act will not suddenly
constitute a demos or unitary public sphere in a polity that is both as
diverse and dispersed as Europe. A more differentiated structure of institutions and procedures is needed if the European Union is to solve the
problem of legal domination democratically. In this respect, the EP could
play a role, but only with respect to specific powers related to reflexively
implementing a new normative framework.

Juridification takes place even in political contexts in which legislative
authority is tied to representative institutions. Here such authority is delegated by legislative principals to various agents in the many situations of
epistemic dependence and asymmetrical information already pervasive in
modern societies (Bohman 2001). The potential for domination lies in the
specific character of the agent–principal relationship that has replaced
formal political authority. Unlike many forms of the agent–principal relationship in economic life, the new transnational agents are acting in a
more general regulatory capacity, regulating primarily the very political
authorities for which they are agents. This produces the well-known
problem of 'the reversal of agency', the transposition of the principal into
the agent and vice versa. The hierarchy of an agency relation may be
defined as 'the asymmetric and *incompletely defined* authority of one actor to
direct the activities of another within certain bounds' (Miller 1992: 16).
The challenge to democracies is precisely that such authority is 'incompletely defined', since it is precisely the incompleteness of the definition of
authority that marks shifts in the structure of accountability away from a
legally defined framework of political authority within the constitutional
state. Some organizations could create their own internal constitution, creating a new hierarchy by assigning a principal to supervise each agent.

Put in this context, the debate about EU constitutionalism is not a
response to any specific historical event or crisis, but about a long-term
learning process concerning the limits of state authority and power. This
problem of domination in modern democracies has been heightened by
the emergence of principal–agent hierarchies and by the new forms of
coordination that larger political structures demand. Constitutionalization

has indeed been the evolutionary response to the pressing problems of internal legitimacy that result from the use of law without institutionalizing the principle of democratic non-domination. The issue of democratic non-domination emerges in this context of multiple demoi in which there is no determinate exercise of a singular popular sovereignty. So long as there are multiple or pooled forms of sovereignty, domination is still possible, even with the features of the formal rule of law present and institutionally protected. The main criterion for successful constitutionalization of the EU is thus whether or not it can democratize the transnational polity, just as representative institutions previously democratized the constitutional state and made its political agents more accountable and diverse. The solution is at a different level of democratic arrangements than simply the delegation of elected legislative authority.

A key feature of democratic constitutions makes them the historically appropriate response to the shifts in authority brought about through juridification: their reflexivity. Constitutions are neither simply institutional designs nor merely first-order legislative practices, but rather also make issues of social order and democracy itself open to deliberative decision-making as it is reflexively institutionalized. Juridification in constitutions has had several stages, including at the very least regularizing expectations in the formal rule of law and creating a private sphere protected from legal intervention. But such constraints on the legal power of the state were not yet democratic. The crucial step in that direction is reflexivity; it entails the 'juridification of the legitimation process' itself, in general and equal suffrage and the recognition of political freedoms of expression and association. These constitute political freedom in such a way that this constitution itself can be challenged and remade; they create rights as conditions of freedom and entitlement, even while opening the interpretation and implementation of these rights to the democratic deliberation of citizens. It is precisely these special reflexive features that are inadequately institutionalized in the EU and thus require a constitutional moment. In the face of juridification, the reflexive feature of democratic accountability and reinterpretation is foreclosed, as law becomes a specialized medium that is adjudicated by delegated experts in its particular semantics.

On this understanding of constitutionalism as a solution to the normative problem of legitimacy, the gap between decision-makers in the EU and the decision-takers in its member states is not that of scale but of the political possibility of reflexive challenge to basic norms, the possible reinterpretation and amendment of which is necessary so that the juridical order is not simply imposed. Reflexivity in this sense is required for the particular form of freedom from the domination, the capacity to resist juridification. As Tully puts it:

> if citizens are to be free, then the procedures by which they deliberate, the reasons they accept as public reasons and the practices of

governance they are permitted to test by these democratic means must not be imposed from the outside but must themselves be open to deliberation and amendment.

(Tully 2002: 217)

Just how this minimal democratic threshold of the possibility of amendment to the normative framework of authority, rights and duties through deliberation might be achieved is the proper democratic question and one criterion of adequacy.

Such *reflexive constitutionalism* does not entail the absence of authority, nor does it always require the devolution of power. Following Sabel, the defining features of a constitutional order include not only the vigorous and deliberative interaction between authority and its constituents, but also a deeper sort of reflexivity that leaves open the possibility of fundamental revision and change. The power of amendment, or the 'reordering of the order itself' (Sabel 1997: 159) is distinctive of a constitutional order. This sort of reflexivity permits not only responses to new circumstances, but also greater responsiveness to changes in the public with whom the institutions interact and depend upon for cooperation. It also permits the terms of cooperation to be dynamic, an especially important feature in an entity composed of diverse groups and constituents who may not share interests and may even have different ideals as to what the appropriate order should be. Thus, the purpose of a *transnational constitutionalism* is to create just such a reflexive, deliberative and dispersed order. Such an order is minimally democratic to the extent that the basic rights and political liberties of the European Union and their implementation must pass through the public deliberation of its citizens, even as this order makes juridical the reflexive conditions for its own democratic legitimacy.

This argument for the deliberation, reflexivity and the non-imposition of a constitutional order shifts the question of the constitutional debate. Rather than constitute a collective will capable of self-legislation, it should create a reflexive order for forming a plural polity. The democratic imperative then depends on the other features of the European polity that we have already mentioned: that it is a polycentric, multilevelled, large-scale and multiperspectival polity. I argue that some, perhaps innovative form of federalism as a regime is necessary in order to attain the minimal democratic requirements of reflexivity and non-domination needed for democracy in a large, diverse and dispersed polity.

Democracy, republicanism and federalism: in with the new

In the last section, I argued that the democratic core of constitutionalism is tied to its reflexive character, that is, its capacity to make the basis of democracy itself the subject of the democratic deliberation of citizens.

From this same criterion of democratic non-domination it also follows that federalism is the proper form of institutional design, provided it also could be shown to be adequate to the democratic minimum of non-domination with respect to the imposition of order. In this section I want to provide a republican justification for such a democratic order and show that it is consistent with republican arguments for pluralistic institutional designs as essential for self-rule by citizens. However, republicanism has traditionally been suspicious of large political units. The reverse is true according to the standard of non-domination that I have been employing: that larger political units are conducive to democracy under certain circumstances, especially if the population is sufficiently diverse to make the domination of minorities less likely in contexts of collective self-determination. Properly organized with dispersed power, there are also deliberative advantages to large and numerous units. It can be shown that some existing practices of the EU exhibit particular institutional structures of cooperation to take advantage of the dispersal of power and deliberation in multilevelled and polycentric polities.

Cosmopolitan proposals of a democratic Euro-polity seem to fall prey to the suspicion that they cannot secure their members from conditions of domination. Kant (1797) already develops the essential republican argument against any strong version of the cosmopolitan political community when he calls a world state a *soulless despotism* with the greatest potential for tyranny. The most direct answer to this objection is that a cosmopolitan political community need not be organized in a state-like manner and hence should not merely replicate on a larger scale the typical modern political form of singular sovereignty with a monopoly on legitimate force. Republican arguments for separation of powers within the state can then be used against classical modern sovereignty and thus can also provide the basis for a democracy of demoi. In this way, republican cosmopolitan institutions further separate power not only by disaggregating state monopolies and functions into a variety of institutional levels and locations but by disaggregating the democratic subject. Republicanism also suggests the appropriate modification of the common institutional form of plural polities and shows how federalism may be extended to the transnational level.

Federalism already provided an institutional solution to the problems of governing extensive and spatially divided political units. As an alternative to the antiquated form of a centralized empire, for many republicans (including Price, Diderot, Turgot and Kant, among many others) federalism had the suitable dispersion of power necessary to overcome the increasingly coercive domination of colonies by the centre (Padgen 1996: 188).[5] The historical story that Padgen suggests sees the emergence of modern federalism and not representative democracy as a central political innovation of the modern period. It challenges the long-held assumption that the large size of a polity necessarily leads to despotism and empire. Similar considerations apply to the number and diversity of the body of citizens. While civic republicans see like-mindedness as a condition of political freedom, cosmopolitan and federalist republicans think that deliberation is in fact more likely to be responsive to claims against domination when the citizenry is large and diverse. More than simply adding a layer of authority, such polities redefine the relationship among the local, the national and the supranational levels of scale.

The constitutional discourse of the European Union has already developed a conception of subsidiarity to attempt to capture the multiplicity of jurisdictions and sites for exercise of power that emerge in such a plural polity. At the same time that the EU has developed into a dispersed and diverse polity with multiple demoi, it must now develop a new interpretation of constitutionalism appropriate to its complex and differentiated structure. This constitutionalism develops political rights as complex forms of membership, the role of which is not merely to constrain the democratic will but to implement democratic authority through the deliberative capacities of citizens to change the constitutional order itself.

One clear instance of this multilevel constitutionalism aimed at non-domination is implicit in its institutionalization of human rights in the European Convention for the Protection of Human Rights and Fundamental Freedoms and the recent Charter of Fundamental Rights (2000). What is the purpose of this new layer of human-rights enforcement beyond the constitutional state? With the accompanying supranational European Court of Human Rights that grants rights of individual petition, at least at the juridical level there are multiple institutions and memberships that can be invoked in making claims about human rights. In this way, the differentiated and polyarchical structure permits greater realization of these rights and their claims against domination, as citizens exercise the rights to make claims given their overlapping memberships. In such a structure, human rights then are constitutive of membership in a democratic community and become a secure basis also on which procedurally to assess new governance institutions, including the transparency of committees and the broad inclusion of participants in deliberations related to committees and methods of policy coordination.

Federalism as a republican form

Various institutional designs have been developed to solve the problem of self-rule with multiple jurisdictions and differentiated democratic institutions. With its iterated levels of representation, liberal constitutional democracy has proven to be a robust solution within certain constraints of pluralism and size. Increasingly, however, second-order issues of the character of the basic units to be represented can no longer be easily and non-controversially decided. Federal states represent a further elaboration of this same set of institutional solutions, but one which was more concerned with the potential domination not just by branches of government but also by the higher levels of institutions. As I argued above, non-domination was previously assured by juridification of the process of legitimation, specifically by entrenching rights to participation and protecting autonomous governance on lower levels. Indeed, as a solution to the problems of domination in an extensive empire of colonies, federalism achieved a transnational scale all the while it aimed at dispersing the increasingly coercive power of the centre over the periphery that undermined the republic. Classic modern federalism became 'a political system which includes a constitutionally entrenched division of powers between a central government and two or more subunits, defined on a territorial basis such that each level of government has sovereign authority over certain issues' (Kymlicka 2001: 94). It is neither merely decentralization in which the central authority decides the framework of directives and basic policies (or, as Held describes it, the general framework), nor a confederation in which the main issue is solving coordination problems through a common set of external policies. To achieve more than these alternatives and create the conditions for robust interaction across various levels and diverse locales, federalism required a written constitution.

Federalism developed hand in hand with the nation state and did not fully develop these institutional possibilities. As the history of the United States shows, classic federal states tend empirically to centralize power as the demands for integration and regulation increase. Note further that, for all its innovation, modern federalism extends (rather than abolishes) the modern state form, to the extent that the subunits are defined territorially. Furthermore, each of its subunits is usually considered to be identical to each other with respect to political culture and the distribution of rights and duties so as to ensure equality. While standard federalism certainly unbundles sovereignty, symmetry demands that the perspective of each of the subunits is considered the same with respect to their interests and autonomy. Thus, it is an extension of the same underlying notion of a polity. While the units of the EU as states with well-defined boundaries are certainly territorial, the EU has not followed the historical path of modern federations, since the polity dimension cannot simply be assumed. Nor has it exhibited the tendency toward centralization and convergence except in specific domains: the greater the centralized power at the federal level, the greater the identification of individuals with political rights associated with *federal citizenship*. This deficit in identification seems to challenge the application of federalism to the EU, as well as the very idea of a distinct European identity. This legal status of European citizenship alone suggests some form of federalism, if not exactly the modern form of centralization and decentralization within a constitutional framework.

What are the alternatives? Some might argue that federalism is simply not the proper framework, since it is too strongly connected to the state form of which it is an extension. However, as Kymlicka and others have argued, there is also a trend toward non-territorial, multinational and thus multicultural and pluralist forms of federalism. In order to overcome the problems of domination within territorial federalism, a *multination federalism* requires that 'decisions about boundaries must consciously reflect the needs and aspirations of minority groups'. Given the character of the European Union, however, there is no such clear distinction between majority and minority groups, even if it could borrow the 'asymmetry' of rights and powers among federal units, including powers of self-government (Kymlicka 2001: 104). What is at stake is not the specific regime suggested by asymmetric federalism, but rather its deeper, constitutional motivation (Dahl 1999: 21). The use of asymmetries must be for the sake of greater democracy within the framework of the European Union, not directly for the self-determination of 'peoples' or 'nations'. Second, it suggests that the European Union should not in every case regard national territorial units as given, since this fixes the purpose of federalism and guides the dispersal of powers and the unbundling of sovereignty. Such a more fluid and negotiable order would be unprecedented in permitting a wide range of constitutionalized plural authority structures along a number of different dimensions, especially where issues present the potential for new forms of domination to emerge at the European level.

For all its innovative character and orientation to the problem of domination within a democratic regime, a modified multination federal scheme does not entirely solve the problem that the EU constitution was supposed to solve: the problem of democracy. If the European Union is already well ordered and institutionally thick, then a new federalism need not reorganize institutions as much as settle the specific constitutional question: how can this structure be sufficiently reflexive so as to make it democratic in the sense that issues of the nature of the polity, of rights and duties, must pass through the public deliberation of citizens? How might a European federation become a democracy and thus provide high levels of legitimacy, accountability and participation? I can here only give some broad suggestions concerning the principles of a reflexive transnational constitutionalism as applied to various institutions. One such example concerns the reflexive and democratic governance of the relations of authority that govern the practice of inquiry upon which institutions depend.

Making democracy transnational: reconstructing publicity and inquiry

This comparative analysis of federalism opens up an alternative interpretation of federalism that is a specifically historical response to emerging European globalization (albeit an inadequate one). It also leads to the development of larger political structures and forms of authority that escape the internal limits on domination within the constitutional state.

One motivation for such republicanism is the delegation of state powers to non-democratic authorities in the European Union and other transnational bodies. As I noted above, one typical approach is to give a greater role to the European Parliament in both setting the policy of the EU as well as opening the development and expansion of the EU to democratic and popular control (Pogge 1997: 171–2; Habermas 2004a: 31). The basic problem is that the parliamentary solution presupposes that there is a feasible territorial and electoral system of representing the European demos, and this has already proven to be a basic stumbling block in the constitutional process. This is not to say that representation has no role. Whatever the scheme, it will have to be complex, functioning more as a mediator among different units, including various functional bodies and interconnected deliberative processes. The more fundamental question than representation is then the question of what the basic units of the polity are in the first place and of creating ones that function to make dispersed self-governance possible. The scheme would have to be flexible and incorporate different sorts of actors with different degrees of interrelatedness not easily subsumed in a hierarchy. If this is the case, parliament is not uniquely connected to the demoi that make up the polity. Federal and deliberative institutions can fulfil the ideal of democratic self-governance without being in every instance self-legislating.

Federalism and European governance: institutions

While it might seem that a more powerful parliament with all the traditional powers of federal systems of representation might make the EU more democratic, it begs the central question of legitimacy: the problem of determining the constituent units of governance within the EU. Federalism goes some way in answering this question, in that it does not merely decentralize power from the central apex, but disperses it in many different sites and centres. Guided by the account of iterated and differentiated democratic structures and the goal of non-domination, other avenues for access to influence are desirable. Indeed, it can be argued that European practices of governance are already '*heterarchical*', in which authority is neither centralized nor decentralized, but shared (Neyer 2003: 689). The Community Method already suggests heterarchy, with highly differentiated roles for the Council, the Commission and for the European Parliament. As a first step, the development and reconstruction of these basic institutions could play a role in the democratic regime of the EU, along with its emerging innovative, decentred institutions and experimental, flexible and dynamic practices in various policy domains.

Given the shape of the European polity, most cosmopolitans argue that the first step is to create a more effective and empowered European Parliament, perhaps with a bicameral structure. This would then clearly locate rights to initiate legislation, to set directives and objectives for administrative bodies, and to review implementation in conjunction with the Commission; as an elected body, it can potentially represent and empower more diverse interests. The European Parliament looks less like an obstacle to a dispersed deliberative polity (as argued in Shaw 1998) if it is thought of not only as an originator of policy proposals and objectives, but also as a deliberative forum for debating important issues of policy and legal interpretation. In this way, EU institutions must be regarded as multiple sites or centres that serve deliberative functions at a European scale. As they also become the focus of a European-wide political public sphere, their forum provides a common focus of public attention for various national and linguistic public spheres that discuss and deliberate upon the nature and scope of the European polity. Thus, so long as EU law has legal supremacy, the EP does more than provide checks and balances with the executive; it also creates the occasions and sites for *large-scale public deliberation*.

This source of legitimacy is crucial to the extent that the EP has already taken on the reflexive role of monitoring the human-rights records of member states and thus testing the legitimacy of their exercise of normative powers. Through these progress reports, conducted since 2002, the status of membership in the European Union is itself open to the test of non-domination. Such a process could be reconstructed as a test for legitimate diversity, based on an ongoing and explicit *overlapping consensus* of the diverse constitutional traditions reflected in the Parliament. This overlapping consensus turns out not to be all that wide, but is restricted in the treaty primarily to principles of liberty, respect for human rights and fundamental freedoms, the 'rule of law' and the diversity of 'national identities' as 'principles common to Member States' (TEU, Article 6). Member states are obligated to respect and implement these rights and principles and are held accountable to this obligation by each other (Article 7). As far as policies are concerned, obligations extend to accepting procedures and methods of coordination, whenever they are deemed necessary.

Similarly, other more standard federal institutions can have deliberative roles. Just as in American case law, one role of the courts is to interpret the doctrine of federalism itself; both the European Court of Justice and national supreme courts have already taken on the judicial task of interpreting the various treaties and their principles, and they will continue to do so even when the sites of deliberation at different scales of governance are more elaborated, including important political principles of jurisdiction and transparency, now interpreted within a multilevel framework. This role also facilitates the democratic process through reviewing procedures and processes of accountability; it could go a step further and demand that various EU institutions fulfil their obligation to deliberate more publicly. Furthermore, such courts continue to have a direct relation to individuals (rather than to publics) across various levels of governance. When individuals may directly petition the European Court of

Human Rights, there is an important analogy to features of constitutional adjudication involved in federal civil-rights prosecutions and suits that Owen Fiss has called 'structural reform'. In confronting these organizations with the basic norms of human rights, such adjudication is part of the process by which the European political community also undertakes to promote the restructuring of large-scale organizations and institutional arrangements that fail to treat individuals as citizens with equal rights and thus do not respect the democratic rule of law (Fiss 1979: 2). The European-level courts could also further protect aliens, immigrants and third-party nationals as bearers of human rights, including various political rights of voice, entry and exit from the Union. Thus, at least judicially, the European Union exhibits the sort of differentiated and *overlapping democratic structure* that not only makes people's basic rights less vulnerable to legal domination, but also provides a means for structural reform in the case of local structures of domination and juridification. It is not simply multilevelled, but realized in overlapping and deliberating promoting institutions that are multiply realized so as to block the domination of the demoi by some particular demos.

Directly deliberative designs

Finally, forms of public deliberation have emerged within the polyarchy of various procedures of responsive implementation of basic policies. As Charles Sabel has argued, a 'directly deliberative' design in many ways incorporates epistemic innovations and increased capabilities of economic organizations, in the same way as the New Deal institutions followed the innovations of industrial organization in the centralized mass production they attempted to administer and regulate (Dorf and Sabel 1998: 292). Roughly, such a form of organization uses nested and cooperative forms of decision-making based on highly collaborative processes of jointly defining problems and setting goals already typical in many large firms with dispersed sites of production. These forms of organization have been established as constitutional orders that do not require uniform policies, but permit a broad range of experimental initiatives with public testing across levels and sites of mutual accountability and authority. This process is often considered to be a form of rule by committee or comitology with deliberative features. Thus, the practices of distributed and coordinated policy formation can become more if we see the purpose of such committees not only in terms of the traditional power of government but as a mode of inquiry essential to experimental and cooperative practices. This mode of inquiry is explicitly recognized by the Constitutional Treaty in Part III, although none of its practices, such as the Open Method of Coordination discussed below, are specifically named (European Council 2004c: Articles III-213, 250, 278, 279) and power of initiative and of policy coordination is still left entirely with the Commission (Cohen and Sabel

2003; Sabel and Zeitlin 2003; Jacobsson and Vifell in this book). Such an overly centralized distribution of powers violates the basic institutional principle of republican federalism, that powers ought to be widely distributed and iterated at various levels to permit access to influence and public testing of practices and policies.

Such a collaborative process of setting goals and defining problems produces a shared body of knowledge, 'federal skills' among EU citizens in negotiating its complex structure, and common goals with diverse practices, so that the solutions need not be uniform across or within various organizations and locations. It cannot assume epistemic superiority if it is to be a non-hierarchical alternative to principal–agent relationships. By contrast, consider the most clearly contested domain of international administration, international financial institutions that broadly speaking function as agents for various member-state principals (including the World Trade Organization, World Bank, International Monetary Fund or the various organizations that set international technological standards).[6] Challenges to expert authority may be seen as leading to the implementation of '*delegative democracy*' (O'Donnell 1999) that aims at undoing the reversal of agency that accountability to such institutions and their fiscal policies tends to produce. This response is insufficient and does not fundamentally alter the problem of legal domination.

The big difference between the EU and such delegative institutions is precisely that the EU is itself a polity and thus already has a constitutional framework for accountability through open and potentially *multiperspectival deliberative inquiry*. Here the explicit recognition of political rights as human rights empowers those affected by authoritative decisions with normative powers, including rights of participation. This makes it possible for citizens of the EU to make claims rather than simply challenge decisions; that is, they may appeal not only to basic principles of democracy and human rights but also to political institutions that should be responsive to their claims and to a political community beyond that constituted by some specific functional task or treaty provision. Constitutionalism then has a wider and more important role, to the extent that it is internalized in non-standard deliberative institutions. Not only does it create some broad institutional distinctions of good and bad reasons, it also creates the demand for *reflective equilibrium* in decision-making. This is because deliberative norms are part of a normative framework, so that at the very least actors are constrained to show the coherence of specific norms and decisions with basic norms. As Neyer put it, for this reason, 'noncompliance with the outcome of a deliberative procedure not only rejects a specific deal, but implicitly opposes the whole normative structure of which the specific norm is a part' (Neyer 2003: 699).

By placing it in a normative framework, delegated authority is embedded in a polity and a reflexive legal order that constrains its exercise by empowering citizens to make legitimate claims beyond the scope of the particular epistemic community typically given authority in functional organizations. However much such *epistemic communities* may constrain the exercise of authority and open decision-making processes to exogenous influences, they filter such influences through their authoritative perspective, usually reflecting current common theoretical commitments. Comitology goes a step further in embedding such deliberative processes in a wider set of political commitments. Even if it does provide incentive for argumentation and reason-giving rather than bargaining among institutional actors, it does not by itself organize sufficient opportunities for empowered discursive interaction to be responsive to a wide range of influences and perspectives. Calls for greater transparency or for participation by civil society are not really the answer, since the weaknesses here are more structural. From the point of view of a federalist republicanism, what is needed is precisely to embed the relation between committees and the Commission in a larger and more public process more widely distributed across levels to encourage greater and more diverse discursive interaction with publics in deliberation. The transnational principle of institutional differentiation once again calls for multiple and iterated processes within a revisable normative framework. Such processes already exist in nascent form.

The European Union as a multiperspectival polity: the open method of coordination

Multiperspectival inquiry could be taken another step further in the EU beyond comitology by employing its 'Open Method of Coordination' (OMC) in a more creative and public way to add a directly deliberative dimension to its polyarchical structure. The growing empirical literature suggests that in its current practice the OMC has not fully solved the problem of transparency that plagues deliberation in comitology even if it has widened the number of actors able to participate.[7] Even so, the structural and procedural differences between the two are most significant in the constitutional context. In its differentiated procedures, directly deliberative processes in the OMC provide a wider public space for ongoing reflection on agendas and problems, as well as an interest in inclusiveness and diversity of perspectives. Many OMC processes are directly related to rights set out in the Charter, including right of access to health care, rights to employment and economic participation and rights against social exclusion (under which are included access to goods, rights and services). These enabling conditions for democracy can take advantage of the intensified interaction across borders that is a by-product of the thickening of the communicative infrastructure across state borders. If governed by the same rights, with particular reflexive concern with political inclusion and participation, transparency and openness have a constitutional basis and provide actors with the capacity to make legitimate claims concerning access to influence. This capacity is then tied to fundamental political rights and normative powers that are the basis of accountability. This accountability is not exercised merely post hoc, but is part of the process of dispersed but coordinated deliberative interaction.

A coordinated but still decentralized federalism provides for modes of accountability in this process itself, even while allowing for local variations that go beyond the assumption of the uniformity of policy over a single bounded territory typical of nation-state regulation. Cohen and Sabel (1997) argue that the European Union already has features of a directly deliberative polyarchy in the implementation of the OMC in its economic, industrial and educational standards. The advantage of such deliberative methods is that interaction at different levels and across many different sites of decision-making promotes robust accountability; accountability operates upwards and downwards and in this way cuts across the typical distinction of vertical and horizontal accountability. Thus, access to influence in such processes that allow for greater variation is more widely distributed across the institutional structure of the EU, and tested by various EU-level institutions such as the Council and the Parliament in their role of implementing the Charter of Fundamental Rights and creating initiatives to achieve shared goals and objectives. These potentially strong connections between the OMC, EU-level federal and community institutions and rights show the republican potential of these dispersed deliberative processes of governance that go beyond epistemic communities to the *building of a decentred polity through deliberation*. At the same time that the OMC promotes deliberation *within* various demoi, it offers a concrete institutional process that achieves deliberation *across* demoi through potentially robust and sustained interaction.

Its primarily democratic deficit, caused by insufficient transparency and openness to publics, lies not in the breadth of its deliberative process, but rather in their democratic depth. The deepening of the democratic features of such deliberation makes the subject for further experimentation. Even on the best interpretation offered by their defenders, committees currently function as 'forums' for political process and as 'coordinating bodies' across various levels of governance; they are, however, only 'semi-public' and related primarily to networks of administrative agencies and private policy experts (Joerges and Neyer 1997a). One possibility is that the deficit could be corrected by use of the strategy of creating *minipublics* to broaden the agenda-setting powers of institutions outside the Commission. In place of an amorphous public at large, minipublics are self-consciously created – representative publics of small bodies of empowered citizens around certain issues or government functions, such as service provision (Fung 2003). Such publics are constructed to be a *minipopulous* in Dahl's sense of the term (Dahl 1989). The possible institutional designs of a minipublic are variegated, depending on the democratic values and institutional goals they seek to fulfil, and on the subject and scope of deliberation: collaboration and problem-solving, innovation and creativity, civic education and engagement, the assessment of policies, opportunities for the less powerful to have voice, and so on. They are not simply made out of pre-existing social partners, but constructed out of more open-ended processes of participation and empowerment of those affected by a policy. A directly deliberative process cannot simply wait to collect responses from the spontaneous and diffuse general public sphere, but must rather continually and iteratively construct a public or publics with which it interacts and which may change its procedures.

By interacting with deliberative institutions at various levels, members of such a public also interact with each other, thereby beginning a deepening process over which the sponsoring institution has no direct control. As empowered members of various polities and of the European Union itself, such participants can make claims to others and to other institutions as they exercise their political rights as members of publics distributed across various roles, boundaries and levels of the European polity. The emergence of such publics in effective democratic governance of this sort does not depend directly on whether or not a 'European public sphere' emerges. Highly differentiated and dispersed public spheres that sometimes overlap and intersect would be sufficient for the requisite interaction between institutions and publics. While such processes go well beyond the current use of committees and the OMC, one of the virtues of the latter is that it organizes diverse and dispersed publics at different interacting sites and levels; and these structures might well permit the emergence of wider and deeper forms of deliberative interaction across institutions and demoi than realized thus far. One function of a minipublic in the context of the OMC would be to monitor the consequences of various policies and problem-solving strategies, thereby increasing both transparency and accountability; similarly monitoring at higher-level institutional sites can increase effectiveness, cooperation and collective learning across publics.

One way that the OMC can achieve this aim is through highly focused deliberation on specific policies and on the goals that set the means and ends contained in the National Action Plans in policy areas, such as employment, regional development or education. This feature also permits publics to identify problems and gaps in accountability. Given that the European Union is similar to most federal states in providing general objectives and frameworks rather than detailed and specific legislation, an OMC equipped with self-consciously created minipublics would lend greater *epistemic advantages* to strategies of implementation and experimentation under the circumstances of politics in a diverse and dispersed polity by combining local knowledge with higher-level learning by comparison across cases. Such benefits emerge, however, only when there is broad participation in the formulation of objectives and in implementation. In recognizing legitimate diversity, such a method of constructing publics may produce significant shifts to local or regional control in areas where it is effective, appropriate and just as the best way to avoid domination. Given competing political demands and the possibility of creative reinterpretation of goals, there need not be any presumption about the best level of governance given these criteria, as seems the case with the principle of subsidiarity.

In this distinctly transnational and republican form, directly deliberative polyarchy is properly distributed and decentred; but its democratic character in the EU needs to be not only widened in dispersed and iterated processes of deliberation, but also deepened in its public character. This transformation will itself require an experimental process of collective learning. It would be a mistake to detach the experimental deliberative arrangements in the EU from the institutions in which they are embedded. Certainly, the process of interactive deliberation must be organized and coordinated administratively; the resources and costs of such processes must be deliberated upon by the same legislative institutions that set the objectives and assess the legitimacy of the process, specifically both national parliaments and the EP. As a result of the community method with its orientation to consensus, they have emerged in order that sovereignty become genuinely pooled; for this to be the case, policies no longer had to be uniform, but the results of structurally similar, interacting but dispersed processes of deliberation at multiple locations. In order to achieve such a pooling and plural authority, the constitutional order of a decentred and thus republican federalism requires institutions, their purpose being to test processes of deliberation for domination and thus for violation of the political rights that all have as members of the European Union and of humanity. These institutions may also test decision-making for its inclusiveness and for the quality of its deliberation compared to other similar sorts of processes. In order to achieve these roles, at least one task of these institutions is to serve as forums for the periodic review and assessment of the overall system of deliberation.

In this way, institutions such as the European Parliament or the European Court of Justice continue to have a democratic role; but their role is precisely transnational, in that they permit and mediate deliberation across various sites and levels of the polity. They are reflexively concerned with the normative framework for democratic deliberation and maintain it by testing for legitimacy in various sorts of ways, not by constituting democratic legislation directly. By contrast, the legitimacy of the decision-making process involving minipublics distributed across various institutions empowered to make policy decisions is dependent on the quality of the deliberation, which can be tested through the perspectives of other publics. Federal institutions are, nonetheless, necessary not only to organize such a dispersed and diverse process, but also to create the multiple channels of influence and communication that enable the deliberation across multiple perspectives needed for a large and diverse polity to be peaceful and democratic. Their legitimacy is thus more *indirect*, dependent on the standards, objectives and membership conditions that make the European Union a polity with a normative, legal framework. In both dispersed and federal institutions, testing and decision-making powers are separated more clearly than in typical federal states. Their role in providing the framework for interactive diversity is nonetheless necessary if coordination, reconciliation and collective learning are to be possible in a dispersed and plural polity. Since deliberation in plural and dispersed polities does not aim at agreement on uniform solutions, it requires only that EU-level institutions serve to establish the domain of legitimate diversity, which would be constitutionalized in provisions related to the normative status of membership, and these in turn based on human rights. In order to institutionalize experimental practices, the constitution must reflect such multilevel and federalist divisions of normative powers.

It might appear that, even if the European Union becomes the 'differentiated, democratic, and constitutional order' that I have argued for here, it still might fall below the level of democracy of the nation state. Since it does not seek to replace but to transform its own distinctive structure, this is not a loss, especially if that level of democracy is not adequate or feasible given the diffuse and diverse character of the polity. If it is able to promote democracy, the role of European citizenship will be tested through the achievement of direct influence in some institutions and the opportunities for deliberative variation and indirect influence in others. In many respects, states too could become more democratic if they incorporate these reflexive, experimental and differentiated features into their deliberative processes as issues become more complex, volatile and transnational in character. In this way, they might for example be able to include non-citizens in deliberations and thus revive new potentials for polity-building even within its institutional form. But this still leaves open an important question: who are the citizens of the Euro-polity? With the new immigration in Europe, the public sphere is undergoing a different 'structural transformation' with the potential for the domination of citizens over residents and immigrants (Habermas 1989a). Finally, the transformation of the inquiry in the EU also depends on incorporating an even broader *cosmopolitan* perspective. Not only does this enable it to deal with individuals such as immigrants and asylum-seekers as bearers of political rights, but it is also necessary internally if it is to be just and responsive to the broad claims of its diverse members. Even if in the short term these dimensions of the EU remain undeveloped, in the long term such a cosmopolitan perspective is already present in the critique of the nation state that motivated its formation and provides the impetus for ongoing collective learning at the constitutional level.

Conclusion: legal non-domination as a transnational constitutional ideal

While many see deliberation in constitutional moments as tied to crises or founding events, I have argued that the proper reconstruction of the current development of the European polity makes the current moment a product of long-term learning processes. The current problem to be solved in the development of the existing normative framework is how to find a feasible democratic solution to a problem of governance. The problems that plague its current form are not the result of some fundamental failure, but come about through the EU's very success at integration through law or its increasing juridification. In this case, judicial institutions are part of this success, thus part of the problem and not directly its solution. This means that the usual linkage between constitutionalism and the rule of law rather than to democracy is incomplete and even misleading. Even if the rule of law does not necessarily give rise to juridification, it cannot solve the problem of legitimacy that it raises on its own, just as it cannot by itself eliminate the possibilities of 'great iniquities' as Hart and others have noted. I have emphasized the democratic and deliberative features of constitutionalism, its reflexivity and capacity to make the very rights and institutional and normative framework of political order open to the deliberation of those citizens who act within them. This reflexivity is also a minimal requirement for political non-domination and for the full exercise of political rights in a constitutional regime. This would require a stronger and more demanding ideal of citizenship, with the danger that the failure to incorporate non-citizens 'may lead to divided societies marked by severe inequalities and conflicts', including permanent minorities and excluded groups at the regional level as well as immigrants from non-member states (Castles and Miller 1999: 39). The expansion of the EU raises a similar potential for inequalities and new forms of domination. In both cases it must remain true to its commitments to democracy, human rights and the sharing of normative powers, even while initiating reflexive and multiperspectival inquiry into these problems. These problems test the European Union's commitment to constitutional toleration and push it toward a cosmopolitan direction in considering the role of the transnational in the transnational polity.

The logic of the argument for non-domination and democracy in the EU can then be iterated in another instance: the European Union can institutionalize non-domination and human rights only if it is a polity of polities within a *polity of polities*. This does not have to do with the logic of scale, but with the differentiated structure that best promotes the reflexive constitutionalization of democracy and the implementation of public deliberation. This next iteration is certainly not going to be made explicit without further political integration and institutionalization at the international level. International institutions generally still lie close to the treaty side of the continuum rather than the constitutional side, although the regime for the implementation of human rights may be an exception. Kant and Kelsen's hope for 'peace through the expansion of international law' heralded by most cosmopolitans did not anticipate the problem of juridification without polity-building deliberation. Moreover, the insufficiency of the rule of law for non-domination suggests that reflexive testing of the normative legal framework requires a process of practical testing only possible if deliberation can be properly organized as a dispersed and diverse process. This is precisely the sort of structure that the European Union embodies in its constitutional order. For reasons related to the epistemic value of publicity (such as a greater capacity for self-correction) and the likelihood of compliance in decisions over which one has had an influence, such an order also results in great rationality and effectiveness of its problem-solving capacities.

With such multi-sited transnational institutions designed for the republican purposes of democratic non-domination, it is plausible to see how they might realistically extend the limits of current political possibilities towards an ever-wider scope of democracy. If this is one of the motivations of constitutional reform, it is easy to see why such a project is the continuation of what is best in the European Union. To be democratic, it must not only achieve a democratic form of regional integration but also meet the repeated challenges of creating the conditions for democratic non-domination under the new circumstances of interdependence and juridification. Given that this is the problem that generates democratic possibilities within transnational polities, the constitutional debates about the European Union could be a precursor to a process that is iterated in many different polities and many different institutions. The model character of EU constitutionalism for transnational democracy more generally may seem surprising, given that the current proposals seem a matter of 'adjusting and improving pre-existing institutions and structures in accordance with principles already immanent in them' (MacCormick 2003: 14). Some of the democratic possibilities that remain implicit in the functional organization will not be directly touched by the new constitution, including a greater role for regional and sub-national actors beyond the committee structure. Once the European Union achieves a more fully reflexive order and if that order is a more differentiated institutional structure, then the question shifts: it is not whether the European Union is democratic, but rather what parts or aspects of it still need to become the subject of ongoing public deliberation. This may lead to yet another, more explicit constitutional moment enacted through '*the people of others*', the European demoi. Such deliberation might become truly feasible only if the current proposals first achieve an order with greater legitimacy, transparency and reflexivity.[8]

Notes

1   Given the variety of constitutional moments in United States history that Acker-
    man discusses, it would be a mistake to see constitutional moments of 'higher
    law-making' in existing democratic polities as always emanating from the
    people. The lack of such a source in the case of the EU Convention is not
    exceptional, although the new constitution will go through a popular ratifica-
    tion procedure in some of the member states.
2   See, for example, the 1941 'Manifesto of Ventotene', by Altiero Spinelli and
    Ernesto Rossi that articulated a federalist vision for Europe on the grounds of
    the crisis of the nation state.
3   Agustín Menéndez has suggested this objection to me.
4   Weiler (2002: 569) puts the difference this way: 'The Quebecois are told: in the
    name of the people of Canada you are obliged to obey. The French or the Ital-
    ians or the Germans are told: in the name of the people of Europe, you are
    invited to obey.' Contrary to Weiler's notion of voluntary acceptance, it might
    be better to say: 'You are invited to amend the constitutional framework, to find
    the appropriate reflective equilibrium in which it is possible for you to obey'.
5   As Anthony Padgen (1996: 200) puts it: 'the Enlightenment was, perhaps more
    than has been recognized, the product of a world which was ridding itself of its
    first, but by no means, alas, its last imperial legacy'.
6   Woods (2000) points out the inadequacy of accountability in international
    financial institutions that seek 'good governance' through accountability, only
    to separate accountability from the formulation of policy goals and their reflex-
    ive implementation. This separation means that accountability will only be post
    hoc and without any political or constitutional basis.
7   This diagnosis of lack of transparency and of broad participation from civil
    society cuts across diverse theoretical perspectives. Hodson and Maher (2001:
    722) see the OMC as inheriting past deficits and as leaving the legitimacy
    problem unsolved, since 'it is debatable whether the open method transcends
    the usual criticisms of governance in the EU, notably elitism and opacity'. This
    criticism may be met by deepening its democratic commitments, even while
    seeing the OMC as a structurally adequate model for transnational governance.
    Another common worry is the scope of the application for the OMC; it works
    best under conditions when options are not constrained. A crucial test case will
    be social welfare and the attempt to develop a 'European Social Model'
    (Scharpf 2002a). Besides leaving the question empirically open, the appropriate
    response is also to concede that the OMC is not a complete model of demo-
    cracy, even if it is a model method for taking advantage of the conditions for
    transnational deliberative interaction. Questions of scope also have to do with
    constitutional constraints on diversity as well as substantive principles of gover-
    nance such as subsidiarity and proportionality.
8   An earlier and shorter version of this chapter was published as 'Constitution
    Making and Democratic Innovation: The European Union and Transnational
    Governance' in *European Journal of Political Theory*, 3, 2004: 315–37.

3 On the political theory of the Euro-polity

*Rainer Schmalz-Bruns**

Introduction

After more than a decade of intense debate about the basic institutional structure of the emerging Euro-polity and the kind of normativity that can or should be built into it, about its unforeseen and 'sui-generis' character as well as about its cultural and historical background conditions, it seems to me that most of these issues are still unresolved. This may – beyond the complexity of the phenomenon itself and the perspectival variations arising from a highly differentiated academic discourse – stem from a challenge that seems to be of a pragmatic and political importance, inviting us to fundamentally reinvestigate and rearticulate even the most fundamental concepts and the overall conceptual framework which for more than 300 years have been used to articulate, shape and develop the political project of modernity. In combination, democracy, constitutionalism and the state have informed the institutional framework which was thought necessary for the realization of the promises of the enlightenment project, namely, as the joint realization of the values of self-consciousness, self-perfection and self-determination (Habermas 1998b: 81). Amongst the challenges that arise from this tradition, not least is the question of precisely why we should advance post-national politics as a solution to the problems we face (Fine and Smith 2003: 478), a move that urges us to go beyond the state as the organizing centre of this conceptual arrangement.

Against this background I shall try to explore the conceptual preconditions that must be met in order to find convincing answers to these fundamental challenges. More specifically, I suggest that a deliberative approach provides the most promising conceptual framework in coming to terms with the major issues of the current debate on democracy, constitutionalism and the state in the European Union. I only assume, but do not prove, that for moral, ethical as well as pragmatic reasons the idea of deliberative democracy is, with regard to its actual competitors (cp. Friese and Wagner 2002; Chalmers 2003), the most plausible candidate for a nascent political philosophy of the Euro-polity. In order to show this I shall proceed in four steps, addressing the issues of democracy, constitutionalism and the state respectively. I start, however, from a more general account of its most fundamental principles.

Deliberative democracy: five components[1]

A generally shared and relatively uncontroversial account of a deliberative understanding of democracy may suggest something like the following: democracy consists of:

> a political practice of argumentation and reason-giving among free and equal citizens, a practice in which individual and collective perspectives and positions are subject to change through deliberation and in which only those norms, rules or decisions which result from some form of reason-based agreement among the citizens are accepted as legitimate.
>
> (Forst 2001: 346)

I agree with Forst that the choice between different model accounts following from the general idea has to be based on the question of which of them adequately conceptualizes democracy as the *rule of reasons*. There are several components to an answer. This is able to shape the specific idea of democracy against the rival communitarian or instrumentalist accounts, as well as helping to decide between the divers versions of a deliberative approach that have played an important role in the debates about the Euro-polity in recent years.

- *Normativity, rationality and reasons.* From a deliberative perspective, the basic justification of democracy is derived from the assumption that it politically mirrors the fact that under modern conditions normativity cannot but be derived from intersubjectivity, i.e. from the rationality assumptions necessarily built into language-mediated social interactions in which individuals acquire a sense of themselves as well as of the ideas of rightness and truth expected to govern their social relationships. If that is the sort of normativity distinctive of modernity, it has immediate implications for our understanding of 'reason' in the light of which we judge a political order as justified or accept political decisions as legitimate. The 'reason' precisely lies in the *reasons* we mutually offer one another in order to collectively convince ourselves of the acceptability of generally binding norms and political decisions; that in turn implies that those reasons must at least meet the formal qualification of being generally and reciprocally justifiable (Forst 2001: 362).
- *The normative ground.* It directly follows that the ultimate ground for a deliberative account of the idea of democracy resides in a basic moral

right to justification – a ground that precludes any instrumental understanding of democracy in which it is thought to serve only as a means to the realization of liberal or libertarian principles, to the realization of communitarian values or to the implementation of best solutions to common problems of action arrived at independently of a democratic procedure (Forst 2001: 374).

- *Conception of political discourse.* This seems to suggest that we should only use procedural and not substantial criteria of legitimacy. But at this point I depart from Forst. Although he is prepared to accept that there might also be substantive criteria that can be derived from the self-application of the principles of reciprocity and generality, his approach does not go far enough. In order for us to accept the outcomes of a procedure as legitimate we must also be able to convince ourselves of the relative weight and merits (their quality as measured by independent standards) of reasons used to justify a concrete decision (Estlund 2000b). So I think it is a misunderstanding to assume that we are prepared to evaluate democratic procedures and outcomes only in the social dimension of inclusiveness. Although any actual procedure can be evaluated in the light of a more inclusive one, inclusiveness does not, by itself, fully exploit the critical idea of doing better (Forst 2001: 373): procedure-dependent and procedure-independent criteria rather have to mutually reinforce one another in order to fully unfold the normative force of democratic proceduralism. And this again, as I have argued elsewhere (Schmalz-Bruns 2002), has two important implications: epistemic proceduralism as defended here suggests that, while it can be translated into different forms of democracy, it certainly does not provide an unequivocal support for direct or participatory democracy as such (see below).

- *Cultural conditions of deliberative democracy.* Having made these points, it is nonetheless obvious that we cannot build democracy on transcendental insights alone (cp. Michelman 2001). Although it is true that the willingness to act on the basis of such insights is itself an important part of our cultural self-understanding, it is not to be regarded simply as given totally independent of the form of the political order under which we live. When we refer to democracy as a culturally embedded form of life, what is distinctive of a deliberative approach is not that it disregards ethical concerns altogether, but that it starts from a normative conception of the 'ethos' of democracy, providing a combination of moral and particular ethical-political components (Forst 2001: 367–8). Part of the answer to this problem is that it seeks to display its rationality assumptions on the collective and not primarily the individual level (cp. Pettit 2001). The other part of the answer is that it emphasizes the ethical role of normatively credible institutions (cp. Offe 1999: 73). This intuitive idea might best be caught in the notion of a *community of responsibility*, which normatively integrates a political community via an institutionally mediated willingness to take over 'discursive responsibilities' for justification, the willingness to take responsibility for the institutional realization of such first-order responsibilities and the willingness to take responsibility for the consequences of decisions and action. Of course, the meaning of willingness in this context is normative and explicatory, not explanatory – but this again highlights another crucial component of discourse ethics in general and deliberative democracy in particular: it provides a primarily structural rather than a motivational account of the force of the better reason (Hitzel-Cassagnes, forthcoming).

- *Institutional presuppositions.* Finally, these remarks lead us to recommend at least some rules for institutional design. The most general conclusion is that deliberative politics is best served if there is a variety of institutional spheres, reflexively acting upon one another. Certainly there should be institutional space for forms of self-government; but there should also be institutional access points for effectively displaying the individual right to justification and contestation, following a principle of 'reciprocal objection' (Forst 2001: 369–70). Further, there should be institutional devices capable of balancing institutional patterns as there is a need to improve the epistemic quality of political decisions on the one hand and a concern for equality on the other. Lastly, there is a need to establish an institutional tier of the polity to make reflexivity visible and allow the citizenry to responsibly act on itself as a whole, and where accountability for decisions concerning the overall institutional arrangement and the management of the interdependence of diverse institutional spheres and forums of decision-making in a differentiated polity can be ensured (cp. Nassehi 2003).

Democratic problem-solving in the EU

Where does it all leave us when it comes to answering the question of how to solve the democratic deficit or dilemma of the European Union? Now, part of the answer to this question lies in the distinction itself: Even if we accept the widely held diagnosis[2] that the EU in its current structure is open to charges of regulatory, expertocratic and legal domination, the democratic deficit only arises once we refer to the democratic tools and institutional devices developed at the level of the nation state, namely, the democratic chain of legitimation which has to run through the various levels of governance. We may realize that, even in the best case, the adoption of standard representational solutions to these problems will lead to a growing alienation of citizens from politics in a social (regarding the incentives for a more elite-driven political process), a factual (regarding the growing dependence on forms of expert knowledge), and a time dimension (regarding the growing spatial and temporal distantiation of citizens from decisive policy choices taken by political elites) (cp. Dahl 1999: 22; see also Offe and Preuss 2003: 201–2). This democratic solution will undermine or overstretch democratic resources, overtaxing the convictions on which the self-identification of a demos as a moral community and the democratic possibilities for the drawing of the boundaries of a larger union must rest. Although there are different articulations of this dilemma, with regard to the EU they all amount to the same suggestion for overcoming the democratic deficit: If the EU is to be a more standard democracy, it must become recognizably like the modern state or federation and will therefore not only face the danger of growing alienation of its citizens or the problem of 'democratic impossibilities', but will have to give up its polycentricity and post-sovereignty. Or, if it is to be a novel form of democracy without sovereignty and hierarchy, then it must give up the standard requirement that its polity constitutes a determinate and sovereign demos.[3] It is precisely this standard assumption of a unified and sovereign demos as the projection of the idea of the sovereign people which lies at the heart of the diagnosis of the EU facing a democratic dilemma; and it is this fusion of a normative principle with a substantialized notion of a demos which the deliberative view tries to confront. This is important because, once we give up this view and allow for a more desubstantialized vision of the idea of a sovereign demos, centred in the normative principle of general and reciprocal justification as stated above, a deliberative approach helps to establish a conceptual alternative based on internally linking the idea of people's sovereignty, the principle of public and inclusive justification, and the idea of a demos. A demos then denotes a reflexively integrated moral (and legal) community, where the sovereignty of dispersed demoi is invested into an order of internally deliberative institutions which are sufficiently reflexive so as to make it democratic in the sense that issues of the nature of the polity, of rights and duties, can be passed through the public deliberation of citizens.[4]

But this provisional answer, which establishes the punchline of deliberative republicanism, thus highlighting its special attractiveness in the attempt to come to terms with the Euro-polity, only triggers a whole series of corollary conceptual questions which have to be answered in order to arrive at a deliberative account of what it would mean to adequately democratize the EU. First of all, any such account has to address the question of those *rationality assumptions* that necessarily underlie the integrative mechanisms on different levels of integration – ranging from problem-solving to polity-building and respecting the demands that arise from moral, ethical-political or pragmatic concerns, which by themselves represent different but related aspects of the overall integration process (see Chapter 1). Second, this is also important for the reason that only against this background can we successfully address another key issue that can be derived from the liberal concern to adequately balance the *private and public autonomy* of citizens, i.e. to balance epistemic proceduralism and democratic voluntarism. Third, this distinction and its institutional corollaries allow for thinking of a *reflexive institutional order*, which at different levels allows for different democratic logics or at least a different mix of the two logics alluded to – provided only that they effectively can reflexively act upon one another. Fourth, this then raises the thorny issue of whether reflexive integration can be realized within the confines of a kind of transnational (or: horizontal or 'societal') constitutionalism alone, or whether some form of hierarchical self-intervention by means of *state-like structures* is also required in order to make citizens' judgments decisive in the respective dimensions of the integration process

These are of course huge questions, and I cannot hope to address them adequately here. But in one way or another, they build the background against which the conceptual problems discussed in the following gain their significance. So, in a first move that is more narrowly confined to the question of how to model democratic processes of problem-solving in a multilevel polity characterized by dispersed and fragmented forms of authorities and a plurality of sites of problem-solving, I shall basically proceed in four steps. First, in order to distinguish the deliberative ideal from more agonal or dialogic accounts, I address one decisive background assumption – namely that there is necessarily an important cognitive or epistemic component to a deliberative account. It is obvious that the basic principle of justification has an epistemic meaning derived from the account of the integrative force of public reasoning, and, what is more, that this meaning is absolutely crucial in providing an explication of the assumption that deliberative democracy is particularly well equipped to come to terms with a *denationalized notion* of a democratic order (cp. Habermas 2001a; Dryzek 2000). Thus, it seems necessary to highlight the epistemic properties of deliberative proceduralism, which at the same time allows the concerns arising from insights into pluralism to be met, on the one hand, and questions about the feasibility of discursive integration to be answered, on the other.

Second, while (auto-)paternalistic solutions to the feasibility concerns figure prominently not only among Euro-technocrats (see for example Majone 1998, 1999), but also among those who share a broad republican outlook on the future of a democratic Euro-polity, I briefly address Pettit's (2004) model account of a *contestatory democracy* which can make (some) democratic sense of the structures of governance developed in the EU, but which finally falls victim to two sorts of criticism: a) it does not take seriously the normative claim for democratic ex ante control of political decision-making and therefore for active and effective participation in collective will formation on the one hand; b) it does not take issue with the concomitant normative claim of effectively determining at least the terms of the democratic division of labour between political elites, policy experts, actors in civil society and the mass electorate.

Third, while this at first sight seems to suggest a more participatory mode of democratic problem-solving, this conceptual inference seems to overdraw the link that exists between the deliberative principle of democratic legitimation on the one hand and participatory governance on the other. *Directly deliberative polyarchy* in this understanding has to be seen as a model account that cannot stand on its own, mainly for the two complementary reasons that it overestimates the democratic credentials of horizontal self-coordination in problem-solving and that it underestimates the normative force of the claim of a demos to be able to collectively judge on the terms of political cooperation. What begins to emerge against this background of conceptual reflections is the vision of a reflexively integrated, multi-layered transnational democracy as an alternative to constitutionally entrenched forms of a federal order, which can make sense not only of democratic self-determination, but which in itself comprises several forms of the realization of the idea of democracy.

Epistemic proceduralism or multiperspectival inquiry?

On the one hand, once we admit that the central task of any political theory is to show how democracy contributes to the moral legitimacy of political decisions (Estlund 2000b: 2; see also 2000a), we are left with the choice of either holding that democratic procedures support the conditions for strong political legitimacy expressed in the epistemic account, or denying that these conditions can be democratically met. But in that case we would either have 'to supply an alternative account of democratic legitimacy or to settle for the fact that democratic decisions have little or no legitimacy at all' (Estlund 2000b: 16). Now, I think that both alternatives to the epistemic account of the moral value of democratic procedures would severely undermine the idea of deliberative democracy, for it must insist that there is a moral dimension to the idea of legitimacy. The fusion of democracy and morality is vested in the idea of reason-giving – a practice that is in turn dependent on raising rationally rejectable validity claims, i.e. on the cognitive content of these claims. I think that we must admit something like this in order to answer the question why political decision-making should depend on public discussion at all and not merely in casting votes or flipping a coin as purely proceduralist accounts of justice (see also Peters' contribution to this volume: 104–6).

On the other hand, we should also understand the reason why democracy cannot simply admit for an idea of truth that is independent of the normative principle of equal and inclusive participation. The argument is simple and straightforward: We should be aware of the dangers of *epistocracy*[5] and we should be sensitive to the dangers of inequality resulting from 'correctness theories' of political decision-making. On balance then, I suggest that we should qualify deliberative proceduralism which holds that we can generate legitimacy for democratic decisions apart from any independent standard of their qualities, in the following sense: An epistemic proceduralism holds that outcomes are legitimate not on the basis of being correct but on the basis of deriving them from a certain procedure:

> *But among the features of the procedure that are held to contribute to the legitimacy of the outcome is the procedure's being, at least as far as can be determined within grounds acceptable to all reasonable citizens, the epistemically best procedure among the procedures that are better than random.*
>
> (Estlund 2000b: 12–13, italics original)

What I have tried to show so far is that any account of the idea of deliberative democracy has to be epistemic in some sense. That might be taken to be rather uncontroversial, and the real question would then be, in what sense and how strong the epistemic conception should be. I suspect that we can come closer to answering this question if we consider two major criticisms of that ideal. That, given its epistemic meaning and content, the principle of justification and the concomitant idea of a rationally motivated consensus are so demanding, reaching so deeply into citizenship competencies and thus into the microfoundation of the democratic process, that they may even alter or invert the idea of democratic self-determination. Moreover, given the fact of pluralism (in the Rawlsian sense of a plurality of equally plausible and rationally defensible comprehensive doctrines), it is not plausible for normative as well as for reasons of feasibility to submit a *rational consensus* as the means by which a political community can be integrated. While both objections in a strong version are misplaced in so far as they fall victim to the fallacy of misplaced concreteness, one can make good sense of them from within the idea of a rationally motivated consensus once one recasts them according to a pivotal distinction between its constitutional and operational role – to indicate how this might work I address them in reverse order.

Concerned as to how to present an account of deliberative democracy that is plausible and viable even under conditions of the complexity of modern societies and its inherent and notorious forms of pluralism, Bohman and Rehg (1996) set the stage for a debate about the normative and practical merits of deliberative politics in a way that very much resonates with the more recent contributions to the European debate on the democratic deficit and the constitutionalization of the Union. They are, on the one hand, inspired by a normative sensitivity to plurality and difference and try to articulate a dialogical vision of a European democracy rooted in a civic republican or broadly constructivist view, and attempts at restructuring the basic institutional set-up of the Union along the lines of a directly deliberative polyarchy on the other hand. The crucial suggestion emerging from their line of reasoning is that, in order to render the deliberative approach in normative and practical terms plausible, i.e. under conditions of the fact of pluralism, and thus to make it safe for the Union, we must take plurality seriously and in any case avoid that (as in the epistemic account) 'real plurality is "transubstantiated" into idealized unanimity, and thereby rationalized' (Bohman and Rehg 1996: 91). This sort of transformation of agreements, the authors contend, would require three rather strong assumptions about the force of argumentation that are, however, open to serious doubts when applied to the conditions of real political deliberation. In particular, they contend that an overly epistemic account of the moral and political force of deliberation cannot take seriously the fact of moral pluralism and disagreement itself. It is thus insufficiently sensitive to the differences between moral, ethical-political and pragmatic aspects of political problems that cannot be rationalized and overcome in a perspective of argumentative rationality alone. Furthermore, they contend that an epistemic account cannot make sense of the notorious observation of the incompleteness of deliberation, i.e. even (or: just) open and inclusive public debate will not necessarily increase the chances of a rational consensus (pp. 91–3). For these reasons, they suggest substituting a more discursive account of rationality for the epistemic one, an idea which is subsequently substantiated by Bohman with reference to the institutional device of a 'multiperspectival inquiry'. This seems to consist of a fusion of the idea of polyarchical forms of problem-solving with dialogical forms of rationality, orientations and virtues that are anchored in a normative idea of pluralism (cp. Chapter 2).

What bothers me here is the conceptual contamination of normative and descriptive aspects of pluralism,[6] and the contamination of an ethical perspective with the forms of rationality on which it is based. Multiperspectivism as a form of making sense of difference is at first precisely that, a perspective, an orientation or a disposition, but one that by itself does not tell us very much about the rationalities on which it rests. So, on closer inspection, one has good reasons to suppose that multiperspectivism based on dialogue cannot, by itself, account for agreement. Its qualifying characteristics such as mutual respect, considerate regard or the solidarity of a non-egoistic commitment can help to achieve agreement but cannot by themselves account for the kind of rationality that forces us to converge on a distinct view. Leaving this point aside, what is more important is that this kind of criticism seems to misconceive the procedural punchline of the argument from rational consensus: It is for internal reasons not meant to bring itself directly to bear on the operational level of achieving agreements, but it only informs those procedural preconditions that must be met in order to qualify factual agreements brought about by different means of argumentation or dialogue or negotiation as legitimate and rationally motivated. This becomes perfectly clear once we turn to those strategies which, for instance, Habermas himself has used to come to terms with the same problems also motivating the dialogical turn of deliberative democracy, and which can be called the *contextual*, the *procedural* and the *epistemological* strategy respectively. The first is based on a distinction between types of problems of political action (moral, ethical or pragmatic in kind) and shall allow for a contextual specification of the principle of justification by establishing different formal and substantive criteria of what should count as a good argument in the respective cases. The second is about the already mentioned procedural transfer of legitimacy from rationally motivated agreement at the constitutional level to modes of interaction and/or forms of political decision-making which, by themselves, cannot match the principle of democratic legitimacy and usually take the form of an 'As-long-as'. The third strategy is built on a fallibilistic account of the cooperative search for truth or rightness.

In short, this amounts to three suggestions. It is difficult to see that dialogical multiperspectivism or dialogical constitutionalism actually establish a conceptual alternative to the epistemic account of deliberative democracy. This would, even if successful, be normatively undesirable because it would loosen the grip of the principle of legitimation on the formal and legally circumscribed aspects of political institutions and the institutional system as a whole. It may nonetheless (and rightly) alter our understanding of what we may (and must) expect to happen at the operational level of problem-solving. This at least is what is behind a complementary attempt by Eriksen (2003) to investigate what he calls the *microfoundations* of supranationalism. His line of reasoning is instructive because, in his attempt to provide a sociologically plausible account of the microfoundations of the European integration process based on communicative action, he convincingly starts from the assumption that the rationality expectations and standards that must be met in political interaction to a certain degree vary with the kind of problems to be solved.[7] This he makes perfectly clear when discussing the merits of experimental deliberation in deliberative polyarchies where, against the background of the distinction between problem-solving on the level of normal politics, on the one hand, and of integration and agreement at the constitutional level of institutional design, on the other (or, alternatively, deliberation with regard to substantial or factual questions in contradistinction to deliberation with respect to procedural questions concerning issues of fairness and justice), he raises two important points. First, as long as problem-solving takes place in the shadow of the normative hierarchy of institutionally established rules and in so far as political conflicts may be thought to be rationally mediated by the mutual regard of (competing) interests or by reference to well-established criteria of validity where opinions about facts are controversial, then actors can moderate their mutual expectations of rationality to a degree falling well below the standards of a rational consensus. Second, once political interaction is confronted with moral questions of justice and fairness (and thus directly addresses the issue of democratic legitimacy), then, he suggests, a rational consensus in the strong sense of an agreement forged in a process of reason-giving and built upon reasons that all can equally share and uphold is normatively imperative (Eriksen 2003: 208–11).

Only against this background, Eriksen contends (and I follow him here), can we identify different modi of reaching an agreement which mainly differ with respect to the respective standards of rationality: a *modus vivendi*-kind of agreement where actors only agree to mutually respect conflicting interests; a *compromise* where agreement is based on different, but convergent reasons; a *working agreement* which tries to make sense of the fact of pluralism in that an agreement is expected to rest on the reasonableness of different understandings of the problem at hand and which may work as a provisional and temporal agreement; and finally, a rationally motivated *consensus* which refers to the epistemic properties of the issues to be dealt with and insists that agreement in this sense is only reached when actors support a common solution to a problem for the same, mutually acceptable reasons (pp. 214–16). This strategy of problem-solving seems to me the most promising attempt to come to terms with the aforementioned objections of pluralism and difference and the feasibility of deliberative democracy, because it allows for analytic and reconstructive force while at the same time keeping the line with the overall epistemic account (or at least: the epistemic content and meaning) of the deliberative approach. But in so doing, it nonetheless provides but a first step in the attempt to outline at least the rough contours of a deliberative model of democracy for the EU.

Contestatory democracy and epistocracy

Although these reflections already point in the direction of reflexive integration, which denotes something like the overall architecture of an adequate institutional structure for a transnational polity like the EU, they nonetheless still leave open the question of institutional design. This is what the rest of the chapter is about; and I start this inquiry by briefly addressing a line of reasoning which you may call a strategy of deliberative insularity. This strategy is premised upon the acknowledgement of the functional role of experts and 'epistemic communities' in the process of democratic will formation. In its paradigmatic form it amounts to a justification of a 'depoliticized democracy' expected to flourish in the shadow of internally deliberative but paternalistic institutions.[8]

In the final lines of his article, Pettit (2004: 64) sums up the overall message of his essay in a very provocative formulation which not incidentally mirrors the motto of the 'Boston Tea Party', thus suggesting a really constitutional moment: 'As war is too important to be left in the hands of the generals, democracy – deliberative democracy – is too important to be left in the hands of the politicians. *No democratization without depoliticization*' (emphasis added). This in part seems to be perfectly understandable from the point of view of the 'republican idea of empowering the common good' (p. 60), which in turn is also at the heart of any deliberative account of the idea of democracy at least in two senses. First, deliberation is indeed taken to be a fact-regarding device meant to shield political problem-solving as far as possible against intrusions from interest-based, competitive and aggregative (party) politics. Second, it also shares with deliberative democracy the civic intuition that politics of the common is best served when it is controlled by civil society under conditions of the public use of reason (p. 59). While this is a widely shared demand, it is not at all clear if this kind of *depoliticization* as the distantiation of politics from 'politicians' really covers the meaning of depoliticization as referred to in other parts of the essay, i.e. if depoliticization is also used in a sense where it also tends to distantiate people from politics. There are several indicators that at least hint in this direction. The first is that his reformulation of the idea of democracy introduces a contradistinction to the idea of popular sovereignty: 'the people should control government because that is the only mode of control under which those reasons can be expected to guide government that are recognized in common deliberation as the valuations relevant to determining public policy'(p. 58). Now, there are two possible readings of what is at stake here – one is that Pettit only wants to deny the accompanying vision of a people that asserts its collective will as a whole; and the other is that he, in the same move, also wants to deprive the people of its active right to determine laws and policies ex ante. If it were the second reading, Pettit would not only compromise any interpretation of democracy as a directly participatory one, but he would also severely restrict the scope of the interpretation of the deliberative ideal. This fits perfectly with the paternalistic institutional devices, which he suggests in the opening pages (p. 53), in order to overcome the deficiencies that arise from self-interested power politics in political decision-making. The contestatory institutions he promotes in order to give meaning and content to the idea of public control are not only meant to 'facilitate', but also to 'forestall' contestation (p. 63), in the sense of reducing the 'contestatory burden' of ex post facto interventional control.

Taken as a whole, it seems to me that Pettit's interpretation of the deliberative ideal is at the least not sensitive enough to the dangers of epistocracy mentioned above. Against this vision a deliberative view, as I understand it here, would have to insist on three things. First, deliberative democracy is not only about contestation as a means of reasoned ex post control of political decision-making, but also, and equally important, about forms of ex ante control via reasoned argumentation by which people may actively shape political decisions. Second, if there should be room for paternalistic institutions in deliberative politics as well, we must be able to effectively relate these institutionalizations to the expressed will of the people, i.e. we must be able to understand them as an instance of democratic *auto-paternalism*. Finally, and for this reason, we cannot remove from the picture of deliberative democracy more generally the idea that the people should control the normative reasons guiding us in justifying and establishing the overall institutional order of a polity – meaning that citizens exert the reflective control in shaping the (institutional) terms of their interactions and cooperation.

Participatory democracy or reflexive constitutionalism?

This might suggest that deliberative and democratic politics in the EU were best served when spelled out as a *directly deliberative polyarchy* (Cohen and Sabel 2003: 345–75; see also Cohen and Sabel 1997; Dorf and Sabel 1998).[9] Very roughly, this is, following Dewey's inspiration of a social inquiry, the attempt to recast the idea of democracy as self-government (and not merely as self-legislation in the republican sense) for purposes of rebuilding (or better: rearticulating) the novel governance structure of a transnational polity like the EU. In order to achieve this end, the authors invite us to the following thought experiment:

> Consider now a world in which sovereignty – legitimate political authorship – is neither unitary nor personified, and politics is about addressing practical problems and not simply about principles, much less performance or identity. In this world, a public is simply an open group of actors, nominally private or public, which constitutes itself as such in coming to address a common problem, and reconstitutes itself as efforts at problem solving redefine the task at hand. The polity is the public formed of these publics.
>
> (Cohen and Sabel 2003: 362)

Now, the merits of this programmatic outlook aside, what is intriguing is the fact that they explicitly cast this vision in contradistinction to a view they ascribe to Habermas, which puts emphasis on the fact that 'the increasing complexity and diversity of the European Union drive public debate to focus more on matters of principle governing life among free and equal citizens, and less on situations of fact' (p. 360). While it seems perfectly reasonable to emphasize the problem-solving dimension of democracy, it seems less plausible to invest all principled expectations and legal safeguards of democratic legitimacy into the (more or less) spontaneous features of cooperation between dispersed sites of problem-solving. In spite of the fact that the authors well acknowledge that, in order to meet the requirements of democratic legitimacy, a deliberative polyarchy should be embedded in a context of enabling and regulating norms of basic political rights, of accountability and of rights to contestation (pp. 367–8), it remains an open question how such an order comes forth. Seeing it as simply emerging from problem-solving is problematic for two reasons. On the one hand, as regards the supposed coordination mechanism, there seems to be neither provision to actually channel dispersed problem-solving in such a way that, from the perspective of the more encompassing general public of citizens, it really addresses the right (and relevant) issues, nor control to ensure that dispersed attention is stable enough in a temporal perspective. On the other hand, and more fundamentally, this model by itself cannot account for how the principles of democratic equality and solidarity are brought to bear onto the self-selective forces on which the dispersed polyarchies should depend (see also Chapter 1 of this volume).

For the current purposes, I leave aside the issue of adequately managing interdependencies at the policy level from within deliberative polyarchies, and instead focus on the presumption that a deliberative perspective should necessarily and unequivocally favour a single democratic form – that of *participatory democracy*. As I see it, this seems to overtax the link that exists between a deliberative account of democracy and participatory politics, and this mainly for two reasons: it depends on an inadequately restricted account of the idea of democratic legitimacy, and it fails to see the normative significance and even desirability of a kind of multi-level democracy where different institutional forms of democracy may reflexively act upon each other. Just in order to briefly illustrate the first point,[10] let us start from one fundamental controversy heading the debate on the Euro-polity: whether the criterion of democratic legitimacy is basically anchored in the voluntaristic principle that everybody should have an equal chance to decisively bring to bear their preferences, or whether the idea of autonomous will formation is better articulated with reference to the epistemic idea that people as autonomous persons are best represented in their ability to demand and give reasons to each other (Habermas 2001a)? It seems to me that it is precisely this alternative account which is at the heart of the enduring controversy about whether to measure the structures of the present or future Euro-polity either against some substantial criteria of 'output legitimacy' or against some formal criteria of procedural (or input) legitimacy. While this is the conventional way to present the alternative, the trouble is that it seems to be wrong in the sense that the distinction between input and output does not adequately represent the alternative between voluntaristic and epistemic accounts of the idea of democratic legitimacy – precisely because this distinction itself can be applied to either side of the input/output divide. Accordingly, we have to draw a more differentiated picture (of at least four basic alternative accounts) which allows for two important points to be made. Counterposing input and output not only leads to an unjustified disjunction of participation on the one hand and the efficiency (or effectiveness) criterion on the other, but it tends to confer a normative dignity to the voluntaristic account of input legitimacy which is hardly warranted by the history of democratic thought.

In order to avoid this confusion and to open up the conceptual space for a more innovative view of the basic institutional infrastructure of the future Euro-polity, we need a closer look at what the idea of democratic legitimacy demands. In a nutshell, the preliminary answer consists of three parts. First, from the perspective of members of a political community taken individually, political authority (a political system, a form of governance) is legitimate if, and only if, its decisions reflect or mirror the dispositions (values, interests, norms, knowledge) of the constituent parts of the society in a way that the reasons for these decisions (can be understood to) meet the uncoerced (and rational)[11] consent of all those concerned. Second, from the perspective of members taken collectively, we must be able to understand the individual judgment as also comprising a guess about what all others would have thought to be a good (acceptable) decision. Third, this reflexive guess leads to a necessary qualification of the process of individual and collective will formation spelled out as a problem of mediation. This problem of mediation for obvious reasons consists of several dimensions and can thus be crudely stated as a problem of mediating judgments about the legitimacy of political decisions:

- with what everybody else (taken individually) wants, thinks, believes or aspires to (i.e. the social dimension);
- with what is correct or true (i.e. the factual dimension); and
- with the future consequences of a political action and its future evaluations by subsequent generations (i.e. the time dimension).

In addition, there seem to be at least two alternative options for how to deal with these problems of mediation, one external and procedural (institutional and rule-based), and the other internal and ethical (based on the virtues of citizens). This still leaves ample space for different combinations of these conceptual components but, instead of spelling these out here,[12] I confine myself to one important conclusion regarding the normative content of the idea of participatory democracy.

What seems to be important in this context is that 'participation' as such is underdetermined in several dimensions that are crucial to the idea of democratic legitimacy. It suffers from problems of selective inclusion (social, spatial or functional) which tend to undermine the normative demand for political equality – this danger of a self-selective exclusion of 'everybody else' can only be addressed within a representative system of delegation. Moreover, it also suffers from problems of 'parochialism' and the (moral and epistemic) underdetermination of its internal procedures. The cure to these problems might be seen in a kind of *reflexive constitutionalism* establishing and structuring the relations of interdependence and independence between participatory settings within and across the borders of specific policy domains, justifying the rules of inclusion and exclusion and privileging internal procedures that favour the deliberative orientations of the actors.

Thus, the question of which model of democracy is adequate for larger polities on the regional scale, the subunits of which are already internally democratized – irrespective of whether these are deliberative polyarchies or nation states – in any case raises many important second-order questions. And this is why a deliberative perspective puts emphasis not only on internally deliberative procedures, but on an institutional system so that the different parts (on different levels) of the system may reflexively act upon each other and where a variety of democratic forms comes into play – a deliberative system which should then also allow for different modes of political interaction and of reaching agreements to play their role.[13]

Reflexive integration: constitutional implications

When it comes to the question of the constitutionalization of the EU we are again confronted with a bewildering complexity of questions. First, there is the question of whether the EU needs to be constitutionalized at all or if it can be taken to be already constitutionalized (and if yes, to what degree)? Even if we answer the second question in the affirmative, there is still room for wondering whether it is constitutionalized in the right way. Is there a model account of the idea of constitutionalism? Finally, even if we were persuaded that there is something like an ideal of constitutionalism, we are torn into debates about its applicability under given circumstances. Taken together, opinions do not only diverge upon the issue of what is to be regarded as the ultimate authority from which a constitution may derive its normative force – i.e. whether we should locate this authority in a moral community, unified and personified in a European demos (Habermas 2004a; Michelman 2001), or whether we can count on dispersed sources of separately legitimated authorities which are multiple demoi (Weiler 1999). There is also disagreement about the scope of constitutionalization as well as about the best means to achieve the aims of constitutionalization.

I cannot engage with all of these questions here, and for the sake of brevity I simply assume that the Union needs to be *re-constitutionalized* in order to render its evolving structures of governance democratically legitimate. The aim of such a project is to build legally circumscribed forms of reflexivity into its structures and to make such forms of reflexive self-regulation democratic, i.e. visible and accessible to all. The reasons for focusing on these points are that, on the one hand, I take these suggestions to be characteristic of any distinctively deliberative approach to constitutionalization, and, on the other, I believe they allow us to come to terms with internal family quarrels within the deliberative camp. In order to show how this might work, I proceed in three steps. First, I indicate four major problems to be solved by (re)constitutionalizing the Euro-polity; second, I briefly introduce the idea of reflexive constitutionalization; and finally, with reference to three criteria, I draw a distinction between two ways of establishing reflexivity, one dispersed and co-evolutionary in nature (the wrong version) and the other one collective and deliberative (the correct version).

Regulated self-regulation

Even if one accepts the suggestion that the most important feature of the European Union as a post-national political order lies in its horizontally dispersed structures of governance with participatory, civic, associational and deliberative underpinnings – which might eventually develop into real normative achievements, provided that these elements can be fused into a normatively convincing form of transnational governance (cp. Joerges 2003) – our expectations concerning the constitutional domestication of these arrangements cannot and should not be too modest. They should also not be too immodest in the wrong way, consisting in simply remodelling the national mode of a strictly hierarchical form of self-intervention on the one hand and evolutionary processes of self-constitutionalization of dispersed polyarchies on the other.[14]

Seen in this light, the first aim of such transnational constitutionalization must consist in eliminating legal domination (cp. Bohman in this volume). Legal domination does not result from the imposition of the arbitrary will of an individual or group, but rather from the use of law 'to impose a cooperative scheme upon others without their being able to influence its terms' (p. 39). This is obviously also the case in the EU where a supranational form of juridification is based on doctrines like those of direct effect and legal supremacy of EU law, while those who interpret the legal meaning of the contractual sources of these laws are not under democratic control. The problem of administrative juridification and domination occurs wherever the constitutive circle between law and legitimate political power is broken, and this in a double sense: Where the jurisgenerative discourses themselves are inadequately institutionalized so that it cannot be taken for granted that public discourses are 'temporally, socially and materially specified in relation to political opinion and will-formation [. . .] in legislative bodies' (Habermas 2001b: 772–3) – that is the problem of administrative domination; or where agents tend to regulate the very political authorities for which they are agents (as in transnational governance arrangements). This is the problem of reversal of agency or 'incompletely defined democratic authority' (see Chapter 2: 40). This demand is a direct corollary to the deliberative principle that, in order for a law to be legitimate, it must be the case that the addressees of the law can plausibly understand themselves as its authors.

Second, it follows from the right to justification that anyone concerned must be effectively able to challenge authoritative political decisions on the ground that they do not meet the criterion of general and reciprocal justification. This right to contestation seems to be best realized when courts judge whether normatively required reasons have been used to justify a political decision, and when they protect the democratic process by reviewing procedures, processes and institutional devices of account-ability (see Bohman in this volume).

From this it directly follows, third, that, if it occurs, the process of a dele-gation of authority itself must be organized in a way that allows people to plausibly interpret it as resulting from their own rational will – i.e. it must be conceived as an autonomous act not externally 'administratively' imposed on them. If there is an *auto-paternalistic dimension* to the idea of democratic self-determination, it implies that it can be reasonably expected that fragmentation between horizontally and vertically dispersed sites of authority can be overcome – i.e. a layer has to be institutionalized at which the interdependencies become visible and from where interactions can be observed, monitored and regulated in order to overcome blind pragma-tism and to provide an alternative to blind co-evolution (cp. Bohman in this volume; Gerstenberg 2002a, 2002b; Cohen and Sabel 2003: 367–8).

While the three aforementioned aims result from the challenge to con-stitutionally rationalize the interplay between institutionalized discourses in the narrower sense and discourses in the broader public as well as instances of self-legislation from within different and dispersed sites of problem-solving and decision-making, a final aim should be to internally democratize them. This aim of *regulated self-regulation* may be best realized through establishing procedural rules to affirm the idea of epistemic pro-ceduralism as stated above, and which put rights to transparency, to access and to accountability as subjective rights to communication, information and participation.

Reflexive constitutionalization

The idea providing the rationale for these four fundamental propositions, which together explain what it means for a process of European constitu-tionalization to be immodest in the right way, is best captured by the notion of *reflexive constitutionalization* as outlined in the previous chapter. For a democratic system of governance to be a fully democratic one, we must be plausibly able to think of it as resulting from the deliberate and deliberatively structured attempts of people continuously and collectively modelling and remodelling the terms of their political interactions. It is important to note that this basic idea has three crucial components to it, all of which must be realized if the system is to be not only reflexive in a formal sense but also in a democratic sense. For one, it must be able to meet the liberal challenge that the Union of constitutionalism and demo-cracy is at best a paradoxical union if not simply a contradiction in terms. In this understanding, by constitutionalizing itself, democracy reacts to the impossibility of founding itself by democratic means (cp. Offe 1998). In order to overcome this paradox, Habermas suggested, and I follow him here, 'we have to understand the regress itself as the understandable expression of the future-oriented character, or openness of the democratic constitution: in my view, a constitution that is democratic – not just in its content but also according to its source of legitimation – is a tradition-building project' that can escape the circle of groundless self-constitution only if it 'can be understood in the long run as a self-correcting learning-process' (Habermas 2001b: 774). Second, once we have accepted this theoretical reason for constitutional reflexivity, I think we also have to admit the implication that reflexivity can only be unfolded at a collective level in two senses: It is collective in the Deweyan sense, i.e. a public is constituted by the very fact that it addresses the combined, but unintended effects and consequences of actions taken separately; and in the sense of the use of public reason, which means that it does so in the light of reasons not only acceptable to all, but requiring acceptability not for distributively, but collectively shared (identical) reasons. Third, it seems to me that, once we have accepted these two implications of the idea of reflexivity, we should also be prepared to admit that there is a *hierarchical dimension* to the idea of reflexive self-intervention: Not only must we be able to sort out moral reasons in the light of which we may be able to devise solutions to the problems at hand, but we should allow them to be decisive – and that is, hierarchically superior.

Dispersed or collective reflexivity?

These conceptual differentiations finally lead me to my last and more substantive point. As I suggested, the understanding of *democratic reflexivity* from a deliberative standpoint as outlined in this chapter helps us to critically distinguish it from its two major competitors: societal constitutionalism as outlined by Teubner (2003) on the one hand and directly deliberative polyarchy on the other. These two perspectives both share the conviction that, in order to make the idea of constitutionalization safe for the postnational order, we have to decouple it from the idea of statehood, but they substitute statehood in different ways. One is the 'anarchical' solution suggested for instance by Cohen and Sabel which basically reads like this:

> In anarchy the alignment of interests and incentives among the actors results in spontaneous coordination without the need for a center to compel provision of information, facilitate the pooling of the information provided, discipline those who abuse the grant of autonomy to victimize some within their own jurisdiction, or take advantage of outsiders acting in good faith.
>
> (Cohen and Sabel 2003: 366)

Here the substitute for the integrative mechanism of the state is the market, and it is hard to see how the authors want to link this integrative mechanism to the idea of democratic deliberation. As opposed to this, Teubner's idea of regulated self-regulation is not premised on the market and economic rationality, but on law – or more precisely on a solution to the paradoxical challenge of establishing rules for the self-generation of law, which are expected to legally regulate the jurisgenerative process from within functionally differentiated subsystems of society (Teubner 2003: 13). In this perspective, his general idea, as far as I understand it, is to suggest that we should understand constitutionalization in a societal sense as a form in which the distinction between state and society is repro-duced within each subsystem by establishing and normatively regulating in itself a formalized and a spontaneous area and their precarious interrela-tions (pp. 17–18). Seen in this light, the promise of *societal constitutionalism* seems to be that we are confronted with phenomena of the inner self-constitutionalization of societal regimes which may substitute for the tradi-tional, i.e. statist mode of constitutionalization. But is this claim justified?

There are, I think, three broad answers to this question. The first is that, while Teubner offers an interesting attempt to generalize and re-specify the idea of constitutionalization, he remains conventional in the sense that his use of the argumentative figure of self-justification is strictly liberal – he refers to a hierarchy of legal norms already built into the idea of right as such. Second, and connected to that, it seems obvious that there are two components to the idea of regulated self-regulation: one is Kantian and symbolizes the conception of freedom and autonomy as self-legislation; and the other is Hegelian and mirrors Hegel's notion of inner statehood as the form in which solidarity and rational integration of a society are achieved (Calliess 2002). The problem is, however, that this is only tacitly and implicitly acknowledged while the approach fails to offer a conceptual tool which might help to re-articulate the Hegelian idea. And third, it seems to me that the concept of *internal reflexivity* (or, in Haber-masian terms: transcendence from within) is underspecified with respect to a third meaning of reflexivity, where it represents a relation between an individual self (actor or group or regime) and an entity that is larger and more encompassing than itself (which, in the confines of a systems-theoretical approach is of course hard to imagine). With respect to this challenge we are left with the idea of only contingent co-evolution, and that of course, for normative reasons cannot be the end of the story in a deliberative perspective.[15]

Reflexive integration and hierarchical self-intervention

Thus far, I have tried to depict the European polity as a polycentric demo-cratic order, integrated by a constitution that gives meaning and structure to the idea of reflexive cooperation which is at the heart of any under-standing of the EU as a new form of transnational political entity. This picture also seems to suggest that such a constitutional order can be established without further reference to the idea of stateness, which is only a conceptual precursor to constitutional theory and, in normative as well as theoretical and functional or practical terms, already absorbed into it. But this is a contentious issue because it confronts us with some important questions about constitutional (self-)justification, (self-)enactment and (self-)application and enforcement. This has led people to take recourse to the state in order to determine the self who shall be constituted; who shall give authority to the constitution; who shall be the addressee of constitutional rights and guarantee its structural provisions. Now, some of these problems can be (and of course have been) solved if we move from the idea of the reason of the state to transcendental insights implied in the very idea of cooperation; if we dismiss the idea of a homogeneous self and put the idea of *a multiple self* in its place, who can reflexively address and constitute itself; and if we substitute a structural and procedural notion of self-application for the legal concept of the personality of the state. The changes these conceptual shifts bring about are significant, because it is no longer the state as a public body that constitutes and constitutionalizes civil society, but it is the civil society that institutes the state as a form by which it can reflexively act upon itself – this is clearly a de-substantialized notion, serving as a civilizing device (Schuppert 2003). Nonetheless, it is important not to forget that a substantial residue of administrative hierarchy and uniform application of law remains crucial for a well-ordered constitutional democracy (Lord 2004a). Without an effective form of organizational law, constitutions are in danger of remaining what they initially are – only words (Brunkhorst 2004: 103).

How then to understand the conceptual relationship of deliberative democracy and the state in normative terms? Even if the notion of stateness acquires some normative content in this respect, it would certainly overstate the issue if we take the state to rest on autonomous sources of normativity as, for example, Hegel would like to have it. Instead, what we have to ask, in taking the relationship between morality and law as an exemplar and where the law has to compensate for the deficiencies of moral coordination alone,[16] is whether the idea of stateness as a means of hierarchical self-intervention into the patterns of societal cooperation is normatively implied in the idea of reflexive integration as outlined so far. However, even if there should be something to this idea, we have to come to terms with the normatively important issue of whether the compensating mechanism (i.e. the state) is in itself sufficiently justified for normative reasons (the strong version), or whether we better understand this as a functional requirement only. The latter is at least consonant with the aims of moral coordination and integration without acquiring a moral value of its own. But before I address this question, let me start by reconsidering the reasons that speak in favour of taking the issue of the state at all seriously in this context.

On statehood

Whenever the issue of a state (or at least of necessary state-like structures) is raised in the context of transnational democratic governance,[17] it is soon confronted with major challenges of at least three kinds. The first is an objection on feasibility grounds, pretending that, whatever the theoretical merits of the argument, this is not a practically conceivable or viable option at least for the mediate and intermediate future. State actors are primarily guided by a sense of the 'reason of the (national) state', inimical to the transnational pooling of their respective sovereignties or to the complete investing of it into a supranational structure. This objection may be at least partially countered by the suggestion that what we really confront is a process of the differentiation of the constitutive components of statehood, which are selectively institutionalized on a level beyond the nation state. Thus we are not confronted with the withering away of stateness or its self-assertion in its traditional form, but with its transformation. But even if we were able to settle the issue at that point, we will soon be confronted with normative concerns, too. And these usually take two forms. One is the second-order problems that arise from superimposing a state form on its constituent units where these units are already internally democratized, and where the normative promise of the idea of the state which resides in fusing statehood, law, constitutionalism, democracy and solidarity into a whole cannot be reproduced.[18] The normative force of this kind of criticism is obviously contingent on the contention that such a system is necessarily undemocratic – a contention that I have tried to reject throughout this chapter. The other is an even more fundamental concern that democracy involves being suspicious of and inimical to any form of hierarchically fixed authority and power.[19] To this objection one could reply (as I presuppose throughout this chapter) that an organized capacity to act is part of the idea of public autonomy as it is understood in the republican tradition and in deliberative democracy respectively.

In the light of these provisional responses to the main charges against the idea of statehood we may rephrase the whole issue and instead ask two different questions: whether we must think of public autonomy as the capacity to effectively act and act upon oneself necessarily in terms of a hierarchy or whether we have reasons to believe that these demands are sufficiently met in horizontal forms of self-coordination, too?[20] In the case of the former, would we have to pay a price for that acknowledgement that is too high in normative terms and that therefore would exceed by far its potential gains? Instead of a full-blown answer to these questions, I conclude with six propositions which show that, for a system of governance to be adequately democratic, there should be hierarchical forms of self-intervention:

*   providing for the possibility to unburden forms of horizontal self-government and coordination and for the possibility to substitute for these if they fail to adequately address political problems at hand;

- providing for an allocative mechanism under which the allocation of rights, duties and responsibilities to problem-solving polyarchies, agencies or expert committees may be thought of as an ideal delegation procedure establishing an institutional link between delegative decisions and the collective will of the people (expressed, for example, in representative institutions) (Pollack 2003; Lord 2004a, 2004b) – and these decisions should also provide 'constitutional' criteria such as procedural norms regulating the internal and external interactions of units of problem-solving, or norms regulating the access to and the composition of the relevant groups;
- providing for the management of interdependencies and independencies, i.e. for a monitoring function which in addition helps to preserve the holistic character of the system;
- guaranteeing that rights and responsibilities within self-governing units are observed and ensuring that structural and organizational demands of democracy are met;
- providing for the visibility of the system as a whole and marking the points of effective access, intervention and contestation; and finally
- providing for the moral credibility of the system as a whole and thus inducing the necessary relation of horizontal trust between citizens (Offe 1999).

Reflexive self-intervention

While this argument so far only tries to establish an internal link between the idea of democracy and some elements of stateness necessary for it to be adequately institutionalized, thus acquiring a normative content only indirectly, it is still an open question how we must understand this link in normative terms. One way of understanding this relationship is in analogy to the relationship between law and morality, according to which law has the function to compensate for the cognitive, motivational or institutional weaknesses of moral coordination alone (Habermas 1992: 135–51). On this account, the compensating mechanism (i.e. the law) must have access to its own source of normativity, which in this case resides in the principle of democracy, holding that only those laws are legitimate which in their origin can be traced back to the collective will of the citizens – i.e. can be reasonably considered as a result of the public use of reason. Now, and although providing for forms of hierarchical self-intervention can, as I said, be regarded to be an essential part of an adequate understanding of the idea of public autonomy, it would surely be taking the issue much too far if we took that to mean that in itself the state is sufficiently morally justified.

So there must be a somewhat weaker version of the contention that a notion of stateness is normatively implied in the idea of deliberative democracy – and this may, as I suggest, consist in the complementary realization of normative principles, which are already implied in the idea of deliberative democracy but which nonetheless remain in a certain tension to the ideal of rationality upon which it is built, i.e. the principle of equality and the principle of private autonomy together with its corollary of democratic voluntarism. The idea then is to say that, only under conditions of hierarchical forms of self-intervention where different forms of democracy reflexively and effectively act upon one another, can we preserve the full meaning of the democratic ideal and acquire an adequate understanding of the full meaning of reflexive integration. And only in this sense then may we also contend that there is no democratization without a state.

Notes

* For especially helpful comments on earlier versions I would like to thank Damian Chalmers, Erik O. Eriksen, Tanja Hitzel-Cassagnes, Daniel Gaus, Oliver Flügel, Rainer Forst, Peter Niesen, Regina Kreide and Hans-Jürgen Puhle.

1 Here I mainly follow Forst 2001, although I shall partly depart from his view in some important respects. These primarily relate to an adequate understanding of democratic proceduralism on the one hand and its institutional repercussions on the other (see below).

2 For an alternative view which denies the reasons normally given in support of the thesis that especially the supranational features of the EU system undermine the normative principles of self-determination, self-legislation and self-government (i.e. the idea of popular sovereignty) in so far as these are (at least up to now) institutionally and ethically realized at the level of already adequately democratized member states (cp. Moravcsik 2003). The problem with this view is not only that it is insufficiently fact-regarding and insufficiently sensitive to normative concerns that cannot be met by efficient problem-solving alone, but that, additionally, it does not take seriously enough the restrictions on democratic self-government that arise from its transnational features such as an incompletely defined structure of dispersed and fragmented forms of authority. For an instructive criticism of this revisionist view see also Ruchet 2004.

3 For this formulation of the dilemma see also Bohman's contribution to this volume.

4 This formulation I owe to James Bohman.

5 This can be justified only if it can be proved beyond any reasonable doubt that the epistemic qualifications of an individual or a small elite by far outreach the epistemic value of broad public and inclusive discussions (cp. Estlund 2000b: 14).

6 Pluralism has, as I see it, moral value without being freestanding in a normative sense (cp. Rawls 1993).

7 Eriksen (2003: 193, 200 and 214–15) – although there remains some unresolved tension in two alternative accounts of the same idea (Eriksen and Weigård 2003).

8 This paradigmatic account is provided by Pettit 2004, although some initial similarities with 'Deliberative Supranationalism' as forged by Joerges and Neyer 1997a might be seen. Especially Joerges (2000, 2003) has, since the initial statement, resolutely tried to reintegrate his earlier view into a framework of trans-

national constitutionalism which also provides a major contribution to the idea of reflexive integration. Cf. also Gerstenberg and Sabel 2002; Schmalz-Bruns 1999.

9 Here I cannot even try to adequately discuss this model, but will instead focus only on two points: the overestimation of its problem-solving potential at the level of everyday politics and thus of participatory politics, and the underestimation of issues of democratic legitimacy raised by it.

10 In the following, I draw on parts of an already published manuscript (Schmalz-Bruns 2002).

11 'Rational' here is taken in the sense Rawls (1993: 48–54) uses it in contradistinction to 'the reasonable': the rationality of a person refers to the capacity to choose and to pursue a conception of the good.

12 For a more detailed account of this suggestion, see Schmalz-Bruns 2002.

13 Bohman in the previous chapter seems to have something very similar in mind, although his way of rendering the issue as 'adequately democratizing' seems to me to be a little bit too defensive, in that 'adequacy' in the way he introduces the idea shall be informed by normative as well as by the emergent structures of the EU, but where it is not quite clear whether this does not also mean that it is the 'ought' that follows the given.

14 Or, to put it once again in Joerges' words, constitutionalizing the Union implies to find a 'third way between constitutionalism "from above" and blind pragmatism' (Joerges 2003: 37).

15 Cf. Joerges 2003, fn. 91 for a very similar conclusion.

16 That is, for weaknesses of the will, for the indeterminacy of moral judgment or at least the cognitive burdens that arise from it, or for its lack of the institutional conditions of a uniform application.

17 A recent prominent example is provided by Alexander Wendt (2003).

18 This is of course a concern originally formulated by Kant in his writing on 'Perpetual peace' and only recently rearticulated and reinvigorated by Habermas (2004b: 135).

19 For a recent articulation of this defensive perspective, compare Abromeit 2002.

20 This, again more defensive question is Habermas' starting-point for developing a vision of a multilevel system of transnational governance which, as a whole, does not and 'for very good reasons' must not adopt the character of a state (Habermas 2004b: 134).

4 Public discourse, identity and the problem of democratic legitimacy

Bernhard Peters

In German debates over the European Union, in general, and its 'democratic deficit' in particular, the following quotation by Peter Graf Kielmansegg has become almost canonical: 'Europe, even limited to Western Europe, is not a community of communications, barely a community of memory, and only a very limited community of experience' (Kielmansegg 1994).[1] The formulation suggests that a political community has to be a community of memory, of experience and of communication as a precondition for having a common, legitimate, democratic political order. Other sceptical objections against further centralization of powers and responsibilities and against the possibilities of further democratization have also pointed to a lack of collective identity and a missing European public sphere. On closer inspection, however, these familiar formulas begin to look somewhat enigmatic. It is not only that the basic terms of these equations are very much contested and used with different meanings. Much has been written, for example, on democracy and legitimacy, and yet there remain not only differences of opinion, quite naturally, but also certain conceptual ambiguities that hinder the debate. Also, there are well-known controversies about the notion of collective identity and the concept of a European public sphere. In addition, the *relationships* between these basic terms are not very well specified. That is, very often even the precise *meanings* of the propositions that supposedly spell out some of these relations remain somewhat fuzzy or ambiguous. So by necessity, the *questions* asked about these relationships remain fuzzy, too. What exactly *are* the supposed relationships between these terms – or between the real phenomena that they denote? Are they conceptual, normative, or empirical? In addition, how should we specify the contents of these different kinds of relationship? The main purpose of this chapter is to clarify some of these terms and some of these problem formulations. I will apply the conceptual framework to the substantive questions about the future of the European Union that form the topic of this volume: what kind of political community or political order should the EU become, what kind of European *project* should we undertake and what might be the basis of the political legitimacy of the projected model of a European political order?

The magic quadrangle of political theory

If we look at the most important and most commonly used of these terms, i.e. democracy, the public sphere (or public discourse), collective identity and legitimacy, it is obvious that a discussion of their relationships to each other is equivalent to a debate on the foundations of any political order. The nexus between these categories can be regarded as the magic quadrangle of political theory, denoting some of the most basic problems of political theory (see Figure 4.1). This kind of problem has traditionally been discussed with reference to the modern nation state. So if we apply them to a new form of transnational political order, like the EU, an additional problem arises: should we adjust the meaning of these basic terms? And should we expect a change of relationships or a *different* nexus between these elements, and possibly a different form of at least some of the elements themselves? The EU certainly shares many features with the modern state – it makes decisions that are binding for all its individual members and over a specified territory. It provides a legal order with rights and obligations and recourse to its own judicial system, produces many regulations and distributes public funds and a few services. On the other hand, it lacks a monopoly controlling the legitimate use of force over its territory and, for now, an army and the right to levy taxes; and it stands generally in a peculiar relationship to its subordinate political units, i.e. the member states. What do these features or similar features of other transnational political institutions mean for democracy, the public sphere, collective identity and the legitimacy of its political and legal institutions and their activities? And should the relationships between these elements look different than in the case of the nation state?

It would be risky, however, to proceed directly to this second set of questions about the peculiarities that the quadrangle may have in the case of a transnational political system. For this presupposes that we already have a clear picture of what the relations between the four corners of the quadrangle are, or should be, in the classical case of the nation state. And

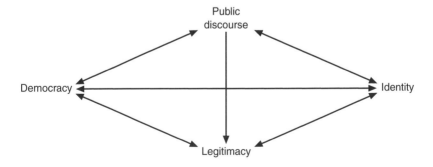

Figure 4.1 The magic quadrangle of political theory.

this might not be entirely true. Therefore, it might be appropriate to look first at the conventional understandings of the four terms and of the relationships between them, before coming back to possible differences between national (or 'single state') and transnational political systems, especially the EU. I will start with a discussion of the four terms and then proceed to the relationships between them. In my exposition, I will generally start with the descriptive usage of the basic terms before proceeding to the normative aspects. This makes it easier to separate the relevant empirical and normative issues.

Democracy

Fortunately, not much has to be said in this context about the notion of democracy. We may note, however, that 'democracy' is often used in two different senses. In one sense, it denotes a whole political order of a certain type (as in 'Western democracies' or 'liberal democracy'). The type of political system is a liberal, constitutional representational one, with parliamentary legislation, free elections, some kind of division of powers, the 'rule of law', guaranteed basic rights and so on. In another usage, 'democracy' more specifically refers to a certain *component* of liberal political orders, namely to the participation of citizens in processes and procedures of political decision-making. This is simple enough, but in some contexts, conflation of these two meanings leads to confusion, as will be discussed later. My own usage will be the second, narrower one. So 'democracy' will refer to all ways in which citizens influence the political decision-making and political action of officials in a way that is generally considered legitimate – not only by voting, but also through the influence of interest groups, political parties and other associations, or by public action or even adjudication. It includes both formalized and informal modes of political participation, but not illegal ones, such as bribing officials or threatening terrorist acts. Obviously this is a descriptive, not a normative concept of democracy. Normative concepts of democracy in this second, narrower sense would spell out how these forms of political participation should look and how they should relate to other parts of the general political order. They would also give an account of the *value* of democracy – a topic to which I will return later. A general normative political theory would include a normative theory of democracy, but would be broader and also include basic constitutional rights other than rights to political participation, basic structures of the legal system and so on.

Public discourse

The notion of a public sphere or of public discourse requires more elaboration. Public political communication and 'public opinion' might of course be considered forms of political participation, as ways of influencing political decision-making and official action. It is common and useful, however, to treat 'public discourse' or the 'public sphere' and 'democracy' as separate categories. One reason for this is that public discourse is much broader than what is usually regarded as political communication. For the purposes of this discussion, it would not matter much if we regarded public discourse as part of the democratic process, so we need not go much further into this question. Now I would like to propose certain meanings for 'public discourse' and the 'public sphere' that seem to be analytically useful and not too far from common usages.

The German term *Öffentlichkeit* may be translated either as *public sphere* or as *public*. *Public sphere* has the connotation of a somehow delineated social space of communication; *the public* denotes some kind of collectivity or community. For reasons that will be explained shortly, I will focus here on *public discourse* in a specific sense. To denote the boundedness of public discourse, I will use terms like *spheres* or *fields* of discourse. *The public* will refer to the participants within a certain sphere of public discourse. What is meant by public discourse here? The *public* feature does not seem to be very controversial. Public communication is freely accessible communication without formal restrictions or special conditions for participation. In public communication, all interested laypersons are free to participate, to listen or to read and to speak their mind. Trivially, *active* participation ('speaking') is a minority affair in most settings, especially in mass communication. But there are no special barriers to 'listening'.

Discourse

Discourse is the more problematic term. It is used with many different meanings in the literature, such as in various sorts of 'discourse analysis' in Foucault and others. My usage is closer to, but not identical to Habermas' notion of 'Diskurs' or to recent uses of the term 'deliberation', especially in theories of 'deliberative democracy' (Bohman and Rehg 1997; Macedo 1999; Fishkin and Laslett 2003). *Discourse*, in this sense, occurs if empirical statements, descriptions or reports, explanations, interpretations, proposals, prescriptions, normative judgments or evaluations are supported by some kind of justification, by some argumentative backing, or by some presentation of evidence. These kinds of argumentative or evidentiary support have to refer to actual or anticipated questions, doubts or objections and they have to be open to further questioning or further objections. Discourse is what we normally understand by debate, or discussion, or argument, interpretation and analysis.

Obviously, we find forms of deliberation or discourse in all kinds of settings, in private communications as well as in organizational or in expert communications. Some of the more clear-cut cases of deliberation we find in certain specialized and institutionalized forms, like scientific communication or court procedures. If we look for public forms of discourse, we

find them partly in discussions during informal encounters and in public
meetings, although speeches during such meetings are not always predominantly deliberative. In the mass media, deliberation is almost
swamped by various forms of entertainment, on the one hand, and by
mere information or reporting of 'news', on the other. But in the electronic media, there are forms of news commentary, news magazines and
documentaries with elements of analysis, commentary and sometimes
advocacy, as well as various discussions and talk shows, many of which are
mainly entertaining or expressive, however. Both in the electronic and
print media, we also find a considerable amount of *reported* opinions with
some deliberative content. In the print media, we find much deliberative
content in non-fiction books as well as in the periodical press in the form
of newspaper commentary, opinion pieces, analytical or advocatory
reporting, essays or other genres of more sustained argument, especially
in the 'Feuilleton' of national German newspapers or in quality journals
or magazines. This media discourse is certainly the most important and
influential part of public discourse.[2]

Why should we focus on the *discursive* part of public communication?
There might be normative as well as empirical reasons. Normative conceptions of public discourse or deliberation play an important role in recent
theories of democracy and legitimacy. Empirically, it might be interesting
to examine the degree to which the reality of public discourse deviates
from the normative model, or what conditions would support or hinder
the realization of the normative model. Apart from that, it seems plausible
to assume that public discourse is the primary medium for the development of public knowledge, values, interpretations and self-understandings
for change and innovation, as well as reproduction or transmission over
time in the inventory of ideas and arguments that are available in a given
public sphere. To put it more generally, public discourse could be
regarded as a primary mechanism for cultural reproduction and change.
This assumption relates to the sphere of public culture and public discourse itself, i.e. to publicly available and circulating ideas. The effects of
public discourse on individual opinions and attitudes throughout the
population, known as 'public opinion', are more uncertain, even if there
is some evidence that changes in mass opinion are influenced to a degree
by elite opinion, which in turn is influenced by the quality press and other
forms of public discourse (Zaller 1992).

Public spheres

Public discourse mostly takes place in certain bounded spheres – 'public
spheres' or 'spheres of public discourse'. Traditionally, individual public
spheres are seen as bounded by nation states, and 'the public' is understood as part of the respective citizenry of each country. National laws and
regulations and national languages put their stamp on each public sphere.

National politics, national governments, parties, intermediary organizations and associations provide topics and input. National mass media function as channels or carriers of public discourse. This is an insufficient description, however. There are more elements of cohesion and boundedness than these mostly external conditions. There are important forms of internal differentiation. Moreover, there is obviously exchange and observation between different national publics or public spheres.

A sphere of public discourse, in this case a national sphere, is characterized by a high density of communication flows, with a higher density internally than that across borders (Deutsch 1956). 'Communication flows' are discursive communications in a broader sense. They are communications between 'speakers' and audiences, such as the reception of discourse by the audience, and they are direct or indirect communications between speakers. Indirect communication consists of observation and 'listening' and may produce indirect reactions, while direct communication consists of addressing each other or each other's positions. Public spheres are also integrated by dominant agendas, sets of issues or topics that turn up simultaneously in the various mass media and other forms of public discourse.[3] In addition, there is a considerable amount of common understanding on the meaning of debated issues, how different positions may be understood and interpreted, what the important and disputed aspects are and what is more or less taken for granted. In cases of dispute, different aspects of a problem might be focused on or different 'frames' might be used, but awareness of these differences is mostly given.

Public culture

In the background of public discourse, there is something like a public culture, which is the repertoire or reservoir of symbols, meanings, knowledge and values that are relevant to a certain public. Part of this is what is commonly called a collective or, better, public identity. 'Relevant' means: known by, accessible to, interesting for, noticed by, directed or addressed to and circulating among a public, but not necessarily 'shared' by the members of these publics in the sense of being universally accepted or internalized. Some important elements of a public culture include huge stocks of common knowledge, especially lots of factual information, many recipes and prescriptions on how to achieve certain results and many norms, mores and conventions for all kinds of situations. There are also certain more general, more prestigious and more elaborated elements: important norms and values, certain general cognitive and evaluative beliefs. There are beliefs about personal life and personal identity, and there are cognitive and normative beliefs about the social world – about history, about basic features of the social and political order, about the future in terms of progress or decline, and about achievements, problems and crises. For lack of a better term, I will call these more general parts of public culture *general interpretations*. The relationship between these general interpretations and collective identities will be discussed in the next section.

At this point, two questions cannot be avoided. First: are there still *distinct* national public cultures in this sense, and how distinct or how different from other national public cultures are they? And second: to what degree is public discourse dependent on or bounded by such a public culture? What are the possibilities for or what are the constraints on public discourse *across* public cultures?

There are familiar objections to the idea of a common culture and to the notion of a *national* culture in particular. To sum them up, in a somewhat oversimplified or exaggerated way: there is no national culture that is a coherent system of beliefs or meanings. Contemporary culture is eclectic, syncretistic, internally fragmented, a jumble of heterogeneous elements, not an organic whole at all. There is no cultural consensus. There are no cognitive and normative belief systems that are widely accepted as valid and binding. There is widespread controversy, dissensus, pluralism, difference, diffidence and at most some fragile acceptance, imposed by the more powerful groups. Therefore, there is no identifiable national culture with a character unique and distinct from other cultures. Because of the incoherent and eclectic character of all culture and because of the widespread diffusion of cultural elements, all differences and boundaries between national cultures have become blurred.

Certainly at least some of these statements have some force and make us wonder whether we should keep looking for that mysterious entity called 'national culture'. And yet, if we travel around different countries, if we read the newspapers, watch television, if we go to public meetings, talk to people, if we live in a country for a while, try to understand its politics, the ways of life we encounter and, even if we talk to colleagues from our discipline, members of our own cosmopolitan profession, don't we feel very distinctly that there *are* very real and consequential cultural differences? And if we look at some of the relevant comparative literature on political culture, value change, social movements and so on, we find at least some confirmation that is not conclusive, but suggestive of the supposed influence of national cultural differences (Hayashi 1998; Hofstede 1998; Inkeles 1998).

Now it is not too difficult to describe in a general manner some kind of middle position between the polemical extremes. We do not have to follow the obviously false alternative between the assumption of national cultural homogeneity and cultural determinism, on the one hand, and the assumption of randomness or total manipulability of cultural variation, on the other. It is more plausible to describe a national public culture as a field of contention. There is a lot of variation of cultural elements, a lot of difference and a lot of disagreement. But the whole ensemble is not simply chaotic, without any kind of order or pattern. Cultural elements are more a repertoire than a definite blueprint for action, but they still form a repertoire with a distinct composition. And a repertoire only exists to the degree that it is already mastered by the actors – who are what they are because of their mastery of or familiarity with that specific repertoire. Contention is widespread, but not random. There are fault-lines, cleavages, camps, central issues and topics, certain inventories of ideas and arguments to support different positions. Despite all disagreements, there are probably some common assumptions, some common language and some shared knowledge of cultural elements. We cannot disagree about everything if we want to argue about our disagreements.

All this has to be properly specified or qualified, of course. There might be further differentiations of the public culture and the public, for instance, in addition to the alignment of adversary camps. Different parts of the public culture might be relevant to different segments of the public. Not all issues are equally important to all people. There might also be some kind of unequal access to the public culture. There might be different degrees of cultural sophistication or unequal distributions of cultural knowledge. Some more elaborate belief systems might be available only to parts of the public, but all of this still allows for basic commonalities, certain common backgrounds and porous boundaries within a diversified national public culture.

The second question asks in what way a national public culture determines the possibility of public discourse and the shape of a national sphere of public discourse. To maintain that there could be no meaningful public discourse, no mutual understanding across the boundaries of public cultures, would be patently wrong. Obviously there are ways in which discourse crosses such borders, and there are ways of mutual understanding between different spheres of public discourse. Much depends, of course, on degrees of cultural distance or familiarity, on degrees of similarity or difference. And always some kind of translation, not only in the literal sense, and thereby possible transformation is necessary. This takes some degree of special effort. So a public culture does not *confine* public discourse to a certain public. But it greatly *facilitates* such discourse, shapes it to a certain degree, influences frames of reference and ways of understanding and takes part in directing attention to certain issues and concerns and in shaping agendas.

Note that this is once again a descriptive account of public discourse or deliberation. Normative accounts would specify institutional conditions and possible norms of conduct for public deliberation. They would also give justifications for the importance of deliberation. In doing this, they might point to the expected *effects* of public discourse. Such an argument, however, would necessarily be based on certain empirical assumptions, to which we will return later.

Collective identities

Public culture, as described above, consists in part of what was called *general interpretations*. Among these general interpretations, there are some that pertain in a special way to the life of the national community and some-times also to national subgroups or to some transnational social unit, such as Western Europe or the Western world in general. These are interpreta-tions or beliefs relating to the community itself – its current state, its char-acter, its problems, its achievements, its history and its future. This is what is commonly called collective or national identity. 'Identity', however, is a somewhat misleading term because of its connotations of homogeneity and permanence. Therefore, it might be preferable to speak of *collective interpretations* or *collective self-understandings*. Because of its familiarity, however, I will also continue to use the term collective identity.

The following is an illustrative list of potential elements that make up those collective interpretations. There are the criteria for the identifica-tion of membership or the distinction between citizens and non-citizens.[4] There are collective self-images: the ascription of characteristics or traits typical of the members or of the collectivity as a whole, generally linked with mostly positive evaluations and with collective ideals or normative models and with notions of collective interests and common problems.[5] Often there are also notions of collective honour or dignity and possibly a sense of violation if the group or certain members are treated with con-tempt or in other ways improperly by outsiders or if members do not live up to the central standards of the group. These collective self-images are often linked with contrasting images of other groups and with compara-tive evaluations, as well as with definitions of the relations to other collec-tivities as friendly or hostile, for example. Within groups, there can also be feelings of special solidarity, commitment and trust toward other group members. Finally, there is the important temporal or historical dimension, relating both to the past and to the future of the collectivity. Collective memories or interpretations of the past, perhaps commitments to certain traditions and collective projects or collective responsibilities derived from the past exist, which link the past to the present and to the future, hopes and aspirations for the future (and not just an individual's future) and possibly even a sense of a collective 'mission'. Not all of these elements need to be present or articulated in particular, of course.

If we use a weak and inclusive notion of collective identity as developed here, and drop the unitary associations of this term, it becomes obvious that we have to ask the same questions about collective identity that have been asked about the role and character of group culture or especially national culture in general. There might be further differentiations of collective identities, in addition to the alignment of adversary camps or the contests between different interpretations or discourses. There might not only be different versions of collective identity, supported by different parts of a national population. There might also be different degrees of interest. Aspects of collective identity might be more important for some people than for others. Public debates about questions of collective identity may be followed primarily by certain segments of the public, and active participation in public will be even more selective.

There is also a great variability in the salience of various elements of collective identity and of collective identity as a whole. In many contexts, these elements remain in the background, as unstated assumptions and beliefs, as taken for granted. Collective beliefs or other elements become more or less explicit, objects of attention or possibly objects of reflection, if they are questioned or disputed or celebrated.

Relations between collective identities

Different collective identities can have special relations. They can be nesting with each other, such as national, subnational or regional identities, or overlapping. The latter is true for collectivities that are at least partly transnational in scope but have national 'wings' or departments or subunits. Examples would be international religious communities or professional organizations of scientists.

Substantively, the relationships between collective identities with overlapping memberships *may* be competing. The strength of the identities in question might be inversely related; one kind of identity would gain strength by weakening allegiance to another. One might also assume, therefore, some kind of competition between national and regional identities, for example, or between national identities in EU member countries on the one hand and some European (or EU) collective identity, on the other. This kind of relationship is not a necessary one, however. Relationships between collective identities might also be indifferent, of a non-rival nature or even mutually supportive. Since group membership and orientation toward a collective identity demand individual attention, commitment and even some kind of active support or participation, there is always some kind of competition. The amounts of energy and attention that individuals can mobilize are certainly variable, but nevertheless limited, and choices about allocation are always necessary. Most of the time these choices may be habitual, however, and made without much reflection. Relationships between group memberships and collective identities can nevertheless be mutually supportive in some respects, especially in the case of nested identities. Family traditions, local and regional attachments, membership in a national church and/or membership in voluntary associations may support people's national identifications.

Incompatible or conflicting relations between collective identities may emerge in several ways. In most cases, there are conflicts between social units, where collective identities are implicated. In certain cases, collective identities may produce conflict because they imply conflicting orientations

and demands. Or conflicts may affect certain elements of collective identity (e.g. collective pride or self-respect), and this may aggravate conflict.
There may be many kinds of conflicts between collectivities with mutually
exclusive memberships, of course. If there are elements of collective identity that give group conflicts a special character and possibly make them
harder to resolve, an important question is how collective identities might
be implicated in such conflicts. In the case of nested or overlapping memberships and collective identities, conflicting demands may simply be
placed on the individual by the respective groups and their collective self-
understandings without open conflict between the groups as a whole. This
is more or less the familiar case of role conflict. Demands of family membership may conflict with patriotic duties. In conflicts between groups,
where overlapping memberships play a role, conflicts of loyalty emerge. In
conflicts between states, for example, class solidarity may conflict with
national loyalty.

Authors have made various statements about competing or conflicting
collective identities (Alonso 1995; Lepsius 1997; Mummendey and Simon
1997; Schauer 1997; Hedetoft 1999). Often assertions are made that
national identity has some primacy over other collective identities, either
in a descriptive or a normative sense. Subnational or transnational collective identities based on ethnicity, class or religion have been seen as dangerous for national unity. On the other hand, national identity has often
been described as the winner in most of these conflicts. National identities
have trumped both international class solidarity and more particularistic
group attachments.

It is, however, not so easy to evaluate general statements of this kind.
The impact of collective identities on people's orientations and actions is
very much influenced by specific contexts, situations and characteristics of
group conflict. It is true, of course, that the stability of a political order
requires that allegiance to the state *on certain matters* is dominant over
competing group loyalties. But modern political orders respect individual
attachments to families, religious communities and other collectivities,
and this is a precondition for their stability. There is some kind of
balance, not simply predominance. Most of the time it is also not evident
to which degree acquiescence to demands of the state is based on national
identifications or on other factors, like power, coercion, various institutional mechanisms for the diffusion of conflict and so on.

Evaluations of collective identities

What about *evaluative* uses of the term collective identity or *normative conceptions* of collective identity? Sometimes, collective identity, like individual
identity, is used as a 'success term' with implicit normative connotations. A
'lack' or 'deficit' of collective identity is then seen as a problem. On the
other hand, there are authors who regard collective identity as a bad

thing, if it exists at all (Niethammer 2000). There are also certain terms that point to certain forms of collective identity clearly considered as bad. These are terms like ethnocentrism, chauvinism and racism. Also typical are familiar typologies of *national identity*, which juxtapose good and bad versions: *ethnic* vs. *civic* identities, *pre-political* vs. *political* identities, *nationalism* vs. *constitutional patriotism*. As I have argued elsewhere, these popular typologies are incoherent and misleading and do not fit the relevant cases (Peters 2002). There is no necessary contradiction between particularistic cultural elements of collective identity, such as specific collective memories, self-interpretations, aspirations and so on, and more political as well as normatively universal elements, normative principles like adherence to human rights, democratic principles and so on. Habermas, who did not invent the term *Verfassungspatriotismus* but gave it its current popular meaning, says as much when he talks of 'contextualizing' universal principles in the context of specific national identities (Habermas 2001a). Understood as such, *constitutional patriotism* means only that constitutional principles like human rights should be one element or maybe the core of collective identities, which are linked to national or transnational political units. But this leaves the matter of the character and importance of their 'context', of other elements of collective identity, entirely open. We still have to judge which other elements are detrimental and which are acceptable, maybe even useful or necessary to give 'flesh' and motivational force to the more abstract normative principles and to strengthen certain forms of collective solidarity. Such judgments apparently call for a complicated mixture of empirical and normative reasoning.

In general, a descriptive and normatively neutral concept of collective identity seems more useful as a starting point. Then, it would become a separate task to identify empirically the consequences or implications of some form of collective identity and to specify explicitly the normative criteria one might wish to apply in the evaluation of collective identities. I will not be able to discuss such normative criteria in a systematic way here. We might consider very briefly, however, some possible criteria for evaluation that are implicitly or explicitly used in descriptions of collective identities.

To the degree that collective identities contain norms, values or, as in the case of national identities, principles of political order, these may be evaluated according to the criteria of some moral or normative political conception. In this sense, we could speak of, for example, 'liberal' and 'non-liberal', or 'democratic' or 'non-democratic' collectivities or national identities. However, the case of *group-specific* moralities or solidarities poses some special normative problems. How do they relate to more general or universal norms or obligations? What kinds of *special* obligations, loyalties or solidarities among the members of some collectivity could be justified? Moreover, how should conflicts between competing loyalties be resolved? These problems have generally been discussed with respect to *national* loyalties or allegiances and their relation to universal moral principles, which we have sometimes framed as questions about the relation between 'nationalism' or 'patriotism' and 'cosmopolitanism'. Many authors have argued that certain special obligations or allegiances could well be justified on universalistic grounds, but there is considerable controversy about these matters (McKim and McMahan 1997).

There are other kinds of evaluations relating to more formal or pragmatic features of collective identity. The following pairs of concepts denote some of these kinds of evaluations. These concepts have both descriptive and evaluative content. They denote certain features of collective identities and at the same time imply a certain evaluation of these features.

Deep or shallow. Deep identities are distinguished by intense commitments or solidarities and by a long time horizon, rich collective memories, and felt collective aspirations for the future. Shallow identities are based on a narrow range of common interests or concerns, low solidarity and short time horizons.[6] It is conceivable that deep collective identities *of a certain kind* might be a preferable basis for a political order. But of course everybody would agree that there could be pretty ugly deep identities in this sense. So this criterion would have to be combined with some of the following.

Coherent or fragmented. These terms may mean two different things. 'Fragmentation' of collective identity may mean that the relevant collectivity is ridden by internal conflicts and divisions and that there are different and incompatible versions of collective identity held by different subgroups. Or it may mean that the elements of collective identity themselves, although widely accepted, are a jumble of incoherent pieces, so that collective identity cannot fulfil its function of giving orientation and meaning to the lives of its members. It is, of course, a matter of judgment how much consensus in the first sense is desirable, depending on the circumstances, and how much coherence in the second sense is possible.

Genuine or manipulated. This one is harder to explain, because 'genuine' or 'authentic' might mean different things. Manipulated collective identities are the result of some kind of deception by interested parties (elites, powerful groups and so on) who somehow, by persuasion, propaganda, compulsory education, control of public communication or other such means, get other people to accept certain forms of collective identity. If these are not freely accepted or if acceptance is not based on some kind of undistorted cultural exchange, this might be regarded as indicating a lack of authenticity. There might also be forms of self-deception in the adoption of collective identities, the acceptance of self-serving beliefs resulting from motives that one hides from oneself. But this is slippery conceptual ground.

Inclusive or exclusive. This could mean greater or lesser readiness to accept newcomers in the group. An inclusive collective identity could also be understood as a tolerant one, with norms of acceptance and respect for a variety of life forms or other orientations and behaviours. An exclusive identity may mean a tendency to stigmatize or exclude members or subgroups that do not conform to the standards of the group. There might of course be very good reasons to disapprove of certain behaviours and no collectivity will or should tolerate everything. So this criterion has to be qualified somehow. Also the readiness to accept newcomers in the group may be normatively contested in various cases.[7]

All of these criteria are still rather vague, as formulated here. They would need to be specified, and the corresponding normative judgments would need to be spelled out and justified much more clearly. It would also be necessary to specify them for different types of groups. Obviously, different criteria should be applied to families, churches and states. This enumeration of concepts that often play a role in the description of collective identities can only hint at the need to make the criteria for evaluation more explicit.[8] I have sketched these criteria here mainly to show that the usual evaluative comparisons between 'bad' cultural or ethnic identities and 'good' civic identities are both descriptively and normatively inadequate, since they do not adequately capture these value dimensions but tend to conflate some of them.

Legitimacy

Relations between normative and empirical uses of the term 'legitimacy' are particularly important and problematic. Again I will start with a descriptive account.

Legitimacy, in the empirical sense, should be understood as a relation between people and whole political orders or certain parts of political systems, such as laws, policies and other binding decisions. The differences between general and specific aspects of legitimacy in this sense are gradual rather than categorical. The relation is one in which people hold certain beliefs or have certain attitudes toward a political system or its components. We could also say that the political system has the support of certain people, usually the members of the political unit in question. What kind of beliefs or attitudes and what kind of support is required to speak of legitimacy? There has to be at least some kind of active support or loyalty, not just passive deference, resigned acceptance and *mere* habit or obedience *merely* out of fear. So, not *all* kinds of compliance with political rules and decisions are necessarily based on legitimacy. Ignoring for now the somewhat complicated relations between beliefs, attitudes and behaviour, we might say that legitimacy requires that people have beliefs about a political order that motivate them to support that order in some way, to accept obligations towards it and to act mainly according to its rules. These beliefs and attitudes should also correspond to public opinion and be articulated in public discourse.

Rational and non-rational empirical legitimacy

There are rational and non-rational kinds of legitimacy, consisting of rational or non-rational beliefs or attitudes. *Rational* here means that beliefs can be articulated and supported by meaningful and intelligible, even if controversial, reasons and considerations. We could try to devise typologies of such beliefs: from a mere calculated pursuit of self-interest, in case this can lead to political obligations, which is controversial, to various kinds of political and moral convictions regarding the collective good, or efficiency, i.e. Pareto-optimality, or the maximizing of utility, or justice and rights and so on. In principle, one could say that there are as many 'types of legitimacy' as there are reasons to support a political system or one of its parts. It might be possible, of course, to sort and classify them in some useful way. It is also possible that such single reasons are embedded in more comprehensive normative frameworks and belief systems held by people in more or less articulated ways. We would then have to identify or reconstruct such belief systems, or alternatively describe the less coherent mixtures of moral and political convictions that might exist instead.

Non-rational kinds of legitimacy cannot be publicly articulated and defended or supported by public reasoning in the same way. Here is an illustrative typology that draws on some of Max Weber's famous types of legitimacy beliefs:

- Traditionalist legitimacy is based on unconditional loyalty to a particular tradition, on beliefs in the sacredness or the superior value of that particular tradition, which is presented in myths, narratives, rituals and other symbolisms.
- Religious legitimacy is based on unconditional belief in sacred, 'revealed' truths (*Offenbarungsglauben*).[9]
- Charismatic legitimacy denotes all kinds of allegiance to political leaders, institutions or collectivities that are based on affective attitudes of a certain kind: unconditional, unreflective identification with powerful individuals or collectives, a mixture of submission and self-aggrandizement through such identifications, and elated feelings of belonging and unconditional loyalty.

These kinds of legitimacy are based on convictions and attitudes that are beyond reason, as it were. They consist in a kind of essentially unquestioned and unquestionable allegiance to the respective political order. Empirically it is of course possible to find mixtures of rational and non-rational kinds of legitimacy. The question whether all such combinations must necessarily be incoherent or self-contradictory can be left open here. Rational forms of legitimacy might be supported by affective elements, like pride in collective achievements, without any contradiction. On the other hand, there are certainly non-rational forms of legitimacy that are also unreasonable or irrational – think of unquestioned allegiance to evil charismatic leaders, for instance.

Normative legitimacy statements – general and applied

If we now look at *normative* propositions, legitimacy means that a political order (or its elements) *deserves* compliance and support in accordance with certain normative criteria or based on certain normative justifications. This implies that a political order is not only acceptable, but also authoritative, and that citizens have a duty to follow its rules and decisions. It implies, on the other hand, that power-holders within the institutions of such a political order have a right to make and enforce binding decisions (Buchanan 2002).[10]

However, we have to distinguish between two types of normative statements about legitimacy. On the one hand, there are general propositions or normative theories that justify certain principles and features of a political order, or that spell out the conditions or criteria under which a political order could be regarded as legitimate. In this general way, all normative theories of political order, or all general theories of justice that include a conception of a political order are theories of legitimacy.

On the other hand, we can judge real political conditions in the light of such normative theories by applying their criteria. We say this or that specific existing political system, this or that institution or this or that law or decision is legitimate or illegitimate. Judgments of this type *combine* normative and empirical elements in sometimes intriguing ways. They can be criticized with respect to the normative criteria applied – by saying either that these criteria are wrong or that they should not be applied to the case in question. Or they can be criticized by maintaining that the empirical description is faulty and that real conditions are not what the critic claims they are. Let us call these two types of normative statements about legitimacy 'general' and 'applied' legitimacy statements. The applied version often poses serious difficulties of its own, even if one relies on some well-articulated general theory. That is because it is not always easy to match normative principles and empirical facts, as lawyers know. There can be dissent not only about the facts of the case, but also dissensus on which principles or criteria are relevant and should 'rule' the case. We must

often take into account different principles that might not be contradictory in their general formulation, but lead to different and contradictory conclusions in a specific application. Some way of weighing,
balancing or reconciling them must be found.

The distinction between general and applied propositions of this kind
seems obvious enough. In practice, however, the applied version is often
confused with empirical statements on legitimacy, or it is at least left somewhat unclear if a certain judgment of legitimacy is meant as a statement of
an empirical fact or as an applied normative statement. So, if one says that
the European Union lacks legitimacy or has a legitimacy deficit, this could
mean that it is not accepted by its citizens (empirical fact) or that it does
not fulfil some normative criteria of legitimacy that the speaker presupposes or takes for granted. Obviously, these two senses of the statement
are very different from each other. If someone criticizes the European
Union for being less than fully legitimate according to criteria he or she
accepts as valid, it does not follow that the citizens of the EU share this
judgment. (They *could*, of course, and for the same reasons, but this would
have to be verified independently.)

Not all criticisms of political systems, rules or decisions are statements
about legitimacy, of course. We can disagree with many aspects of a political order, with many rules and policies, without denying its general legitimacy or without even denying the legitimacy of specific decisions – we
oppose them, work for their change or appeal, and at the same time
regard them as binding or authoritative, for the time being. This is what
makes legitimate opposition within a liberal democratic system possible.
Only in the most serious cases will we deny legitimacy – which then poses
the well-known normative questions of disobedience or even resistance.

What is 'procedural legitimacy'?

The literature contains various typologies of legitimacy that are mostly,
but not exclusively applied to *empirical* legitimacy. I will mention only two
of these. One is the distinction between 'input' and 'output' legitimacy,
which has been made popular above all by the work of Fritz Scharpf
(1975). This dual typology of input and output legitimacy is somehow
related but not identical to another distinction, which is used, however,
mainly in a normative sense or with reference to normative grounds of
legitimacy. This is the distinction between 'procedural' and 'substantive'
legitimacy and grounds of legitimacy. It is a tricky one, especially if one
tries to favour procedural over substantive legitimacy, or wants to see procedural legitimacy as a substitute for 'substantive' grounds of legitimacy,
presumably not available any more because we live in a post-metaphysical
age or in multicultural societies with deep normative divisions.

One problem with this kind of position is that it does not distinguish
between legitimation or justification *through* procedures and the legiti-

macy or justification *of* procedures. Another problem is that it overrates the role or importance of procedural legitimacy, or its ability to stand alone, as it were.

We can regard certain *procedures*, above all democratic procedures, as a necessary condition for the legitimacy of a political order in the normative sense. For this assumption, however, we have to give *substantive* reasons – arguments from equality, liberty or autonomy, for instance, or more instrumental ones. If we now look at the ways certain procedures, e.g. democratic procedures or processes, or the workings of other institutions, such as courts, in a very general sense confer legitimacy to their outcomes, we can distinguish between cases where certain procedures are *necessary* and cases where they are *sufficient* for legitimacy. If we think that a certain democratic legislative procedure is a necessary condition for the legitimacy of a legal rule or that democratic procedures have to be an element of a constitutional order for it to be regarded as legitimate, we have the 'necessary, but not sufficient' case. However, if we accept certain binding decisions as legitimate and binding for no other reason than that they are the result of certain procedures, we have the second case, in which following the procedure is sufficient by itself. This latter case can happen in two ways. If we look at a certain binding political decision, we might abstain from judging on the merits of the case. We just do not have enough information or competence to judge, and we lack the time, energy or interest to achieve it. We accept the decision, however, either because we think that the procedures that were followed mostly get it right substantively or for the more principled reason that we think it is a legitimate procedure that would bind us even if we disagreed with the result on substantive grounds. This brings us to the second version of procedural legitimacy: the situation where we disagree with the merits of the decision. We find it wrong, we oppose it; we may have opposed it before it was made, but we lost. We lost to a majority with different opinions, for example. We may continue to oppose the decision, but we feel bound by it, we consider it legitimate, because it was brought about in a way that we think is generally legitimate, appropriate and maybe necessary. This is pretty familiar, of course, because the most important example of this kind of procedural legitimacy is the so-called majority principle in democratic decision-making.

It is quite obvious, however, that this kind of procedural legitimacy cannot be a general substitute for substantive legitimacy, which is based on substantive judgments on the merits of a political decision or proposal. Apart from the fact that we probably want substantive reasons for the acceptance of certain procedures (as stated above), we could hardly also be persuaded to accept every possible decision as legitimate merely because the rules of procedure were followed, even if they are the rules of democratic participation in political decision-making. We would always reserve judgment to deny legitimacy to political decisions and, in cases of egregious substantive errors, to think about legitimate forms of disobedience or resistance. In most cases we would also find it difficult to accept the outcomes of procedures, where no intelligible substantive reasoning was employed in the process itself. Would we still accept political majority decisions, if majorities always decided on a whim or merely followed their own private preferences, or followed reasons not intelligible to us? In this way, 'procedural legitimacy' can certainly be regarded as an important element of modern political orders. But procedures cannot be the only basis for legitimacy. This is plausible neither as a normative position, nor as an empirical assumption about the general basis of legitimacy of today's liberal democratic systems.

But what if we regard *argumentation* or *deliberation* as the fundamental procedure that confers legitimacy upon political outcomes in a post-metaphysical age? Well, this is just a sleight of hand. If we consider deliberation a 'procedure' for making decisions by consent necessary, the whole distinction between procedure and substance collapses. Deliberation is 'substantive' in itself – it cannot work without substantive reasons and without reasons that have at least the potential to be convincing for every participant. And how can deliberation confer legitimacy on political decisions? Not by the 'procedure' of arguing by itself, but either by convincing people that these decisions are right on the merits, or by preparing a majority decision. But then we are back to procedural legitimacy in the sense that was discussed above, and, therefore, back to its limits.

'Input' vs. 'output' legitimacy?

Despite their popularity, the meanings of the terms 'input' and 'output' legitimacy are not very clear. 'Input' is certainly meant as a reference to democratic procedures and political participation. 'Output' suggests something like policies or public services. This may be fine as it goes but, understood as such, this is certainly not an exhaustive classification of types or grounds of empirical legitimacy. It seems to be an empirical fact that in Western constitutional democracies some decisions are accepted on a different basis, not because they are the result of *democratic* procedures, but because they are made by institutions that are considered legitimate and authoritative on other grounds. Consider courts, in particular constitutional courts, independent central banks and regulatory agencies.[11] To a large degree, these institutions are considered legitimate in their own right, and this confers legitimacy on their decisions. Even if the legitimacy of, say, a regulatory agency is seen as dependent on a mandate by the legislature, this is not the only source of its legitimacy. People also have to see it as competent and fair. This is even truer for constitutional courts. Also, these liberal democracies are considered legitimate because they guarantee a range of certain rights and generally uphold and adjust a system of laws, rules and regulations that govern above all the relations and transactions *among* citizens or more generally, legal subjects. The fact that they do this, that they define and guarantee basic rights, for example, is certainly an elementary basis for their legitimacy. Now one *could* call guarantees of human rights, basic civil rights, and liberties 'outputs' of the political system, of course (even if this does not seem a very natural way of speaking), in light of the fact that many of these regulations are constitutive elements of the political and social order itself. If one wanted to give 'output legitimacy' this broad meaning, one would have to do it more explicitly than is usually done, and the notion might then lose the whiff of opprobrium that often seems to come with it. It would also be misleading to connect 'output legitimacy' with efficiency as a criterion for legitimacy. Not only the general structure of legal rights and obligations, but also particular policies, as well as regulations, are often judged not just by standards of efficiency, but also by standards of fairness or justice. Even 'market constituting' rules and policies, which to a very large degree consist in definitions of property rights, allocations of risk or other ways of distributing responsibilities for economic externalities, and thereby have distributive effects, can be judged in this way and often are.

We should abandon the popular juxtaposition of 'input' and 'output legitimacy', however, because it is overly simplistic and potentially misleading. I propose to use the terms 'institutional' and 'substantive' legitimacy instead. Institutional legitimacy would denote all aspects of legitimacy which are derived from trust in decision-making institutions and their competence – be these democratic institutions or procedures of various kinds, regulatory agencies, expert committees or courts (Majone 1998). Substantive legitimacy would refer to support for legal structures or policies based on substantive assessments of their merits and demerits.

Relationships within the quadrangle: the national case

Now let us go back to the *relationships* between these elements. It will not be possible to examine all combinations, so I will concentrate on some of them. This time, I will not treat empirical and normative aspects separately, but will deal with them as we go along, with different emphases in each case. I will first discuss these relations with the familiar case of the single state or nation state in mind, although many aspects might be generally applicable to all kinds of political orders with state-like qualities. Whether other cases, e.g. of transnational political systems, show different relations between democracy, legitimacy, public discourse and collective identity, and what those differences might be, will be briefly discussed at the end, using the example of the European Union.

Legitimacy and democracy

Not much can be said here about this relationship beyond what was said in the preceding paragraphs. Just note that the often-used term 'democratic legitimacy' is ambiguous. Does it mean the legitimacy of democratic procedures, or of a democratic but also liberal or constitutional political system as a whole? Or does it mean the legitimacy provided by democratic procedures? If the latter, the term becomes problematic if 'democratic legitimacy' is the *only* kind or basis of legitimacy mentioned. For reasons mentioned above, it is not very plausible, normatively, to regard those procedures in themselves as the only basis for legitimacy. As an illustration, a legitimate political system should not only guarantee certain democratic procedures and corresponding rights, but also see to it that other human rights and basic liberties are respected – and this not only for the sake of democracy, which would then quite mistakenly become the supreme or sole value.

The normative problems of giving a more detailed account of desirable and justified legitimate democratic institutions and procedures and their relationship to other elements of the political order are very complex, but also quite well known and cannot be discussed here. The same is true for the empirical relations between democracy and legitimacy. It is widely and plausibly assumed that democratic participation is *one* important condition of the legitimacy of political systems. But how important it is and *what kinds* or *what features* of democratic participation support political legitimacy *in what areas* is much less clear.[12]

Democracy and public discourse

Theories of democracy regularly assume an elementary conceptual connection between democracy, the public sphere and legitimacy. Appropriate forms of democracy require appropriate forms of the public sphere; the public sphere, with appropriate forms of public discourse, and democracy are indispensable presuppositions for the legitimacy of political orders (Habermas 1973; Manin 1987; Habermas 1992).

Contemporary normative political theory exhibits both fundamental agreement and varying detailed specifications of normative expectations and demands on the public sphere. In *all* versions of normative democratic theory, a public sphere providing sufficient information and transparency of political decisions as well as competition of ideas and arguments is considered a basic presupposition of democratic participation. Some classical conceptions, such as that of John Stuart Mill, as well as more recent normative conceptions of the public sphere and democracy give special emphasis to public discourse or *deliberation* (Cohen 1989; Dryzek 1990; Schmalz-Bruns 1995; Nino 1996; Bohman and Rehg 1997; Elster 1998). Public deliberation means a collaborative argumentative effort to obtain collectively acceptable solutions to problems or resolutions of conflict. Even where a consensus is not obtained or expected, public deliberation should lead to learning effects, to an enrichment of the collective 'stock' of arguments and ideas, to a reflective examination and possibly transformation of one's own convictions and preferences, to a certain degree of understanding and respect for opposing positions, and with all that, to a higher degree of rationality and legitimacy of political decisions.

Upon closer inspection, however, different notions of the role of public discourse or deliberation can be found within the deliberative camp. These are distinguished by the function that they ascribe to public deliberation. First, there is the *informational function*: citizens have to have the option to gather sufficient information on contested political matters to make informed decisions. They also have to have information on the dealings of their political representatives and authorities, and the representatives and authorities should have information on the preferences and opinions of the citizens, beyond the very limited kinds of information they get from elections and popular votes.

Then there is an *opinion-formation model* of public communication in a somewhat stronger sense. In this view, citizens not only have to receive necessary information individually, as it were. They also need an opportunity to *engage in debate* in order to get to reasonable, considered decisions. They have to encounter different opinions, test their own viewpoints and arguments, expose them to counter-arguments, and so on. They do so by either watching public debates or listening to them, or reading about them and forming their judgments on the various positions presented, or preferably, by participating in debates themselves, as active speakers. For most citizens, the opportunity for active participation can present itself only in smaller forums, of course, such as in informal meetings, citizens' assemblies or juries, town hall meetings and so on.

These variants of an 'opinion-formation model' of public deliberation, as I would call it, are at the base of many normative conceptions of public deliberation or deliberative democracy. These models are all about citizens making up their minds in the best possible way about some political decision before them – using the best available evidence, information, arguments or interpretations to come to their own conclusions, or possibly to come to a collective conclusion within the particular community of communication in which they are actively engaged.[13]

The 'opinion-formation model' of public deliberation is certainly right. It specifies essential functions that public deliberation should provide in a democracy. But as such, it only gives *a severely truncated version of what public deliberation is or should be about*. Public deliberation is not *just* about people making up their minds on topics that are on the public agenda, using available information and opinions. Public deliberation is or should be much more.

It should not just be about decisions. It should also be about the setting of a common, collective agenda. It should be about the *identification* of problems and about a *collective search for new solutions*. It should not just be about the resolution of immediate political questions. It should also involve a more general debate about worldviews, values and principles and collective self-understandings. It is about collective solutions, but it is also about *intellectual and cultural innovation* and producing and distributing new ideas and interpretations. It should not and cannot lead to consensus within the deliberating public. But it should lead to something like a common horizon, a *common* and *shared field of contestation.* And this requires some kind of communicative exchange within a larger public, some flow of ideas, arguments and counter-arguments, propositions and interpretations within the whole public sphere.

Public discourse and legitimacy

If connections are made between public deliberation and political legitimacy, how should these be understood? Some alternative understandings are not always clearly distinguished. In a normative view, we could make public deliberation a *condition* of legitimacy – where legitimacy is understood as something like acceptability based on good, compelling reasons. We could accept that a political order is only legitimate (acceptable) if it includes a measure of public deliberation as an integral part of the political process, or that a good level of public deliberation makes a political system better, i.e. more acceptable or legitimate. This seems to be quite plausible, depending, of course, upon the specifics. We might also say that individual political decisions within an ongoing democratic political system are normatively acceptable only if prepared by public deliberation. This proposition seems to be more doubtful, or at least in somewhat greater need of elaboration, but I will let it stand for the moment.

The connection between deliberation and legitimacy could also be understood in a different way, however, as already indicated at the beginning. We could say that public deliberation is necessary to produce a high degree of reasoned acceptance about basic features or actual policy decisions within a political system. To put it differently: a higher level of public deliberation will, on average, produce more reasoned and stable agreement on contested political matters than will a lower level, all other things being equal. Now this is a somewhat more problematic empirical proposition.

As we have noted above, some normative conceptions of public deliberation seem to suggest that deliberation is a precondition for legitimacy, where legitimacy itself is understood as something like a reasoned consensus about political matters. A notion of consensus (ideal consensus) was also an important, if not always very well understood part of Habermas' writings on 'Diskurs'. This has led to many critical or polemical reactions.

Repeatedly, consensus has been associated with denial of conflict, conformism and cultural homogenization. These suspicions have been aptly criticized elsewhere (Honneth 1991; Chambers 1996). The very idea of public deliberation is to strive toward consensus by moving through dissidence. Criticism and problematization are just as much a part of discourse as the attempt at rational dissolution of dissent. Any discussion where the participants do not intend in some way or another to convince their opponents by putting forward arguments and, if need be, to be convinced by the arguments of others, can hardly be taken seriously. Also certain over-generalized social-theoretical objections against a positive evaluation of public consensus are way off track. The notion that contemporary societies are no longer capable of integration via consensus is either trivial or implausible. No one maintains that social integration or order could be generally ensured by consensus. Does anyone really imagine that widely shared convictions, for instance, about certain fundamental norms or constitutional principles, can no longer play a relevant role for social integration? There is certainly a lack of any evidence to support this.

More interesting, though, are specific pointers to the constraints which restrict the possibility of arriving at rational consensus in current public discourse. Two sorts of reasons are put forward here. In the first case, sceptical philosophical objections against the rational, generally acceptable decidability of normative or evaluative questions are put forward. These objections may be partly based on empirical assumptions about cultural differentiations or cultural pluralism in contemporary societies, whose reconciliation by means of cultural consensus appears to be impossible, or at least improbable. In the second case, we find mainly empirical pointers to certain social dynamics and other social characteristics of public communication processes that make reaching consensus extremely improbable. Some new empirical studies on public controversies or publicized conflicts reveal that neither the attainment of consensus nor explicit efforts in that direction are usually registered (Gerhards *et al.* 1998; Wessler 1999). The literature also provides indications of plausible explanations of such phenomena. Typically, public controversies, especially in the mass media, have a triadic structure: the adversaries address a public to gain its endorsement. Seldom do they address each other directly. There is also a lack of social constraints, which would press for an agreement. This is different from many other situations in which practical decisions have to be reached out of necessity and from close social relationships or milieus where unresolved dissidence may create a disturbance. Quite to the contrary, public actors thrive on controversy and dissidence. They may strive toward agreement and endorsement as a rule, not against majorities, but rather against specific segments of the public, often against certain milieus, political or cultural movements to which they feel bound. Not only the struggle for public attention, but also the struggle for intellectual and moral leadership in their own camp often puts a premium on intransigence and the demonstration of particular sensitivities. The speakers present themselves as honourable and committed protagonists of the values they represent; they seek to demonstrate profound diagnostic capabilities and powers of observation. This often leads to a somewhat dramatized or accusatory style. Sometimes this may not prove very helpful in gaining agreement or endorsement beyond the boundaries of one's own camp.

Empirical evidence thus seems to indicate that public discourse very seldom leads to the harmonious solution of real conflicts. Argumentative processes of persuasion may not even lead to reciprocal and explicitly confessed definitive changes in the opinions of the participating protagonists. One therefore cannot expect any automatic increase in legitimacy for controversial political decisions.[14]

A lively discursive public sphere would first of all appear to multiply questions and uncertainties and increase dissidence. In so far as it produces innovative ideas and proposals, it would probably bring about an increase in the variation of opinions rather than a reduction. This variation may be reduced in the course of the development of public controversies by virtue of polarizations, simplifications, generalizations and camp-building, initially leading to a consolidation of dissent.

On the other hand, debates that do not lead to generally accepted solutions or general accord may still clarify the difficulties and different aspects of the topic under debate, at the very least discrediting some of the bad arguments and clarifying some other aspects. Under favourable circumstances, such debates may not end up exerting such a polarizing effect, but perhaps lead to a certain mutual recognition of the differences or the seriousness of respective positions. This, in turn, may facilitate the search for institutional compromises or the acceptance of such compromises.

Above all, though, one should imagine the effect of public discourse – with regard to the influence of ideas or to convictions held by the public – more as a *shift* of the opinion spectrum, rather than as a *contraction* of this spectrum. Certain positions or arguments will eventually become implausible, lose influence or disappear altogether from the public stock of argumentation. Others will gain in influence within the spectrum. At the same time, new ideas, new problems or problematizations and new controversies will appear. Notwithstanding, this process may contain elements of convergence, of reaching consensus in a very general sense. Certain ideas, convictions, normative principles and stocks of knowledge sediment themselves out more or less as generally, or even universally acceptable, proven and convincing – without consensus necessarily being explicitly declared.

Some cultural processes of change that have emerged or are in the process of emerging in the West over the past decades provide us with plausible examples. Just think of the changed attitudes toward gender or familial relations, of environmental issues or minority rights, or – to mention a more specific example – the development of the public view of Nazi history in Germany.[15]

It is these more gradual and diffuse changes in the cultural repertoire, rather than short-term agreement on specific controversial political issues, that we should expect as the potential effects of public discourse. These effects include changes in the stock of public argumentation, shifts in the spectrum of controversies on the basis of sedimentation of a stock of widely accepted convictions, developments in the interpretation of central principles or values, as well as changes in specific collective self-interpretations. The extent to which these changes can be understood as enlightenment or cultural learning processes can only be clarified by means of internal post-constructions in which the achieved rationality gain itself can be argumentatively identified.

Following the account of public discourse just given, it seems likely that public discourse influences above all the general normative expectations and criteria by which people judge political orders. Consensus or convergence in this respect is a long-term process, and the resulting convergence in normative standards may provide one condition of political legitimacy. A decent and lively public discourse may, in the end, also support some general mutual respect and tolerance despite continuing disagreements over many of the questions debated. But this effect seems to be more contingent and to depend very much on the specific qualities of public discourse and the nature of the disagreements.

Public discourse, democracy and collective identity

Let us finally take a look at some relationships between collective identity, on the one hand, and democracy and public discourse, on the other. Some of these relationships are conceptual – as described above, beliefs in legitimacy make up a *component* of collective identities, but they do not make up the whole of collective self-understandings and a public culture. Normatively, we would of course ask that certain normative convictions become part of a collective identity, convictions corresponding to the principles of a just social and political order. This might be one understanding of the concept of constitutional patriotism. A more difficult question is which other features of a collective identity could be justified as generally desirable for a properly functioning democracy and public sphere. This depends to a considerable degree on assumptions about empirical, causal connections between these elements of the social world. It seems plausible that a collective identity with shared memories, but also a critical and reflective stance toward the past, with accumulated collective experiences, and with certain visions about the collective future, would further democratic decision-making in various ways. Such a collective identity might also provide or at least support certain forms of mutual civic trust and solidarity required to overcome divisions of interests or values. Similarly, it might be said that a shared cultural background, including elements of collective identity and some kind of collective self-understanding about shared responsibilities and possibilities for joint action and problem-solving would greatly facilitate the working of an internally integrated sphere of public discourse. We can assume, on the other hand, that public discourse is a very important mechanism for the production, change and intergenerational transmission of collective identities. Very little is known empirically, however, about these relationships. We have certain narratives or theoretical models of nation-building, where the development of liberal democracy and its broad acceptance as legitimate, the development of a national collective identity and a common sphere of public discourse go hand in hand. We can assume that all these components are interdependent in some way and that their development requires some kind of bootstrapping operation to get the necessary synergies to work. The precise connections remain largely unspecified, however. And it is even more difficult to say how we could transform such knowledge to the degree we might acquire it, into workable practical prescriptions.

Relationships within the quadrangle: the transnational case, with some remarks on the European Union

The foregoing discussion has largely proceeded in the 'classical' framework of discussions about national, single-state political systems. If we move to other forms of political order, in particular transnational ones, would we have to revise our basic concepts of the four corners of the quadrangle? And would we have to change our assumptions about the relationships between these elements, i.e. between democracy, legitimacy, identity and public discourse, either in an empirical or in a normative sense?

The answers are far from obvious. Here, I can articulate only a few suggestions, guesses and questions, taking the European Union as my prime example.

There does not seem to be any need for a new concept of *legitimacy*, for the explications of the term given above – both for its empirical and normative uses – are completely general. The question then becomes whether the grounds of legitimacy will shift in the case of transnational political institutions – whether some kinds of procedural or institutional legitimacy become more important, or some other elements, such as the acceptance of certain legal frameworks on substantive grounds of justice and efficiency.

In institutional legitimacy, support would go to transnational decision-making procedures and institutions, democratically elected bodies like the European Parliament, intergovernmental bodies, courts or regulatory agencies. Substantive legitimacy would be ascribed to the general legal framework which defines rights and obligations, as well as to political management or 'steering', the provision of services and so on. It would be based on various normative assessments, be it efficiency in the technical sense (Pareto-optimality), normative criteria like aggregate utility, justice or some conception of the common good. The overall legitimacy of a trans- or supranational political framework like the EU has to be based on a mixture of these forms or criteria of legitimacy with a different combination of criteria applied to different parts of the framework. In some areas, institutional competence of a non-democratic kind might be most important, in other areas certain forms of democratic participation may be deemed to be desirable, and still other parts of the framework might be judged on various substantive normative grounds.[16]

Things look similar with the concept of *democracy*. The general terms of the discussion do not really change. Let us just note that there is a very strong tendency in the literature about democracy on the transnational level to shift the emphasis from the classical models of representative democracy, with their emphasis on the role of elections, parties and parliaments, to concepts of functional, or segmented representation. Here, associations and interest groups, as well as committees or networks of experts, are expected to represent, or potentially represent, if not 'the people', then at least 'civil society' or group interests or maybe the common good. This is often garnished with some notion of deliberation, though not always strictly *public* deliberation. Whatever one may think about these approaches, all of their concepts and theoretical elements are fairly well known from the literature on national democracies – including both praise for and criticism of 'corporatism' or 'associative democracy'. The shift in emphasis is quite interesting, however. In the past, democratic-minded theorists were often quite critical of interest-group influence, lobbying or corporatism (Offe 1984). This may have changed a little with the growing influence of social movements and 'public interest groups'. The danger with this is that the *democratic* aspect tends to be superseded by partisan substantive judgments. Group participation in political decision-making is good as long as the right (i.e. progressive) groups, associations or organizations are involved. The question of selective representation or the non-representation of certain parts of the electorate tends to be neglected.[17] One could argue, of course, that the participation of organized 'stakeholders' in political decision-making in different areas is under the circumstances the best remaining means of guaranteeing that relevant interests are represented and are taken into account in decision-making. But that is an open empirical question. It might very well be that there are varying degrees of selectivity of representation, depending on the characteristics of the policy area and the institutional features of the decision-making process (Majone 1996b), and that this selectivity is quite biased and problematic, at least in some cases. Apart from this serious deficit, one might consider this development as a laudable pragmatic adaptation of concepts of democracy to the circumstances of transnational political systems. This pragmatic version of democratic participation, however, does not square with an emphasis on *individual* political equality and *broad* political participation often also inherent in concepts of transnational democracy, or at least implied in strong notions of democracy where democratic participation is seen as *the* central or possibly *only* foundation of legitimacy (see below). It is also remarkably insensitive to the fact that this version of interest-group democracy might very well *weaken* the 'classical' parliamentary form of democratic participation and decision-making and thereby the path of legitimacy which leads from the decisions of national parliaments via government representatives to the decisions or agreements of transnational bodies.[18]

With the *public sphere* and with *collective identity*, the case is slightly different. Here we have extended discussions about the need for new concepts. In the debate on the development or possibility of a *European public sphere*, the assertion that such a sphere should not be modelled upon national publics and public discourse has become almost canonical (Eder 2000). Instead we should look for a Europeanization of national public spheres. This is an interesting proposition with possible applications to democratic participation in general (see below). However, in much of the literature, Europeanization means that these national public spheres become more similar to each other. National European publics, it is said, transform themselves into a differentiated European public sphere by debating the same issues, above all issues concerning the EU itself, at the same time and in roughly comparable terms (Eder and Kantner 2000). However, parallel universes of discourse do not make a common public sphere. They may fulfil what I have called above the 'opinion-formation' function of public discourse. But they cannot fulfil the further functions of genuine *public* discourse. We can speak of a *shared* universe of discourse only if there are communication flows, flows of ideas and arguments across national borders, crisscrossing the whole European sphere. Such an intensified circulation of ideas, contributions or 'speakers' (authors) can take place in several ways. One elementary form is the reception of such ideas and arguments in another country and the reference to it in one's own contributions through quotations or other references in agreement or opposition. Another elementary form of communication beyond national borders is the import and export of cultural products or contributions *in toto*. These communication processes are evident if books, press products (periodicals or single articles), films or television commentary are imported or exported in original or translated versions. Contributions by foreign authors in print or electronic media can also be a sort of cultural export and transnational communication. Such flows of communication are more hidden, however, if the diffusion of ideas or other cultural elements takes place in personal contacts or individual observations of other countries' public spheres (e.g. by reading periodicals or books). Such encounters or observations might influence authors or other cultural producers, but they might not explicitly refer to them. Of further interest is coverage of supporting or critical comments on deliberative contributions from other national contexts, from simple quotations to foreign-press reviews to explicit discussion.

To some degree, these ways of cultural diffusion and exchange are taking place between many national publics around the world. To speak of a *European public space* requires the fulfilment of at least two additional conditions. First, such communication flows *within* Europe, or more precisely, between the member states of the European Union and its respective publics, should be markedly denser than communication flows across the outside boundaries of the EU (e.g. denser than communicative exchanges between EU member states themselves and the United States). This will probably require some convergence of the public cultures of the member countries in order to facilitate mutual understanding and the coordination of debates. And second, there should be something like a common public identity as a background to the debates. Common membership in the EU should be some kind of reference point. In national public debates, we find not only references to one's own national political entity and political institutions, but also an implicit or explicit self-identification as a national public endeavouring to form an opinion. Thereby certain forms of common cultural characteristics and collective identity work as an assumed or actually shared background, for example, references to shared historical experiences that are taken for granted. This is frequently but not necessarily accompanied by demarcation from other groups. A critical condition for a genuine Europeanization of public debates would be the enlargement of the imagined collective 'we' beyond national borders (for example, to 'Europe' or 'the Western community') and a growing importance of corresponding disassociations (from 'East' or 'South' or possibly from 'America').

Is such a genuine European communicative space developing, to what degree and with what speed? On the matter of empirical fact, the jury is still out. Published empirical results are meagre, inconclusive and partly contradictory (Trenz 2002; van de Steeg 2002). My guess is that in the near future (the next two decades or so), the Europeanization of public discourse will remain quite limited, still mostly restricted to certain elites, and in no way comparable to the density and intensity of national discourses. Behind this expectation are certain theoretical assumptions: national public spheres are characterized by specific communication infrastructures as well as by features of their public culture as described above. These features manifest themselves in interpretation patterns, relevancy structures, collective memories and other cultural resources. These differences are linked to social practices and institutional structures that impact the character of the public sphere and the mode of cultural reproduction. Put differently: public spheres have a social and cultural foundation that extends well beyond the framework of media markets and media organizations. Many other structures that are of importance affect intellectual production and its reception, collective interests and problem definition. These structures include educational and research facilities, journalism and other professions, networks and cliques of producers of cultural and intellectual property, structures for interest articulation and aggregation such as political parties, interest groups and social organizations and milieus. All these conditions are not at all easily reproduced on a European level. Thus, the development of a genuinely common sphere of public discourse will be impeded.[19]

This brings us again to the topic of *collective identity*. Here we often find in the literature a reworking of the already mentioned dualism of 'cultural' or even 'ethnic' and 'civic' identities, with a recommendation to rely upon a version of *Verfassungspatriotismus*, preferably produced by public deliberation, as a basis for loyalty to and solidarity within the European Union. We have to ask, of course, if these alternatives are mutually exclusive, and if they are exhaustive. Do they give a good description of the most relevant possibilities or desiderata? And what exactly are the arguments for or against the various alternatives? As argued above, the juxtaposition between a universal and 'thin' political identity, on the one hand, and a 'pre-political' and 'thick' cultural identity on the other is quite misleading, especially if connected to a claim of normative superiority of the former type. National identities as we know them are all somewhat cultural and thick, and they can have 'good' and 'bad' aspects or features quite independent from their degree of thick- or thinness. On the other hand, there can be serious doubts about the viability of a somewhat disembedded 'constitutional patriotism', principally based on adherence to universal normative principles. Habermas himself seems to say as much in his attempts to describe 'contextualized' versions of constitutional patriotism (Habermas 2001a). With this, the implied incompatibility between 'cultural' and 'civic' models of collective identity begins to dissolve. What kind of shared identity would suffice to support a European political community with vastly extended political competencies depends on somewhat uncertain empirical estimates. This question cannot be settled by normative arguments. Probably only some process of trial and error with a close watch on errors and more positive experiences and an open mind towards both possibilities and limitations can be helpful here. The same is true for the relationships between national identities and a common European identity. It is of course possible that these two kinds of collective identity go together in a non-conflicting or even mutually supportive way, just as many German regional identities rarely come into conflict with national identity. But of course this need not be so. National identities could very well reinforce themselves in opposition to a common European identity, especially in cases of disagreements and conflicts between member states. It is a matter of fact that national identities in Western Europe have been forged by profound common experiences and shared cultural histories, and that they still have a strong influence on current frames of reference in public discourse and political action (Jachtenfuchs

2002). In this role, they will not easily be replaced or superseded by a shared European Union identity. At least this is a plausible empirical assumption; no amount of normative or conceptual reasoning is going to settle this question.

If we now look further at the *relationship* between the development of a *European public sphere* and the *legitimacy* of the European Union, we should remember that most statements about a lack of legitimacy because of an underdeveloped or missing common public sphere and a 'democratic deficit' are of the kind that I have called applied normative judgments. The EU has a 'legitimacy problem' or 'legitimacy deficit' because it does not have the normatively required features of democracy and the public sphere (Banchoff and Smith 1999; Scharpf 1999b). One could of course point to survey results showing declining support for the EU to uphold the thesis that EU citizens also perceive this normative deficit. So the legitimacy deficit also seems to be an empirical fact. It is not clear, however, whether this fact is caused by a perceived democratic deficit or even the lack or underdevelopment of a common public sphere. Maybe many people do not want to see their national public spheres and democratic arrangements supplanted by European ones? We can of course assume that, in the long run, working forms of political participation as well as a common public sphere and joint public deliberation would produce more stable political support. In the short or medium term, however, empirical effects of an increasing Europeanization of public discourse are much less certain. There are several reasons for this. One is the fact that public debates tend to increase dissensus on practical questions in the short or medium term, as described above. Also, increasing communicative exchange between member countries may lead to increasing awareness of differences and a wish to preserve them or keep a healthy distance. And most importantly, the result of a more vibrant and open public debate on the whole EU project is very much open indeed. Maybe 'the people', unlike most political, economic and apparently academic elites as well, do not really like the idea of further political and administrative centralization.

Similar considerations apply to the relationship between democratization and legitimacy. As for normative positions on transnational democracy, an interesting contradiction has emerged. On the one hand, there are many attempts to base the legitimacy of a transnational political system like the EU, either on elements of legitimacy other than democratic ones (e.g. on other kinds of institutional legitimacy, or on guarantees of basic rights, or on functional necessities) or on forms of democracy in which individual participation is less important, as in the concepts of functional representation or group participation mentioned above. On the other hand, we find a strand of argument that derives a demand for transnational political institutions with enhanced competencies from a principle of popular sovereignty (*Volkssouveränität*). The argument goes roughly like this: We should not be governed by anonymous social mechanisms, like markets, but should direct most of our common affairs collectively. If social processes and those anonymous mechanisms spread beyond national borders, collective control exercised by national democracies diminishes greatly. So we need to re-establish democratic controls on a transnational level. Note that the argument in its pure form does not rely primarily on negative *effects* of international markets. These would have to be proven. This is often attempted, of course, if not always in the most persuasive and rigorous manner, and there might be other institutional ways of dealing with them. On the most basic level, it is the lack of democratic control over social and economic processes that matters (Zürn 1996; Brunkhorst and Kettner 2000; Habermas 2001a, 2004a). In this way, democratic self-government, or popular sovereignty, tends to become the most important or sole basis of legitimacy.

These two strands of argument concerning transnational democracy are not easily reconciled. The second kind of argument is also problematic in itself, for normative reasons mentioned above. The importance of popular sovereignty or self-government is generally derived from some notion of equality and individual liberty or autonomy. The individual (each individual) should be able to regard himself or herself as a producer of the laws governing his political community. In a situation where each individual's influence on political decisions is literally marginal in the strict economic sense, it is not easy to make sense of such a notion, especially when we talk about transferring political powers and responsibilities to transnational bodies, where democratic control and accountability are on a whole even more difficult to achieve than on a national level. Democracy should be seen as a mechanism for accountability and control, and also as a mechanism for innovation and collective learning, rather than as a realization of individual and collective autonomy.

So the question should not be how can we save democracy or popular sovereignty in a globalizing world? Rather: what kinds of political institutions, on what level (subnational, national, trans- or supranational) do we need to secure basic rights and achieve other normatively desirable goals, and what role can various kinds of democratic participation and control have on each level? Once again, possible answers depend to a considerable degree on empirical facts that we know too little about and that need more attention than hitherto given to them.

Some conclusions

Let us now briefly look back to the position of 'Euroskeptics' like Kielmansegg, Grimm or Scharpf, whose 'scepticism' is quite modest, to be sure (Kielmansegg 1994; Grimm 1995b; Scharpf 2002b, 2003a, 2003b). We can take Kielmansegg's formula, quoted above, to mean that a working democracy, a functioning public sphere and a sufficiently rich and shared cultural framework as well as a common stock of historically grounded self-understandings are mutually interdependent and have to evolve concomitantly. We can add Scharpf and Grimm's observation that democracy requires certain social, organizational and institutional infrastructures (mediating organizations and associations, structures of cultural reproduction and so on) as well as include a common public sphere. We can observe that these features are still largely missing at the European level, or at most are developing very slowly. What follows for the European project?

One possible move would be to dismiss one or some of these premises. This has been done in various ways. One way is to criticize or denigrate the notion of a shared culture or a collective identity and to deny that they are necessary for a well-functioning polity. In addition, one assumes that they could be supplanted by some kind of overarching consensus on general moral and political principles, supported by pan-European public deliberation. Another way would be to point to an existing or emerging European identity. This is mostly done by pointing to a European 'community of values', by referring to the fact that the member states share certain basic democratic, individualistic, egalitarian values or normative principles and self-critical ways to deal with them. However, on a general level, these values are not just shared by Western Europeans and, on a more specific level, there seems to be at least as much variation between different EU members or prospective EU members as between the EU and other Western countries. In any case, agreement on general values does not yet constitute a common identity, as explained above. A similar move has been to reformulate the notion of a European public sphere in a way that makes its emergence rather less demanding and problematic. This is not very convincing, for reasons indicated earlier.[20]

Another possible stratagem is what I would call institutional avant-gardism. Let us make a constitution, with more advanced features than the one just produced by the Council. It should implement immediate European citizenship, an extensive list of guaranteed rights and institutional reforms which supposedly give more power to the European people, not peoples (EU-wide referenda, an elected president of the Commission, more power to the European Parliament, more important responsibilities to the EU as a whole, etc.). After that, the rest will follow. Culture, identities, public discourse and social and organizational infrastructures will adapt to the possibilities. This cannot be ruled out a priori, of course. Naturally, we have to act in the face of uncertainty. But doesn't this look like a rather risky strategy? Pointing to historical examples of 'nation-building from above', or possibly to the example of the United States is not really helpful. For Europe is different. It already *has* strong nation states, most of them working reasonably and enjoying fairly stable support. So what if the masses and the circumstances do *not* follow? Experiences so far, such as with the European Parliament, are not encouraging at all.

There is a third possible consequence. It consists of two parts. The *first part* is commonly known by the name of *devolution*. This would mean getting serious about checking further political centralization, about checking and maybe reducing the powers and competencies of the EU. It would mean making the famous principle of 'subsidiarity' intelligible – leave as many tasks as possible to the national democracies and give as few as necessary to the EU. This would have to be spelled out in much more detail, of course. 'Leaving it to the national democracies' could both mean leaving it to national policy-making or to intergovernmental policy-making. And the meaning of 'necessary' is wide open, of course. But let it here roughly mean: only if there are strong arguments for the proposition that certain goals, widely accepted by EU citizens, cannot be reached by national political systems or by intergovernmental policy-making, or not in a sufficient way, and if there are strong arguments that supranational policy-making has a distinctively better chance, should political tasks be delegated to supranational European authorities. This is still pretty vague, of course. For now, the main function of this principle is to shift the burden of proof. And this seems quite necessary. In current debates, too many assumptions concerning these matters go unquestioned much of the time. In fact, the whole political or normative discussion about the future of the EU tends to sidestep this aspect. Instead, further political integration or centralization is taken for granted, either as a normative goal or as an unavoidable fact. The main question then is how one could guarantee the legitimacy of this development or its democratic character. If the question whether we should really strive for an ever-closer union is really taken up, it is usually done in a very feeble way. Do we still need European federalism to keep Europeans from going to war against each other? That, as somebody has remarked, looks like yesteryear's answer to yesterday's problems, and is rarely put forward today. Do we need a federal union with a constitution and a bill of rights to secure basic, including social, rights? But why should such a system be a better guarantor of all kinds of rights than Western European liberal democracies, each with their own constitution and institutional means of safeguarding those rights? Do we really need a 'common' foreign and security policy, i.e. one that is more 'common' and centralized than hitherto with a more unified political and military command? For what exactly? To check the latest unilateral tendencies of the United States? What difference would this kind of political and military structure have made to such controversies as the Iraq war? What difference would it have made internally, and what difference in our relations with the US, which was ready to go it alone anyway, regardless of how strong or weak the Europeans? Do we need common rule-making on education and related matters? Do we really need the Europeanization of social welfare, health and social security systems in order to defend a European alternative to some actual or fictitious 'neoliberal world order'? Why are centralization and homogenization needed for that and how would homogenization be possible, given the very different conditions and traditions within the EU?[21]

There are basically two more specific answers to these questions. One is that the internationalization of economic and social processes and interdependencies hampers the capabilities of the nation state and that international cooperation or transnational organization is necessary to deliver the goods. In its most general form, this is undoubtedly a valid argument. But in detail there are many more open questions than is often assumed. It is known from the literature that assumptions about the deleterious effects of international competition and factor mobility on the abilities of the state for taxation, regulation, redistribution and the provision of certain goods and services need to be examined much more closely. The evaluation of these effects is also very much dependent on normative and empirical assumptions about the desirability and the likely outcomes of state or trans-state interventions or various kinds of political intervention or regulation in various areas. We cannot assume that there is consensus about these things and that *étatisme* is just part of the European model which we are supposed to defend. Much more open political debates on these issues seem necessary and sometimes more useful than some of the more abstract controversies currently dominating normative discussions in the academic field.

Another answer refers to the spillover and other effects of transnational political systems, in particular the EU. Scharpf (2003a) has presented a concise version. Upon closer examination, it consists of two parts. First, negative integration must spill over into positive integration, at least in the form of regulation, to guarantee factor mobility, unfettered competition and a level playing field. Second, the institutional structure that was created to secure market freedoms has developed its own, seemingly unstoppable, dynamic. The ratchet-effect of the treaty mechanism, where treaty provisions can only be revised unanimously, and the competencies assumed by the Commission and the European Court of Justice lead to ever-growing *legal and political* constraints for member states in areas like public services or some kinds of social provision, i.e. with respect to certain 'market-correcting' policies. An answer to that, not entirely favoured by Scharpf, would be to reconstitute the ability for political decision-making in these areas on the EU level. Now, the first assumption again requires both closer empirical investigation and a normative debate. For example, do we really need uniform European rule-making on *all kinds* of risks associated with economic activities? And to the second proposition, an alternative exists that was already mentioned: containing the powers of the Commission, the Court, and maybe the European Parliament, for that matter. This could be done in various ways and, in any case, may not be easy to achieve. But that is no good reason to ignore the possibility in normative political discussions.[22] In general, there is more than one good reason to leave many of these matters to national democracies, as far as possible. Variety is one reason, viability is a second. Transparency, accountability and responsiveness are additional reasons.[23]

The last reason gets us to the *second part* of the strategy: *strengthening national democracies* and their grip on EU affairs (and other transnational political matters). Let us look for ways of 'Europeanizing' *them*. Make EU institutions more transparent and accountable to *them*. Let national parliaments more regularly debate EU matters. Maybe put other kinds of national checks and balances into place. Let the path of legitimation for EU decisions and policies continue to run primarily through national political systems, and strengthen this path, instead of trying to bypass it.[24] This means, among other things, no further powers and responsibilities for the European Parliament and no more direct links between 'regions' and the EU, one of the least democratic and most dubious aspects of the EU anyway. Why should one do this? Not because of some dubious essentialist reasoning about national *demoi* and popular sovereignty. But because national democracies in Western Europe *are*, by and large, working reasonably well, and because they rely on formative historical experiences and accumulated stocks of institutional, political, cultural and social 'capital' – stocks that should not be squandered. Because, for the time being, it does not seem likely that the EU as a whole, as some kind of federal system, would be able to replicate the conditions which keep the national democracies working and stable, all their faults notwithstanding.

A final thought: legitimacy is not all

To come back to the general topic of this chapter: it should have become clear by now that the question whether an existing political order or a normative model for such a political order is *legitimate*, and the question whether it is a *good* political arrangement, or the *best* under current circumstances, have to be distinguished. Empirically, a political system *can* enjoy legitimacy even though it may have serious defects and better political arrangements may be possible. Normatively, a good political system has to be legitimate. No political order that could not be justified on normative grounds could be considered good. However, there may be various different hypothetical political systems that could be considered justified in terms of justice or on some other normative grounds, but which would differ in their overall goodness. One might just work better than the other, be more stable, be more able to solve problems and conflicts, provide better conditions for social cohesion and cooperation, be more suitable for the pursuit of collective goals, such as prosperity, the flourishing of cultures and so on.[25] These aspects of goodness depend on other factors in addition to the justice or legitimacy of the basic features or principles of a political order. Some of these features have been touched upon (certain features of the public culture and collective identity, some kinds of accumulated social and cultural 'capital'), others may be added (workable, problem-solving institutional and organizational arrangements and so on). Some of these conditions may also be instrumental in producing or sustaining beliefs on legitimacy without in themselves being conditions of legitimacy, i.e. fulfilments of normative criteria of legitimacy. Here it must suffice to point out that legitimacy is in a sense the most basic, but not the only, or not a general, encompassing normative standard for the evaluation of political orders.

Notes

1 *'Europa, auch das engere Westeuropa, ist keine Kommunikationsgemeinschaft, kaum eine Erinnerungsgemeinschaft und nur sehr begrenzt eine Erfahrungsgemeinschaft.'* (Author's translation.)
2 The *public sphere* might be understood as a bounded field of public communication in general. Since *public discourse* is a special segment of public communication, the field of national public discourse (to take the standard example) is only one part of the national public sphere.
3 Beneath national agendas, as it were, there are of course also specific regional or local agendas, or special agendas of subgroups of the population.
4 In many cases, especially in the case of modern states, there are of course institutionalized rules for the attainment of membership; collective interpretations relate to the interpretation and justification of those rules.
5 Beliefs about political legitimacy, i.e. evaluations of the political system that one belongs to as more or less acceptable and worthy of support or loyalty can be part of these collective self-images. They might be linked, however, with more general political and moral beliefs that are applicable also to other political systems; these are part of what I call general interpretations.
6 The distinction between 'life-style enclaves' and 'communities of memory' in Bellah *et al.* 1985, is an example of this kind of evaluation.
7 There might be additional criteria, some of which can be found in the literature on ethnocentrism and group prejudice: aggressiveness toward other groups, for example, or dogmatism concerning collective beliefs and self-images.
8 A more complete account of the notion of collective identity and some related problems is given in Peters 2002. Some passages here have been taken from that text.
9 Contemporary religions do not necessarily see political legitimacy as solely derived from revealed religious truth, but may claim rational justifications for the moral and political beliefs that they support. These complex relationships between faith and reason cannot be analysed here.
10 Evidently, normative arguments about legitimacy cannot be based on the non-rational beliefs and attitudes mentioned above. This would be a contradiction in terms. This is an important asymmetry between the two accounts. For rational forms of legitimacy, there is a closer correspondence, as empirical accounts of rational legitimacy describe the normative beliefs or convictions that people hold. Normative conceptions of legitimacy can, therefore, serve as some kind of heuristic for the description and interpretation of such beliefs.
11 Somewhat confusingly, Scharpf (2003a: 4) has classified legitimacy based on acceptance of these kinds of institutions or procedures as 'output legitimacy'. Apparently he wants to argue that the legitimacy of these kinds of institutions is based on the outcomes they are expected to produce. In general, however, output legitimacy has been understood as referring to a political system in general, not just to its 'non-majoritarian' parts.

12 Remember, for example, the once popular thesis that democracy, or at least a certain kind of democracy, necessarily leads to a 'crisis of legitimacy', at least under free-market or 'capitalist' conditions.

13 A wonderful example for this model is Bruce Ackerman and James Fishkin's idea of a 'national deliberation day' (Ackerman and Fishkin 2004).

14 This may be different in the case of local, transparent public spheres or in the case of advisory panels, which are under great pressure to arrive at solutions and which, by means of repeated co-presence, exert great reciprocal pressure for persuasion and accommodation.

15 Case studies of the abortion debate and of the public discussion of surrounding narcotics policy did not, however, reveal any change in the balance of argumentation during the periods investigated. But it remains rather unclear just how typical these two examples may be (Wessler 1999).

16 Institutional and substantive legitimacy are interdependent, of course: institutional competence will at least partly be judged by the actual performance and the effects of institutions and procedures.

17 Is the emphasis on rational deliberation in these contexts (i.e. in consultations, committee work and so on between politicians, administrators, experts and group or movement representatives) a sufficient corrective? It may well be that deliberation enhances the quality of decisions, not only in cognitive, but also in normative terms. But this does not relate to the *democratic* aspect of these proceedings, except in so far as these deliberations also lead to *public justifications* of agreements and decisions. But how often do we find sufficiently clear and intelligible public justifications as a result of this kind of decision-making?

18 This can be seen, e.g. in the attempts of the European Commission to surround itself with lobby groups of various kinds. It seems likely that one of the reasons for this strategy is a wish to strengthen its position against the Council and by implication against the influence of national parliaments.

19 Jens Steffek has pointed out to me that transnational European debates on important policy matters (like the 'stability and growth pact') actually do take place and that disagreements and cleavages are not necessarily determined by specific features of national public cultures. That may well be the case. The argument here is that most public debates even on common European affairs are still conducted within national public spheres and are often, if not always, influenced by features of these public spheres and public cultures. This does not imply that these national spheres are mutually closed and national discourses are not mutually intelligible.

20 Similarly, general philosophical arguments, based on theories of meaning and interpretation and so on, which maintain that intercultural communication and understanding are possible, are somewhat beside the point (Kantner 2004). Obviously they do not deal with the more specific social and cultural conditions perhaps not needed for transcultural communication in general, but necessary for a functioning transcultural and transnational public sphere.

21 One could also argue that, for the EU *in its present form*, the thesis of a 'deficit' with regard to legitimacy or democracy is largely a red herring, and that it is precisely the character of EU competencies and policies that a) explains a certain lack of interest in EU affairs in the general public(s) and b) makes this lack of interest less pressing than it may seem. Andrew Moravcsik has recently put forward such an argument in a way that is, for me, entirely convincing. He points out that 'the EU's current activities are restricted by treaty and practice to a modest subset of the substantive activities pursued by modern states', that it is this subset of regulations and policies that gets least attention from the

public also on the national level and that is most suitable for delegation to specialized administrative and similar bodies (Moravcsik 2003).

22 I leave out some other possible grounds for common EU policies, like the goal of redistribution between countries or regions, or squarely protectionist positions (internal opening, external closure). I have also to neglect the question of which kinds of decision-making (intergovernmental, joint decision-making, supranational) might be desirable in which areas (Scharpf 2003b), apart from my remarks in the next paragraph.

23 With respect to EU enlargement, this would lead to a recommendation of 'widening and flattening'. It would make superfluous many arguments about the question if Turkey (Europe's defining enemy for a long historical period) now belongs to (a Christian?) Europe or not. Such a perspective would also lead to some questioning of the EU as an economic bloc – with internal economic openness, but closure vis-à-vis third parties.

24 This is somewhat akin to Fossum's concepts of a 'Union of deep diversity' (adopting a concept of Charles Taylor) and of an 'audit democracy' – not *his* favoured alternative, though (see Fossum 2004; Eriksen and Fossum 2002). However, it entails some elements of the problem-solving entity as defined in this volume. Calls for strengthening the control of national parliaments over EU affairs are not new, of course. They have mainly come from certain political camps, both left and right, in Britain and France (Jachtenfuchs 2002). But to my knowledge, they have not been taken very seriously in our highbrow intellectual and academic circles.

25 Note that goodness in this sense is not necessarily identical with efficiency, a notion that must be defined with reference to given individual preferences (and their Pareto-optimal fulfilment). Trivially, efficiency is not identical with justice or legitimacy. But in a normative perspective at least, it is not necessarily identical with the goodness of a political arrangement either, for similar reasons. But the initial situation relative to which efficiency has to be defined, as well as given individual preferences, might be criticized as not good enough or capable of improvement, as it were. If 'effectiveness' is defined as 'problem-solving capacity', it may become more or less identical with goodness, as the term is used here (and has to include efficiency, by the way).

Part II

The Euro-polity in the making

5 The quest for European identity

Gerard Delanty

Can the European Union have an identity and if so, what kind of identity? Does a European identity have to be an EU identity? This is a question that has become of increasing interest in recent years. There is a growing number of publications on the question of European identity in the context of the increasing consolidation of the EU.[1] Given the scale of Europeanization, it is not surprising that culture and identity would sooner or later enter the agenda of the EU. The EU has evolved much of the apparatus of a state, as argued in other chapters in this volume; since 2004 it occupies a significant and much enlarged territory, and is one of the major economic regions of the world. A project that began as a means of integrating the economies of France and Germany in the early 1950s has now become a polity, although still lacking an army and an identity (on other missing elements, such as taxing capacity, see the contributions by Menéndez and Peters in this book).

According to Julia Kristeva (2000), in a view that is now widely shared, Europe must become not just useful, but also meaningful. The normative conception of society that this entails has rarely been considered and yet is implicit in notions of cultural identity, the European model of society. According to Jeremy Rifkin, there is now a 'European dream' in the making which will rival the 'American dream' in its capacity to articulate a new vision of society (Rifkin 2004). Implicit in these views is the fact that the European project cannot be separated from normative considerations concerning its identity.

This chapter is concerned with the question of identity and whether a post-national polity can have an identity and what, in normative terms, is the desirable kind of identity. In the context of the theme of this book, an attempt will be made to relate post-national European identity to reflexive integration and a rights-based conception of the EU post-national polity. However, the perspective on identity outlined in this chapter suggests a stronger emphasis on participation. Participation is as central to citizenship as rights – especially where identity figures as a consideration – and it requires arenas for giving voice and for reflexive contestation about Europe.

Debating European identity

Positions on the question of European post-national identity differ greatly, the debate polarizing into two positions. On the one side are those embattled post-nationalists who believe the European Union can, and should, articulate a post-national identity and, on the other side, those Eurosceptics and pessimists who think that a European identity cannot compete with national identities and is therefore destined at best to a marginal existence. In this latter view, Europeanization should be confined to political and economic management with identity left to nation states, hence the EU as merely a *problem-solving entity*. The defenders of European identity occupy an ambivalent position between a normative defence of the idea of a post-national supra European identity and an optimism that such an identity actually exists or can be created. Two issues are central to the debate: the notion of collective identity being underpinned by a demos and by ethnos. These options reflect two different views on the EU, namely the EU as a *rights-based post-national union* or a *value-based union*, respectively.

In general, the critics claim a political identity must be rooted in a political community, or *demos*, which must be anchored in a cultural identity, or *ethnos*. The defenders claim that a demos need not be based on such a cultural community and, moreover, that Europe can articulate a post-national identity based only on a transnational or supra demos. In essence, then, the question concerns the nature and relation of cultural and political identity within the European context. It is a question concerning the possibility and limits of a supranational identity. Does this identity arise from the proliferation of individual Europeanized identities or are these identities created by a supranational identity?

I argue in this chapter that this way of posing the question leads to a zero sum situation and fails to appreciate the distinctive features of European post-national identity, which cannot be reduced to the demos or ethnos and, moreover, does not necessarily take the form of a supranational identity from which will flow new European identities. Against reductive attempts to define European identity as a cultural or political identity based on peoplehood in the traditional sense, a proposal is made to see it in terms of a socio-cognitive *form* consisting of repertoires of evaluation, discursive practices, a plurality of identity projects which could be characterized in terms of a dialogic identity. In this respect there are clear parallels with notions of deliberative democracy and what may be called a cosmopolitan European identity. In essence, then, a cosmopolitan European identity is not a supranational identity that transcends other identities but one that exists within and alongside them.

The chapter proceeds as follows. Some initial questions relating to identity are critically discussed in order to clarify the terms of the debate. This leads to a discussion on the nature and limits of a cultural identity for the EU. Arguing that this can only be very limited, the next section concerns the nature of a political identity for the EU based on a demos. The last section argues for the salience of a cosmopolitan conception of postnational identity where the focus is on identities in the plural rather than on a singular supranational identity.

Problems in defining identity: a constructivist perspective

The term identity presents so many problems that many critics have simply argued against it. Some say it is incoherent; others claim the notion of a collective identity contains a latent authoritarianism (Niethammer 2000; Brubaker and Cooper 2000). Do we mean a collective identity, a variety of interlinking collective identities, an aggregation of personal identities, a broadly defined cultural category or civilizational idea or an official EU cultural or political identity? European identity can mean many different things. Nevertheless, given its widespread use, simply dropping the term is not very helpful, as it would have to be replaced by something else. Whether Europe is unable to compete with national societies because national identities are more real or powerful than collective ones depends on what kind of collective identity we mean when we refer to large-scale social groups or societal complexes having an identity.

Properly defined, identity can be used to refer to collective 'we-feelings', collective consciousness, belonging and group attachments. The following characteristics can be noted.

1   Identity is constructed, rather than being simply given. Identities are constantly shaped and reshaped. While they may appear natural or given to those who possess them, the social-scientific perspective requires a constructive view.
2   One dimension of this processual formation of identity is narrative. Identities are articulated discursively as well as being objectified in symbolic and cognitive forms. For this reason, the role of self-identification is particularly important. Identities are thus forms of self-understanding.
3   Identities mark the boundary between self and other; they have an inside and outside. Yet, people rarely have just one identity; they have many. Identities thus exist in situations of multiple identifications and as a result are overlapping, nested, coexisting.
4   In so far as identities entail the making of a distinction between self and other, difference plays a central role. This can range from positive identification to negative identification.[2]

Two other distinctions must be made. First, identities can be personal – the identity of a person – or collective – group identity. The nature and dynamics of the identities of groups are very different from the identities of individual persons. Conflating these levels results in conceptional confusion. A group – a firm, an association, a movement – may have a collective identity based on one single purpose or a symbol whereas an individual, such as the individuals who make up the group in question, will have many identities depending on their lifestyle and activities. Group identities do not always translate directly into individual identities. It is important to note, too, that a collective identity will not necessarily directly result from personal identities and can exist without a direct relation to them. A collective identity requires the existence of a social group with a collective project, thus more than just the aggregation of personal identities.

Second, concerning collective identity, it is helpful to distinguish between the collective identity of a group and the identity of a large-scale entity such as a nation. Although there is no necessary difference, the larger the group the more diffuse the identity will be. The danger is to over-generalize collective identities. The collective identities of coherent groups and wider societal or civilizational identities are frequently confused, with the result that what in fact are broad societal categories are attributed the status of fully articulated collective identities. The notions of an Irish identity, a Chinese identity, Jewish identity, black identity, etc., represent categories which can be the basis of different collective identities, but are not themselves identities in the same sense as more concrete collective identities. In the case of these diasporic identities, the term may cover a broad cultural spectrum of diverse groups or possibly a whole society. It is therefore important to distinguish between personal identities, collective identities and societal identities.

The implications of these distinctions for European identity are the following. First, the extent of personal identifications with Europe does not in itself amount to a collective European identity as such. The proliferation of Europeanized personal identities does not produce a European collective identity even though it may offer the basis for such an identity. A collective identity derives not from numerous personal identities, but from a distinctive social group or institutional framework that articulates a collective self-identification or objectifies the identities of individuals. For such an identity to exist there must be a means of expressing an explicit collective self-understanding.

Second, European identity as a collective identity can exist on the level of a distinctive, official supranational EU identity, but it can also take the form of a broad cultural conception of Europe. Here, European identity is a generalized mode of self-understanding through which groups, whole societies, movements, as well as individual citizens, define themselves and their relation to others. On this latter point, it is also important to distinguish between European identity and what is often called the idea of Europe. Many accounts of European identity in fact concern the history of the idea of Europe.

European identity exists on different levels (personal identities, collective identities and wider cultural models of identity) which need to be carefully differentiated. It is possible to conceive of European identity as a cosmopolitan identity embodied in the cultural models of a societal or civilizational identity rather than as a supranational identity or an official EU identity in tension with national identities. The argument proposed in this chapter is that there is enough evidence to speak of a *Europeanization of identities*, in the sense of a growing number of personal identifications with Europe and which have a resonance in cosmopolitanism. Although this does not at the moment translate into a political or cultural supranational EU identity, it exists as a significant current within the vast array of processes that constitute Europeanization and has the potential to be a basis of reflexive integration. The implication of this is that, as a cosmopolitan societal identity, European identity is a form of post-national self-understanding that expresses itself within, as much as beyond, national identities. It is not therefore a question of whether the EU can create its own version of a national identity. In short, a supra-national identity is the wrong model for European identity.

This approach to European identity suggests a constructivist perspective, highlighting the transformative capacity of societies, the expression of new conceptions of social reality, normative models and imaginaries, which are not yet fully embodied in a political order or institutional framework. From a constructivist perspective, the notion of a European identity can only be understood with reference to a discourse in which competing claims are worked out rather than as a straightforward notion of culture (see Orchard 2002). Discursive transformation leads to socio-cognitive transformation whereby social imaginaries are articulated that go beyond the immediate context and have learning possibilities.

The argument is that the state does not define a people's imaginary. New conceptions of peoplehood can be found in the currents that are now a feature of Europeanization. One such imaginary which is currently emerging is the cosmopolitan. But there are also others, which can be called, following Boltanski and Thévenot (1991), 'orders of justification', that is different cultural repertoires or regimes of evaluation. This is an under-theorized and under-researched dimension of Europeanization, where the most fruitful application of constructivism can be applied in a way that reconciles micro and macro analysis. Europeanization can thus be conceived of in terms of multiple and competing orders of justification articulated through different cultural and political repertoires (national, transnational, cosmopolitan, etc.) and forms of sociality.

Cultural identity and Europeanization

The capacity of the EU to articulate a cultural identity has become increasingly evident since the mid 1980s (Shore 2000; Roche 2001; Banús 2002). The Maastricht Treaty makes a vague reference to the goal of 'reinforcing

European identity and its independence in order to promote security and progress in Europe and the world'. European collective identity in this sense has clearly become more pronounced in recent times with the proliferation of symbols of Europeanness and an emerging EU cultural policy, along with scientific and educational policies aimed at enhancing a consciousness of Europe.

The European cultural policy was developed in the context of the regional policy as reflected in the Cohesion Fund and the Committee of the Regions. Together, the EU's regional and cultural policy laid the basis of a notion of a cultural identity based on *unity in diversity*. This was reflected in the Maastricht Treaty, which stated: 'The Community shall contribute to the flowering of the cultures of the member states, while respecting their national and regional diversity and at the same time bringing the common cultural heritage to the fore.' Cultural programmes such as the Capital of Culture Award moved the emphasis away from notions of unity to diversity. The EU thus gradually embraced notions of cultural diversity (Barnett 2001; Pantel 1999; Schlesinger 2001). This all naturally tended to reinforce a weak notion of cultural identity, as opposed to a strong one based on unity. Moreover, this tendency suggested a shift from a concern with unity to one of integration.

Given the recognition of diversity, it is evident that European cultural identity cannot be a challenge, let alone an alternative to national identities. Critics such as Anthony Smith (1992) and Cris Shore (2000, 2004) have argued strongly against the viability of EU policy-making in the domain of culture leading to an alternative to national identity. In their work, Europeanization is variously presented as an elite project that cannot translate political and economic imperatives into culture without losing a connection with identity. Shore (2000: 225) argues that the EU model of identity is flawed in two respects. One, it makes the false assumption that, by producing awareness of cultural diversity, the various identities will fit together harmoniously. This is flawed because it ignores politics in that, once identities become politicized, tiers of loyalty become enmeshed in issues of power and sovereignty. A second flaw is that the European historical heritage can simply be used to build a pan European identity. This is flawed, Shore argues, since many of the values that define it are, aside from being elitist, precisely what divides people.

There is also the problem of language. The post-2004 EU now has a population of 450 million, with 20 official languages in its 25 countries. The EU has found it easier to create a common currency than a common language (de Swaan 2001: 144). So long as Europeans do not share a common language, the possibility of a common European culture is limited. The European elites once were educated to be multilingual and to master ancient languages. Today's Europeans are mostly monolingual, aside from the use of English as a lingua franca in the domain of work and consumption and bilingualism in northern Europe.

Some argue that Christianity is what defines and unites Europe's cultural heritage. Siedentop (2000) for example claims that Europe's democratic heritage has come from Christianity while Islam is based on a different cultural heritage. While there is some basis to it, a closer look reveals some problems with this view. Christianity has been a divisive force in Europe. The greatest division in this regard is not the schism brought about by the Reformation – and the many divisions within the reformed churches – but the one that resulted from the separation of Latin and Greek Christianity in the eleventh century (see Delanty 1995; see also Asad 2002). In light of the incorporation of parts of Europe with large Orthodox populations into the European Union and the growing multiculturalism of Europe, which includes more than 15 million Muslims, this is a matter of considerable significance (Vertovec and Rogers 1998). Although there can be no doubt that Christianity has been immensely important in shaping European history, it is difficult to see how it offers a basis for a cultural identification and an orientation for European self-understanding. In this context the role of Islam in the making of European civilization cannot be neglected, as Jack Goody (2004) has argued. Moreover, Europe today – despite the existence of Christian monarchies, political parties and Christian commemoration days – has become predominantly secular. European secularism has its origins in the Peace of Westphalia, and even in earlier developments within Christendom, which established the institutionalization of the principle of toleration, the basis of freedom on thought and belief.

A further consideration on European cultural identity concerns the question of memory. Memory is central to the cultural identity of nations but, when it comes to European cultural identity, there are few European-wide memories. The EU is relatively memory-less. It is unlikely that the EU will be able to create powerful memories, given the absence of a 'European people'. The founding events of the EU have resulted in relatively undramatic treaties with little if any symbolic content. The 'founding fathers' were not great charismatic figures, but pragmatic administrators whose experience of war in Europe predisposed them to forget rather than remember the past. There were no revolutionary episodes in the formative moments in the history of the EU, just piecemeal organizational expansion unconnected with ideology and the zeal that had been a characteristic feature of nation-building. In this sense the EU has largely been a problem-solving organization that did not need a cultural memory.

In view of these considerations – the absence of a basis of identity in religion, in language, in memories – an additional point can be made: a European people does not exist as an ethnos. There is no shared understanding of a sense of European peoplehood. At most, Europeans are united in recognition of their diversity and occasionally in response to an 'other'.

In terms of cultural identity, the conclusion can be drawn that, while there is an emerging EU cultural identity, it is relatively weak in comparison to national identities. Moreover, the nature of this identity is one that, in embracing diversity, in the positive sense, cannot be a foundation for a robust collective identity.

Political identity and Europeanization

If cultural identity is weak at the European level, is there a stronger kind of political identity? One of the strongest statements of a political identity was the Declaration on European Identity of 1973, signed in Copenhagen by the then nine member states.[3] The Declaration stated:

> The Nine member countries of the European Communities have decided that the time has come to draw up a document on the European Identity. This will enable them to achieve a better definition of the relations with other countries and of their responsibilities and the place which they occupy in world affairs.
>
> (Council of Ministers 1973)

The Copenhagen Declaration was more explicitly designed to elucidate the doctrine of unity than diversity. It referred to a 'common European civilization' based on a 'common heritage' and 'converging' attitudes and ways of life. The Declaration strongly emphasized the notion of 'Identity' with a capital 'I' as an official identity – 'The European Identity' – to define the political structure of what was then the EEC in its relation with the external world:

> The diversity of cultures within the framework of common European civilization, the attachment to common values and principles, the increasing convergence of attitudes to life, the awareness of having specific interests in common and the determination to take part in the construction of a united Europe, all give the European Identity its originality and its own dynamism.
>
> (Council of Ministers 1973)

With the growing consolidation of the EU a political identity has increasingly come to the fore. However, it has been somewhat relativized by cultural policies which, as previously argued, tended to emphasize the diversity of Europe. The notion of unity has served a weak political identity, but is not enough to constitute a strong identity. Robert Schuman looked to a higher unity and introduced the 'High Authority' of the Coal and Steel Community, which became the model for EU supranationalism. But there was no master plan for European unity in all societal dimensions. The French-dominated project saw Europeanization as the culmination of those very republican values upon which the nation state was founded. Catholic social modernism, to be sure, added another, more social and economic, dimension to this otherwise largely liberal project, but one that was easily contained within the liberal principles of the modern state. The principle of subsidiarity, borrowed from the Catholic states, was never seen as uprooting the national state and the republican principle of sovereignty.

Notwithstanding these considerations, there is no doubt that a European demos has come into existence. The European space has increased enormously (Eder and Giesen 2001). The European Constitutional Treaty is itself an example of the political reality of Europeanization. But what kind of a political identity can this be?

Habermas' (1994, 1998a, 2001a, 2004a) argument concerning 'constitutional patriotism' is the most sophisticated conception of a European political identity. Constitutional patriotism, as the normative content of post-national identity, refers to an identification with democratic or constitutional norms and not with the state, territory, nation or cultural traditions. For this reason it is a political identity as opposed to a cultural identity. The basis of Habermas' argument is that political identity does not have to be based on a cultural identity. Culture is thus particular, while political identity offers in principle the possibility of a limited universalism. Originally advocated in the context of German debates on the viability of national identity, it is relevant to the wider European debate about the limits and possibility of a post-national Europe. Given the limits of a stronger cultural identity on the European level, it is pertinent in so far as it avoids the problems of a narrow collective identity for such a large-scale and diverse system of societies and states. Moreover, the multicultural reality of Europe makes it impossible for European identity to be based on particularistic conceptions of peoplehood.

Despite these advantageous characteristics, constitutional patriotism is not without problems. To begin with, the Habermasian position is in effect an argument for a post-national legal identity, with only weak political significance; it is an identity focused on the universalistic principles of the constitution rather than with any specific content, whether political or cultural. Constitutional patriotism is therefore a minimal identification with normative criteria. The notion of constitutional patriotism, when taken out of the German context, loses its symbolic power on a European level where it must distance itself from substantive expressions of peoplehood. The idea of a cosmopolitan European people is thus caught up in the paradox of having to appeal to notions of commonality while denying the existence of an underlying 'we'. If all that binds Europeans together in the post-national constellation is the renunciation of history, there is nothing left to define them as a people.

As a political identity there is also the possibility that, without a clear sense of who the people of Europe are, European political identity will be defined as anti-American. Habermas and Derrida's (2003) joint declaration of a European identity was also significantly couched in the language of European anti-Americanism. In a newspaper article published in Germany in 2003, Habermas explicitly stated: 'Let us have no illusions: the normative authority of the United States of America lies in ruins' (Habermas 2003). Europeans may not know who they are, but they know who they are not. This is clearly an unsatisfactory conception of European identity.

Is there another sense in which Europe could have a political identity? Bernd Giesen (2003, 2004a, 2004b) has argued that the memory of *collective trauma* is becoming the mark of European identity and gaining a role comparable to the role that the memory of revolutions had in the past. It is important to note that this is not an EU memory, but a wider European identity. But for Europe today, there is no European-wide memory of a heroic uprising including all Europeans. Instead of the heroic revolutionary tradition of modernity, there is a new European culture of apologies, mourning and collective guilt for national crimes such as the Holocaust and other acts of violence against minorities. This culture of forgiveness is epitomized by the former German chancellor Willy Brandt's symbolic act of kneeling in front of the Warsaw Ghetto memorial in 1970. This new cultural development could indeed be seen as more profound than a constitutionally based, 'thin' European identity. The Holocaust memory remains the paradigmatic instance of such forms of commemoration. Until now a German post-national memory, there is evidence of it becoming a European cosmopolitan memory (Levy and Sznaider 2002). According to Giesen, the shift from triumphant to traumatic memories has a distinctively European character, as opposed to a national character, in that only in Europe is there public and official recognition for victimhood, he argues, and, moreover, this is the expression of the Judeo–Christian tradition of the confession of guilt through which the individual is purified of wrongdoing.

A more plausible explanation for such developments is simply a more advanced degree of *democratization*. The incorporation of more perspectives into the public sphere inevitably results in a pluralization of memories. In any case, atonement for the collective guilt of the past could offer only a very limited kind of European identity and it would be difficult, as argued in the previous section, for this to be a specifically EU memory. The thesis that cultural trauma might be the basis of a collective identity for Europeans generalizes from the German post-war experience where there were only victims and perpetrators. This is a collective identity for perpetrators and may paradoxically be in contradiction with a genuine multicultural collective identity or of limited relevance to the EU. For such a project to become inclusive, it would have to include memories that are not only cultural traumas, which in the cultural-trauma theory is a trauma only for the guilty perpetrators in their attempt to create a new national identity through coming to terms with the past. While some critics are sceptical that memory can be extended to large groups who have little in common (Margalit 2002), others believe that a politics of cosmopolitan memory is possible (Derrida 1994; Ricoeur 1995).

In conclusion, then, it can be argued that there is no 'European people' in any of the three senses the term can be used: the people as a *Volk* or *ethnos*, that is a culturally constituted community of memory and descent; the people as a national community defined by the political boundaries of the state and its territory; and the republican or Kantian notion of people defined by the civic consciousness of a *demos* as opposed to a state. The EU has solved the problem of defining the European people, as Etienne Balibar has argued, by simply stating that only those who already possess national citizenship belong to it. In this way the notion of peoplehood is reduced to a legal category based on exclusion rather than inclusion (Balibar 2004: 122). The first sense of peoplehood as an ethos is also clearly absent and there is no desire to create it. Peoplehood is constituted in stories and narratives, according to Rogers Smith (2003). As argued above, nothing like this has yet been articulated on a European level. Widespread racism, xenophobia and discrimination against migrants, along with national hostilities, undermine the possibility of an inclusive European people emerging. To a degree there is an emerging political identity, but what is absent is a clearly defined sense of peoplehood.

Cosmopolitan identity and Europeanization

So far it has been established that, as a supra collective identity, only a limited cultural and political identity is possible for the EU. This is not as insignificant as the critics make out, but it is certainly not very extensive and not a basis for reflexive integration, except in the relatively weak sense of a general acceptance of diversity and support for universalistic constitutional principles. Once the EU becomes a constitutional polity, such a post-national identity is highly appropriate as a supranational identity. But how effective will it be in terms of loyalties? Will it offer a significant reference point for identification?

The argument of this chapter is that European identity can be conceived in a different and equally real sense and one which is relevant to reflexive integration as opposed to functional or systemic integration. This is to address the societal dimension of collective identities as opposed to the exclusively institutional, pointing to a view of collective identity as a process or a developmental logic with learning possibilities rather than as a fixed and unchangeable state. European identity is a form of self-recognition and exists as a constellation of diverse elements articulated through emerging repertoires of evaluation and social imaginaries. The kind of European identity that this suggests is one that expresses cosmopolitan currents in contemporary society, such as new repertoires of evaluation in loyalties, memories and dialogue. In other words, it is not a supranational identity, but a *cosmopolitan identity*.[4]

It is possible to conceive of European identity as a cosmopolitan identity embodied in the pluralized cultural models of a societal identity rather than as a supranational or an official EU identity in a relation of tension with national identities. As a cosmopolitan societal identity, European identity is a form of post-national self-understanding that expresses itself within, as much as beyond, national identities. Post-national and cosmopolitan currents are evident within national identities and are given cultural form by what we have been calling new European repertoires of evaluation.

Both European identity and national identity are embroiled in each other and reflect some of the major shifts in culture and identity that have occurred in recent times. The most significant of these shifts is the move from substantive to what Zygmunt Bauman (2001) has termed *liquid identities*. Viewed in this perspective, there is no tension between national identity and European identity. National identities are not closed to cosmopolitan influences or based entirely on non-negotiable cultural assumptions. The relativizing of cultural values in late modernity has led to a greater self-scrutiny in national identity, which is no longer codified exclusively by political elites or reflective of the cultural form of the nation state. There are few national identities that do not contain critical, reflexive and cosmopolitan forms of self-understanding. The idea of a morally superior European identity that somehow transcends national identity must be rejected as an implausible construction. To varying degrees, all national identities in Europe contain elements of a European identity, which is not an identity that exists beyond or outside national identities (see Malmborg and Stråth 2002). For example, the major expressions of German national identity today contain a strong sense of a European Germany; national identity and European identity do not exist in a relation of tension, but of complementarity. This is also the case with regard to Finnish, French, Irish, Greek and Italian identity, as well as others. In these cases, the nation already contains within it a post-national moment.

There is little doubt that the EU is having an impact on personal identities, with more and more people expressing an identity with Europe. Undoubtedly this is in part due to the Europeanization of lifestyles (Borneman and Fowler 1997). Eurobarometer surveys (June 2003) show that 54 per cent of EU citizens think that their country benefits from membership of the EU; and in 2004 as many as 77 per cent approved of the draft European Constitution. While people support the EU for pragmatic reasons (Christin and Trechsel 2002), it is evident that they also support it because they identify with the values they associate with it rather than with the EU as such. Studies have shown that, while identifications with Europe are not as intense as national identification, complementary attachments to the nation and to Europe are increasing. While relatively less than 10 per cent put Europe first, a significant and increasing number express equal attachment to Europe and the nation (Citrin and Sides 2004; Kohli 2000: 125).

In a study of the national and European identities in football, King finds growing evidence of a European identity emerging amongst English football supporters (King 2003). Thus, there are declining numbers who identify exclusively with the nation, suggesting that Europe has become a viable and positive supplementary identity for many people who do not see it as eroding national identity. A strong cognitive dimension to European identity can also be noted: the more the EU appears to exist as a real entity, the more identification with it occurs (Castano 2004). Laffan (2004) argues that the EU is now a major component of the cognitive and normative structures in contemporary Europe. The cognitive dimension is embedded in the symbolic culture of the EU. This leads to a transformative relation between the different aspects of the configuration of identities which act on each other. The relation is more than one of coexistence, for the various identities co-evolve. It is in this sense that Risse (2004: 271) argues for the relevance of a constructivist approach. European cosmopolitan identity is expressed not just in the awareness of the cultural diversity that constitutes Europe, but in the formation of new and more reflexive kinds of identity, which draw from many different kinds of collective identity, ranging from ethnic to national to EU.

It is often suggested that European identity exists within a pyramid of identities, whereby the European component is at the top. This might account for the existence of a supra EU identity, but does not account for what is being termed a European cosmopolitan identity, which, while being to a degree layered, or nested, is not necessarily ordered into a harmonious structure of allegiances that become progressively thinner and more culturally anonymous as one departs from the 'secure' foundations of ethnicity and nationality. With the enlargement of the EU, there is likely to be a further pluralization of identities, making a single supra European identity less likely but the absence of this does not preclude other expressions of European identity (Fuchs and Klingemann 2002; Laitin 2002). There is a strong contentious movement of European environmentalism, for instance, and there is a consolidating European public sphere around particular issues, such as anti-war feeling. Cross-national solidarities cannot be underestimated, as is illustrated by the public acknowledgement placed in *Le Monde* by the Spanish Government thanking the French people for the support following the terrorist attack in Madrid in March 2004. These are examples not of a supra European national identity, but a cosmopolitan identity. The cultural foundations of this identity are not in a consensual but in a communicative conception of culture (see Eder 2001).

The upshot of this argument is that if a European self-understanding exists, it is one that is not premised on an underlying identity as such or on the fictive myth of a 'people'. To be European is not to identify with the EU or to have a common identity comparable to a national identity. This suggests a cosmopolitan identity that is particularly relevant to reflexive forms of integration: the national and the European, as well as other levels of identity, are being constantly negotiated and at the same time transformed. Whatever the specific content of European identity, the important point is that it is not an identity rooted in a cultural form of life that might be the expression of a 'European People'. This communitarian and republican vision of Europe does not offer an alternative to the instrumentalist view of Europe based on the market and efficiency. A cosmopolitan identity suggests a collective identity beyond both values and interests. As a societal identity, it is a 'thin' identity and sustained by dialogic or discursive structures rather than a pre-established cultural foundation. I have earlier described this as a sense of collective identity closer to a cultural category than an identity of a specific social group. Identity in general, but specifically this sense of identity, cannot be seen as a 'thing'; it is a system of relations and a capacity for communication. The Europeanization of identities can thus be seen less as a new supra identity than as a growing reflexivity within existing identities, including personal, national and supranational identities, as well as in other kinds of identities. This reflexivity rests on functioning communication spaces and is consistent with the deliberative view of democracy.

The argument of this chapter is that European identity exists on different levels, cultural and political, and is contested. As a result of the ongoing process of Europeanization as well as wider processes of globalization and the cross-fertilization of cultures, there is an increase in the number of European personal identities within the populations of European societies; but there is less evidence of the existence of a European collective identity. Nevertheless, there are discernible signs of such a collective identity, which in general can be related to the cultural and political identity of the European Union.

A more diffuse kind of European societal identity exists on the level of a cultural model in which new forms of European self-understanding and self-recognition are expressed. It is only from the perspective of this societal identity that the shape of Europe can be discerned. European identity in all these senses – personal, collective and societal, especially the latter – is not in competition with national identities; indeed, it is arguably the case that national identities are becoming more cosmopolitan, as are personal identities. Both national identity and European identity should be seen, like most collective identities today, as fluid or 'thin' identities rather than as hard or 'thick' identities that are rooted in pristine cultures or historical logics.

Conclusion

The implication of this sociological view of collective identities in Europe as 'thin' is that cosmopolitan forms of understanding can take root in a variety of ways. Rather than an overarching, all-embracing or supra European collective identity reminiscent of the nineteenth-century nation state, European identity should be sought in the cosmopolitan currents of European societies in which new forms of self-understanding are emerging.

For the EU, this suggests that a future European post-national and constitutional order will have to reconcile itself with the fact that the identity of Europe is not easily codified in a cultural package or an official EU identity. Identity is about *giving voice*, and this requires neither a clearly defined ethnos nor a demos but discursive spaces. This view of Europe seems to accord with the deliberative theory of democracy and its concern with communicative power. For the European Union, therefore, the challenge is less to anchor its constitutional order in an underlying identity or overarching collective identity than to create spaces for communication (one of the themes discussed by Bernhard Peters in Chapter 4). This will require more than a constitutional patriotism.

It can be inferred from the current research on post-national identifications that a post-national EU based on rights and citizenship does not require a fully articulated cultural or political identity comparable to national societies; rather what it needs is the creation of public spheres in which people – individual citizens, social movements, collectivities of various kinds – can raise their voices. This suggests a model of the EU based on participation in public discourse. One of the striking features of *European* identities, that is, identities that have a recognizable European character, is that they arise in discursive contexts; they are highly diverse and often *reflexively* articulated. Central to this is the recognition that some of the most important expressions of European identity are *within* national and regional contexts, rather than beyond them on a supra-national level. The Europeanness of these identities consists as much in the ways in which values, interests, beliefs, modes of justification, etc., are mediated and negotiated in discursive situations, as in a specific package of identifications. Europeanness refers less to an identity as such than to a category within which different collective identities exist.

Rights themselves do not give rise directly to identities, nor are rights simply based on underlying identities. The historical experience has been that identities arise in the context of struggles for recognition. In this, participation is the key, for citizenship is based not only on rights but also on participation in civil society. Europe is being socially constructed out of disparate projects, discourses, models of societies, imaginaries and in conditions of contestation and resistances. A rights-based EU must therefore be anchored in participation and in the creation of reflexive spaces for public communication, including communication and contestation about Europe. At the moment the EU promotes itself as a rights-based entity, especially advocating human rights. However, for the EU to become anchored in an actively constructed identity, as opposed to an ideology, it will need to be more closely related to an emphasis on participation. In short, this points to a discursive conception of the post-national polity as a cultural foundation for the EU.

Notes

1 See, e.g. Brague 2002; Cederman 2001; Cerutti 1992, 2003; Delanty 1995; García 1993; Herrmann *et al.* 2004; Mikkeli 1998; Soysal 2002; Viehoff and Segers 1999; Wintle 1996.
2 On theories of identity, see Calhoun 1994; Eisenstadt and Giesen 1995; Eder *et al.* 2002; Jenkins 1996; Melucci 1996; Somers 1994.
3 Declaration by the nine foreign ministers in Copenhagen, 14 December 1973 (Council of Ministers 1973).
4 On the growing literature on cosmopolitanism, see Archibugi *et al.* 1998; Breckenridge *et al.* 2002; Cheah and Robbins 1998.

6 Contemporary European constitution-making

Constrained or reflexive?

John Erik Fossum

Introduction

The European integration process is still, after five decades, a highly contested terrain. The EU in its present state is generally held to suffer from important legitimacy deficiencies.[1] In response to this (and in preparation for large-scale enlargement), the Union, in late 2000, embarked on a comprehensive process of reform. A central element here was the Convention on the Future of Europe. It forged the Draft Treaty establishing a Constitution for Europe (European Convention 2003d) that the specially convened Intergovernmental Conference (IGC) adopted in Brussels in June 2004 (now awaiting ratification in the 25 member states).[2]

This process was launched by an EU that had consistently abstained from spelling out the *finalité* of the integration process. The academic and political debate that had sought to fill this lacunae, had thrown up very different conceptions of the EU, such as: common market; regulatory state; value-based community; and federal union (state-based as well as non-state-based). These conceptions are grounded on distinctly different notions of the EU's constitutional character, and of its basis of legitimacy.

The question is whether the Laeken process (after the Laeken Declaration of 2001 that gave the Convention its mandate) has managed to come up with a solution to the EU's legitimacy deficit. If we look at the Convention's draft, some analysts claim that it merely dresses up the EU's existing legal structure in constitutional cloth and garb. To some this means that it does little to rectify the Union's legitimacy deficit, whereas to others it holds out the promise of preserving the Union's unique structure and achievements.[3] Others claim that it represents a further step in the gradual constitutionalization of the Union.[4] What this entails is also disputed. It raises questions about the presuppositions behind as well as the effects of constitutionalization. In one reading, the issue is whether such a process can contribute to forge a European demos, as a vital prerequisite for democracy. In another reading, the issue is whether it contributes to constitutional reflexivity, in that it makes issues of social order and democracy itself open to deliberative decision-making, as Bohman maintains in Chapter 2.

It is not only the constitutional dimension that is contested. So also is the nature of the Convention exercise itself. Was it a body initially set up to examine the best ways of extending the Common Market to the new members, but which was subsequently redirected? Was it rather a body that established the functions of a *European regulatory entity* and entrenched this in a Constitutional Treaty, with the member states as the constitutional stalwarts? Was it instead a *value commission* that embarked on a hermeneutic process of self-examination, so as to ascertain the character of Europe's value foundation? Or was it a *constitutional assembly* that forged the Constitution for Europe?

The range of positions reflects not only different interpretations of the process and the draft, but also different underlying conceptions of what is and what should be a legitimate EU. With the aid of normative theory, these positions can be formalized into a set of legitimation strategies, each of which yields an explicit set of principles, institutional-constitutional arrangements and modes of allegiance that the EU's legitimacy can be based on (Table 6.1). The first two strategies both understand the EU in problem-solving terms. The first strategy does not envision the EU as a polity, but rather as a Single Market.[5] The second is the *regulatory* strategy, which conceives of the EU as made up of a range of relatively independent regulatory institutions, whose powers and prerogatives have been delegated to them. It envisages the EU as a partial polity, labelled a *problem-solving entity*, and whose democratic legitimacy is derived from the member states.[6] The third, *value-based*, strategy speaks to the EU as a value-based *community*, founded on a common European identity and conception of the European heritage and value basis.[7] The fourth, *rights-based*, strategy highlights the role of civil and political rights as critical vehicles in the development of a constitutionally entrenched *democratic political union*.[8]

This chapter addresses the following question: which legitimation strategy is the Convention exercise reflective of? I present and evaluate the Convention exercise in relation to these four legitimation strategies.[9] This assessment does not include the IGC and the changes it made to the draft (European Council 2004c). The strategies are all based on deliberative theory, but vary with regard to the deliberative virtues that they privilege, i.e. *epistemic, transformative* and *moral* (see Chapter 1). In the following I develop diagnoses of the EU's legitimacy deficit from each of the three latter strategies. This serves as a focal point for assessing the purpose of the reform; a depiction of how the strategy envisages the reform body and the reform process; and a characterization of the constitutional nature of the output.

In the following pages, each strategy is outlined and applied to the Convention exercise in a sequential manner. The concluding section provides a brief summary of the overarching implications we can discern from this for the EU's legitimacy.

Table 6.1 Legitimation strategies for the European Union

	Market problem-solving	Regulatory problem-solving	Value-founding	Rights-entrenching
Polity type	Common Market	Derived regulatory entity	Value community	Federal–democratic union
Deliberative merits	Epistemic	Epistemic	Ethical/transformative	Moral/transformative
Purpose of reform	Extend the Common Market to the new members	Extend the 'regulatory state' to the new members	Hermeneutic self-clarification	'Fuse' Europe's constitutional horizons
Type of body envisaged	Expert body	Stakeholder body	Value commission	Constituent assembly
Anticipated output	Proposals for extending the Common Market	Member-state-based constitutional treaty	Assurance of the Union's value foundation	Constitutional proposal

The legitimacy of the Convention exercise

Although some continue to cling to the notion that the Union is a Common Market, and some at the outset also thought that the Convention would confine itself to dealing with market extension, the Convention exercise clearly demonstrates that the first strategy (as outlined in Table 6.1) has very limited applicability.

Extending the 'regulatory state' beyond Western Europe

The second legitimation strategy (as the first) is based on a consequentialist notion of legitimation. It conceives of the EU as a problem-solving entity, but one which has taken on a wider range of functions than those of market-making and maintenance. The EU is often considered as a regulatory state, made up of a wide range of specialist agencies and regulatory bodies (Majone 1996a, 1998). Its remit of action is limited to certain critical problem-solving tasks. It offloads and compensates for the declining problem-solving ability of the nation state in a globalizing context within areas such as environmental and social regulation (not redistribution), migration and cross-border crime.

The strategy posits that the EU's legitimacy relates to its performance, i.e. the EU's ability to produce substantive results (Wallace 1993: 100). This strategy highlights the epistemic value of deliberation.[10] The idea is that deliberation increases the rationality of decision-making and thus contributes to problem-solving. To this strategy, support for the EU is highly conditional. When expectations are not met, support is withdrawn. The types of issues that such an entity can handle are generally confined to those associated with weak evaluations (Taylor 1985). Accordingly, the institutional apparatus operates on an intergovernmental, not a supranational, logic. This mode of legitimation is also often referred to as output legitimation (Scharpf 1999a). In democratic terms, the EU is *derived from* the European nation states – hence indirect legitimation is sufficient. This line of reasoning is consistent with Robert Dahl's (1999: 21) view that, beyond a certain scale, and the EU is beyond this, representative democracy cannot work.

This strategy sees the legitimacy deficit as an expectations–performance gap, and as a hollowing out of national democracy. Each nation state faces risks and challenges that it can no longer handle alone in a manner consistent with citizens' needs and expectations. Union action is often ineffective, as it is constrained by the member states. Barring such constraints, Union action could undermine national democracy, through untrammelled juridification.

To address this dilemma, the strategy posits that the Union set up a body to clarify its remit of problem-solving within an enlarged Europe, so as to ensure the best match possible between expectations and performance. The mandate would contain a set of issue areas or substantive matters that the body would address. It would also offer a set of guidelines to help the body in its assessments of which tasks should be allocated where, so as to ensure effective problem-solving. The mandate would underline that the Union's democratic legitimacy is derived from the member states. It would ask the body to justify that its recommendations do not threaten or undermine the democratic legitimacy of the member states, and instruct it to consider solutions to the Union's hollowing out of national democracy.

The type of body most consistent with this strategy would be an *expert committee* or a corporatist body (with representation from the main affected interests). The body's composition would reflect the nature and range of issues: the more salient, the more broadly based (experts, affected interests and representatives from the member states). A broadly based body set up to deal with issues of vital importance to national democracy could be subdivided into expert committees to handle pragmatic issues and make recommendations to an overarching body, and with national representatives who would have a special obligation to protect national democracy. The output would be in the form of proposals or recommendations (even in the form of a constitutional treaty) that would be put to the member states for final acceptance.

The applied strategy assessed

There is some support for this strategy in the Laeken mandate (Lenaerts and Desomer 2002: 1224). Several of the participants, notably the British government, started out from this position (European Convention 2002c). At Laeken, the European Council instructed the Convention to discuss a wide range of substantive issues and stressed the practical nature of European cooperation. 'Practical' also referred to the type of polity: 'What they [citizens] expect is more results, better responses to practical issues and not a European superstate or European institutions inveigling their way into every nook and cranny of life' (European Council 2001b). The Laeken Declaration also expressed concern with the remit of Union action:

> There is the question of how to ensure that a redefined division of competence does not lead to a creeping expansion of the competence of the Union or to encroachment upon the exclusive areas of competence of the Member States and, where there is provision for this, regions.
>
> (European Council 2001b)

But the declaration did not confine itself to substantive issues; neither did it cast the Union as a mere instrument of the member states. The mandate is 'surprisingly wide' (Lenaerts and Desomer 2002: 1213) and framed as a *response to citizens' demands and expectations*, which relate not only to practical issues but also to democracy, transparency and fundamental rights. In line with this, the Laeken Declaration instructed the Convention to consider (but not determine) the fundamental issue of a constitution for Europe, including its value basis, the rights and obligations of citizens and the role of the member states.

The Convention was not composed of experts, neither was it set up as a corporatist body.[11] As with the Charter Convention, it was mainly composed of representatives from the Union's (including member states') institutions, and a majority of the Convention members were parliamentarians (46 out of 66 voting members, and 26 out of 39 from the candidate countries). The broad national representation (through national parliamentarians, government representatives and to some extent also EP parliamentarians) meant that no single actor could legitimately claim to reflect the national position in case of conflict. Such conflicts would also be highly visible, as the Convention was instructed to conduct its affairs in public, and to make the debates and documents available to the public. Its composition and the very use of the term 'Convention' to designate the body are evocative of something more and different than can be assumed from this strategy.

The Convention format, as a method of treaty reform, was distinctly different from the EU's well-established, bargaining approach to treaty change (Curtin 1993; Moravcsik 1991, 1998), the Intergovernmental Conference (IGC), which consisted of member-state officials and was the body formally in charge of treaty change. However, the Convention was not set up as a free-standing vehicle. Instead, it was set up to prepare proposals for the subsequent IGC, where each member state would retain its veto. Given this structure, an important issue is whether the member states would seek to determine what the Convention would propose to the IGC, or whether they would permit it to come up with its own proposals. Even if left relatively free-standing, the Convention, to ensure that its proposals would go through the IGC, would have to anticipate or enlist the support of the member states. This way of structuring the process could therefore leave the member states in control of the process.

The Convention was not given a free rein. The European Council appointed its leadership. Each member (and candidate) state had a government representative personally appointed by the respective head of state or government, so as to ensure a measure of control. The Convention leadership was instructed to inform the Council at regular intervals, and the Council determined its time-frame of operations.[12] But neither the Council, nor any member state, could place restrictions on the Convention's access to information or expertise[13] or regulate its interactions with other actors.

But although faced with strong external controls, Valéry Giscard d'Estaing, at the opening meeting, spelled out an ambitious vision for the Convention and its work which, by underlining the essential constitutional character of the undertaking, also suggested that it might take on a more independent role than set out in the mandate, a role that would take it farther away from the type of body prescribed by this strategy. This role conception was consistent with the view of a great majority of Convention members (Magnette 2004a: 213). Giscard, in his opening speech, underlined the importance of the undertaking, a point further amplified through the invocation of the Convention spirit (European Convention 2002a; Magnette 2004a: 214, 2004b: 212). The stakeholders were *all Europeans*, and the Convention was a unique body, distinctly different from an IGC. This difference was reflected in its working methods. It would work as a deliberative body, according to an argumentative rather than a bargaining style, and was devised to emphasize the power of argument over that of the status and position of the speaker, so as to de-legitimate situated interests (Magnette 2004a: 216).[14] It would abstain from voting, and its purpose would be to reach agreement on a common proposal. This provision on voting also directly affected the representatives from the applicant countries, whose status was that of observers, and who did not have the right to vote. In the absence of voting, force of argument would count more than status as applicant.

These decisions went well beyond the Laeken mandate, but they were not consistently adhered to. The Praesidium and the President made proposals,[15] whose origins were not based on the Convention's deliberations. Members also detected a strong bias in the President's portrayal of issues, and the President and the Praesidium at times appeared as mere extensions of the member states.[16]

The Convention's initial rules of procedure were similar to the Council's standard procedures[17] and were not consistent with an open deliberative assembly. Their introduction sparked great uproar and opposition, and they were subsequently changed.[18] This shows that the members of the Convention came to see it as an independent body early on, one which should not only formulate its working methods, but also operate in accordance with the norms of a deliberative body.

The many and strong levers that the member states had to influence the Convention with could confine the endeavour to that of narrow problem-solving, to ensure subsequent acceptance by the IGC. If we look more closely at the Convention's work, its initial phase was a sounding-out phase, which lasted for several months, and dealt with central issues of principle. The second phase, the working-group one, was far more practical. Here, three rounds of working groups dealt with substantive issues (such as defence, economic governance, freedom, security and justice and social Europe), as well as with institutional-procedural ones (subsidiarity, the Charter, legal personality, national parliaments, complementary competences and simplification). Members could choose which working group to join. This process was not strictly orchestrated by the member states. The discussions were intended to cover all aspects of the mandate and, although there was no explicit group on legitimacy and democracy, these issues crept into most of the discussions. Members generally found the working groups useful, as their smaller format helped foster more open deliberation, and their work helped provide suggestions and inputs to the final phase, the proposal phase, where the draft was produced. Through these three phases, the Convention combined attention to principles with detailed examinations of specific issues and sought to fuse these together into a draft proposal.

The Convention's (Praesidium excepted) deliberations were open and public, with thousands of documents available. In addition to its final draft, the Convention produced a comprehensive body of descriptions and assessments of virtually all aspects of the EU; political visions; assessments of its normative quality; and concrete constitutional proposals. Through a system of rapid and updated translation and publication of almost all available documents, the participants and the public had information on all actors' views and positions throughout the process. These traits testify to the epistemic quality of the process, a point which participants also stress.

But there were limits to this, as well. The draft was developed in a piecemeal fashion, with batches of articles released at a time, and with very little time to respond to each set.[19] Participants lacked an adequate overview of the process – what the end product would be and how the different parts would fit together. Since the Council refused to extend the time-frame of the Convention's work, when requested by Giscard to do so, there was not enough time for the participants to establish with any degree of certainty whether the structure in place properly reflected their views and stances.

Beyond problem-solving?

The Convention operated as a deliberative body. But it *did not confine itself* to the handling of substantive problems. At the same time, the fact that it was inserted into the IGC structure did affect its work. The Council was not only tightly consulted; it also used its power to direct the Convention's work. Albeit many political leaders had held low expectations of the Convention at the beginning,[20] over time they realized that they had to take it more seriously and did so through inserting politically accountable, central government figures (13 such changes took place (Closa 2004: 199)). Some of the government representatives at times took on the role of 'national fire-walls' or 'red-line drawers'.[21]

The Council's strong influence, through forward linkage of the Convention to the IGC, helps explain how the Convention – stimulated by its President – sought to reach settlements that had a chance of gaining acceptance in the IGC (Closa 2004; Eriksen and Fossum 2004; Magnette

2004b). This orientation was revealed in its working quite close to the text of the treaties, so that much of its work revolved around assessing the provisions in place (adding, revising, embracing and slashing such). The forward-linkage orientation also served to ensure tight links to the respective governments and served to shift some of the inevitable intergovernmental bargaining onto the Convention in the final stages of its work. The Convention, less from its own design and more from its being inserted into the IGC, came to place special onus on member-state concerns. It conducted its deliberations 'under the shadow of the veto' (Magnette 2004a: 220).

The result of the Convention's deliberations, the Draft Treaty establishing a Constitution for Europe, should therefore be expected to reflect member-state concerns. The draft does contain protocols on subsidiarity and national parliaments, both of which can protect the member states from EU encroachments, and also preserves national veto in the amendment procedure.[22] But the Convention's deliberations had shown that national positions differed greatly. There was no agreement on what the Union's remit of action should be, neither on how national democracy should be protected. Further, the Convention opted for a flexible approach to division of powers and competences, which could weaken national preponderance (Craig 2003).

Magnette argues that the result can best be summarized under the heading of *simplification*. This ambiguous term helped unite integration-friendly federalists and Euro sceptics, who otherwise disagreed on many fundamental issues, in striking a compromise, or what Magnette (2004b: 210) labels an 'ambivalent agreement'. This is an 'agreement based on preference differences and belief differences that cancel each other.[...] It implies that when deliberation reduces disagreement either about ends or about factual matters, it may increase disagreement about the decision to be taken' (Elster 1998: 101).

This depiction of the result as an ambivalent agreement reveals first, that the process of deliberation revolved around far more than pragmatic issues; it came to touch on core normative issues that pertain to what is good and what is right. Second, it also suggests that the process of deliberation served to increase dissidence and stimulate greater variation in opinions and views (see Chapter 4). But this is not the whole story, as an agreement emerged to *frame the issues in explicit constitutional terms*. Kokott and Rüth note that, although Joschka Fischer gave a vital impetus to such a framing in his 2000 speech:

> not even the most daring would have imagined that only three years later a general consensus could be reached to adopt a Treaty, in the title of which the word 'Constitution' figures. In fact, it was widely believed that those Member States which were rather critical towards further integration, would never agree to such a step, as the idea of

giving a Constitution to the Union was often equated to completing
the decisive step towards a Federation or at least perceived as an allu-
sion to a federal future of the Union. The term 'constitution' was
therefore, especially for the British, as much a taboo as the term
'federal' itself.

(Kokott and Rüth 2003: 1319–20)[23]

This change in framing suggests that there might be a greater contraction
in the range of positions than that implied in the notion of ambiguous
agreement. Further, simplification, as understood by the Convention, did
not amount to scaling down, but could actually lead to more integration.
The structure that was to be simplified was also already more comprehensive than what this strategy envisages.

We can therefore conclude that the Convention exercise was only
partly reflective of the second strategy. The issue is how different it was.
That the Convention succeeded in framing its work in explicit constitutional terms, requires us to go beyond assessing its epistemic role to also
consider it as a body capable of *transforming* opinions and viewpoints. Its
constitutional orientation and inclusive conception of its stakeholders
also requires assessment of how well it harnessed the *moral value* of
deliberation.

Value-based self-clarification

The third strategy is based on a contextual mode of rationality and presents the EU as an emerging value community. The EU is not a state, but
it is clearly more than an international organization. It makes collective
decisions, with deep implications for values and identifications in Europe.
The critical challenge facing the Union, the strategy posits, is to clarify the
Union's value basis, through a collective process of self-interpretation.
This presupposes clarification, both of who the peoples of Europe are, as
well as who they want to be. This process must reach back in time and
establish that there is a set of common traditions and memories that can
be seen as constitutive of Europe. These must then be revitalized and
drawn upon to support and sustain further integration and to foster a
common identity. This means that the process has to extend beyond institutional reform. It has to reach into people's hearts and passions, and
turn them into compatriots, who are willing to embrace those collective
obligations important to each other's wellbeing.

A common identity does not only help to stabilize the Union's goals
and visions, it is also necessary for securing *trust*. Trust is an essential condition for deep and binding cooperation and for the settlement of conflicts by neutral procedures (see Eriksen's and Schmalz-Bruns' chapters in
this book). A critical source of trust is a common cultural substrate, which
can help foster allegiance and respect for laws.

This strategy presupposes a constitution, but this is a 'rooted' constitution, i.e. it is a body of laws and norms with deep roots in a pre-political community of values and a common identity. The constitution is the legal embodiment of a community of values, where Europeans address and see themselves as fellow compatriots (and not as market actors). The constitution emanates from these socio-cultural roots, over a considerable period of time. Thus, 'the juridical presupposition of a constitutional *demos* [coheres] with political and social reality'. But the *conditions* have to be present. 'In many instances, constitutional doctrine presupposes the existence of that which it creates...' (Weiler 2001b: 56).

The reform process, according to this strategy, has to take as its point of departure that the EU's legitimacy deficit stems from an underdeveloped constitutional support structure: the lack of a truly European identity and a sense of community (Grimm 1995a, 2004; Guéhenno 1996; Offe 1998). Necessary ingredients for ensuring the requisite trust are lacking. In the absence of such, institutional reforms would amount to reforming empty shells. From this perspective, the questions currently facing the EU are:

- Does the legal-institutional structure that has been established by a set of elites and which has emerged almost through stealth actually rest on a set of European values?
- Does it cohere with and can it sustain a European identity?
- Is it conducive to further constitutionalization in Europe?

Applied to the Convention, for it to play such a hermeneutic self-clarifying role, its mandate would have to instruct it to go beyond the universal principles that the Union already appeals to.[24] The Convention would need to establish, not only that a set of European values exist, but also that they are sufficiently deep and delimiting so as to serve as a foundation for a genuine European community and identity. Only then could they serve as the requisite leitmotif for Europe's constitutional development within the framework of the EU. The assessment would also have to serve as a test as to whether the EU has progressed *further than warranted* in value and identity terms.

Such a 'value commission' could be composed of those best equipped to define and rediscover the EU's value foundation: its most authentic *value articulators*. These could be Europe's intellectual leaders (poets and journalists and academics – all of those with an alleged special ability to capture 'Europe's soul'), under the assumption that they would be best equipped to clarify and articulate the values. Such a body could also include a significant contingent of religious leaders and movements. Those selected would be required to articulate the idea of Europe, and the notion of a Europe of values, in a language that all would understand. Given Europe's diversity, however, no constellation can readily be found that would reflect a set of distinctive and Europe-defining values. For this reason, the Convention would have to be set up to tap the *transformative* aspect of deliberation.

But in this complex setting, transformation without proper community authorization would not be enough. The process of self-clarification could not be undertaken by the Convention alone, but would require assurance through consultation with the relevant intermediary bodies (parties, social movements and interest groups and other stakeholders) that the values amplified by the Convention are the ones that Europeans cherish and endorse. This body would come up with recommendations, as its role would be preparatory only.

The applied strategy assessed

The Laeken mandate asked the Convention to discuss what value foundation a future European constitution could be based on. This hardly adds up to seeing the Convention as a body whose *main task* would be to undertake a hermeneutic self-clarification of the EU as a value community, as the Convention was asked to address a wide range of questions, and was not required to come up with a constitutional proposal. The Laeken mandate (forged by the then 15 members) further left to the Convention the task of establishing the relevant *scope* of the community of values: should it refer to the values of the community of present members, or to those of the expanded Community as well? If the latter, the exercise would not simply be one of looking backwards to the present community, but would also have to be future-oriented so as to establish the values that a greatly reconfigured EU *post-enlargement* would embrace, with all the ambiguities entailed in terms of the Union's scope and character, as the debate on Turkey amply demonstrates (Sjursen 2002). The Convention, as noted, had decided to include the voices of the applicants; therefore the process of hermeneutic clarification revolved around an enlarged, ambiguous and other-regarding self, which also meant that the Convention exercise went beyond the core tenets of this strategy.

This is further reflected in the Convention's composition. It was not made up of value articulators (no special procedures for the Convention to interact with and consult with such existed either). It included some of the most strongly institutionalized divisions in Europe, but far from all of the most important of Europe's divisions.[25] Notably absent were representatives from Europe's numerous religious communities.

It was nevertheless so broadly composed as to contain widely different conceptions of what a legitimate Europe entails in value terms. But whereas the Laeken mandate at most asked it to reach a common understanding of the requisite value foundation, Giscard's and the majority's intention went further: to foster consensus on a common proposal. Hence the need for members to distance themselves from those who appointed them: 'This Convention cannot succeed if it is only a place for expressing divergent opinions. It needs to become the melting-pot in which, month by month, a common approach is worked out' (European Convention 2002a: 12).

The question was how such a composite body could foster agreement. Would this not amount to overtaxing the body's ability to foster the transformative aspects of deliberation? To understand this we need to distinguish between two critical aspects of transformation: common understanding vs. common agreement. Deliberation can foster common understanding, without this leading to agreement through changed preferences.

Giscard spoke of the need for the Convention to forge an agreement of a strong kind: 'We must ensure that governments and citizens develop a strong, recognized, European "affectio societatis", while retaining their natural attachment to their national identity' (European Convention 2002a: 7). However, what was underlined was *not* unity as such, but a more complex, inclusive and essentially *federal*, sense of commonality, one imbued with respect for difference and diversity. This was not a vision of the Union as one community, but is better thought of as a 'community of communities'. The onus was on the need for participants to enlarge their positions and stances, so as to include a European dimension in their sense of self. Such an enlarging did not require explicit shifts in loyalties and allegiances. The requisite transformation was more of a *morally inclusive* character.

A significant contingent of the Convention's members nevertheless wanted to go further than Giscard had encouraged, in value terms. They argued that the European constitutional edifice not only rested on a set of pre-political values, but also that these were of a religious kind. The Convention's task, to them, was to make sure that these were sufficiently well articulated and represented in the text so that Europeans would associate the constitution with them.[26] A considerable number of Convention members, strongly supported by the Pope, and much of the European People's Party (EPP), sought to insert a reference to Europe's religious foundation. Opinions differed as to how to do this. Some sought a reference to God modelled on the Polish Constitution, others to Christianity, others to Europe's Judaeo–Christian roots and others again to Europe's Greco–Roman roots (European Convention 2003b: 18).

However, no agreement could be found on a common European religious value foundation. Those favouring a reference to Christianity met strong opposition and failed to convince the majority of Convention members. The preamble has no reference to Christianity, but does refer to Europe's religious inheritance.

Some members of the Convention still wanted to include religious criteria in the membership requirements, which would exclude Turkey. The EU's established membership requirements have been based on universal principles (confined to Europe), not Europe-specific values (Sjursen

2002). Giscard, outside the Convention, recommended against Turkish membership, and sparked uproar. The draft retains the present membership requirements.

Beyond a value community?

The debates revealed that there was no consensus on a set of Europe-specific and exclusive Europe-defining values, neither at the outset of the Convention's work nor at its concluding debates. Rather, the Convention's debates brought out the complex configuration of values found in the EU. The debates touched on at least four dimensions: the EU as made up of universal and secular values; the EU as a harbinger of religious values, but without this being confined to a specific religion; the EU as a bearer of Christian values; and the EU as made up of national (and regional) communities. The conceptions of Europe ranged from cosmopolitan to communitarian. There were appeals both to the need to forge a European constitutional patriotism and to protect the deep diversity of Europe (Fossum 2004).

The resultant draft portrayed the Union's values (as expressed in Article I–2 on the Union's values) in largely the same morally inclusive way as were found in the treaties. Consensus was reached on the same universal values as were presented in Amsterdam, and reiterated at numerous occasions, namely, human dignity, liberty, democracy, the rule of law and respect for human rights. The notion of equality had been added to the final draft, after considerable pressure. There was also agreement on the need for the Union to respect Europe's rich cultural and linguistic diversity (cp. Article I–3.3). The notion of a Europe of nation states, so well entrenched in the treaties, was also clearly evident in the debates and in the resultant draft (cp. Article I–5). This brief recapitulation reveals that the Convention had a limited transformative effect in narrow ethical terms. But, despite its highly composite nature, the Convention confirmed the morally inclusive values that were entrenched in the treaties. The draft underlines the highly inclusive nature of the community of values that the Union embraces.

The Laeken mandate had not set the Convention up to foster a deep value transformation. The deep sense of *trust* that this strategy presupposes probably also requires a different, smaller and more intimate body, where people work closely together over a lengthy period of time so as to ensure proximity, and close and continuous interaction. Then participants can reciprocally establish their mutual truthfulness and trustworthiness. The very size of the Convention (de facto 207 persons, as the substitutes were very active) was too large to ensure such familiarity. This was exacerbated by the Convention operating as a part-time body. The format of the plenary debates was not very conducive, either to authentic expressions of individual views, or to *exchanges* among the interlocutors, as the Praesidium set the order of speakers in advance and left very little opportunity for responses to interventions, as well as for clarifying questions.[27] Further, of even more importance was the short length of each intervention (generally three to four minutes), which was enough to make one or several points, but not enough to provide adequate justifications for these. It was certainly not enough time for each participant to delve into the past, conjure up evocative images and crystallize that person's view of what constitutes a common vision of Europe.

At the same time, an assessment of the deliberative quality of the plenaries only, would greatly distort the comprehensive deliberative process that the Convention exercise fostered. This consists of other officially established Convention-related forums, as well as numerous other official forums, both of which spawned a range of more spontaneous encounters, through networks and contacts. Among the official convention forums, the working groups provided a more conducive atmosphere; and participants found them very useful, both to clarify issues and to establish consensus. But they were devised so as to respond to limited aspects of the mandate, none of which explicitly dealt with the issue of a European identity or Europe's value foundation.

In sum, the Convention was not instructed to re-create the set of European values that are designative of a value community, in its communitarian-republication trapping. The Convention, as a deliberative body, permitted a thorough examination of the Union's value basis. This included efforts to establish a set of more specific *European*, in the sense of Europe-confined, values. But, rather than getting bogged down in struggles over competing visions of precisely what it means to be a European, the Convention agreed on a set of values that are universal in orientation and that correspond to the values that can be discerned from the *common* constitutional traditions of the member states. The general thrust that runs through the debates and the draft is the need for reconciling universal values with Europe's diversity. 'These [universal] values are common to the Member States in a society of pluralism, tolerance, justice, solidarity and non-discrimination' (European Convention 2003d: Article I–2).

The Convention exercise, rather than forging significant *shifts* in values, nevertheless confirms Peters' notion of a contraction of the range of views (see Chapter 4). This is reflected in the endorsement of the Union as based on universal principles, and in the framing of the exercise as one of constitutional importance. Here we see both elements of agreement and of a shared understanding of the exercise. The question is how far this agreement carried in terms of what is meant by constitutional; in terms of its specific character; and in terms of reflecting the interests of the main stakeholders, the citizens of Europe.

Developing a rights-based federal union

The fourth strategy rests on the moral value of deliberation and pro-pounds a rights-based, procedural notion of legitimation. It envisages a European Union based on a wider, cosmopolitan conception of demo-cracy, and one which embodies the core principles of the constitutional democratic state, but with a *post-national* vocation. Its support resides in a *constitutional patriotism*, where a set of legally entrenched fundamental rights and democratic procedures are embedded within a particular socio-cultural context so as to make for political affect and identification (Habermas 1994, 1998a, 2001b). This strategy therefore also speaks to the shaping of a European *demos*, but this process occurs through different means than those presented in the third strategy.

The strategy is critically dependent on the EU harnessing the norm-ative essence of the modern democratic constitution: the respect for the individual – its integrity and dignity. These are also critical conditions for constitutional reflexivity, upheld by the following conditions: a political culture based on tolerance of difference; a set of rights that protect the integrity of the individual – private freedom – and that also enable partici-pation in the opinion- and will-formation processes and make for public freedom – political rights (Habermas 1996); a set of institutions that enable the citizens to consider themselves not only as the subjects but also as the authors of the law; and a viable public sphere. In this view, demo-cracy is not only an organizational arrangement – parliamentary or presi-dential democracy – but also a legitimation principle. In other words, democracy is a procedure which sets the terms for reaching legitimate decisions.

This strategy would take as its point of departure that the EU's legiti-macy deficit stems from the following aspects. First, whilst the EU has a material constitution, this amounts to juridification bereft of adequate democratic controls and absent a proper democratic justification. Second, whereas the EU is a granter of rights, the citizens have not given the rights to themselves.

The strategy presupposes that a *democratic* constitution is forged through a constitutional moment,[28] i.e. through a process that has an explicit democratic sanction, permitting citizens to be seen as, and see themselves, in normative terms, not only as the addressees, but also as the authors of the laws that affect them. But the Union is *not* involved in con-stitution-making from scratch. It might be more appropriate to think of what is happening as a 'fusion' of Europe's constitutional horizons. Such a fusion builds on the justified principles already entrenched in the national constitutional traditions. For this process to comply with demo-cratic requirements, the Convention's deliberations and results would have to comply with the basic interests and concerns of its stakeholders, the citizens of Europe, i.e. with the general requirements of democratic constitutionalism, pertaining to basic rights, democracy and the rule of law.[29]

Such a process-oriented approach can be consistent with constitutional reflexivity, which speaks to a dynamic notion of the constitution, rather than a notion of the constitution as a contractual arrangement established and fixed *at a particular point in time*. This might also be more relevant to the highly complex and contested EU which, as we have seen, does not rest on and cannot draw on a set of pre-political values or a clearly developed European identity. This also suggests that the constitutional agreement struck might not rest on a rational consensus but might instead be a working agreement, i.e. 'an agreement which has come about argumentatively, but where the actors may have different but still reasonable and acceptable grounds for their support' (Eriksen 2003). Working agreement is an intermediary category, between compromise and consensual agreement. Such an agreement is more a temporary resting-point, than a fixed-for-all agreement, and therefore also presumes procedures that do not throw up overly high thresholds against subsequent change.

If this is a more adequate description of the EU case, it is important to underline that the strategy presumes *further EU constitution-making* so as to ensure that the principles and institutional arrangements do provide the EU with the democratic legitimacy that this strategy requires. The critical issue is how far this process needs to go. Here opinions differ. Bohman argues that two elements are critical (see Chapter 2). The first is to ensure the basic conditions for constitutional reflexivity. Second, these need to be entrenched in a transnational structure. This line of argument is premised on the EU as distinct from, and as not having the vocation to become, a state. This both means that it cannot rely on a hierarchical system of authority, and further that its polycentric structure is conducive to reflexivity, in that it stimulates democratic experimentation. The substantive and procedural requirements for constitutional reflexivity that Bohman lists are significantly weaker than those that, for instance, Schmalz-Bruns finds necessary (cp. Chapter 3). The latter argues that the only way in which constitutional reflexivity can be ensured is through basic democratic requirements which, to be effective, *also* presuppose a kind of hierarchical structure. At issue therefore is whether the Convention exercise does take the EU closer to the requisite conditions, and further, what kind of structure these are embedded within: polycentric, polycephalous (as a type of intermediate arrangement) or hierarchical.

This difference in positions would also be reflected in different views of the Convention exercise, as Bohman's position would be compatible with the Convention as a preparatory body only and where the IGC remains as the formal proposing body. Schmalz-Bruns' position would instead presuppose that the Convention rather than the IGC would be the formal proposing body. The Convention would then be a *strong public*,[30] a body which embodies both deliberation and decision-making. This also entails that the Convention's foremost responsibility is not to the European Council or to the member states, rather it is directly responsible to and must answer to the public.

The applied strategy assessed

As noted, the mandate asked the Convention to consider core constitutional issues. But the Convention was *not* set up to serve as a constituent assembly. Such a constitutional moment was not now, but might be precipitated by its work.[31] The Laeken mandate, however, portrayed the Convention as an *extension of the public debate* on the future of the European Union. The Convention's rationale, from this perspective, was to give structure to, and to take this debate further. The mandate sought to build on and continue, but also to open up and render more transparent, the Union's established process-oriented approach to constitution-making. But it did so within a framework that privileges states, not citizens.

The Laeken Declaration's attempt to institutionalize the public debate through the Convention conceived of it as a preparatory body and not as a strong public. The Convention, nevertheless, decided to go further and produce a Draft Constitution. Thus, its resolve to forge a consensual decision on a common constitutional text effectively redefined the Convention into an 'as if' strong public.[32] The Convention claimed to have popular authorization for this decision to proceed beyond that of a mere preparatory body. Thus, it in effect appropriated a democratic mandate. This means first, that we should evaluate the body according to the same deliberative-democratic standards as were set out above. Second, we should evaluate the outcome in relation to the process-oriented approach rather than against the standards of a fully fledged democratic constitution, as the Convention was *not* in a position to ensure democratic authorization. The draft should therefore be assessed in terms of how well it complies with the requirements for constitutional reflexivity: a set of procedures and rights that ensure an ongoing process of discursive validation of the structure in place, as well as provisions that permit its change in response to reflexively fostered future agreements.

When the Convention is considered in relation to the first point, we have seen that it did comply with many of these deliberative requirements; and this is also confirmed by numerous analyses (cp. Magnette 2004a, 2004b; Maurer 2003; Lenaerts and Desomer 2002: 1240; Fossum and Menéndez 2005; Eriksen and Fossum 2004). The process was open and quite transparent and did permit different views to come to the fore. There is also evidence to show that opinions and positions have changed.[33] The draft was accepted by a very large majority of Convention members. But it was also evident that the full power of deliberation was not unleashed. This was particularly the case during the final stages of the

process, when it started to resemble an IGC, in that there was both bargaining and brinkmanship.

With regard to the second point, the title 'Draft Treaty establishing a
Constitution for Europe' is evocative of the process approach to constitution-making. Its title reflects what many of the participants expressed,
namely that this was as far as could be got, but also that the draft can serve
as a vehicle to foster the constitution for Europe. The question is what this
amounts to in constitutional reflexivity terms.

The draft reflects the majority of the Convention's great concern with
citizens' rights, as reflected in the inclusion of the Charter of Fundamental Rights. On this issue there had been a change in positions, in particular on the part of the British government, which initially did not want the
Charter to be a fully incorporated part of the draft (European Convention
2002c: 13; 2002d). The Convention did not consider the substantive contents of the Charter, as this had already been agreed upon by the Charter
Convention (2000). But this also means that the draft carries forth the
Charter's limitations as a vehicle to ensure self-legislating citizens (Eriksen
et al. 2003a; Fossum 2003).

What is also important to recognize is that the draft (if ratified and
adopted) would move the EU from a polycentric to a bi-cephalous entity,
through the formal abolition of the pillars (portions of which are nevertheless retained in various provisions), the instituting of legal personality
and numerous other unifying and simplifying provisions. The early-
warning system for national parliaments would for instance pull them into
the Union's ambit of operations and thus further entrench this comprehensive multilevel institutional structure. It would be a structure with two
heads (bi-cephalous) framed on top of one common legal body (but with
certain issue areas still outside it). The two-headed structure would
emanate from the retention of a Council-led decision-making system
within a number of issue areas still subject to unanimity provisions. This
structure is further entrenched in the amendment provisions for national
veto. The draft thus takes the Union closer to statehood by consolidating
the legal-institutional structure, but this process does not extend all the
way. This unifying thrust serves to underline that the draft will move the
Union further beyond the status of a polycentric structure (which is the
conception of the EU that Bohman's position rests on).

The draft also contains a number of institutional proposals that will
increase the democratic quality of the EU, through provisions that
strengthen the European Parliament as a legislative body, albeit still not to
a par with the Council.[34] Greatly strengthened transparency requirements
(Articles I–49, III–304, 305) will also improve individual and inter-
institutional lines of accountability. The popular right of initiative (Article
I–46.4) will improve citizens' access to the system. The draft moves the EU
closer to a parliamentary model, but this thrust is modified by a number
of provisions, such as those that will probably strengthen the Council and

entrench a bi-cephalous structure. The draft can be seen as equipping the Union with a dual basis of legitimacy: a Union of citizens and of states (European Parliament 2003). But although the Constitution is seen to emanate from both, numerous provisions will place the member states in a privileged position.[35]

Participants and analysts have presented the draft as a compromise,[36] or an ambiguous agreement, but it is closer to a *working agreement*.[37] The draft was the result of a long, preceding, argumentative process, where different reasons had been presented, sought justification for and assessed and tested. This procedure had made a final settlement possible, although the settlement was supported by different reasons.[38] There were shortcomings in the process, but it had permitted a rather thorough vetting of arguments. Further, standpoints and positions had changed. The results were also acknowledged to amount to more than what would have been achieved in an IGC,[39] which testifies to the importance of this process.

A working agreement entrenching citizens' rights can foster or sustain constitutional reflexivity. It was pointed out above that this agreement contains provisions likely to limit the reflexive character of certain of its rights and institutional procedures. Two further elements require mention. First, although the draft held different parts, with constitutional and normal legislative acts, respectively, this difference was not reflected in differentiated amendment procedures.[40] The draft was a seamless web, which could be construed either as over-constitutionalization or as de-constitutionalization. The former, over-constitutionalization, occurs when the detailed provisions in Part III become intrinsic parts of the constitution. This could make the constitution into a straitjacket and serve as an important constraint on the democratic decision-making process.[41] However, this assessment is also a matter of which evaluative standard is chosen. From a normative perspective, drawing on the notion of revolutionary constitution (see Brunkhorst 2004), the relevance of the term over-constitutionalization hinges on the constitution's compliance with basic constitutional norms (basic rights, egalitarian organizational and procedural norms and a viable public sphere) in the first place. The Union's Constitutional Treaty does not comply with such, given its democratic deficiencies (Fossum 2004; Menéndez 2005; Peters 2004). Further, when the constitutional provisions proper are not superior to the non-constitutional ones, which applies when the non-constitutional and democratically deficient provisions in Parts III and IV regulate and determine the operation of the constitutional provisions in Parts I and II, then, from a normative perspective, we may talk not of over-constitutionalization but of de-constitutionalization. Whichever reading is most relevant, either way, the problem would be exacerbated by a second element, the retention of national veto in amendment. In a Union of 25 this would probably mean a high threshold against further constitutional changes. This combination (draft as seamless web with high thresholds) could render the entire structure – constitutional and non-constitutional provisions alike – highly resilient to change, with negative effects on reflexivity.

Conclusion

This chapter has assessed the question of the EU's legitimacy with particular attention to the Convention. It has shown that the Convention took on the role, not only of staging a constitutional discussion, but also taking this process further to come up with a Draft Constitutional Treaty. This exercise has moved the Union closer to the fourth strategy. The Convention was able to tap the virtues of democratic deliberation to an unprecedented degree in EU constitution-making; and the draft also moved the process of constitutionalization forwards, as it holds numerous provisions to strengthen the EU's democratic quality.

The Convention adopted an 'as if' it were a constitution-making body approach, as it had not been authorized to serve as one. It appropriated a democratic mandate, thus greatly raising the stakes of the undertaking. But this appropriation could not be democratically authorized, as it had to carry out its deliberations under the shadow of the veto in the IGC. A process which the Convention thus sought to stage within the framework of strategy four was reined in and made subject to several of the core constraints inbuilt in strategy two.

This analysis provides us with three more general conclusions pertaining to the EU's legitimacy. First, the EU has adopted an approach to constitution-making that has become increasingly reflexive. The Convention exercise is the most explicit manifestation of this, but closer analysis of previous instances has revealed a certain built-up momentum. The approach adopted has been one of constitution-making as ongoing process. The legitimacy of the process and its products depends on the EU's ability to draw on justified norms and to entrench these in institutional form and practice, with a concomitant strengthening of the conditions that safeguard and promote reflexivity.

Second, this gradualist approach is still embedded in a framework with strong built-in safeguards for member states. These are justified by the need to retain nationally based democracy (albeit these arrangements represent weak safeguards in practice).

Third, the results are curious mixtures. On the one hand, in terms of overarching principles, the EU draws on those that mark the *common* constitutional traditions of the member states. But, as the Convention exercise showed, although it could draw on justified norms, its work continued the Union's unique blending of creative consolidation of the common constitutional traditions of the member states with the effort to distil out a constitution from the *acquis*, one which would highlight the unique features of the Union. The draft's bi-cephalous character underlines this careful blending.

The Constitutional Treaty can best be seen as a working agreement, which sought to forge a balance between a Europe of states and a Europe of citizens. It has moved closer to addressing citizens' concerns than before, but nevertheless ends up privileging states. Its main shortcoming, however, is comprised in its overly high thresholds against change. It risks ossification and could threaten the constitutional reflexivity thus far the hallmark of the Union's emerging post-national constitutionalism. 'Reflexivity constrained' is thus the most appropriate label for this.

Notes

1 See for example Abromeit 1998; Beetham and Lord 1998; Eriksen and Fossum 2000; Weiler 1995, 1999.
2 The draft was eventually adopted by the IGC, after an initial round where it was rejected. The basic structure of the draft survived the IGC, although there were several important substantive changes. See European Council 2003a, 2004a and 2004b which provide overviews of all the changes.
3 For more on these achievements see Weiler 2001a, 2001b, 2002.
4 See Bernhard Peters' contribution to this volume; Fossum 2004; Fossum and Menéndez 2005; Kokott and Rüth 2003.
5 Cp. Mestmäcker (1994), cited in Gerstenberg 1997. This position was also reflected in the debate, in particular espoused by some UK Tories and Euro sceptics, but also by some East Europeans.
6 Cp. Majone 1996a. This conception was well reflected in the debate.
7 The Pope pressed hard to have a reference to Christianity in the draft. Several members in the debate also spoke of the need for the Union to develop a clearer value foundation.
8 This position is held, with many shades, by most of the federalists in the Convention. See for instance Lamassoure and Duff. See also contributions by Jo Leinen, president of the Union of European Federalists.
9 On the strategies, see Fossum 2000, Eriksen and Fossum 2004, and Chapter 1 in this book. The evaluation of the Convention is based on personal attendance at six Convention plenary sessions, attendance at a range of Convention-related meetings in the European Parliament, as well as personal interviews with Convention members, secretariat member, European ombudsman and civil society representatives. I have also drawn on 23 structured interviews with Convention members conducted by CIDEL-funded staff in Brussels. Documents used include plenary debates, Convention submissions (to the plenary and to all the working groups and discussion circles), together with constitutional draft proposals from Convention and non-Convention members. Also helpful was attendance at various seminars and workshops with Convention-related membership and academic analysts working on the Convention.
10 Cohen and Sabel (1997) and Gerstenberg (1997) are deliberationists but do not think of the EU in explicit derivative terms. Majone does not work from an explicit deliberative perspective but highlights the epistemic value of deliberation (cp. Majone 1996a: 292).
11 Representatives of civil society and the Committee of the Regions were present as observers. It was also set up with several outreach functions, such as a Forum and a Youth Convention.
12 See Schönlau 2004 for a more detailed assessment of the role of time and timing in the Convention process.

13 This was the case at IGCs (cp. Beach 2003 and the Council Secretariat's central role).
14 What Magnette here refers to as situated interests is similar to Elster's (1992, 1998) notion of bootstrapping.
15 See Zanon 2003 who cites numerous examples. The origins of the skeletal draft (European Convention 2002e) remain somewhat mysterious but came from the close circle around Giscard (interview with Convention observer).
16 Consider in particular their handling of the Franco–German proposal (European Convention 2003a) on the Council Presidency, where it chose to disregard the majority position and support the large states. See Zanon 2003.
17 Interviews with Convention member and staff.
18 See Closa 2003. Interview with secretariat official. See also Lenaerts and Desomer 2002.
19 This is evident from the sequencing of articles, and was confirmed in interviews with participants, as well as often stated by the same in plenary debates.
20 Proponents of a delimited EU, based on intergovernmental cooperation, generally opposed a Convention. The Swedish government initially opposed the idea of a Convention (Petersson *et al.* 2003: 75) as did the UK one, which initially had no clear strategy in relation to the Convention. Interview with Convention member, 22 January 2003.
21 The British government representative, Peter Hain, spoke frequently of 'red lines', i.e. British positions on issues that could only go so far. Other similar instances of red-line drawing were by the Polish, Spanish and Benelux countries (Closa 2004).
22 Giscard was cited to the effect that 'The substance of the text under discussion is a constitution, but one which takes the legal form of a treaty since, in contrast to a national constitution, the powers conferred on the Union derive from the States which conclude the treaty' (European Convention 2003c: 1).
23 A Convention member also noted in interview that few of the representatives from the applicant countries had thought about the EU as a constitutional order before they came to the Convention.
24 These are liberty, democracy, respect for human rights and fundamental freedoms and the rule of law. <http://europa.eu.int/eur-lex/en/treaties/dat/C_2002325EN.000501.html>
25 The percentage share of women was very low. It also failed to even faintly reflect the increasingly multicultural nature of many of its member states (Shaw 2003).
26 There were some suggestions to insert them in Article 2. This was closely associated with Article 45, which sets out the procedure for initiating procedures against a member state which breaches the Union's principles and values (European Convention 2003c: 5).
27 This arrangement was subsequently supplemented with the so-called blue-card system, which allowed interventions from the floor and sparked a more open debate (European Convention 2002b).
28 For this notion consider Ackerman 1991, 1998.
29 A critical issue is whether this conception of the EU has to be state-based. For incisive accounts of this issue consider Schmalz-Bruns (Chapter 3), who works from this strategy perspective. See also Brunkhorst 2004.
30 *Strong public* refers to institutionalized deliberations 'whose discourse encompasses both opinion formation and decision-making' – as different from *weak public* (or what has elsewhere been termed as *general public* (cp. Eriksen and Fossum 2002)) and which refers to public spheres 'whose deliberative practice consists exclusively in opinion formation and does not also encompass decision-making' (Fraser 1992: 134).

31 'The question ultimately arises as to whether this simplification and reorganization might not lead in the long run to the adoption of a constitutional text in
the Union' (European Council 2001b).

32 It might be added that the Laeken Convention did use the Charter experience
as a reference point, including the consensus method implicit in the Cologne
mandate, which became explicit in the Laeken mandate.

33 Twenty-three members of the Convention were asked if they had changed their
minds in the course of the debates in the Convention, and whether they saw
the Convention exercise foremost as a bargaining or as a learning experience
and what its main lessons were. The results show considerable movement on a
number of issues. Many said they had changed their minds during the work of
the Convention. The participants generally confirmed the epistemic value of
this form of deliberation. None reported any great personal transformation,
although many pointed out that the views of the representatives from the applicant states changed and also underlined the importance of fully including
them.

34 Such provisions are: co-decision as the main legislative procedure (Article I–33,
with reference to Article III–302); far more use of qualified majority voting in
the Council (cp. Article I–24); and the formal abolition of the pillar system
(not quite so in practice, though).

35 See Fossum 2004.

36 Cp. Plenary debate 12 June 2003. Convention members, when asked whether
the Convention exercise was a bargaining process or a learning process, generally came up with responses to the effect that it was both but they all (23)
particularly stressed the learning aspect.

37 For this category, see Eriksen 2003 and Schmalz-Bruns (Chapter 3).

38 There was no final vote but most likely 195 out of 207 members and substitutes
supported the draft, whereas nine signed the so-called minority report.

39 Participants' accounts. See also Kokott and Rüth 2003: 1317, Fossum and
Menéndez 2005.

40 But note that Articles IV–444 and 445 of the final IGC version do envisage simplified revision procedures for limited aspects (after a unanimous vote by the
Council) of Part III (European Council 2004c).

41 For a more detailed description of this problem, see Menéndez 2005.

7 Towards a post-national foreign and security policy?

Helene Sjursen[1]

Introduction

As recognized by the Laeken European Council, the European Union stands at a crossroads. There is considerable uncertainty as to what type of entity the EU will become, as to what kind of order is emerging in Europe; and several possibilities arise. On the basis of the polity options developed in Chapter 1, I identify three ideal types for the emerging European order. First, the EU might be on its way to being reduced to a mere *problem-solving entity* based on economic citizenship. Here, membership would be derived from its discernible benefits and the purpose of the organization would be to promote the material interests of the member states. Second, the EU might be moving towards becoming a *value-based community* premised on social and cultural citizenship. From such a perspective, the EU would be a geographically delimited entity seeking to revitalize traditions, mores and memories of whatever common European values and affiliations exist in order to forge a *we-feeling* as a basis for integration. A third possibility would be that the EU could become a *rights-based post-national union* based on a full-fledged political citizenship. Public support for this option might be motivated by a constitutional patriotism, emanating from a set of legally entrenched fundamental rights and democratic procedures that are deeply entrenched in the 'collective psyche' of Europeans and in the institutional framework of the European Union.[2]

The main purpose of this chapter is to discuss to which of these ideal types the EU's foreign and security policy (EFP) speaks.[3] Often, answers to questions about the emerging European order are sought by analysing the building and reforming of the EU's overall institutions. However, when it comes to identifying the nature of the EU, it is not enough to look at its emerging governance structures and its basic, overarching institutional features. We must also look more closely at developments in particular policy fields. Different actors have different interests, visions and values that they wish to project onto the European level, different ideas about what the EU ought to be about. The importance and relevance of these different interests, values and visions might become more visible through analyses of how different policy issues are conceived of and incorporated into the EU. Often, it is here, in the processes of determining what should be done with regard to concrete policy issues and areas, that the fundamental features of the EU are actually defined. Thus, analysing the principal reasons for including particular policy issues, as well as the reasons for particular policy decisions, might contribute to a better understanding of what kind of order is emerging in Europe. To what extent can we identify a break with the core principle of the Westphalian order (i.e. the sovereign equality of states) and the development of a higher order law – above the states?

The question of foreign and security policy is particularly interesting in this regard because expectations that member states will move beyond national sovereignty on this policy issue are low. Foreign and security policy is in many ways the *hard case* for those expecting that the EU will move beyond mere problem-solving. The very nature of foreign and security policy is by many considered alien to supranationalism and thus it is widely believed to be self-evident which ideal type of the EU the development of a common foreign policy speaks to. What is more, cooperation in foreign and security policy within the EU is chiefly confined to a separate pillar (although this will change with the Constitutional Treaty), where decision-making procedures differ from those in the Community pillar in several and crucial ways. Hence the predominant perception of the foreign-policy field within the EU is that it would speak to the first ideal type of the EU as a problem-solving entity, with little onus on collective tasks and obligations beyond the interests and preferences of the member states and where the output is accordingly limited. However, this might not be the whole story. Discussions about creating a foreign and security policy have been a central part of the agenda of European integration since the early 1950s, and since the early 1970s a gradual building of common institutions, positions and policies has taken place. If it is the case that there are so few discernible results from cooperation in foreign and security policy, why then do the member states spend so much time attempting to organize and define this policy? Why do they not concentrate their efforts on those issue areas where the benefits are clear and evident? Such questions gained importance against the backdrop of the work of the Convention on the Future of Europe where not only one, but two working groups focused on issues related to foreign and security policy, and where the question of increased majority voting in this issue area was debated to the very end.

In order to discuss to which of the above ideal types the EU's foreign and security policy speaks, it is necessary, however, to work out more precisely what kind of foreign and security policy one might expect according to each of them. Hence, in this chapter I have sought to work out three analytically distinct conceptions of the EU's foreign policy based on the problem-solving, value-based and rights-based ideal types of the EU. In working out these three conceptions, I have focused on three core indicators:

1   the institutional structure of the common foreign policy;
2   the legitimacy basis of the common foreign policy; and
3   the conception of international relations on which collective foreign-policy initiatives (towards states outside the EU) might rely.

Based on the first ideal type of the EU, the principal hypothesis would be that the emphasis on developing a common European foreign and security policy is the result of an expectation of long- or medium-term gains of such cooperation for individual member states, outweighing any short-term costs involved in building cooperation in this policy field. However, given the potential reservations to this problem-solving conception of EFP, two alternative hypotheses that speak to the second and the third ideal types are also being considered. Hence, consistent with the second ideal type of the EU, the second hypothesis is that the desire for a 'truly' value-based community would require a common foreign and security policy whose purpose would be to ensure and protect the sustainability of the European *community*. Finally, consistent with the third ideal type of the EU, we would expect that efforts to build a common foreign policy would be mobilized by a concern for promoting certain binding and constraining principles not only inside the EU but also at the international stage.

In the first part of this chapter the principal hypothesis is discussed in more detail. What might a problem-solving foreign and security policy look like? Based on the conclusions of this analysis, I discuss, with reference to some empirical examples, to what extent this might be a plausible conception of the EU's foreign and security policy. Subsequently, similar discussions are developed based on the second and third hypotheses. Is it so that, even with regard to a *hard case* such as foreign and security policy, where national sovereignty and national interests are considered to be most difficult to curb, developments point in a different direction than towards the EU as a problem-solving entity?

Problem-solving in foreign and security policy

As noted in the introduction, conventional wisdom and the predominant view of the EU's foreign policy conveyed in the academic literature would suggest that it speaks to the first ideal type of the EU as a *problem-solving entity*. There are several reasons why this is so. Perhaps most important is the fact that in foreign and security policy the national veto is fiercely protected and the supranational institutions (in particular the European Parliament and the Court) formally have only limited influence. The emphasis on the primacy of national interests could be considered the cause, for example, of the breakdown of European cooperation over the war in Iraq. The obligation to consult is in principle part of the rules and norms of the Common Foreign and Security Policy (CFSP) framework. The signatories of the so-called 'letter of the eight' that supported the position of the United States' government, simply ignored this obligation when it was considered a hindrance to the expression of what those states considered to be in their particular interest.[4] Hence this seems to confirm the principal hypothesis, linked to the ideal type of the EU as a problem-solving entity, that cooperation will only take place on foreign and security issues when there are visible benefits from such cooperation and that, when such benefits are not in evidence, member states will choose to go their own way (i.e. to defect), or cooperate within other fora.

In more precise terms, what kind of institutional structure and decision-making processes would we expect a problem-solving entity to have in foreign and security policy? What would be the legitimacy basis for such a policy and what kind of perspective on international relations would its policy initiatives be based upon?

Institutional arrangements

The ideal type of the EU as a problem-solving entity rests on particular theoretical assumptions about the nature of political processes and actor rationality. At the core is the definition of actors as utility-maximizers. Actors are considered as rational in the sense that they seek to maximize their own interests. Following from this, politics is considered to be the outcome of adverse self-interested behaviour. Furthermore, the under-lying scientific position of this perspective emphasizes material rather than normative or social structures. Actors are conceived of as monologi-cal and they consider that 'other people are just external, objective facts of reality, on the line with material things, only with the distinctive quality that they carry out strategic actions too' (Eriksen and Weigård 1997: 221). In international relations it is the state that is considered to be the rele-vant actor category and the above assumptions about rationality are trans-ferred to this unit. The sovereignty of the state and its wish to remain autonomous are taken as given. The expectation is that, even though states may seek to establish decision-making processes and institutions allowing them to maximize utility in a particular sector or on a particular issue, they will always seek arrangements that allow them to maintain or enhance their autonomy. Hence a core expectation will be that states will mostly choose to establish *intergovernmental* institutional arrangements rather than supranational ones. Such institutional arrangements would allow states to maintain their autonomy yet at the same time reduce the costs of cooperation when this would be considered beneficial to state interests.

One might, however, imagine different forms of intergovernmental arrangements, or attribute more or less importance to collective institutions in the bargaining process that leads to their establishment. In the literature on international relations, there is disagreement between neo-realists and neo-liberal institutionalists on this issue. Whereas the former have little faith in the role of collective institutions, the latter attribute considerable importance to institutions as instruments for reducing transaction costs. Applied to the EU, it has thus been suggested that one might expect a certain willingness from states to pool or delegate power in order to ensure credible commitments from other actors (Moravcsik 1998). Delegation or pooling might, according to this perspective, chiefly take place in 'issue areas where joint gains are high and distributional conflicts are moderate, and where there is uncertainty about future decisions' (p. 75). Furthermore, one would expect governments to commit themselves to collective institutions in policy areas where this would commit other governments to policies favoured by key domestic constituencies, or perhaps to pre-commit the government to policies unpopular with domestic constituencies that do not support the government. Finally, the expectation would be that governments would be 'nesting specific decisions inside a set of larger decisions reached by unanimity' (p. 76). The fundamental assumption of actor rationality is, however, also maintained in this neo-liberal institutionalist perspective; and the emphasis on states' ability to, or preference for, controlling institutional developments is not reduced or weakened. As Risse-Kappen (1995: 26) has argued, 'neo-liberal institutionalism should not be regarded as part of the liberal paradigm. This "co-operation under anarchy" perspective shares all realist core assumptions, but disagrees with structural realists on the likelihood of international co-operation among self-interested actors.' Hence, with regard to the type of institutional arrangements, it seems reasonable to argue that this perspective would consider intergovernmental institutional arrangements more likely than supranational ones.

Legitimacy basis

The question of the value basis or legitimacy basis of the foreign policy conceived of as problem-solving would probably not be considered particularly relevant, as this would be enshrined in the nation state. Given that all power is considered to remain with the state, other sources of legitimacy than the ones produced domestically would not be required. With regard to the intergovernmental unit, focus would be on the extent to which joint problem-solving would be more effective in terms of maximizing the specific interests of each individual member state than separate, national problem-solving. As long as such effectiveness is in evidence, further requirements for legitimation would most probably not be considered important.

Perspective on international relations

Finally, with regard to the perspective on international relations, interstate conflict is a natural ingredient. This is so not only with regard to relations between member states, but also with regard to these states' collective relations with third states, i.e. in the international system. In such a system, there is no focus on justice or on fair distribution. Decisions will reflect the will of the strongest. This means that the perspective on international relations that might underpin the initiatives of a problem-solving foreign policy at best would be inspired by a concern for ensuring stability within the established Westphalian system through a balance of power – that is, to the extent that it is possible to expect the establishment of common European interests from this perspective. However, different scholars have different expectations with regard to the strategies that states would choose in an anarchical international system. Hence, whereas some would emphasize that actors would seek security through an international balance of power, others would expect that states' rational calculations would lead them to act offensively to acquire more power than others (Mearsheimer 2001). Neo-liberal institutionalists, on their part, would expect EFP to put a greater emphasis on cooperative regimes also in the international system; however, such regimes would not challenge the fundamental nature of the system. Hence all the above perspectives share the assumption that states have no choice in an anarchical international system other than to act as if they were power-hungry. Furthermore, they share a focus on great powers as the relevant players, as well as an emphasis on rules and norms as simply reflecting the interests of the most powerful.

In sum, foreign and security policy within a problem-solving entity would be formulated with the help of *intergovernmental institutions* (within which decisions are made through processes of bargaining). There is *no need for direct legitimation* of the choices made in foreign and security policy, as all power remains with the nation state and normative or legitimacy questions are considered to be confined to the domestic political sphere. Finally, with regard to the perspective of such an entity on international relations, the emphasis would (at best) be on a need to ensure stability within the established, anarchical, Westphalian system through a *balance of power.*

To what extent can such a conception be said to be satisfactory in terms of capturing the core elements of the EU's foreign and security policy?

Empirical relevance

To many, principal characteristics of the EU's foreign and security policy are indecisiveness and ineffectiveness. It is argued that little is happening in the field of foreign and security policy within the EU. In fact the very existence of a common European foreign and security policy is questioned. Such ineffectiveness would be consistent with the expectations of a problem-solving conception of the EU's foreign policy, where one would only expect cooperation in situations where discernible benefits for each member state are visible, hence on a limited number of issues. However, to what extent do such analyses become a self-fulfilling prophecy? If there is no alternative conception of cooperation on the table, certain dimensions of the empirical reality might be lost, or their importance or relevance ruled out without being considered. To what extent, for example, is the argument that it is not really meaningful to talk about a common foreign and security policy within the EU, as it only exists on paper and has no real substance, simply a reflection of a particular view of which kind of actions or initiatives are relevant in international politics? That is, might there be a theoretical bias to this approach? It is possible that the conception of EU foreign policy as 'problem-solving' and the theoretical assumptions that this conception relies upon, say much, or perhaps more, about what is *not* possible, than what is possible in terms of integration and cooperation in foreign and security policy. What become particularly visible, and under-standable, from this perspective are the limitations to this policy area in, for example, situations of international crises, whereas day-to-day policy-making and potential incremental change might slide out of focus.

Another general comment to the perspective outlined above might be that its relevance or applicability to foreign and security policy is limited, given that there are few concrete material gains or costs in foreign and security policy. There are obvious exceptions to this, for example, with regard to building and sustaining a military capability and national intelli-gence network, as well as with regard to the building and sustaining of a national defence industry.[5] Here the potential material gains would be easy to measure and it is possible to rationally calculate gains or losses entailed by different choices. Most importantly, however, the above argu-ment is not a relevant one for rejecting this approach because utility can be defined either in terms of increased international influence or in terms of increased (territorial) security rather than as material economic gains. In order to ensure the relevance of the perspective for analysis of foreign and security policy, 'utility' then needs to be operationalized in a different way – not as economic gains, but as international influence or increased (territorial) security.

The most important question for this chapter, however, is to what extent the three indicators related to the conception of foreign policy as problem-solving fit with what we know about the EU's foreign policy? At first sight, the fit seems to be fairly good. This is particularly so with regard to the *institutional structures*. Despite the Commission's persistent efforts to take over as much as possible of the foreign-policy dossier and to put its personal mark on the EU's relations with the rest of the world, member states retain their national veto on most issues and have built institutions to facilitate a process of cooperation in which they retain control, instead of delegating power to the Commission.

However, a number of empirical observations suggest that something more is going on within this, mainly intergovernmental, structure than what might be captured through a focus on member states' fixed preferences defined as a desire for increased international influence or increased (territorial) security (Tonra 2001; Aggestam 2000; Pijpers 1996; Allen 1998; Howorth 2000). It is perhaps in particular the assumption of the rational-choice perspective of the stability of preferences within an intergovernmental framework that (implicitly) is challenged by this literature. Several authors suggest that the CFSP seems to have a certain transformatory capacity vis-à-vis national foreign policies. They suggest that it is not only the strategies of the member states that have changed, but that their perception of which types of problems and issues are relevant and of the appropriate way to resolve them has evolved (Tonra 2001; Smith 2000; Aggestam 2000, 2004; Pijpers 1996). Furthermore, some write about processes of 'Brusselsisation' (Allen 1998) or 'Brussels-based intergovernmentalism' (Howorth 2000) in the CFSP. By this they mean that, although national governments are still formally in control of foreign policy, in practice much of the foreign-policy-making process has been moved to Brussels, thus making it more difficult for national ministries to fully control what is being decided. These observations imply that, although the first indicator seems to be strongly confirmed by what we know about the formal institutional arrangements of the EU's foreign policy, there might, in practice, be moves in a different direction and towards something that might be more difficult to explain with the theoretical tools that this conception of the EU's foreign and security policy relies upon. The institutional arrangements, even if we refer only to the second pillar and not to external relations, may not be merely intergovernmental.

With regard to the *legitimacy basis* of the foreign and security policy, there is substantial evidence that the problem-solving conception fits with what we know about the EU's foreign policy. The lack of democratic control of the foreign-policy process at the EU-level is well documented. Although the European Parliament is active in terms of producing statements and documenting its views on international issues, it has a very limited role in the actual making of foreign and security policy. Some would argue, however, that the issue of democratic legitimacy in foreign and security policy is not as relevant or important in the nation-state context either, due to the particular nature of foreign policy as opposed to domestic policy. Hence the crucial test to this indicator might be evidence of a sense of common identity, rather than of procedures that ensure democratic control. However, here also the evidence at first sight appears to be in the negative, as the EU is composed of a number of nation states with different historical experiences and cultural reference points providing the legitimacy basis for national foreign policy. One reservation can be added to this: the systematic references made to a common European heritage and a 'European family' during discussions about enlargement to

Central and Eastern Europe might suggest that there are elements of a perception of common identity in place (Sjursen 2002). It would still, however, be necessary to show that this comes into play in foreign and security policy and not only in enlargement. I will return to this later in the chapter.

Finally, with regard to the *perspective on international relations*, this is perhaps where the evidence supporting the conception of the EU as a problem-solving entity is the weakest. It is increasingly argued that the EU and its foreign policy has a particular impact and that the EU's particular role in the international system distinguishes it from other international actors (Rosecrance 1998; Aggestam 2000; Menéndez 2004a; Manners 2002; Sjursen 2003). One of the characteristics of its policy is an effort to strengthen those dimensions of the international system that contribute to constrain power politics. Such observations could be considered to be a reflection of the limited achievements of the foreign-policy cooperation in a problem-solving EU. Kagan (2003), for example, has argued that it is because the EU does not have the resources to use force that it espouses Kantian ideals in its relations with the rest of the world. The problem with Kagan's argument, however, is that he does not investigate any alternative hypothesis. He does not consider for example the possibility that an emphasis on other instruments than military force may be the result of a normative assessment of the appropriateness of the use of such instruments, rather than of their availability.[6]

At a more general level it can be argued that, with regard to the relevance of a problem-solving conception of EU foreign policy, what is at stake is not only the existence of a rest category of empirical observations that do not seem to 'fit' completely. Rather, the issue might be that parts of the empirical world of inter-state interaction are sliced off before the analysis begins, hence a theoretical bias. In fact, in order to achieve agreement to undertake efforts to seek collective problem-solving in the first place, a considerable level of understanding between the actors is necessary. They must agree on the object of their dispute as well as have a similar understanding of how to measure the power potentials that determine the outcome of the bargaining process, i.e. the compromise. Finally, they must have some, minimal, shared normative framework. Otherwise it will not be possible for them to agree that the results are valid and to ensure that all parties put them into practice. Many authors have argued that, in order to understand how these 'prior' understandings come about, we may need a different conception of actor rationality and political processes than the one provided for by rational-choice theories (Müller 2001: 163; Eriksen 2003). The bargaining process that leads to a compromise in the distribution of costs and benefits is only one part of the process of cooperation between states. This would also suggest then that, in order to properly capture the reasons for these efforts to build a common foreign and security policy, we cannot limit ourselves to this perspective.

Beyond strategic rationality?

The above discussion suggests that it might be worth taking a closer look at the two alternative hypotheses outlined in the introduction and that speak to the second and third ideal types of the EU (the EU as a value-based community or as a rights-based post-national union). Whereas the second hypothesis would suggest that a common foreign and security policy would be established mainly to ensure and protect the sustainability of a particular community with a particular European identity, the third hypothesis would suggest that the efforts to build a common foreign policy could be understood as the expression of a concern for promoting certain principles not only inside the EU but also on the international stage. These two hypotheses rest on different theoretical assumptions about the nature of political processes and about actor rationality than those relied upon in the first ideal type.

Central to both hypotheses is the conception of actors as communicatively rational and not just strategic. This conception contends that actors are considered rational when they are able to justify and explain their actions in relation to intersubjectively valid norms, that is, norms that cannot be reasonably rejected in a rational debate, and not only when they seek to maximize their own interests (Eriksen and Weigård 2003).[7] There is, in other words, an explicit emphasis on language in this perspective that we do not find in the rational-choice approach. This builds on Jürgen Habermas's theory of 'speech acts' and communicative action. Habermas considers that our communication through linguistic expressions – speech acts – plays a central role in regulating and reproducing forms of social life and the identities of actors (Habermas 1998a). The process of argumentation is considered to be the crucial mechanism of social coordination. Arguably this is also so in a rational-choice perspective. The actors may not always be mute in a bargaining process – such processes obviously entail exchanges of information between actors – however, the type of information conveyed in a bargaining process is different (Heath 2001). Here it is mainly a matter of signalling preferences that are backed by threats and promises, whereas the definition of actors as communicatively rational suggests that they are also capable of providing reasons for particular choices and that others are in turn capable of assessing the validity of those reasons. This opens up the *theoretical* possibility of an agreement between actors based on an understanding supported by mutually acceptable or identical reasons, rather than individual utility calculations.

This perspective is similar to a rational-choice analysis in the sense that they are both action-theoretical approaches. Social phenomena are considered to be products of interaction between individuals. However, rather than focusing on monological actors with fixed preferences, the theory of communicative action focuses on dialogical actors 'who co-ordinate their plans through argumentation, aimed at reaching mutual agreement' (Eriksen and Weigård 1997: 221). In addition to the concept of actors as strategic and oriented towards realizing self-interest, we have then a conception of actors as understanding-oriented and seeking to reach agreement with other actors through argumentation. Here it is posited 'that co-operation comes about when the process of reason-giving generates a capacity for change of viewpoints' (Eriksen and Fossum 2000: 257).

The reasons for a particular policy choice could be material gain, but they could also be formulated with reference to an actor's sense of identity or understanding of the common good. This is the form of justification that we would expect in the value-based foreign policy. From this perspective, communicative processes are context-bound; they are only possible in collectivities that have a 'thick' sense of identity. In such collectivities the relevant form of justification would be referring to what the appropriate conduct is, given the particular identity of the particular community in question.

Furthermore, actors could explain their actions with reference to principles that, all things considered, can be recognized as just by all parties, irrespective of their particular interests, perceptions of the good life or cultural identity. This would be the form of justification that one would expect in a rights-based foreign policy. Whereas the concern for material gains could be accounted for through a rational-choice perspective, answers to questions regarding 'who we are' (identity questions) or what is the right conduct from a moral perspective are more difficult to reconstruct from such premises. Consequently, this conception of actors as communicatively rational might help us in particular to bring the potential communal and/or normative dimension in the EU's foreign and security policy out more clearly (Sjursen 2004).

This conception of actors as understanding-oriented and thus able to shift from a purely self-regarding to an other-regarding mode of interaction is not the same thing as a conception of actors as altruistic. Rather the actor is conceived of as having:

> the ability to critically reflect on her own understandings of reality, interests, preferences, and maxims of behaviour; to estimate the consequences for other actors should she decide to pursue her own interests; and to participate in a discourse with others regarding the interpretation of interest and norms for the coordination of behaviour and interaction.
>
> (Lose 2001: 185)

This opens not only for the possibility of a change of preferences as a result of interaction and communication, but also for the possibility of actors agreeing to certain decisions even if they go against their own material interest.

Indicators of a value-based or a rights-based foreign policy

What kind of expectations might we have then of the institutional arrangements in a value-based and a rights-based foreign and security policy? What would be the legitimacy basis for such foreign and security policies and what kind of perspective on international relations would their policy initiatives be based upon?

Institutional arrangements

If we start with the *rights-based* foreign policy, it follows from the definition of actors as communicatively rational and understanding-oriented that they will be capable of agreeing to establish institutions and rules for interaction that are mutually binding and that may constrain their ability to promote particular interests. The mobilizing factor for the establishment of such institutions or rules would be the joint conviction of the actors involved that they would provide the best way, or the best procedures, for solving common problems. It is perhaps less obvious whether or not this perspective would lead to expectations of supranational or, rather, intergovernmental institutions and international governance (Bohman 1999). However, the most likely option would probably be *supranationalism*, defined as the establishment of a mutually binding legal arrangement, connected to sanctions, between the actors. Such mutually binding institutions would be necessary in order to ensure collective action, to take away the motives for actors not to comply with common rules. They impose sanctions for non-compliance; hence make it less costly to act in a morally adequate way. Without mutually binding legal norms, there is always a risk of defection and a concern that some actors contribute more than they receive (whereas others are free riders). In order to avoid such risks common rules are necessary. Here, the rational-choice perspective might agree with the communicative perspective – however, it diverges on the potential for actors to actually come to agreement on common rules. Furthermore, the two perspectives differ on the reasons why actors might agree in the first place, as well as comply once they have come to agreement. Whereas the rational-choice perspective would expect agreement only if the rational utility calculations of each individual actor suggest that agreement is beneficial, the communicative perspective assumes that agreement is possible on the basis of the better argument. In the aftermath, then, the legal agreement is maintained not only because of its ultimate ability to force actors to comply but because it is considered legitimate – it is considered to provide fair terms of cooperation for all actors involved. Regardless of their material resources, they are subjected to the same duties and have the same rights. The law is considered to have a moral element that makes it possible to obey it based on a moral assessment about what is fair, or what is in the interest of the common good (Eriksen and Weigård 2003). It ensures a fair process of decision-making.

With regard to a *value-based* conception, the consensus that would provide the basis for compliance is limited as it is based upon a we-feeling, a sense of common identity and the idea of special obligations to fellow members within the unit. Allegiance to a common foreign and security policy would be the result of a sense of common destiny and a clear distinction between what is European as opposed to membership in other human collectives. In such a unit, supranational institutions would be unproblematic, indeed a necessary requirement for a foreign and security policy with a mandate to protect and sustain the collective 'us' and 'our' particular way of life from other units in the international system.

Legitimacy basis

With regard to the legitimacy basis for a value-based and a rights-based conception, there would also be differences. In both cases, however, the democratic checks and balances of the member states would not be a sufficient source of legitimacy, as both conceptions are considered to entail a degree of supranationality. In the case of a *value-based* conception, one would rely on the sense of solidarity as the principal source of legitimacy for the foreign and security policy. The requirements for democratic checks and balances would perhaps be considered less strong, as the need for a common foreign and security policy would be justified in terms of defending and protecting a particular life-form from potential threats and intrusions. The value- or identity-based conception does not as such presuppose democracy. It is only if the community in question endorses democratic principles as a constitutive part of their common identity that democratic legitimacy would be expected. Hence what one would expect first of all is a certain requirement of consistency between the particular understanding of the characteristics of a particular entity and the policy choices made. To many, such a perspective might be particularly relevant with regard to foreign and security policy. Indeed, it is sometimes even argued that, particularly with regard to issues that pertain to national security, openness and democratic accountability can be problematic, and efficiency requirements are more important. Physical survival – national sovereignty – is what is ultimately considered to be at stake, and is thus considered to take primacy over requirements for democratic checks and balances.[8] This is also reflected in the national constitutions of some states, in the sense that foreign and security policy is often considered to be the prerogative of the executive and the decision to go to war is sometimes even almost exclusively in the hands of this branch. National parliaments on the whole spend less time scrutinizing foreign-policy issues than traditional domestic political matters. The advocates of the limited need for democratic controls and procedures in foreign and security policy seem, however, to lean not only on criteria of efficiency but also on assumptions of cultural and ethnic cohesion within a nation state. Questions of foreign policy are often framed in terms of 'us' and 'them', most likely in an attempt to make it legitimate and appropriate to expect a reflex of solidarity and unity of purpose, one not requiring the same kind of democratic checks and balances as those issues that only pertain to relations within the collective 'us'.

With regard to the legitimacy basis for a *rights-based* conception of foreign and security policy it would, as noted, also need to draw on something else than the domestic political processes in the member states, due to its supranational elements. However, it would not, in the same way as in a value-based conception, be possible to expect an automatic sense of solidarity and support for a common foreign and security policy due to a common identity. A rights-based common foreign and security policy would need to be accountable to a wide variety of interests and perspectives. In order to ensure such accountability a broad public debate, where all those affected could in principle be heard, would be required. This presupposes a European public sphere as well as legally entrenched rights of citizenship at the supranational level, not only at the national level.

Finally, what kinds of perspective on international relations would we expect in a rights-based and a value-based foreign policy?

Perspective on international relations

With regard to the *value-based* foreign policy, the similarities might be stronger with the problem-solving foreign policy than with the rights-based one. In both cases the perspective would rest on a sense of potential for conflict with other actors. In a problem-solving entity this would take the form of a perceived need for protecting self-interests in an anarchical international system whereas in the case of the latter it would be a matter of protecting specific values and a particular way of life. As already noted, with regard to the foreign policies of states, it is often the case that the questions of protecting particular interests and a particular identity are rolled into one. This is very well illustrated if we consider the concept of 'national interest', which is constantly used by national foreign-policy-makers to justify what they do. Although the existence of a clearly identifiable national interest is in many cases an illusion, the implicit assumption of the existence of such a national interest lurks behind many analyses and discussions of foreign policy.[9] Hence some might consider it artificial to draw an analytical distinction between an interest-based and identity-based foreign policy. And in terms of the perspective on international relations, the difference is perhaps not that big: in the case of a value-based foreign policy, the emphasis is likely to be on the world perceived in categories of 'us' and 'them', and organized in accordance with particular cultural understandings of differences and similarities. The perspective on international relations is likely to be that it consists of various culturally integrated spheres. However, in concrete cases, foreign policy choices might differ according to whether the identity aspect or the interest dimension is the dominant one.

With regard to the perspective or understanding of international relations that one might expect in a *rights-based* foreign policy on the other hand, this would differ quite radically from that in a problem-solving foreign policy. In the former it is reasonable to expect that the emphasis would be on the cosmopolitan elements in the international system and on the need to further strengthen these. The emphasis would be on overcoming power politics, rather than on contributing to the power-political game through the strengthening of existing (perceived) balances of power or establishing a new balance of power. More concretely, this would mean a focus on multilateral institutions and the need for a strengthening of international law. The onus would be on arrangements that would bind actors at the international level also and put (legal) constraints on the ability of actors to pursue self-interested behaviour and exercise power for their own material or political gain. However, a rights-based foreign policy would not only emphasize the value of international law but also the importance of a re-orientation of international law towards a strengthening of the status of human rights. It is on the basis of human rights that a supranational legal structure can be established. Hence one might expect that a search for a redefinition of state sovereignty that would allow for a certain reconciliation between the principle of external sovereignty, which in practice can lead to the acceptance of tyranny, and the principles of human rights, would be a central part of this perspective on international relations. New developments such as the establishment of the International Criminal Court would be an example of the kind of initiatives that a rights-based foreign policy would put emphasis on.

Beyond problem-solving?

To what extent, if at all, do the things we know about the EU's foreign and security policy fit with the conception of a value-based and/or a rights-based foreign policy as outlined above? Do these conceptions fare better than the problem-solving conception of EU foreign policy, and, in particular, do they speak to those observations about the EU's foreign policy that were not captured, or less well captured, by the problem-solving conception?

Intuitively, the answer would be that such conceptions of foreign policy have little empirical relevance. We are not used to thinking or talking about foreign policies in terms that explicitly highlight their normative dimension. Practitioners who do so are at best considered naive and ignorant of the 'realities' of international politics, at worst dangerous idealists, promoting moral principles without regard for political and cultural particularities. With regard to political scientists who emphasize such dimensions, they are suspected of uncritically accepting the arguments of cynical policy-makers who hide their real agendas behind rhetorical statements about the importance of rights and values. The arguments in favour of rejecting the empirical relevance of a value-based or rights-based conception of European foreign policy are further strengthened by the fact that the institutional structure of the CFSP remains intergovernmental and that, in both a value-based and a rights-based foreign policy, we would expect intergovernmentalism to be overcome, or at least supplemented by other institutional arrangements. Even the outcome of the Convention on the Future of Europe seemed to confirm that intergovernmentalism is firmly entrenched in European foreign, security and defence policy.

However, as noted earlier in the chapter, there are some signs of change with regard to this first indicator of *institutional arrangements*. Although these changes are not translated into formal institutional structures, the institutional nexus of policy-making and the many actors involved in the field of foreign and security policy depart from a simple intergovernmental organizing model. The Commission's activities affect traditional foreign-policy issues; and it is often difficult to distinguish between its domain and that of the member states. Further, the frequency of meetings amongst national representatives in the various institutional settings organized under the Council and located in Brussels may have contributed to what observers refer to as processes of 'Brusselsisation', which suggest a de facto move in the direction of supranationalism (Allen 1998; Howorth 2000). The time spent on the preparation of these meetings as well as their duration may imply a deliberative mode of interaction. Committee studies of other EU areas, as well as IR studies, have documented change in role perception, learning and alteration of preferences in such sites (Joerges and Vos 1999; Egeberg *et al.* 2003; Risse 2000). And, as noted earlier, the transformative capacity of the CFPS vis-à-vis national foreign policies is highlighted by several authors. The existence of clearly distinguishable national preferences has become less obvious. The so-called 'coordination reflex' between diplomats has become habitual in the foreign-policy field and the accumulation of previous stances provides a common framework for action and decision. The planned abolition of the pillar system, the new post of Foreign Minister and the plans to develop a diplomatic corps all seem to take EU foreign policy beyond intergovernmentalism. The new Foreign Minister, for example, will have a mandate from the Council but will spend most of his/her time in the Commission, only intermittently meeting with the national Foreign Ministers. From an organizational perspective this would imply that his/her prime reference and identity will be linked to the Commission rather than the member states.

With regard to the *legitimacy basis*, we have already noted that there seems to be substantial evidence to support the problem-solving ideal type of the EU's foreign and security policy and little to support the rights-based ideal type. This is so in particular if we define 'all interested parties' as we have done here, as the European citizens rather than the member states. There is little evidence, so far, of a European public space in foreign policy.[10] One exception would be the public response in Europe to the United States' war in Iraq. However, this was not translated into a common policy at the European level.

Does the conception of the EU's foreign and security policy as value-based fare any better with regard to the issue of legitimacy basis? Interestingly, here, when the then US Secretary of State Henry Kissinger, fearful of European discussions of establishing closer cooperation in foreign policy within the EC, launched what he called the Year of Europe, in an attempt to strengthen transatlantic relations, the response of the European Community was to issue, in July 1973, the Copenhagen Declaration on European Identity. Whilst stressing the importance of the United States' nuclear umbrella for Europe, the Declaration states not only the importance of equality between the United States and Europe but also that the transatlantic dimension should not affect the then Nine EC member states' determination to establish themselves as a distinct and original entity.[11] The way in which the issue of participation in the European Security and Defence Policy (ESDP) for non-EU NATO members has been dealt with is perhaps also an illustration of the existence of a sense of a common EU identity. The arguments that the EU presented for excluding these states from full participation in ESDP decision-making rely on a clear idea of insiders and outsiders. The decision on inclusion or exclusion is not described as a matter of costs and benefits to the EU, but as a matter of principle. Full participation in the decision-making processes related to security and defence policy is only granted to those states that are members of the European Union. The fact that non-EU NATO members commit military personnel to the EU's headline goals does not provide rights to participate in decision-making. However, the argument is not couched in terms of culture and identity, but rather in formal legal terms, so again the basis for arguing that this indicates a common ethical, cultural identity basis is not particularly strong. This also goes for the Declaration on European Identity in which the diversity of cultures within the framework of a common European civilization is stressed.[12]

Finally, with regard to the *perspective on international relations*, are the value-based or rights-based conceptions of a European foreign and security policy matched by empirical observations? The discussion here will focus on the rights-based conception, as it has already been suggested that the value-based one would not differ very much from a problem-solving foreign policy. Here it would seem that there is more support for the rights-based conception of EU foreign policy than on the two other indicators. EU foreign policy increasingly emphasizes the importance of respect for human rights for peace and security, thus 'chipping away' at the principle of external sovereignty.[13] This is reflected in much recent academic literature on the EU's foreign policy where the emphasis is not only on the EU having an impact on the international system but on it having a particular type of impact. This suggests that the perspective on the international system is different from the one we would expect in a problem-solving entity, as well as a value-based entity, and that this perspective would be more akin to what one would expect from a rights-based entity. Several authors (Maull 2000; Manners 2002; Rosecrance 1998; Aggestam 2000) suggest that the EU's foreign policy has a normative dimension that is difficult to understand based on a cost–benefit calculation. This is clearly so with regard to enlargement, where the political criteria for membership have been crucial in terms of deciding which states are eligible to join (Sedelmeier 2000; Sjursen 2002). However, there is also evidence of such concerns in the EU's broader foreign policy. As Ian Manners (2002: 248) shows in his study of the EU's campaign for the abolition of the death penalty, the EU 'has played an important, if not crucial, role in bringing about abolition'. Manners here points to the EU's activities not only towards countries that are or seek to become members of the EU, but also to states without this ambition. Furthermore, protection of human rights is included as an important goal in the European Union's development policy. This has, amongst other things, led to a human-rights clause becoming standard content of all trade agreements established with third countries since 1992 (Menéndez 2004a). Even more important perhaps is the EU's particular approach in its pursuit of human rights, which is characterized by a strong emphasis on diplomatic instruments and economic aid. As Karen Smith (2003: 111) argues: 'the EU still clearly prefers positive civilian to coercive military measures'. This is also visible in the EU's security strategy, where the emphasis is on 'preventive engagement'. Diplomatic action and multilateralism are highlighted as cornerstones of the EU's approach to international security (European Council 2003b).

Conclusion

The main aim of this chapter has been to contribute to a discussion about what characterizes the emerging European order through analysing the EU's foreign and security policy. Taking three ideal types of the EU, reflecting different core aspects of political organization, as a starting point, the question asked was to which of these types do the developments in foreign policy speak? In order to answer this question, the main task of the chapter was to work out more concretely what might be the core characteristics of a foreign and security policy based on the problem-solving, value-based and rights-based ideal types of the EU.

Consequently, this chapter contributes to the debate about what characterizes the emerging European order however at the same time it enters into discussion with existing analyses of the EU's foreign and security policy. In this respect it has been suggested that it would be useful, not only to open up additional perspectives on EU foreign policy to the realist/intergovernmentalist ones, but also to specify more clearly what kind of theoretical underpinnings such alternative perspectives might have as well as what might be coherent alternative conceptions of European foreign policy.

Whereas the first, problem-solving, conception of EFP is consistent with what might be referred to as the mainstream perspective of the EU's foreign policy, as dominated by the member states and producing weak responses merely covering the lowest common denominator of national interests, the second and third conceptions can be connected to a more recent literature, arguing not only that there is an element of autonomy to the EU's foreign and security policy but also that a core characteristic of this policy is that it has a certain normative dimension. However, whereas the theoretical tools that allow us to account for the first conception of EU foreign policy are fairly well developed, those that would allow us to account for the idea of the EU's putative normative dimension are perhaps less so. What is particularly lacking is a clearer analytical distinction between a foreign policy that is strongly underpinned by identity-inspired norms and one that is influenced by more cosmopolitan or universally acceptable norms. This might be a particularly important distinction in today's international affairs.

Although much of what we know about the EU's foreign and security policy no doubt fits with the problem-solving conception, there do seem to be gaps. This is particularly so with regard to the perspective of the EU on the international system and the strong emphasis on norms and principles in the EU's foreign-policy initiatives. However, also with regard to the process of decision-making, and the nature of the institutional arrangements, there are developments that need to be better accounted for. This suggests then that, even in foreign and security policy, the EU has moved beyond mere problem-solving, as it has been defined in this chapter. What, then, is it moving towards? Traits of the rights-based ideal type are visible in the EU's perspective on international relations. One of the characteristics of its policy is an effort to strengthen those dimensions of the international system that help to constrain power politics. With regard to the institutional structures, developments are indicative of a move beyond intergovernmentalism and thus weaken the link to the problem-solving ideal type. However, as the findings appear consistent mostly with transnationalism rather than supranationalism, they do not confirm the rights-based ideal type.

Notes

1 Many thanks to Erik Oddvar Eriksen, Agustín Menéndez, Karen Smith, Anne Elizabeth Stie, Marianne Takle, Wolfgang Wagner, Alisdair Young and Cathleen Kantner for comments and advice on previous versions of this chapter. The financial support from the Norwegian Ministry of Defence is gratefully acknowledged.
2 As these are ideal types, it should be clear that in empirical terms they may coexist, or be considered cumulative (i.e. a rights-based entity is for example likely to contain at least a problem-solving capacity, however, a problem-solving entity will not necessarily be rights-based).
3 Following amongst others Hill 1993, Smith 1998 and White 2001, the EU's foreign policy is considered here to encompass not only the activities of the second pillar (CFSP) but also the external activities that emerge through the so-called 'external relations' of the first pillar.
4 Of course, to many this was not a matter of interests at all but of values or principles, but that is not how it would be seen in this perspective.
5 One could also add that, from pure efficiency concerns, one might actually expect more than a pooling of sovereignty on some issues. With regard to the defence industry or intelligence, it would no doubt be more cost-effective to have a European army than to maintain national military forces. Arguments in this direction are occasionally heard in the EU, although they are not the most predominant. However, this would entail abandoning the autonomy of the individual units. Thus, *effectiveness* in this perspective is defined as 'more effective than what it might be to conduct only a national foreign and security policy'. This does, however, suggest that there are certain assumptions about mutually recognized norms, such as the principle of external sovereignty, built into this perspective that it cannot fully explain.
6 On a different note, it might be added that the lack of resources or instruments is perhaps not the only problem for the EU's foreign and security policy. The desire of the US to prevent such policies materializing has increasingly become a challenge as well. Hence the EU's ambitions to take over NATO's operations in Bosnia, for example, appear to have been hampered as much by the United States' reluctance to see the EU in this role as by the EU's inability to fulfil it.
7 See also Habermas' discourse principle, discussed in Eriksen and Weigård (2003: 147) and based on Habermas (1996: 107).
8 This is of course problematic from a normative perspective, but that is not the issue here.
9 Or, to quote a former state secretary in the Norwegian Ministry of Foreign Affairs, 'the national interest is something you invent on your way to the airport'.
10 It is of course possible that this is partly due to the fact that such a question has not been systematically investigated in studies of European foreign policy.
11 Declaration on European Identity by the nine Foreign Ministers (Council of Ministers 1973).
12 Ibid., paragraph 2.
13 See in particular *Human Rights in Third Countries. Summaries of Legislation*: <http://europa.eu.int/scadplus/leg/en/lvb/r10100.htm>, but also European Council 2003b.

8   The purse of the polity

Agustín José Menéndez

> The economic basis for the creation and preservation of democracy is the
> distribution of wealth and income among the majority of the people in
> such a fashion that no elite can permanently dominate the community.
>
> Ratner (1967: 22)

Introduction

The power to tax entails the power to create and consolidate political
communities. Solid civic ties between the members of a political community can only be forged and renewed with the help of the power to tax. It
creates the financial basis of the provision of public goods and services to
all citizens, and enables the redistribution of economic resources. In this
sense, taxes are not only the price of civilization, but the very sinews of
liberty and community. The power to tax is, indeed, the first and strongest
component of the financial powers of any political community.[1] Neo-
liberals ignore that the lack of normative legitimacy is likely to lead to an
actual loss of *social legitimacy*, to social discontent and, eventually, to unrest
and violence (Rawls 1971; Ackerman 1980; Holmes and Sunstein 1999;
Murphy and Nagel 2002). Indeed, both the provision of essential public
services and the guarantee of a certain degree of economic equality
among citizens are essential in order to ensure the stability of a political
community. In modern, post-industrial societies, individuals deprived of a
fair access to essential public services and of public insurance against
unemployment, sickness, old age and bad luck will, sooner or later, come
to the conclusion that the political and legal order is tilted in favour of the
powerful few to the detriment of the many. The tax system plays an essential political role, by means of operationalizing what citizens owe to each
other, and by establishing legal and administrative procedures to ensure
compliance with such obligations (Menéndez 2001). It is thus necessary to
have a close look at the tax powers of the European Union in order to
understand what kind of entity it is.

This chapter is organized in five sections. The aim of the first section is to unpack the very concept of the power to tax by reference to a general theory of democratic taxation. This allows for a separation of the different aspects of the concept, necessary for an analysis of the division of tax powers among institutions and levels of government. The second section lays down the basic conceptual framework upon which the rest of the chapter is built. In general terms, there are three basic ways of characterizing the European Union: as a problem-solving entity, as a community of cultural or pre-political values or as a rights-based community (cf. Chapter 1). On such a basis, I reconstruct the central discourses on the power to tax of the European Union, relating both to the theoretical framework and to the empirically prevalent characterizations of the EU's taxing powers. In the third section, I describe the actual tax powers of the EU. Contrary to what is usually assumed, the Union has substantive powers to tax, although not controlling a substantive tax yield of its own: the Union has constitutional and legislative tax powers which exert a major influence upon the power to tax of the member states and its regions. In the fourth section, I claim that the analysis of the taxing powers of the Union disproves the claim that characterizes the Union as a community of values, and that a dynamic reading of such powers points, although ambiguously, to the characterization of the Union as a rights-based community. The actual content and consequences of the transfers of Union tax powers underpin the hypothesis that the Union is in transition from a problem-solving organization to a political community. The last part holds the conclusion.

Unpacking the power to tax

Any analysis of the power to tax *of* (and *in*) the EU requires a conceptual framework which allows us to separate the different aspects of the power to tax – the components into which it can be divided, and thus shared among different levels of government.

Traditional tax-law dogmatics and classical state theory are not very helpful in this regard. First, they have a propensity to present tax power as an unlimited prerogative of the sovereign.[2] This is reflected in the implicit affirmation that the justification of the power to tax is the very existence of the state, and in the tendency to focus on the study of concrete tax figures, downplaying the systematic aspects of taxation, at which the connection between the power to tax and political and social citizenship becomes clearer. Second, the power to tax tends to be aggregated rather than disaggregated. The very close connection between the state and tax power prevents a clear distinction between the different aspects of taxing powers, and consequently neglects power-sharing arrangements among different institutions and levels of government. Indeed, the division of tax powers between the organs of the state is part and parcel of the standard operationalization of the democratic principle. Budgetary processes are typically characterized by the assignment of wide powers of initiative to the executive while the last word is reserved to the parliamentary assembly. Moreover, a monolithic understanding of the power to tax is clearly inapt when dealing with democratic states which are organized along quasi-federal lines, and thus characterized by a division of powers, including tax powers, not only among institutions, but also among different levels of government.

An alternative theoretical and conceptual framework would have to be provided by a general theory of democratic tax law, integrating insights from legal theory, normative political theory, the public-finance literature on fiscal federalism (Musgrave 1965, 1969) and, last but not least, political-science studies on federal polities, including the EU (Lindberg 1970; Wright 1957). But for our present purposes, it may suffice to consider three of the elements of such a general democratic tax theory.

First, in procedural terms, democratic taxes are characterized by being decided by citizens themselves (in Kantian fashion, citizens are expected to tax themselves). This general and abstract idea triggers the more concrete one of the different aspects of the power to tax. A first distinction must be made between the *normative design* of tax systems and the *effective power* to apply the general norms which define them to *specific cases* – between defining taxes and collecting taxes. The very idea of the tax system as a formula which quantifies our obligations towards others requires a general and abstract definition of each tax figure, later to be applied to concrete cases by citizens themselves, under the monitoring and subsidiary enforcing powers of the tax administration. At any rate, the action of the tax administration should be fully determined by the normative tax framework. This is, as is well known, an idea central to the rule of law. A second distinction concerns the different aspects of the normative tax power. In line with general democratic constitutional theory, one should distinguish between the *constitutional*, the *statutory*, and the *regulatory* normative powers to tax. At the constitutional level, citizens define the general *procedural* and *substantive* principles according to which taxes should be collected. These include the principle of legality of taxation and the principle of *non-retroactivity of taxation*. At the *statutory level*, citizens' representatives define the essential elements defining each tax figure, the tax base, the tax rate and the elements defining when the tax obligation is due. The *regulatory level* comprises all questions of detail, which are decided by executive powers on the basis of the general framework defined by the legislature. The key distinction is perhaps the one between the *statutory* and the *regulatory* powers to tax. Trusting too much to the regulatory work of the executive would imperil the democratic character of tax law, but deciding too much at the statutory level would be to deprive the legislature of the time and energy needed to legislate on other issues (Menéndez 2001: 308).

Second, the characterization of the tax system as a complex formula which operationalizes what citizens owe to each other is indicative of the close connection between taxes and conceptions of distributive justice. The assessment of tax systems requires distinguishing three main possible conceptions of distributive tax justice: the *liberist* or libertarian (which equates taxes with the prices of public goods), the *republican* (which equates taxes with the sacrifice due to fellow citizens) and the *liberal or social-democratic* one, which considers that taxes are better conceptualized as a combination of prices of public goods and public insurance premiums (see further Menéndez 2001: 149ff). According to *liberists*, taxes are a device to split the costs of the provision of public services among citizens, and taxes should be distributed according to the principle of commutative justice, because they quantify the benefits we derive from the functioning of public institutions. This could make us wonder why taxes are necessary at all, and whether the costs of public goods and services could not be met with the help of the market-price system. However, the features which define pure or quasi-pure public goods render it impossible to allocate their costs through market prices. Taxes which aim at redistribution of economic resources among citizens are to be avoided. In contrast, *republicans* regard taxes as the institutionalization of the sacrifices we have to make in favour of our co-citizens. The sharing of pre-political or cultural values creates a basic resemblance between citizens, and renders possible a degree of empathy necessary to ensure solidaristic predispositions. According to *social democrats*, taxes represent both the best possible criterion for the allocation of the prices of public services[3] and a public insurance premium. The legitimacy of the political order is crucially dependent on the legitimacy of the basic ethical choices which underlie the socio-economic order. If the order chosen is one in which economic resources are allocated through a system of private property rights, in which economic exchange takes place according to market rules, legitimacy requires a system of mutual insurance against economic risks, to be funded through a redistributive tax system.

Third, the division of powers among different levels of government in federal political communities should be arranged in such a manner as to ensure the political character of decision-making at each level of government. This entails that, in general, the level of expenditure undertaken at each level of government should be matched by a roughly similar set of taxing powers in its *legislative, regulatory* and *collecting* dimensions. Thus, the principle of *no taxation without representation* should be coupled with the principle of *no representation without taxation*. But how to conceive of the EU as a taxing polity?

Theoretical models

In order to spell out different policy options I rely on the reconstruction of three ideal types of the EU as a polity outlined in Chapter 1. That is, the regulatory or problem-solving entity, the value-based or communitarian, and the rights-based conception of the European Union. But I am also sensitive to actual discourses on the justification and extent of the tax powers of the Union, something which requires distinguishing two different variants of the *communitarian* conception of the EU.

The problem-solving conception

The *problem-solving* conception of the European Union characterizes it as a functional organization and, more specifically, as a *functional international organization*, created to address pragmatic problems which members could not resolve acting independently. Institutionalization, and the consequential appearance of the Union to be a kind of *polity in the making*, would have been prompted by the need to render credible the commitment to common rules. This *description* is shared by intergovernmentalists, neo-functionalists and regulatory accounts of the Union (Moravcsik 1993, 1998; Haas 1958; Schmitter 2003; Majone 1996a). What differentiates them is their analysis of the *causal mechanisms* behind integration and the *normative* basis of the process. Thus, intergovernmentalists and regulatory variants of the problem-solving conception of the EU would claim that member states are the main agents of integration, and that the Union is justified by serving the interests of its member states. The legitimacy of EU institutions and legal norms would be either derivative from the member states or based on *performance* – output legitimacy (Scharpf 1999a; Moravcsik 2003).

This characterization of the Union has clear and direct consequences for which tax powers would be *justifiable* to transfer to the Union, namely only those required by the general problem-solving tasks of the Union, and those required to solve specific tax problems accruing in the relations between member states.

The breadth and scope of the tax powers granted to the Union is related to the powers needed to create a *common market* first, and a *single market* later, between the members of the Union. Ex hypothesi, massive welfare gains are to be derived from the integration of markets of goods (and to different degrees, of labour, services and capital). Economic integration requires first and foremost the abolition of import taxes and of domestic taxes which discriminate against imported goods. This implies a close connection between the functional objective of creating a common market and the transfer of certain tax powers to the federal or supra-national level, basically of (i) negative constitutional tax powers (the prohibition of customs duties, the prohibition of national taxation which discriminates exclusively on the basis of nationality) and (ii) positive legislative tax powers (to determine the tax base and tax rates of external customs duties first, and of sales or turnover taxes later). Further transfer of tax powers is to be expected once integrating states agree on tackling additional common problems through the institutional structure of the organization they have constituted. This would explain the accrual of further, even if limited, legislative powers over corporate income taxation, personal income taxation or excises, closely related to the completion or perfecting of a *single market*. Additionally, the very implementation of the economic freedoms essential to the establishment of the single market creates the conditions under which the effective power to tax of member states and regions might be factually eroded. This creates a new problem which can only be solved by means of establishing framework rules, and which requires the assignment of further powers to the supranational institutions, mainly on what concerns the flow of information between tax authorities and the extent to which national tax authorities must act in defence of the revenue interest of other member states.

In negative terms, the problem-solving conception predicts that the Union will not be assigned any general *collecting* taxing powers. Problem-solving conceptions would thus consider that the European budget is strictly speaking a matter of justice between member states, and not between individuals. The costs of the policies implemented at the Union level will be met by the member states and, while the budget of the Union will be larger than that of a typical international organization, this only reflects the firmer will of member states to render credible their commitment to problem-solving through common institutions. This entails that the taxing powers of the Union would not necessarily be exerted according to a coherent tax distributive justice conception, but merely in order to *solve* the specific problems which member states agree to decide at the European level. This is so either because the very idea of a tax system is considered as a reconstructive device and not as a regulative ideal to be imposed upon the congeries of norms through general tax principles (as liberists will claim), or because such a task should be left in the hands of the nation states, which would have the competence to *systematize* taxes by means of adapting the regulatory ideal to the need of common problem-solving at the European level. As long as the Union remains a tax-problem-solving organization, the conception of tax justice prevailing in the inter-state relationships will be a *liberist* one, grounded on principles of commutative justice.

On what concerns the appropriate procedure of decision-making on the functional powers assigned to the Union, the problem-solving conception clearly favours a procedure which is as *intergovernmental* as possible, with national governments in the Council having the last word on tax matters. In the absence of a political decision-making process at the European level, only unanimous intergovernmental decision-making can ensure an *indirect democratic legitimacy* to these decisions.

The *derivative legitimacy* of the Union implies that the limited tax powers granted to the Union should be circumscribed to taxes which pursue *regulatory*, not *redistributive* purposes. This is so because redistribution is an overtly *political task* which can only be properly undertaken by a community which has direct and transparent political legitimation.[4] This is not the case, either for the time being, or indefinitely, if the Union is merely a problem-solving regulatory regime. The limited tax powers of the Union cannot be authorized by a sufficiently legitimate decision-making process, if only because the Union is not, strictly speaking, a full-blown political community.

The communitarian conception

The *communitarian* conception of the European Union characterizes it as a community based on a set of ethical values, shared by all European citizens on account of pre-political factors and predispositions, typically a common culture (Benda 1993; cf. Weiler 2003). According to communitarians, being a citizen is not a mere act of will, but something which is rendered possible by the pre-political sharing of 'something' (i.e. a 'culture'); turning individuals into next of kin predisposed to make sacrifices for others. A pre-political we-feeling ties citizens to the political community as a whole and consequently to all its members, and renders them ready to assume their duties, because they all belong to the political unity that transcends into unity the singleness of each individual.

Such an ideal type of the Union as a political community leads to two contrasting judgments on the actual political character of the Union, and very clearly, on the tax powers which should be in the hands of the Union.

The first one is the *Euro-nationalist* variant, which leads to the characterization of the EU as a super nation state, to which Europeans should show allegiance; eventually, they should shift their ultimate loyalty to the Union. However, such a characterization of the Union rarely underpins actual discourses on the European power to tax.[5] If this position becomes the one advocated by political and social movements, it will lead them to defend the transfer of a good deal of the constitutional and legislative powers to tax from member states and regions to the European Union. This would be so because the common *nationality* shared by Europeans would have to be translated into the shifting of redistributive policies to the European level.

The second variant is the *Euro-sceptic* one, according to which the European Union cannot become a political community (in a communitarian sense) in the foreseeable future. Europeans do not share the pre-political elements which forge a community, and for such pre-political commonality to emerge will require a long process which cannot be manufactured or controlled. There is no common history or language that Europeans share (the most extreme versions claim that there is no common ethnicity). Under such conditions, Europe cannot be regarded as a political community, as a *common political will* cannot be formed (thus, the so-called *no demos thesis*) and the pre-conditions for Europeans sacrificing for co-Europeans cannot be met. It is a Union of 'deep diversity' (Fossum 2004). Despite the fact that the present institutional and legal reality of the Union actually contradicts the basic claims of Euro sceptics, this conception underlies influential discourses on European tax powers. Communitarian Euro sceptics consistently oppose the granting of any substantive tax powers to the Union, and would claim that, not being a political community at all, its functions should be limited to being an institutionalized forum in which member states could cooperate and exchange information and best practices. This is typically the case with British Euro-sceptic arguments against any common European regulation of taxes, a paradigmatic example of which is the recent pamphlet by Theresa Villiers (2001) and the document CONV 782/03 submitted to the Laeken Convention.

The rights-based conception

The cosmopolitan conception of the European Union characterizes it as a building block in the process of global institution-building. The Union would occupy an intermediate position between the United Nations and nation states as a regional political community, based on the mutual acknowledgement of rights needed to establish decision-making processes in which all those affected have the right to participate. As such, the European Union should be regarded as a *political community* which is part of a cosmopolitan order (cp. Eriksen 2004). Even if originally created as an international organization, its purpose clearly transcends those typically assigned to intergovernmental organizations. It has a full-blown institutional structure and a legal system into which national legal systems have increasingly fused, something which explains the *primacy* of European over national and regional laws. Decisions taken at the European level widely affect the citizens, something which requires that the democratic legitimacy of the Union be based on the democratic credentials of its decision-making procedures and the protection of the fundamental rights of European citizens.

A rights-based European Union would have wide constitutional, legislative and collecting tax powers aimed at creating the financial basis with which the Union could ensure the protection of the values of dignity, freedom, equality and solidarity. These are at the very foundational basis of the Union, as a complex political community, as reflected in its Charter of Fundamental Rights.

The Union would be expected to acquire the constitutional tax powers framing national and regional tax systems with a view not only to solving *functional problems*, but also to ensuring the *autonomy* of each level of government to make meaningful tax choices within its scope of competence.

Concerning legislative tax powers, the Union would be expected to acquire full competencies over the tax figures which would be collected by the Union itself, while being assigned a variety of legislative powers, aimed at harmonizing bases and rates of taxation, coordinating the exercise of national tax powers, or merely gathering data with a view to ensure a sound macro-economic policy,

Concerning collecting powers, the Union would have powers corresponding to the *financial needs* equal to the tasks assigned to it. Moreover, as is typical in federal systems, the Union could act as the collecting agent of nation states and regions. This solution could be especially pertinent in areas such as the *corporation income tax*. At any rate, the Union would have wide powers concerning the information-sharing of national and regional tax administrations.

This implies that the EU should have a budget of its own, mostly funded by taxes directly collected by the Union (i.e. *genuine* own resources, and not national transfers which are called own resources). This should be complemented with a power to borrow in order to finance expenditures with an inter-generational dimension, and to meet cyclical imbalances between revenue and expenditure.

The characterization of the Union as a political community which is part of a cosmopolitan order entails that the taxing powers of the Union should be exerted with a view to ensure the *coherence* of the overall tax system applicable in the Union, that is, the *coherence of the Union, national and regional tax systems*. This requires sheltering, and not hampering, the allocative, redistributive and macro-economic decisions adopted at the national and regional level, especially from the disruptive effects of corporate power.[6]

The main features of the four polity options as outlined above are summarized in Table 8.1 with regard to the different conceptions of European tax power.

The actual tax powers of the European Union

In the following section I will analyse the constitutional, legislative and tax-collecting powers of the Union and the economic importance of such powers. This is basically done by means of considering the relative weight of each tax figure over which the Union has powers, both by reference to the Union's GDP and by reference to the total tax collected in the Union. In the absence of a full quantification of the Union's tax powers,[7] it seems to me that the figures highlight the breadth and scope of *Union actual tax powers*, and thus prove wrong the usual assumptions about its negligible tax powers.

The constitutional power to tax

The European Union has a wide and extensive *constitutional power to tax*, which affects all European, national and regional taxes. However, the power is basically *negative*, as it does not establish any direct mandate to the legislature concerning the shape of the tax system (as is typical in

Table 8.1 Different conceptions of European powers to tax

	Problem-solving	Communitarian Euro-sceptic	Communitarian Euro-nationalist	Rights-based
Background distributive justice conception	Liberist	Liberist at the intergovernmental level	Communitarian	Liberal
Constitutional power to tax (EU)	Negative objectives	None	Negative and positive objectives	Negative and positive objectives
Legislative power to tax (EU)	Setting frameworks if needed (preferably tax bases, not rates)	None	Legislating (leaving power to raise additional rates to nation states)	Co-legislative powers: defining tax bases; fixing rates in some cases
Power to collect (EU)	None; transfers from member states to collect costs	None; transfers from member states to cover administration costs	Most taxes	Taxes which fund the federal level
Systemic relevance	No concern for systemic coherence	No system beyond national tax system	Coherence a task for the federal level	Coherence ensured by joint efforts of all levels of government

national constitutions). Moreover, this power is not *exclusive,* but is *over-lapping* with the constitutional powers to tax of member states.

European constitutional norms are an essential part of the *parameter* of constitutionality of European, national and regional tax norms.[8] European constitutional principles *bind* the legislature on the three levels without exception when drafting tax norms. Indeed, European constitutional principles even extend to the external relations of member states, framing the exercise of the power of member states to enter into agreements with other states (be they member states or third parties) on tax matters (Pistone 2002). There are five groups of prominent principles.

First, the most salient European constitutional norm with tax relevance is the *principle of non-discrimination on the basis of nationality* (Art. 12 TEC). The European Court of Justice (ECJ) has rendered scores of judgments in which national tax norms have been found to be void on account of their formal or material infringement of this principle (see Farmer 2003; Lyal 2003). The Court has declared void not only internal sales taxes which were discriminatory (thus, on the basis of Art. 95 TEC),[9] but also personal income tax provisions[10] and corporate income tax provisions.[11]

Second are the four main economic freedoms inscribed in the treaty, namely, the free movement of goods, persons, services and capital, along with the principle of free competition.[12] Indeed, many of the referred judgments of the Court declare national or regional tax norms void on account of a simultaneous violation of the principle of non-discrimination on the basis of nationality and an infringement of one or several of the economic freedoms. The principle of free competition has been increasingly invoked by the Commission as foundation of the claim that some national tax measures qualify as *unlawful* state aid, and therefore should be considered void (European Commission 1996; Schön 1999; Nannetti and Mameli 2002).[13] The relevance of state aid derives from the extensive practice of having resort to tax expenditures, that is, deductions from the tax liability as a means of fostering certain economic activities or certain products.

Third, the basic principles underlying the Economic and Monetary Union,[14] and especially the *companion* Growth and Stability Pact,[15] result, *de facto*, in the framing of the power to tax. The consolidation of the Economic and Monetary Union, as established in the Maastricht Treaty, requires a progressive convergence of national macro-economic policies. Specific monitoring and sanctioning mechanisms were annexed to the Amsterdam Treaty concerning excessive budgetary deficits. Moreover, rather detailed broad policy guidelines of economic policy are formulated every year, and the Commission is in charge of reviewing the compliance of national budgets and macro-economic policies with these (see Art. 99 TEC; see also TEPSA 2003; Hodson 2004). Even if all these provisions do not ground any concrete European constitutional tax power, it is obvious that they result in a further framing of national tax powers, on account of the *conditions* they impose on macro-economic policy, including tax policy. This was clearly proved by the 2001 opinion of the Council on the stability programme of Ireland and, more recently and pungently, by the early warnings addressed to Portugal, Germany, Italy and France and since then, to several other member states.[16]

Fourth, European tax norms, or national norms which implement European tax legislation (i.e. national VAT legislation), are also bound by the principle of protection of fundamental rights, as spelled out in the solemnly proclaimed Charter of Fundamental Rights. As is the case in many national constitutional systems, fundamental rights establish the *European unconstitutionality* of any tax norms which run foul of them.

Finally, it must be noted that European constitutional norms establish a basic *distribution of legislative and collecting tax competencies*, which bind European, national and regional legislatures. Some of these provisions reflect a basic constitutional choice, as does the prohibition of customs duties affecting trade between member states (Art. 25 TEC). This is akin to a *negative* constitutional tax principle, which extends to quantitative restrictions both to exports and imports, and measures having an equivalent effect (Arts 27 and 28 TEC). The same can be said of the prohibition to regulate or collect customs on imports from third countries addressed to national and regional legislatures (Art. 26 TEC).

The European-relevant constitutional principles regarding tax thus ground the claim that the Union has *constitutional tax powers* that frame European, national and regional legislation. However, it must be added that most of these powers are *negative*, that is, they set limits to the tax norms that can be written into statutes, without mandating positive legislative objectives, as is usually the case in national constitutions. This is so because the constitutional power to tax is shared with the member states (and regions) on a rather equal basis. National constitutions and *national constitutional traditions* establish principles that frame all *European* taxes (be they *legally established* by Union, national or regional laws), and that can limit the scope of application of Community principles. Even if these national constitutional traditions are *common*, and as such, cannot be said to imply some kind of primacy of national over Community law, they prevent anyone raising the claim that the power to frame tax norms belongs within the European Union to the *institutions* of the Union exclusively. Change in the shape and direction of *national constitutional traditions* can actually alter the contents of the framing principles of tax norms in the EU. Further, constitutional principles might come into conflict with each other. Such conflicts require an appropriate *weighing and balancing* of the principles, in order to determine the concrete rule applicable to the concrete case (cp. Alexy 2002). In case of a conflict between a European constitutional principle established at the Community level (e.g. the free movement of capital) and a principle stemming from a national constitutional tradition, the former does not necessarily have preference.

This complex structure is occasionally reflected in the construction of the European legal system by the ECJ. Consider the judgment in *Bachmann*,[17] in which the Court argued that a principle of 'coherence of national tax systems', unwritten and unknown until then, required that the contested Belgian national tax norm be considered as *constitutional*, even if it contradicted *prima facie* the principle of non-discrimination on the basis of nationality and at the very least two fundamental economic freedoms.

The results are mixed. On the one hand, certain principles formulated at the Community level frame the national power to decide the shape of concrete taxes. On the other hand, legislative and collecting tax powers granted to Community institutions must be interpreted in the light of the *common constitutional traditions*. Such common traditions play a major role in deciding potential conflicts between the whole set of principles that frame the European power to tax, be they established through the European or the national constitution-making process.

The legislative power to tax

The European Union also has extensive legislative powers to tax. It has exclusive competence concerning customs duties and agricultural levies. It has a framing legislative power concerning the definition of the tax base of Value Added Tax, and considerable powers concerning the determination of VAT rates. It has framing legislative powers concerning the definition of the tax base of excise duties on alcohol, tobacco and mineral oils, taxes collected at rates framed by Union legislation. Furthermore, the Union has limited and fragmentary, but still relevant powers concerning the definition of the corporate income tax and the personal income tax.

The Union has full legislative power over *customs duties*, including agricultural, isoglucose and sugar levies. Union powers extend to both the definition of the tax base and the setting of tax rates.[18]

The Union also has extensive legislative powers on turnover taxes, which have resulted in a long series of directives on VAT.[19] Such powers are pretty exhaustive concerning the definition of the tax base. Not only do all member states collect VAT, but VAT liability is essentially triggered by the very same economic transactions. Union legislative powers are more of a framing character on what concerns the definition of tax rates. This is so on three accounts. First, member states retain the power to fix the *standard rate* at which VAT is collected within the limits fixed by the Union when setting maximum and minimum VAT rates. Second, member states retain the power to keep up to two reduced rates (see Table 8.2 for the standard and reduced rates in force in the member states).[20] Third, they can exempt a series of goods and services from a list drawn in European legislation.[21] Thus, national autonomy is prevalent, even if it can be exercised only within the limits set by Union law (but such limits are, for the time being, rather wide).

Table 8.2 VAT rates on 1 May 2003: standard, super-reduced and reduced

Member state	Super-reduced	Reduced	Standard
Austria	–	10.0	20.0
Belgium	–	6.0	21.0
Denmark	–	–	25.0
Finland	–	8.0/17.0	22.0
France	2.1	5.5	19.6
Germany	–	7.0	16.0
Greece	4.0	8.0	18.0
Ireland	4.3	13.5	21.0
Italy	4.0	10.0	20.0
Luxembourg	3.0	6.0	15.0
Netherlands	–	6.0	19.0
Portugal	–	5.0/12.0	19.0
Spain	4.0	7.0	16.0
Sweden	–	6.0/12.0	25.0
United Kingdom	–	5.0	17.5

Source: *Structures of the Taxation Systems in the EU Countries, 1995–2002*, Luxembourg: Office for the Publications of the European Communities, 2004.

The *legislative* powers of the Union over turnover taxes are of major economic importance, given that VAT is one of the three major sources of tax revenue in all national tax systems, representing on average 17.2 per cent of the total tax collected in the EU in 2002. Ireland is the country in which VAT represents a higher percentage of the tax yield (24.8 per cent) while Luxembourg is where VAT is of lesser relative importance (14.9 per cent). Table 8.3 proves that VAT has been one of the major tax figures in the last twenty years. It has consistently represented between one-fourth and one-fifth of the total tax yield. It can also be noticed that, with the single exception of France (due to the reduction of the standard VAT rate implemented by the 'gauche plurielle' coalition led by Lionel Jospin), VAT seems to be on the increase in terms relative to the total tax yield.

The European Union has extensive legislative powers concerning the definition of the tax base of the main *excise taxes* in all member states, namely *excises on alcoholic beverages, tobacco and mineral oils.*[22] Table 8.4 shows these excises as a percentage of the total tax revenue of the member states. The Union also has framing power concerning the determination of such tax rates. It has not only established the minimum rates,[23] but it has also specified its structure. Union norms are rather exhaustive in this regard.[24] All this implies that the Union has legislative tax powers which extend to taxes yielding between 4 and 10 per cent of the total tax revenue, while the legislative power of the member states is confined to setting the rate of excise.[25]

The Union has fragmentary legislative powers limiting the tax liability which member states can establish on account of *corporate income taxes*. Such

Table 8.3 Percentage of total tax revenue stemming from VAT: 1980, 1998 and 2002

Member state	1980	Average 1995–2002	2002
Austria	20.1	18.6	18.7
Belgium	16.8	15.3	15.4
Denmark	22.3	19.5	19.9
Finland	18.7	17.8	18.2
France	21.1	16.8	16.3
Germany	16.6	16.2	16.2
Greece	13.2	21.3	21.9
Ireland	14.8	22.6	24.8
Italy	15.6	14.2	15.2
Luxembourg	16.4	14.4	14.9
Netherlands	15.8	17.4	19.1
Portugal	16.2	22.7	22.7
Spain	10.2	16.8	16.9
Sweden	13.4	17.2	18.1
United Kingdom	14.7	18.8	19.3

Source: 1980 data: OECD Revenue Statistics; 2002 data and average 1995–2002 data: *Structures of the Taxation Systems in the EU Countries, 1995–2002*, Luxembourg: Office for the Publications of the European Communities, 2004.

powers have been exercised through three directives.[26] However, it must be acknowledged that such directives are specific concretizations of the Union constitutional tax principle of non-discrimination on the basis of nationality, specifically on what concerns cross-border economic activities undertaken by companies, and of the freedom of establishment and the free movement of capital. As such, they reflect the constitutional tax powers more than the legislative tax powers of the Union. In addition, a Code of Conduct on business taxation was approved in 1997,[27] and a report on its basis published in 2000.[28] This Code had a limited but not irrelevant impact on the definition of national corporate income tax bases. However, the Code was not presented as a *binding piece of legislation*, but as a piece of soft law, from which no further tax powers accrued to the Union.

Another area where the Union has fragmentary legislative powers concerns the definition of *personal income taxation*, more specifically on what concerns *income stemming from savings in the form of interest payments*.[29] This power (see Art. 6 of the Directive) comes hand in hand with a power to fix the rate at which a withholding tax should be collected on savings income obtained in a member state by a national of another member state. The EU rate (35 per cent at the end of the transitional period) is applicable only if the member state where the interest payments take place does not *automatically report* to the member state of residence of the person receiving the payment that such income has accrued to her (Arts 8 and 9).

This implies the affirmation of a positive legislative power concerning the definition of the *personal income tax base*, and the accrual of a

Table 8.4 Percentage of total tax revenue stemming from excises on alcohol, mineral oils and tobacco, 1998

Member state	Tobacco	Alcohol	Mineral oils	Total
Austria	1.30	0.79	3.07	5.16
Belgium	1.12	0.55	3.28	4.95
Denmark	1.28	0.74	1.54	3.56
Finland	1.06	2.26	4.82	8.14
France	1.18	0.48	4.07	5.73
Germany	1.54	0.48	4.76	6.78
Greece	4.27	0.80	8.94	14.01
Ireland	3.20	3.15	5.34	11.69
Italy	1.09	0.15	5.08	6.32
Luxembourg	4.17	0.39	6.39	10.95
Netherlands	0.96	0.38	3.47	4.81
Portugal	2.87	0.54	7.51	10.92
Spain	n.d.	n.d.	n.d.	n.d.
Sweden	0.76	1.01	2.45	4.22
United Kingdom	2.40	1.87	6.65	10.92

conditional full legislative power in case one member state does not opt for the automatic exchange of information with another member state. The *economic* importance of this power cannot be properly established by reference to the present relative weight of capital income taxation, if only because the levels of tax avoidance are rampant (in part as a result of the affirmation of free movement of capital as an autonomous economic freedom since 1988). However, some estimate that the measure, if fully functional, will report between 2 and 3 per cent of the present total tax revenue yield (Drèze and Malinvaud 1994).

With the only exception being customs duties, agricultural, sugar and isoglucose duties, all these legislative powers are subject to the law-making procedure established in Art. 94 TEC, in conjunction with Art. 95.1 TEC. This subjects the approval of the proposals made by the Commission to unanimous agreement in the Council. Such a procedure clearly favours the maintenance of the status quo, and casts a shadow upon the strength of Union legislative tax powers. However, this is not exactly the same as pre-serving *national tax sovereignty*. Once legislative powers have been exercised, member states are bound by Union legislation until it is amended. Given that all member states retain a veto power and unanimous agreement is hard to obtain, legislation tends to remain unchanged for long periods of time. This might have entailed a *de facto* transfer of power from public institutions to markets, which can indulge in tax-shopping practices. But I would like to insist that it would be wrong to derive from this state of affairs that *nation states* have retained most of their national tax sovereignty. Finally, it must be added that in the case of customs and agricultural duties, a qualified majority in the Council is sufficient (Art. 36 TEC).

The tax-collecting power

The third dimension of the power to tax corresponds to the power to actually collect taxes. The powers of the Union are limited, but still far from negligible. The Union has tax-collecting powers over customs and agricultural duties, in addition to having established a framework within which national tax administrations must act in defence of the revenue interest of the Union and of other national tax administrations.

The tax bases of the Union

Leaving aside the power to collect personal income taxes over the wages paid to its own employees, characteristically granted to all international organizations, the Union is entitled to collect all customs duties on goods and services imported in the Union from third countries (with basis on Art. 26 TEC), as well as agricultural, sugar and isoglucose levies. It also has a legal title to a percentage of the VAT collected in all member states.[30] These powers are usually neglected or unknown because the taxes are *effectively collected* by public servants which taxpayers perceive as *exclusively national public servants*.

In the case of VAT, the fact that a part of the yield goes to the Union is obscured by the fact that this is not advertised to citizens in any European country, and even more by the fact that the concrete amount is not directly determined in each and every transaction, but by reference to a complex, aggregate formula. This is due to the very simple fact that the definition of the tax base and of the products and services subject to VAT is not fully harmonized (in that member states retain some marginal discretionary powers). VAT is thus in practice *transferred* from the budget of each member state to Union coffers, in exactly the same manner as the national contributions proportional to the national income are handed over. Indeed, this is usually marked as a *national transfer* in *national budgets*. This can only breed confusion over the *Europeanness* of the EU VAT rate. To make things even worse, the decision over the specific EU VAT rate is subject to a decision-making procedure equivalent to a treaty amendment (the own resources decision) (see Art. 269 TEC). Nothing could render the existence of an actual power to collect VAT more obscure to European citizens. Similar observations can be made regarding customs and agricultural levies, collected by national agents *acting on behalf of the Union*, but whose institutional identity in the eyes of the public remains national.

Moreover, the Union is constitutionally precluded from issuing debt, and must have a balanced budget (Art. TEC 268).

These arrangements give the Union a modest power to collect taxes. The aggregate yield represents less than 1 per cent of the European GDP (0.5 per cent of the GDP of the EU–15 in 2002, an average 0.7 per cent in the period 1995–2002), which amounts to less than 2 per cent of the total

Table 8.5 Customs duties as percentage of total tax revenue

Country	1965	1998
Belgium	4.24	1.17
France	1.82	0.23
Germany	2.23	0.46
Italy	2.57	0.26
Luxembourg	0.45	0.35
Netherlands	6.40	1.30

Source: OECD 1999 Revenue Statistics.

amount of taxes paid in the Union (a meagre 1.23 per cent in 2002, and an average 1.72 per cent in the period 1995–2002).[31]

However, to come to the conclusion that such powers are basically negligible, as many do, is a trifle precipitate.[32] Regarding the power to collect customs duties, the *importance* of the decision taken *in principle* in the Rome Treaty of 1957, and actually implemented in 1970, can only be fully appreciated if one considers the *actual* relative weight of customs duties in the 1950s and 1970s, and not their present weight. Otherwise, one incurs an anachronistic reading of the decisions. As late as 1965, customs duties yielded to member states well over 2 per cent of their tax revenues; with the Netherlands (over 6 per cent) and Luxembourg (under 0.5 per cent) being the two deviant cases (see Table 8.5). It was not fully unpredictable that the yield of customs duties would decline as international trade in goods and services became increasingly deregulated, but this supposed a joining-together of a small but far from insignificant amount of the tax revenues of member states.

Powers instrumental to tax collection

A 1976 directive marked a clear break with two ideas central to national tax administrations, namely, that they had to monitor compliance with national tax laws and defend the national revenue interest – *national* in both cases being exhaustive of the laws to be applied and of the revenue interest to be protected. Indeed, the directive required national tax administrations to treat requests from other member states almost as if they stemmed from their own national tax administration, thus *recognizing and enforcing the tax claims made by the tax administrations of other member states.* At first, the scope of application of the norm was limited to the taxes over which the Community had been assigned tax-collecting powers: customs duties and agricultural duties.[33] However, the field of direct taxation was covered by a directive approved the following year, which imposed a duty to share information among national tax administrations.[34] As time has passed, the scope of both directives has tended to increase, thus reinforcing the process of Europeanization of national tax administrations.[35]

The net upshot of this analysis is that the taxing powers of the EU include: wide constitutional tax powers affecting all tax norms, but which are mainly negative and non-exclusive, as national constitutional tax principles continue to play a major role; extensive legislative powers affecting the definition of the tax base of almost half the total amount of taxes collected in the Union, although such powers are weaker regarding personal and corporate income taxation, and the economic importance of which is somehow relativized by the requirement of Council unanimity for their exercise; and, finally, rather limited tax-collecting powers, although coupled with a thick normative framework which reconfigures the very institutional identity of national tax administrations.

Which model fits better?

I started this chapter by sketching three different conceptions of the European Union, and postulating the corresponding characteristics of the Union's tax powers. I then proceeded with an analysis of the actual constitutional, legislative and collecting tax powers of the Union. I am thus now in a position to discuss which of the three conceptions corresponds more closely to the actual powers of the Union.

The communitarian model

A first conclusion is rather easy to reach. The communitarian conception of the Union, either in its Euro-sceptic or Euro-national model, is clearly not one which corresponds to the present taxing powers of the Union. The Euro-sceptic variant fails to explain the extensive constitutional, legislative and collecting taxing powers of the Union. Further, the present taxing powers of the Union fall short of what is implied by the Euro-national communitarian conception. One would expect more *positive* constitutional powers, more extensive *legislative* powers and clearly far-reaching tax-collecting powers. It must be concluded that, while the Euro-sceptic conception has been factually transcended, the Euro-nationalist conception seems a rather far-away normative vision, not least because respect for the identity of member states as political communities is part and parcel of positive constitutional Union law.

This leaves us with two paradigms competing as the most plausible framework within which to reconstruct the present taxing powers of the Union, the *problem-solving* and the *rights-based* conceptions. While a *static* reconstruction seems to indicate that the former conception fits better the present shape of the taxing powers of the Union, a *dynamic* reconstruction of the taxing powers of the Union increases the salience of the rights-based conception. This leads me to the conclusion that the taxing powers of the Union are in transition from a *problem-solving* paradigm to a *rights-based* one.

The problem-solving model

The EU's most outstanding powers are no other than negative constitutional tax powers and limited legislative powers specifically aimed at establishing the tax conditions under which the common, and later, single market could function. The completion of the common market, and also the resolution of the problems deriving from the success of market-making, explain why powers have been transferred to the Union. Tax-collecting powers in the hands of the Union are limited, and they are closely related to the financing of a limited range of policies which are in themselves indicative of the commitment to a common institutional framework.

Advocates of regulatory governance can argue in support of their claims that official discourses on the taxing powers of the Union clearly reflect the conception of the Union as a tax problem-solver. Even a superficial reading of the Commission's policy papers and proposals of the last decade points in this direction. Indeed, the Commission's discourse has focused on justifying its proposals by reference to possible welfare gains. In this regard, the emphasis on so-called tax coordination comes hand in hand with the abandonment of legislative proposals of a more systematic character. The very idea of a 'tax package', comprising the late 1990s' tax initiatives, does not point to the construction of a *European tax system*, even in a piecemeal fashion, but merely to a package deal. Finally, one could argue that not much has been done to reduce the levels of tax fraud rendered possible by the very process of European integration. Indeed, even the call to curb *harmful* tax competition has not yet translated into the adoption of concrete measures, something which might be said to indicate that the very idea of national tax sovereignty trumps the characterization of the Union as a true political community. Member states can see themselves as players in a competitive game where *self-interest* and *self-gains* prevail over a *communal* sense of fairness. One must, however, adjust for the very *dynamics* through which the present configuration of the taxing powers of the Union has come about.

The rights-based model

First, one must take into account that the assignment of additional legislative taxing capacities to the Union has not always been justified with reference to narrow and specific problems; and that the exercise of the existing, transferred powers is usually motivated by more comprehensive goals. It is clear that the transfer of legislative competencies over the definition of the savings-income tax base, or plans to assign legislative competencies over the definition of the corporate tax, have been justified and discussed, not only by reference to the consequences the lack of harmon-ization has over competition in the single market, but mainly by reference to the erosion of the tax powers of member states and the consequences of this in terms of vertical and horizontal tax equality, and especially on the financial basis of welfare states. The evolution of Union powers on VAT offers good examples of this. The approval of the Sixth VAT Direc-tive in the early 1970s resulted in the harmonization of the definition of the tax base of turnover taxation. This was actually required not so much by the need to perfect the common market (as this was essentially achieved with the First and Second VAT Directives of the late 1960s), but by the decision to assign to the Union a rate of the VAT collected in the whole Union, as part of its own resources. Moreover, the Union has recently started to make use of VAT as a macro-economic lever. More specifically, reduced VAT rates were allowed on two types of services which were labour-intensive; the overall goal was to make use of the legislative tax power of the Union in order to reduce unemployment.[36]

Second, it might be the case that public discourses on European tax powers and norms are constructed upon a problem-solving conception of the Union. However, this might be somewhat misleading. It is clear that, as the treaties stand, the accrual of new tax powers to the Union must be justified by reference to the very idea of single-market-making. However, the definition of the problems and challenges which the Union confronts requires solutions which clearly transcend its problem-solving conception. In brief, we might be close to the point in which spillovers become *political.* A good illustration of this point is provided by present discourses on European corporate taxation. True, the repeated failures of attempts at harmonizing even limited parts of the corporate income tax,[37] and the limited scope of legislative tax powers actually held by the Union could be explained by the rationales behind the problem-solving conception. More-over, a first reading of the most recent communications and studies of the Commission on the matter seems to justify the accrual of further compe-tencies to the Union by reference to specific problems of an economic or technical character.[38] In the official (and dominant) discourse, the corporate income tax is a question that the Union has to address because the present state of affairs leads to a distortion of the levelled playing field which the single market should provide to economic actors. As things stand, efficiency losses are incurred, and the international competitiveness of European companies is hampered. A technical, welfare-based argument is clearly made when reference is made to cross-national companies incur-ring losses due to compliance with as many accounting systems as the member states they operate in, when corporations are sometimes double-taxed, or when cross-border restructuring is penalized by taxes not due on purely internal operations. Still, what is hard to explain from the problem-solving perspective is that the discourse has increasingly focused on the need of transcending targeted solutions (as the parent-subsidiary or merger directives). A structural reform of corporate income taxation, nothing less, is required in order to solve present problems. This implies a quantitative leap in the discourse. True, the discourse continues to affirm that the very reason why this reform should be undertaken is the idea of completing the single market. But the concrete measures have open political implications, as is simultaneously acknowledged. More specifically, the Commission argues that there is a need for a European definition of the corporate income tax base applicable at the very least to the corporations making use of the European Company Statute, and eventually to all big companies.[39] Further, a mutual recognition of national tax-base definitions should be the solution applicable to small and medium-sized corporations, or at the very least, experimented with for some years.[40]

This explains why the harmonization of corporate tax bases is back on the Council agenda.[41] The mutual recognition of national tax systems or some form or another of European corporate tax might be justified with a view to *render perfect* the common market, but such developments are much more than ordinary spillovers. Indeed, as neo-functionalists could agree, they are spillovers which reveal the open political character of the whole process of market-making since its very beginning. Similarly, problem-solving conceptions also have a hard time explaining new elements in the corporate-tax discourse. For example, there is a growing number of references to the mismatch between the existence of a 'single market' and 25 corporate tax systems; if profits are made on a European-wide scale, why should they be taxed on a national scale? Such questions clearly raise the issue of which is the relevant community of economic risk in a single market. Furthermore, these new lines of argument are openly supported by several national governments, which simultaneously invoke *market-making* arguments (the need to complete the common market), and *political reasons*, which reveal the connections between corporate taxation and distributive justice (tax dumping leads to social dumping).[42] Hence the emergence of social movements and political platforms which request a degree of corporate tax harmonization *mainly* of political reasons.[43] It does not take much ingenuity to realize that the Eastern enlargement will probably exacerbate tensions, and further render explicit the political character of the discourse on the matter. The fact that some of the new member states (significantly, Cyprus, Latvia and Lithuania) have an effective corporate tax rate which represents one-third to half of the effective tax rate of present member states ensures that the issue will not simply go away.[44]

Third, the fragmented and asystematic character of the legislative and collecting tax powers of the Union reflects the disjointed character of public expenditure of the Union. However, it is no less true that apparently disparate programmes can be reconstructed from the standpoint of basic legal principles in order to justify a further expansion of taxing and expenditure in the hands of the Union. In that regard, the introduction of the principle of social and economic cohesion in the Single European Act (Arts TEC 158 to 162) has served to provide a common focus to the expenditure programmes approved since then, and might play an essential role in further moving the European tax powers in the direction of a rights-based political order.

Fourth and finally, European tax powers are exercised within the constitutional and legal framework provided by the European Union legal order. This is founded on the basic principle of loyalty among member states, which points towards a sense of solidarity and commonality which goes far beyond the idea of a mutual advantage contract. It implies a commitment to institutionalization which goes beyond the mere projection of credibility. This contributes to a formal or thin *we-feeling*, upon which European tax norms can build. Indeed, the *Europeanization* of national tax administrations, the obligation to defend the revenue interest of the Union and of the other national tax administrations create *some of the conditions* under which a we-feeling can be forged in a civic, solidaristic fashion.

Conclusions

On the background of a theoretical framework for analysing the division of taxing powers between the EU and its member states, I examined the actual constitutional, legislative and collecting tax powers of the Union. What do such powers tell us about the nature of the Union as a political community? I analysed which of the three basic polity models of the EU (as a problem-solving, communitarian or rights-based polity) fits better the set of tax competencies in the hands of the Union. While it is concluded that the EU's tax powers are far wider than commonly asserted – partly due to the influence exerted on national and regional taxing powers by the Union's constitutional and legislative tax powers – it is found that the Union still presents most of the features characteristic of a regulatory entity.

Having said that, a dynamic reconstruction of these same powers indicates that the Union is moving towards a rights-based polity, with regard to its taxing powers as well. There are clear indications that the *problem-solving* paradigm is not enough (and will continue to fall short in this regard) to explain and ground the tax powers of the Union. This is because:

- the assignment of tax powers to the Union, and their actual exercise, is increasingly justified by reference to conceptions of tax and economic justice;
- even in those cases in which the assignment of new taxing powers is justified by reference to functional purposes, the solutions proposed

imply a transcendence of a pure problem-solving paradigm, as they entail a *political spillover*;

- the affirmation of the principle of social and economic cohesion as part and parcel of European constitutional law might trigger a recharacterization of the purpose of EU taxing powers;
- the regulation of EU taxing powers by an increasingly constitutionalized Union legal order points to a sense of solidarity and commitment which transcends the mutual-gain basis of a problem-solving conception.

Our political representatives and most fellow citizens might still think of the EU as a tax problem-solving entity; it might even be true that they feel at ease discussing tax questions within the confines of such a paradigm. But it is increasingly difficult to pretend that the issues raised can be dealt with in mainly non-political terms, in brief, in terms different from those in which tax questions are posed within member states. Basic principles of Union constitutional law, not to mention the factual dynamics of economic integration, rule out many tax decisions which were perfectly conceivable only two or three decades ago. The introduction of reduced VAT rates to foster the creation of employment, the definition of savings-income tax bases or the fixation of corporate income tax bases are the kind of questions around which elections are fought and decided; they have been set or are in the process of being set at the European level, through a European decision-making process. Moreover, the taxing powers of the Union are but a part, even if an essential one, of the set of public powers in the hands of the Union. The constitutional turn of the Union as a whole seems to point towards its transformation into a political community, which cannot be stable and sustainable without a we-feeling created and regenerated through the exercise of taxing powers.

Taxation without representation is tyrannical, but representation without taxation cannot but end up putting into jeopardy the fabric of the Social Rechtsstaat which the Union claims to be.

Notes

1 A distinction is made between the power to tax and the power to spend. For an analysis of the budgetary powers of the EU, see Menéndez 2004c.
2 Although there are many exceptions. See Menéndez (2001: 191ff) for the three main strategies of justification followed by tax-law dogmatics: procedural, substantive and through guaranteed implementation of the tax system.
3 The main difference with liberists being the very definition of what is to count as a public good.
4 Thus, Majone (1993: 160) claims to distinguish clearly between social regulation and social policy, the latter being focused on redistribution, and being properly beyond the reach of the Union for both normative and prudential reasons: 'It is fortunate that the normative case for a European welfare state is

not compelling, for the practical prospects are extremely poor.'

5 Except possibly for discussions on the need to further harmonize 'sin taxes' (on alcohol and cigarettes), which are very closely related to the ethical conceptions of a community.

6 Paradigmatic examples of rights-based discourses on the European tax powers can be found in the federalist and social-democratic literature (Collignon 2004; Strauss-Kahn 2004; see also Menéndez 2004c).

7 This would require measuring the power weight of constitutional, legislative and collecting tax powers, so that all figures could be reduced to one single scale, and added.

8 There are also tax implications for EEA members. On this, see e.g. van den Hurk and Theunissen 2001.

9 See e.g. Case 433/85, *Feldain v. Directeur des Services Fiscaux*, [1987] ECR 3536, which was a more sophisticated version of Case 112/84, *Humblot v. Directeur des Services Fiscaux*, [1985] ECR 1367.

10 See Farmer 2003; Lyal 2003. Among the cases, see C-175/88, *Biehl*, [1990] ECR I-1779; although the Court finds that national tax measures were contrary to the free movement of workers, in par. 14 it considers as very relevant the fact that the regimes entail a discrimination on the basis of nationality; C-279/92, *Finanzamt Köln-Altstadt v. Roland Schumacker*, [1995] ECR I-225; C-80/94, *Wielockx v. Inspecteur der Directe Belastingen*, [1995] ECR I-2493, the leading cases on the taxation of non-residents' income; and C-136/00, *Rolf Dieter Danner*, [2002] ECR I-8147 on deductibility of pension-plan contributions.

11 See Farmer 2003; Lyal 2003; Jiménez 1999; and, among others, the following cases: Case C-264/96, *Imperial Chemical Industries (ICI)*, [1998] ECR I-4695; Case C-118/96, *Safir*, [1998] ECR I-1897; Case C-307/97, *Saint-Gobain*, [1999] ECR I-6161.

12 See e.g. Case 270/83, *Commission v. France*, [1986] ECR 273; Case C-330/91, *Commerzbank*, [1993] ECR I-4017; Case C-484/93, *Svensson & Gustavsson*, [1995] ECR I-3955; Case C-250/95, *Futura Participations*, [1997] ECR I-2471; Case C-311/97, *Royal Bank of Scotland v. Elliniko Dimosio*, judgment of 29 April 1999.

13 See also the 'Commission notice on the application of the State aid rules to measures relating to direct business taxation' of 28 November 1998, OJ C 384 (1998): 3.

14 See Arts C 99 and 104 TEC, the protocol on the excessive deficit procedure, annexed to the Treaty of Maastricht.

15 See 'Resolution of the European Council on the Stability and Growth Pact Amsterdam', OJ C 236 (1997): 1–2; Council Regulation (EC) 1466/97, OJ L 209 (1997): 1–5; Council Regulation (EC) 1467/97, OJ L 209 (1997): 6–11.

16 On Ireland, see Council Opinion of 12 February 2001, OJ C 77 (2001) and ECOFIN Council Conclusions of 29 October 2001, SN 4404/01; on Portugal and Germany, see Council Opinion of 12 February 2002, 6108/02 (Presse 28); on Italy, see Council Press Release of 5 July 2004, 10888/04 (Presse 213); on France, see Council Recommendation of 21 January 2003, OJ L 34 (2003): 18–19.

17 Case C-204/90, *Hanns Martin Bachmann v. Belgian State*, [1992] ECR I-249: pars 21–3; Case C-300/900, *Commission v. Belgium*, [1992] ECR I-305: pars 14–16, 20–2.

18 See Council Regulation (EEC) 2913/92, OJ L 302 (1992): 1–50, containing the Community Customs Code.

19 The Sixth VAT Directive (Directive 77/388/EEC) of 17 May 1977, OJ L 145 (1977), is the central piece in the European VAT system, as it contains the basic definition of the tax base.

20 See Article 12.3A of the Sixth Directive. As established by Council Directive 92/77/EEC, OJ L 316 (1992): 1–4, the standard rate has to be at least 15 per cent, while reduced rates should be at least 5 per cent.

21 See Article 13B of the Sixth Directive.

22 See Council Directives 92/83/EEC of 19 October 1992; 95/59/EC of 27 November 1995; and 92/81/EEC of 19 October 1992.

23 See Council Directives 92/79/EEC, 92/82/EEC and 92/84/EEC of 19 October 1992; and 1999/81/EC of 29 July 1999, OJ L 211 (1999): 47.

24 Consider, for example, excise duties levied on cigarettes, which account for at least 57 per cent of the retail selling price (including all taxes, cigarettes belonging to the most popular price category).

25 See also Council Directive 92/12/EEC, OJ L 76 (1992): 1, as last amended by Directive 2000/44/EC, OJ L 161 (2000): 82.

26 The merger directive (Council Directive 90/434/EEC, OJ L 225 [1990]: 1–5) articulates a basic negative legislative decision. The parent–subsidiary directive (Council Directive 90/435/EEC, OJ L 225 [1990]: 6–9) determines the tax treatment that national tax legislations should give to benefits transferred from a subsidiary to a parent company established in another member state. The directive on a common system of taxation applicable to interest and royalty payments made between associated companies of different member states (Council Directive 2003/49/EC, OJ L 157 [2003]: 49–54) aims to avoid double taxation of interest and royalty payments in cross-border payments between associated companies, which implies a legislative measure aimed at allocating the power to tax certain corporate income tax bases among member states.

27 Annex to the Conclusions of the ECOFIN Council Meeting on 1 December 1997, concerning taxation policy, OJ C 2 (1998): 2–5.

28 See the report of the ensuing group (the Primarolo Group) to the ECOFIN Council, Press Release 4901/99 of 29 February 2000; see also Radaelli 2003.

29 Council Directive 2003/48/EC, OJ L 157 (2003): 38–48, for its application, see OJ L 257 (2004): 7. See further Larking 2001; Dassesse 2004; and the well-argued criticism in Pires 2002. Holzinger 2003 contains a political-science analysis.

30 See Council Decision 2000/597EC, EURATOM on the system of the European Communities' own resources, OJ L 253 (2000): 42–6.

31 The data is taken from *Structures of the Taxation Systems in the EU Countries*.

32 For example Moravcsik (2003: 608): 'At a first approximation, the EU does not tax, spend, implement or coerce and, in many areas, it does not hold a legal monopoly of public authority [...] The ability to tax and spend is what most strikingly distinguishes the modern European state from its predecessors, yet the EU's ability to tax is capped at about 2–3 per cent of national and local government spending (1.3 per cent of GDP) and is unlikely to change soon.'

33 Council Directive 76/308/EEC, OJ L 73 (1976): 18–23.

34 Council Directive 77/799/EEC, OJ L 336 (1977): 15–20.

35 Council Directive 2001/44/EC, OJ L 175 (2001): 17–20; the Commission Directive 2002/94/EC, OJ L 337 (2002): 41–54, lays down detailed rules for implementing certain provisions of Council Directive 76/308/EEC on mutual assistance for the recovery of claims relating to certain levies, duties, taxes and other measures.

36 Council Directive 1999/85/EC, OJ L 277 (1999): 34–6; prolonged by Council Directive 2002/92/EC, OJ L 331 (2002): 27. Detailed information on its application can be found in the Commission press release (IP/99/1002) of 20 December 1999.

37 Proposals of corporate tax harmonization were already formulated in the early

1960s; see Regul and Renner 1966: 116–17. A comprehensive proposal was made in 1975 (European Commission 1975). While some support seemed to exist for the harmonization of tax rates (with the Commission proposing rates between 45 and 55 per cent), the same could not be said about the harmonization of tax bases, which was regarded as the exclusive competence of the member states. The failure of the proposal entailed that, until very recently, proposals were very limited in breadth and scope.

38 See European Commission 2001b; the companion and more thorough working paper of the Commission staff (SEC/2001/1681); and the recent follow-up by the European Commission 2003.

39 For a study on tax implications, see the 'Survey on the Taxation of the Societas Europaea' of 2003, by the Internation Bureau of Fiscal Documentation.

40 See the Commission's 'Outline of a possible experimental application of Home State Taxation to small and medium-sized enterprises', DG XXI, TAXAUD C.1/doc (04) 1410, 24 June 2004.

41 See 'Commission Non-paper to Informal Ecofin Council of 10 and 11 September 2004: A Common Consolidated EU Corporate Tax Base', of 7 July 2004; 'Commission Non-paper to Informal Ecofin Council of 10 and 11 September 2004: Home State Taxation for Small and Medium-Sized Enterprises', of 7 July 2004; 'Results of Informal Meeting of Economics and Finance Ministers, The Hague, 10–11th September 2004 – Banking and Company Taxation', MEMO/04/214 of 13 September 2004.

42 The discussion is old, but was revived by enlargement. On the eve of enlargement, Gerhard Schroeder openly linked corporate tax harmonization and solidarity between member states of the European Union. See 'A Double Edge Sword', *The Economist*, 30 April 2004. This claim was also made by the French Chancellor of the Exchequer, see 'The Nicholas v Jacques Show', *The Economist*, 11 September 2004. See also 'Tax Wars in the EU', *The Economist*, 24 July 2004. Political pressures based on the connection between tax dumping and social policy were acknowledged by the Director General for Taxation, Robert Verrue, before the Economic and Monetary Committee of the European Parliament; see 'Commission Hopes to Launch Co-operation on Company Tax', *Agence Europe*, 2 September 2004. See also 'Le dumping fiscal empoisonne les relations franco-polonaises', *Le Monde*, 11 September 2004; 'La Pologne revendique l'utilisation de l'arme fiscale pour créer des emplois', *Le Monde*, 14 September 2004; 'Bruxelles songe à harmoniser l'assiette de l'impôt sur les sociétés', *Le Monde*, 14 September 2004: 'Officially, relocations were not on the agenda at the meeting of the European finance ministers in The Hague on Friday 10 and Saturday 11 September. But the topic was on everybody's minds'. (Author's translation.)

43 Which ends up affecting the political platforms of traditional political parties. See e.g. the European Socialists' manifesto on globalization, 'Europe 2004: Changing the Future', of 5 February 2004.

44 On effective corporate-tax rates in the new member states, see the 2004 report of Ernst and Young, 'Company Taxation in the New EU Member States: Survey of the Tax Regimes and Effective Tax Burdens for Multinational Investors'.

9 Soft governance, employment policy and committee deliberation

Kerstin Jacobsson and Åsa Vifell

Since the mid-1990s, innovative forms of governance have been developed in the EU. These forms of governance are based on other mechanisms of policy coordination than supranational law-making, and they include the type of soft governance framed as 'the Open Method of Coordination' (OMC) at the Lisbon summit in 2000. The OMC is a procedure for policy coordination based on common guidelines or objectives, which leaves the decision-making capacities on national policy to the member states. Although the soft coordination procedures vary between policy areas, common denominators are the use of cyclical processes, soft law and peer review and pressure (Borrás and Jacobsson 2004; Hodson and Maher 2001).

This method of cooperation has made possible a coordinated European strategy in policy areas which fall under the jurisdiction of the member states, such as policies of employment and social inclusion. The definition of employment promotion as 'an area of common concern' and the commitment to coordinate national policies accordingly (Art. 126 TEC), already tells us something of the polity development of the EU. Here institutions are developed, if not to counterbalance, at least to complement the economic integration process. Moreover, they are founded on the notion that in an integrated market it is no longer appropriate to view problems as national rather than transnational. Common responses are needed. Yet since member states are not ready to give up jurisdiction in these fields, innovative forms of soft governance have provided the solution.

The system of soft governance builds on a systematic exchange of information and on dialogue, which, ideally, will allow for coordination where all parties strive towards the same objective. To what extent is it reasonable to view the OMC as a 'process of communicative action, which helps participants to internalize new norms and agree on ideas and objectives' (Meyer 2002: 7)? Since actors cannot be forced to comply in the case of soft coordination, as preconditions such as sanctions and the threat of exclusion are absent, we assume that deliberation gains in importance as an action-coordinating mechanism. Indeed, the OMC may be considered a test case for the *power of deliberation*. This chapter investigates to what extent this type of soft governance is supportive of a deliberative mode of policy-making. We focus in particular on employment-policy coordination, as the European Employment Strategy (EES) is possibly the most developed example of the new type of soft coordination.

The chapter investigates four committees which are central to the policy process of the OMC. In particular we study the Employment Committee (EMCO) but we also look at three other committees involved in employment policy-making. The role of committees in EU governance has been given extensive attention.[1] Still, empirical studies from diverse fields are needed to determine if, and in what way, committees and administrative networks can be said to contribute to a *deliberative mode of governance*. Focusing on the role of committee interaction in fostering dialogue and learning based on the exchange and evaluation of arguments, provides a useful way of examining how soft coordination could perhaps provide favourable conditions for deliberation.

We focus on the administrative and political process preceding the formal political decision-making, because this is where EU policy is, in practice, forged. The EU system is characterized by constant interaction and negotiation; and borders between national and supranational, but also between politics and administration, are blurred. In transnational networks, governmental actors and civil servants from the member states interact closely with representatives of EU institutions and sometimes with private actors. Investigating the role and nature of such networking is important in order to understand how European integration is in practice achieved. Committees exist in all phases of EU policy-making: decision preparation, decision-making and implementation. A number of previous studies have shown that EU committees tend to develop into team-spirited working groups in which the participants work closely together and gain confidence in one another (Hanny and Wessels 1998; Beyers and Dierickx 1998). Joerges and Neyer (1997a, 1997b) even see the EU committees as examples of the development of a cooperative and deliberative culture in the EU. We will investigate to what extent this is true of the Employment Committee and the other committees involved in employment-policy coordination. How conducive are they to the development of the EU as a polity in its own right?

This chapter shows that there are indeed indications that soft coordination could support a deliberative mode of governance. However, there are also structures and factors that limit the scope for deliberative interaction. There are limits to deliberation both as a mode of problem-solving and action coordination as well as a legitimacy-providing mechanism. Nevertheless, the committee interaction studied can be said to contribute to a cooperative integration process in several related respects: The committees serve as central nodes of administrative networks, providing policy-makers with contacts and *forums* for exchanging experiences

and knowledge, and increasing awareness of policy options. The committee interaction contributes to trust-building, facilitating interaction and
creating common understandings and notions of problems and challenges, as a base for expanded cooperation in the future.

Deliberative supranationalism

It is in the search for supranational legitimacy that the deliberative democratic tradition has gained salience in EU studies in recent years (Habermas 1996, 2004a; Cohen and Sabel 1997, 2003; Eriksen and Fossum 2000).
The argument has been that the EU cannot solely rely on deriving its legitimacy from the member states. As the EU is developing as a polity in its
own right, it has to develop its own base for legitimacy (Eriksen and
Fossum 2000). The deliberative ideal, then, provides an alternative both
to the instrumental and functionalist view that sees effective problem-
solving and output legitimacy as the key to legitimacy (Scharpf 1999a) *and*
to the culturalist view that argues that supranational legitimacy requires a
common identity and sense of solidarity, that is, a European demos. In
addition, deliberative theory is not only providing a normative theory
about democratic legitimation, but also a positive theory about the nature
and integrative mechanisms of the European integration process (see
Chapter 1).

Deliberative democracy pertains to the procedural requirements of
legitimacy. It is through public argument and reasoning among free and
equal citizens that proposals can be justified. In public deliberation, the
reasonableness of proposals and ideas can be assessed. Reasons must be
provided for proposals and they must be acceptable to others, ideally to all
affected. Such a conception of democracy favours a specific principle of
justification, namely the deliberative one, instead of a particular organizational form. It emphasizes that collective choices should be made in a
deliberative way and not just that those choices should fit with the preferences of the citizens (Cohen 1989; Jacobsson 1997). This is in contrast to
the conception of collective choice as the aggregation of individual non-
deliberative preferences. A common will is *formed* in a process of deliberation, in which new perspectives may be taken into account, new
information added and preferences changed. One of the functions of
deliberative will formation – of having to present reasons that must be
acceptable to others if they are to survive the deliberative process – is precisely to mould preferences. The outcome of a deliberative process may
well be a compromise and/or a majority decision. However, voting is
more rational, less arbitrary and more legitimate if it is preceded by deliberation. Whether it results in changed preferences or not, deliberation
promotes reflectively held preferences. It functions to clarify lines of conflict and to foster a common view of the problem and of what is at stake,
and thus the scope of disagreement may be reduced (Knight and Johnson

1994). This is one example of how deliberative theory may be helpful in explaining political integration, by pointing to the role of deliberation in cooperation.

Joerges and Neyer (1997a, 1997b) have argued that there are core institutional features of the EU which can be read as supranational versions of the deliberationist ideals. They argue that comitology is indicative of the emergence of a deliberative style of EU policy-making. They point to the 'development of co-ordination capacities between the Commission and Member State administrations with the aim of establishing a culture of inter-administrative partnership which relies on persuasion, argument and discursive processes rather than on command, control and strategic interaction' (Joerges and Neyer 1997b: 620). While Joerges and Neyer do little to substantiate the claim that committee interaction can in any meaningful sense contribute to improving the *democratic* character of EU governance, their identification of the emergence of a deliberative style of policy-making is still interesting from the perspective of deliberation as an action-coordinating mechanism in the European integration process. Based on empirical research and with a focus on EU employment policy, we try to answer if and how the OMC has supported a deliberative mode of policy-making. The criteria are:

1   the extent to which the OMC fosters deliberative problem-solving, based on reason-giving and evaluation of arguments, rather than strategic bargaining, and thus the extent to which interaction is characterized by a communicative rationality rather than a strategic rationality;
2   the extent to which action coordination based on fair arguing rather than on coercion and power relations takes place, and thus the extent to which the principle of equality of participants is being respected;
3   and the extent to which all affected parties have the chance to present their arguments.

Strategic action is, according to Habermas, oriented towards successful realization of preferences, and its rationality depicts the match between chosen means and given ends. Communicative action is oriented towards mutual understanding and its rationality depends on the ability to reach agreement with others. While both action types may use language as a means, in the latter case, action coordination follows from the unforced power of the argument, the power to *convince*. Bargaining processes are tailored to situations where power relations cannot be neutralized in the way rational discourse presupposes. As explained in Chapter 1, both bargaining and arguing are cooperative solutions. While a rational consensus rests on reasons that can convince all parties in the same way, a bargained compromise can be accepted by different parties for different reasons (Habermas 1996: 165f). Habermas' concept of rational consensus is a strong one. As argued by Eriksen and Weigård (2003: 222f), we need a concept which can capture situations where agreement is reached based on arguments and reasons but where participants can have *different* but *mutually acceptable* reasons to consent. A *working agreement* is more than a negotiated compromise as it can be supported by 'reasonable arguments' because deliberation has been conducive to learning and trust enhancement (Eriksen 2003: 212). In this chapter, we therefore distinguish between a rational consensus, a provisional consensus in the form of a working agreement and a (bargained) compromise. Rational consensus can serve as a normative standard but is unlikely to take place in practice. Working agreement and compromise are two types of agreements, where the former is reached after deliberation oriented towards mutual understanding but where the outcome is based on different but acceptable reasons.

We focus on four EU committees involved in EU employment-policy coordination, looking at both their formal role and their actual working methods and informal and formal interaction. Empirically, the following questions are addressed: Does modification of outlooks and positions take place, and are there indications that positions are moved by arguments? Are common and shared notions of the need for action developed and common frames of reference adopted, indicating that convictions are changed? Does arguing rather than bargaining characterize the interactions in the committees? How open is the OMC, both in the sense that the discussion is open-ended and in the sense that it is open to insight and contribution from a wider circle of participants?

The OMC as an enabling structure

In terms of procedures, the Open Method of Coordination, as outlined at the Lisbon summit, builds upon common EU objectives. These are in turn to be translated into national policy targets or objectives and, combined with periodic monitoring, evaluation and peer review, organized as mutual learning processes and accompanied by indicators and benchmarks as means of comparing best practice. In the case of employment policy, the coordination procedures include the setting of common guidelines by a qualified majority vote (QMV) in the Council; the delivery of National Action Plans (NAPs) where national implementation of the guidelines is to be reported; the evaluation of the NAPs by the Commission and the Council in the Joint Employment Report; country-specific recommendations decided by the Council by QMV; and peer exchanges by civil servants in the Employment Committee.

The OMC is interesting from a deliberative perspective for several reasons. Without formal sanction mechanisms, deliberation gains in importance, as does the need to support arguments with solid data such as empirical evidence and well-developed statistics as a base for evaluating and comparing performances. In principle, the OMC allows for debate on the nature of problems, the best way to solve them and how to implement them in different contexts. Since norms and guidelines are easy to change and thus revisable in the light of evaluation, the OMC is both a flexible and a potentially reflexive instrument. Moreover, it is open to diversity and adaptation to local contexts. It also builds on the sharing of knowledge and experiences and on learning from others.

The OMC is open to the participation of a wide range of actors at all levels. The Lisbon summit explicitly acknowledged this participatory dimension of the OMC. In addition, the OMC is compatible with both functional and territorial subsidiarity, being open to the decision-making of national parliaments and subnational authorities as well as to contractual agreements between non-state actors, such as the social partners. The European Employment Strategy (EES) provides opportunities for social partners and other civil-society actors to be heard, as well as encouraging learning and cooperative efforts through a variety of organizational practices, such as partnerships and local or regional action plans. The OMC offers a role to subnational actors and non-state actors, not only in the implementation phase, but also in the policy-formulating phase. It recognizes the need for coordination of action at many levels of government. To that extent it contributes to multilevel and multi-actor integration (Jacobsson and Schmid 2003; Scott and Trubek 2002).

In principle, the OMC could function as a structure supporting a more deliberative mode of policy-making. The lack of formal sanctions is likely to facilitate agreements and avoid 'horse-trading' situations – it lowers the degree of political conflict. The fact that no direct allocation of resources is at stake may also support a consensus orientation. The OMC can be considered a good test case for the power of deliberation. Generally, in the case of Community legislation, voting – whether by QMV or unanimity – may encourage deliberation but also advance package deals and horse-trading. In the case of the OMC, power pressure is useless since it is ultimately up to the member state to implement the agreements or not. This means that bargaining and compromises cannot, in the absence of binding rules and sanctions, be expected to coordinate action, in contrast to a consensus where actors are convinced of having attained the best solution for all. In the discussion, arguments must be general enough to persuade everyone if implementation is to take place. In order to be effective, the OMC must foster *commitment* to the common goals, and not just a superficial consensus with no real obligations involved – hence actors must be *convinced*.

Committee governance

Four advisory committees are involved, to a greater or lesser extent, in the system of governance developed around the EES. These committees are unique in the sense that they hold a position in between the Council and the Commission. Although formally preparatory committees under the Council, the secretariats are hosted by the Commission which is also a full member of each committee. The committees are to supply opinions on request of either the Council or the Commission. In addition, these committees do not fit the traditional pattern of the EU policy process in yet another respect: since the OMC is not a legislative process, normally there are no other Commission working groups to prepare the Commission proposals and no comitology committees involved in the implementation phase. There are normally no other Council working groups involved, and the Permanent Representatives Committee (COREPER) is also largely left outside the process. This means that EMCO, as the other committees, is the only preparatory body before Council level, and is thus granted an important role in the policy process.[2] The main features of the four advisory committees are outlined in Table 9.1.

When investigating the nature of the committee discussions, we ask how committee members express their opinions – from the point of view of the problems and interests of individual member states or from the point of view of common EU challenges and interests? Is there time for open discussions, and are the meetings mainly characterized by arguing or bargaining? The main sources of information are interviews with civil servants both at EU level (the Commission, the COREPER and the European Parliament), and at national level conducted during 2001–2. We also draw on the participant observation of one of our colleagues (Thedvall 2004).[3]

The Employment Committee

The Treaty of Amsterdam called for the setting up of an Employment Committee, the purpose of which is to promote coordination of employment and labour-market policies between member states. EMCO as well as the other three committees studied here have advisory status, and its tasks include: monitoring the employment situation and employment policies in the member states and the Community; formulating opinions at the request of either the Council or the Commission or on its own initiative; and contributing to the preparation of the Council proceedings. EMCO, as well as the other three committees, is a preparatory forum for the Council, but is closely linked to the respective Commission Directorate General (DG), the Employment and Social Affairs DG in the case of EMCO, where the secretariats are located. The secretariat prepares all documents that are to be discussed in the committee and drafts the committee opinions. It is responsible for preparing the agenda with the chairman and for circulating documents. While its task is to support the committee, the secretariat relies heavily on the expertise provided by the Commission. The Commission generally provides the background material and formally employs the officials at the secretariat. Yet, the Commis-

Table 9.1 The four advisory committees involved in European employment policy

	Employment Committee (EMCO)	Economic Policy Committee (EPC)	Economic and Financial Committee (EFC)	Social Protection Committee (SPC)
Treaty base Council configuration	Art. 130 TEC Employment, social policy, health and consumer affairs (4–6 meetings/year)	Art. 272 TEC Economic and financial affairs (10–12 meetings/year)	Art. 114 TEC Economic and financial affairs	Art. 144 TEC Employment, social policy, health and consumer affairs
Commission DG and location of secretariat	Employment and social affairs	Economic and financial affairs	Economic and financial affairs	Employment and social affairs
Members	2/member state 2 from the Commission	2/member state 2 from the Commission and the ECB[1]	2/member state 2 from the Commission and the ECB[2]	2/member state 2 from the Commission
Main tasks	Contributes to the employment policy coordination and other related processes. Employment guidelines, review of the NAPs, Peer Review Programme, contributes to the broad economic-policy guidelines (BEPGs) and to the macro-economic dialogue.	Contributes to BEPGs and the employment guidelines, prepares the macro-economic dialogue and acts as a preparatory group for the EFC.	Follows the financial situation in the member states, examines the freedom of movement of capital and the balance of payments. Important functions with regards to the Stability and Growth Pact and the Excessive Deficit Procedure (Art. 104 TEC). Preparatory body for the Eurogroup.	Monitors the development of social protection policy in the member states, promotes exchange of best practice and of information, prepares reports and opinions.
Members' domestic ministry affiliation	Labour market and financial affairs	Financial or economic affairs	Financial or economic affairs	Social policy and labour market
Number of meetings per year	6–7	10–12	10–14	10–11

Notes
1 According to the statutes, member states as well as the ECB and the Commission should each appoint four members; however, common practice is now to have only two members present each.
2 Until 2003 the national Central Banks were also represented. Today they may only participate in the main committee when stability of financial markets is discussed. This change was brought about mainly due to the enlargement.

sion is also a member of the committee, something which makes the role of the secretariats somewhat ambiguous.

EMCO consists of two ordinary and two alternate members from each member state and two members from the Commission. A chairman elected from the member-state representatives heads it for two years, assisted by a steering group. EMCO has two subgroups, the indicators group and the ad hoc group, both headed by members of EMCO. Membership in these groups usually does not overlap with membership in EMCO. The indicators group consists mainly of lower-level officials, such as technical experts from ministries, and occasionally experts from other agencies or organizations.

Usually the meetings last for one or two days. Apart from the ordinary meetings in Brussels, EMCO normally meets once during each Presidency in the country holding the Presidency. These are called informal meetings; and give the Presidency a chance of presenting the main issues which it wants the Commission to develop. Some interviewees claim that these meetings are a good way to meet and discuss in a more relaxed manner outside the 'Brussels structure', and that this enhances willingness to learn and 'take in' good examples. Over the years, the nature of these meetings has changed. In the beginning, they tended to be a kind of discussion session on policy, without any aim of producing a written contribution or an opinion. According to our interviews, the Presidency's priorities have gradually taken over the informal meetings; and the committee is increasingly asked to supply a written statement on certain political issues close to the Presidency's priorities.

Demand for written contributions generally makes national positions clearer and discussion less open-ended. Negotiations then tend to focus on wordings instead of policy. One Commission official interviewed held the Presidencies responsible for this development since the latter want to give more 'weight' to the committee in preparing issues for the Council. Without a written contribution, it is generally difficult to submit anything to the Council, and conversely, a committee's opinion can serve as a basis for discussion at ministerial level. The committee has increasingly come to be used by members as a clearly preparatory semi-political forum. Originally, EMCO had areas where it produced opinions, but it also had more exchanges of views and discussions on policy issues without any written result going to the Council.

Moreover, since the agenda has become more packed, it is hard to find time for discussions on best practices and similar topics. The overburdened agenda causes the more relaxed and open discussions to suffer. Some interviewees consider this a natural development, since the group is now largely aware of differences and policy choices in the respective member states. It seems that the sharing of experiences takes place in the Peer Review Programme instead, where participation is optional, or in bilateral exchanges between countries.

In EMCO, the hierarchial level of civil servants participating is fairly high (which it should be, according to the founding Council decision), which gives the group certain characteristics. In the working groups, the hierarchical level of participants is lower, consisting mainly of technical experts. The ambience in the indicators group is described as much more relaxed since the agenda is not as full as in EMCO. There is more time for discussion and less pressure to reach a decision or joint position since there is no obligation to supply written statements within a given time-frame. The main task is to supply EMCO with information about what kind of comparative data can be used. The indicators group handles tech-nical issues, such as development of indicators and ways of comparing stat-istics, but these are highly *political* numbers, since they provide the base for comparisons between countries.

In the committee discussions, it does not seem to matter whether a par-ticipant is a member of a small or a large country. Substantive knowledge and experience are more important. Whether the discussion takes more of a bargaining character than a deliberative one is highly dependent on the issues on the agenda. In the work on country-specific recommenda-tions, national standpoints and negotiation on wordings completely domi-nate the discussions, while other, less politically sensitive matters may generate more open-ended discussion.

In our interviews with committee members, it is clear that they speak and reflect in terms of the political mandates given to them 'back home'. Moreover, the fact that several countries changed their representatives after elections with changed parliamentary majorities indicates that members are there on political and not personal mandates, in contrast to the Council's intentions when establishing the committee.

The economic committees

Another important committee in the employment field – and even more so in the economic-policy field – is the Economic Policy Committee (EPC), which served as a model when EMCO was established. The EPC and the Economic and Financial Committee (EFC) share a secretariat and a secretary. This secretary does not perform any practical tasks for the EPC, such as circulating documents or maintaining contact with the secre-taries of the other committees. This work is done by a lower-ranking civil servant, who works closely with the personnel at the DG for Economic and Financial Affairs (ECFIN). Unlike EMCO and the EFC, the EPC's compo-sition and mission is not spelled out in the treaty and thus its treaty base is weaker (Art. 272 TEC).

The members of the EPC are mainly economists with similar educational backgrounds, a number of which have high academic qualifications. Among interviewed officials at the DG ECFIN, it is considered a privilege to be able to discuss ideas with the highly articulate, educated and experienced members in the EPC. The discussions seem to run smoothly, with seldom any confusion about expressions and terminology. The participants all identify themselves with the same theoretical approach and their background supplies them with the framework for their discussions. To this extent they constitute an 'epistemic community' (Haas 1992).

There is mostly consensus on the issues on the agenda, but on occasion, discussion takes the form of negotiations over national standpoints and political mandates. This is the case when addressing country-specific recommendations, which always tend to be politically sensitive – not because the members of the committee disagree on the substantive matters, but because their political mandates to act as representatives of their governments come to the fore.

The EFC, as specified in the treaty (Art. 114 TEC), replaced the earlier Monetary Committee. It is not so closely related to employment-policy matters, but it pertains to the employment guidelines. The EFC differs from the other committees studied here, although it formally displays some similarities to them. The most obvious similarities are the secretariat, which is shared with the EPC, and the 'in-between-ness' in relation to the Council and the Commission. It is, however, very clear that this committee is much closer to the Council, and thus represents a more intergovernmental form of cooperation. All members are high-ranking senior civil servants from the finance ministries and, although not formally political actors, very closely linked to the political power in their ministries, a fact which also serves to reinforce the perceived higher status of this committee. It takes the shape of a more informal 'Council', in which government representatives meet in a preparatory body. These properties make the committee highly political in comparison to the others.

The EFC has no permanent working groups but these can be established ad hoc if necessary. However, an alternates group has been established and consists of all the alternate members of the committee and works as something close to a preparatory body for the full committee. This development is due to the relatively full agenda of the committee and the limited time that the high-ranking senior civil servants are able to devote to meetings.

In preparing documents and providing background material for EMCO, the EPC or the Social Protection Committee (SPC), there is at times close cooperation between the DG ECFIN and DG Employment and Social Affairs. However, this is not the case with the DG ECFIN officials preparing material for the EFC who have few contacts outside the DG. The working methods in terms of meetings and procedures have always been secret in this committee. Hanny and Wessels (1998) refer to the committee as 'an animal of a particular nature in the jungle of committees', as 'decision-makers in the dark', and as an 'old boys club' (see also Verdun 2000). The reason for the secrecy of the EFC stems from the times when it was called the Monetary Committee and handled issues concerning EMU. Secrecy was considered necessary in order to avoid speculation and to create financial stability. According to several officials, the issues handled by the committee today do not require the same degree of secrecy. But the status of the committee is partly due to its secretive nature; and the secrecy seems to provide the framework for free exchanges and confidence between the members. As one committee member put it:

> If you discuss politically sensitive matters, and if you are a tight group where everyone knows each other and you are not bothered by diplomats reporting everything you can, of course, be more open [...] As group pressure is created, you can't see it as your mission to divert all the unpleasant things said about your country.

This official believes that, while there is an element of competition, the members are quite clear about the fact that they cannot always win. In his view, the closed nature of the EFC, in combination with the peer pressure, means that you 'drop your guard' with respect to criticism.

The group enjoys close cooperation and informal and personal contacts work smoothly. The participants have little trouble understanding each other and the terminology used is common to all. The working style is highly consensus-oriented and agreement seems common even before issues are explicitly addressed and discussed. However, when issues become politically sensitive or controversial, for instance in the formulation of country-specific recommendations, the discussions enter into negotiations over wordings and become less open-minded. As in EMCO, the political mandate of the members is clearly stated. Members might very well agree personally on the recommendations yet add comments such as: 'We all know that this is the appropriate way but that is unfortunately not the way we have chosen to organize it in my country.' Positions and preferences may be revised through the discussions at the level of individual officials, but it is far from certain whether these changes are translated into national policy.

Recently, however, there are signs that the EFC has become more politicized, and that discussions are becoming *renationalized* (Linsenmann and Meyer 2003), as with the committee discussions on the Growth and Stability Pact and the failure of some countries to follow the common rules. Possibly the controversy between large and small member states will be sharpened in the coming years. Contrary to the case with other committees, nationality seems significant, indicating that power relations are important. During the meetings, representatives of small countries do not speak as much as those of the larger ones. The larger countries also have unofficial lunch meetings in which the small member states do not participate (Hanny and Wessels 1998). The lunches are nowadays mostly used for the preparation of the Eurogroup.

The Social Protection Committee

The latest committee to be established was the Social Protection Committee (SPC). It relates to the same Council constellation and DG as EMCO. When the Treaty of Nice came into force in 2003, the SPC became treaty-based (Art. 144 TEC). There is also support in the treaty for cooperation in the area of social exclusion. This does not apply to pensions or health care, which clearly fall under the principle of subsidiarity. Still, the member states have agreed to look at possibilities for cooperation on these issues along the lines of the OMC. There is one subgroup, which has been working on indicators for social inclusion and is currently focusing on indicators for pensions.

The very idea of balancing the financial side of the debate and giving social protection a concerted voice at EU level was an important explanation for why the social ministries came together. However, the committee members have not pushed for the subsequent development of social-policy coordination. Rather, the Commission has responded to the high-level mandates given by the spring summits. Moreover, the member states have been reluctant to introduce some aspects of the OMC used in other fields, such as the use of recommendations and ranking of countries.

It might, perhaps, have been expected that the SPC would be the committee where participants have most trouble in understanding each other in the discussions, since welfare regimes vary considerably between countries. However, this has not been a major problem. The motivation to find common ground has been high and members have worked hard to explain their national features. A common conceptual understanding has developed through the meetings.

While EMCO seems to have experienced a shift from more open-ended discussions to negotiations on wording because of a tight agenda and the demand for written opinions, the agenda of the SPC has been busy from the start. It is considered important to provide written documents in order for the SPC to make itself heard at EU level. This is, however, a difficult balance to keep since it also implies stronger cooperation at EU level, to which some member states are averse.

Since issues often overlap in the various committees, interaction and coordination between them are well developed at the level of civil servants. The secretaries provide their agenda to each other before committee meetings and they can participate in each other's meetings. This is true of EMCO, the SPC and EPC. The EFC, with its more secretive relation to the other committees, does not participate in this collaboration of circulation of drafts, agendas or steering-group coordination. There have been attempts to establish more contacts between the other committees and the EFC. However, such projects are looked upon as somewhat of a 'mission impossible' by most interviewed. Several interviewees contested the need for secrecy. Most topics bear on administrative issues and only a small amount touches upon questions related to exchange rates or sensitive economic policies. Even though all the committees are central for the OMC and for effective policy coordination, there exists a *hierarchy* between them. This perception stems both from the formal rules surrounding them and from the more subtle notions derived from the relationship between the treasuries and the spending ministries at national level. Most members of the EPC and EFC represent the ministries of finance or economy at home and therefore hold a strong position nationally. This has led to a belief amongst the members of the economic committees that they might not benefit from cooperation with EMCO and the SPC since they represent weaker ministries at home.

Committee governance in practice – deliberative or not?

There is evidence pointing to ways in which the OMC supports a more deliberative mode of governance. However, there are also factors that undermine and limit the possibilities for the committees to function as deliberative *forums*.

Arguing or bargaining?

Are the committee discussions characterized by argumentation aimed at reaching mutual agreement, or by bargaining aimed at the successful defence of pre-determined national positions? Or, put differently, what is decisive: power relations or good arguments? Our results indicate that the committee discussions take on quite different features depending on the issues on the agenda. Generally, discussion is open-ended, where all members can present their arguments and try to find common ground. Except for the EFC, it is not of great importance whether one represents a small or a large country. Instead, the one who presents arguments which build on substantive knowledge and experience on the topic at stake, for instance a country with a good record in economic or labour-market policy, gets his or her arguments thoroughly considered. There is also a will to listen and to learn from the experiences of others. Strategic bargaining is not the general mode of interaction in the committees.

However, contacts to create coalitions with like-minded members before meetings do take place, usually concerning issues that might become politically sensitive. When it comes down to the formulation of recommendations or the exact definition of indicators, the discussion in the committees or in the bilateral consultations with the Commission, takes the form of negotiations and bargaining. The member states try to influence the exact wordings of the recommendations in order to make them acceptable at home.

Although the committees are formally advisory, they have great influence in that their proposals are often identical to the eventual Council decisions. This has led member states to use the committees increasingly as *forums* to place issues on the political agenda. This is especially true for EMCO. Because the committee in this respect has become more political, discussions have become more like negotiations on the basis of national standpoints than open-ended discussions on best practices and exchange of opinions. Limited time-frames and the demand to produce written statements in order to influence policies seem to have made discussions less open-ended and more focused on bargaining on wordings than on openly addressing common problems or different policy choices.

Certain deliberative features seem more prevalent in the discussions taking place in the EPC and EFC, given the way views are exchanged: a common terminology is used and a will exists to understand the position of others. One explanation is that these committees are much more closed to outside actors. There are no contacts with social partners or NGOs, and the EFC does not even have regular contacts with EMCO or the SPC. Moreover, being trained economists, the members of these committees constitute an *epistemic community* with shared theoretical frames of reference, which facilitate discussion. On the other hand, large countries have a greater say, which indicates that power relations rather than the 'power of the good' argument is decisive when sensitive issues are at stake.

Shared frames of reference and consensus orientation?

At a general level, shared understandings of common problems and challenges have developed. This is true both of the need for stable public finances and the need to handle the demographical challenge, including the need for increased rates of employment and the reform of tax and social-benefit systems. While these correspond to problems in the real world, part of this development is a result of cooperation and arguing. Common policy approaches, such as a preventive and activating labour-market policy and the 'make work pay' principle, have been developed. Other examples are the common indicators agreed upon for instance with regard to quality in work as well as various targets for employment levels. However, a complete agreement on policy does not exist, especially not for concrete measures. Yet there is an awareness of the expectations of the others, and that there will be reactions against failure to respond to the common objectives. Non-compliance must be explained and reasons and arguments provided. Critical comments and recommendations from other member states are becoming increasingly acceptable.

Our empirical material suggests that the ability of the committees to find common ground and to agree on proposals is for the most part high. Being an epistemic community (of economists) is helpful in this respect. The members in the economic committees seem to agree more easily than EMCO and the SPC and use less bargaining, partly because of their common professional background and theoretical approach. For instance, members of the economic committees express satisfaction that they do not have to discuss such 'irrelevant' issues as lifelong learning. What is relevant for the discussion and what is not is here partly determined by the established frames of reference (or by the discourse in a Foucaultian sense). EMCO and the SPC contain greater variation in internal views as a consequence of more differentiated membership. Agreements reached in the economic committees seem to be achieved at the expense of excluding alternative voices.

Even though the rules of procedure in the committees allow for voting, the ambition is to reach consensus. If the chairman is uncertain about whether there is consensus or not, a round is called where each member makes a statement. If consensus is not reached, there is usually no decision or the issue is removed to be settled elsewhere. On issues of particular national sensitivity, member states may insist on a specific wording, but often the representatives are content with making a symbolic remark on the national position before adjusting to a common line. Committee members are dedicated to reaching agreement.

However, in sensitive areas and when it comes to the written output of committee deliberations, it is difficult to find evidence of national positions actually being modified during committee interaction. Ultimately, the members have political mandates from the ministries 'back home', as proposals must be negotiated and decided at national level in the OMC areas. The member-state representative may well agree that a certain measure might be the best for his/her country, but might also know that this is not what is considered to be the best solution nationally for political reasons. Thus, even if the individual civil servant becomes convinced during committee interaction, this will not necessarily result in actual policy change in the member state. While *reasoned argument* can indeed transform individuals' preferences, the structural conditions of committee interaction – members being delegations of national representatives and the exclusiveness in relation to outside interests – limit what deliberation can achieve. Even if one should not underestimate the immediate influence that committee members might have on national politicians, this is a development to be envisaged more in a long-term perspective.

Inclusiveness and transparency?

As the deliberative ideal prescribes that all interested parties should have the opportunity to present their standpoints and arguments, the question of openness to insight and input becomes important. Most interviewees perceive the OMC processes as being closed not only to the broader public but also to other interested parties. The overall knowledge of the processes within the public administration in the member states has been shown to be low outside the core group of civil servants working directly with the issues. The broader public in the member states has almost no knowledge of the new policy-coordination processes taking place and even the national parliaments are only sporadically involved. They usually do not have a decisive say on the national action plans since the OMC is perceived to be a governmental concern (Jacobsson and Schmid 2002, 2003; Jacobsson and Vifell, forthcoming). A study of discussion in the national quality press of the European Employment Strategy showed very discouraging results (Meyer and Kunstein, forthcoming). There is so far little connection between the EU policy-coordination process and the national public spheres.

As regards social-partner and NGO participation, relations vary considerably between the committees. The SPC and EMCO are the most open to outside participants. On the financial side, there is no participation from NGOs, while the social partners are heard occasionally. EMCO and the SPC are more open to other interests, partly because of the formal mandate, according to which both committees are obliged to consult the social partners, but also because of the working methods established with exchanges of 'good practice' and informal meetings where NGOs and others sometimes take part. One explanation for this is that there is, although not formally, a hierarchy in which the economic committees have a stronger position – a position that makes it possible to ignore demands for the participation of other stakeholders without losing legitimacy. In contrast, the social-policy side needs the support of other stakeholders.

Compared with the economic committees and their staff, the Commission officials working with EMCO and the SPC are more interested in contacts with interest groups, also recognizing the value of such contacts. Nationally, through the NAP processes related to both employment policy and social inclusion, there is an expressed will to involve civil-society actors. This is much less so on the economic-policy side (Foden and Magnusson 2002). Even so, the macro-economic dialogue, involving the European-level social partners, has been established to ensure consistency between monetary policy, fiscal policy and wage policy in the monetary union.

One major drawback in the committee governance within the OMC is the lack of transparency in the decision-making process. Besides the fact that not all stakeholders have the opportunity of presenting their arguments, it is hard for outsiders to know how policy is being made. The EFC is the clearest example, since its meetings are not documented in any way. Even if the committees are formally only advisory, in reality they have a much stronger role in the policy process, which makes the question of accountability pertinent.

This chapter has focused on the role of the committees in developing a more deliberative mode of governance in the EU. The committees studied are interesting since they are an expression of a close cooperation between the Commission and the Council, and since they are central actors – nodes of networking – in the governance of the OMC. However, it is important to acknowledge that there are other aspects of the EES which are relevant to focus on from a deliberative perspective. These include the encouragement to build *partnerships* nationally and subnationally, to develop local and regional action plans and to mobilize relevant actors. Arenas for dialogue between stakeholders have been established at all levels, from the macro-economic dialogue to local partnerships. While far from being fully exploited, the EES has provided new opportunities for actors to be heard and opened space for new cooperative initiatives. Nevertheless, the EES still leaves much to be desired with respect to transparency and participation (de la Porte and Nanz 2004).

Prospects and limits of deliberative supranationalism

What conclusions can we draw on the prospects of deliberative suprana-tionalism, based on our study of the role of committee deliberation in soft coordination?

Enabling features of the OMC

There is some empirical evidence that the OMC in employment policy is supportive of a consensus-oriented process of policy-making. Participants enter the committee discussions with the ambition of finding common points on which cooperation can be developed. Participants acknowledge that there are common problems which require coordinated action, and in which the experiences of others may be useful; and they try to present their arguments in such a way as to make them applicable in other con-texts. The work of developing common indicators to measure progress is an attempt to build common frames of reference and standards, even though the discussion about indicators has so far been coloured by national positions and negotiations.

The non-binding character of the discussions seems to facilitate a delib-erative mode – openness towards arguments – and a culture of listening and learning, rather than meeting criticism with defensive attitudes. In the absence of legal force, reason-giving gains in importance – in order to become 'binding' on practice, participants must be convinced that a pro-posal is reasonable and worth implementing. Comments from someone with experience from the field and with well-founded arguments are generally considered more important in the committee discussions than, for instance, the size of the country of the speaker. The member-state representatives increasingly accept the fact that they will receive peer criticism.

The common project of developing and coordinating employment pol-icies has been generally accepted. A *European perspective* is gradually devel-oping in which policy actors, at least at elite level, increasingly 'think politics' and policy with European frames of reference rather than exclusively national ones. They have begun to rethink national employment policies in the light of 'common problems' and understand them in terms of 'common concerns', which may require coordination and cooperation (Jacobsson 2004). Norms of action, both norms of cooperation and substantive norms of certain policy principles, have developed. To this extent it is accurate to speak of deliberative *supranationalism*. The OMC contributes to *normative* integration to the extent that mutual understanding is fostered and convictions about the reasonableness of common guidelines are developed. This is in itself a form of social and political integration.

The limits of committee deliberation

However, there are obvious limits to this receptiveness to be moved by arguments. Positions are partly 'locked' beforehand due to the political mandates from national governments. This becomes clear when the topic for discussion concerns recommendations or other issues that might become more binding. Then bargaining instead of open-ended discussion tends to dominate the interaction. If it is the case that, the more direct effects on decisions on substantive policy or the allocation of resources, the less open the discussion based on exchanges of experience and knowledge becomes, then there are limits to deliberation as the sole or main action-coordinating mechanism. However, deliberation may still be the key to improved legitimacy and justification of decisions.

It seems easier to reach consensus with more technical and less politicized issues. The subcommittees handling mainly technical issues also fit into this pattern. This may explain Joerges and Neyer's (1997a, 1997b) positive results from a committee concerned with risk regulation in the foodstuff sector consisting mainly of lower-level civil servants working on highly specialized issues requiring scientific assessments (see also Hasselgård 2003). It is likely that it is easier to reach consensus in the comitology committees than in committees in the preparatory phase studied here, especially since these committees are the only ones involved in the employment-policy process. Hence the political agreements will need to be reached within them. Comitology committees mainly consist of lower-level national experts, for instance from agencies, who often share professional backgrounds and technical competencies. In the committees studied here, the representatives are higher officials from ministries more closely linked to the political level. It seems more relevant to study these preparatory committees, rather than the committees in the implementation phase, in order to test the action-coordinating power of deliberation. It is also more relevant from a democratic perspective, since the legitimacy question is more burning in policy-making than in implementation.

Our results show that it facilitates the reaching of consensus if members share the same professional background or theoretical frames of reference. Again, this may explain Joerges and Neyer's positive results from looking at committees working on specific technical, although sometimes politically sensitive, issues in the food sector where the participants, due to the scientific discourse, focus on the best technical solution rather than on control and distributional matters (Pollack 2003). The exchange within epistemic communities tends to be less open to considering other perspectives. It tends to build on a pre-political consensus. Strictly speaking, it would be questionable allowing discussion that is closed to alternative perspectives to qualify as deliberation at all. Committee discussion has limits when it comes to solving political problems and conflicts of interest or value – the type of issues that cannot easily be resolved by scientific evidence.

It also seems to be the case that, the more closed the forums, the more likely the committee members are to give up positions during discussion. Again it is worth highlighting the difference between the economic committees and EMCO and the SPC, where the discussions in the EFC in particular seem to benefit from the limited openness of the committee. This means that transparency in the transgovernmental process might increase bargaining rather than arguing.

Elster (1998) has argued that confidentiality may be useful in certain phases of policy-making since transparency may hinder representatives from transforming their initial positions. Committee governance, in its capacity to develop a cooperative regime, may have an important function to fulfil in a certain phase of the policy-making process but will formation, in order to be *legitimate*, must ultimately be developed with input from forums with *public deliberation* (Eriksen and Weigård 2003: 219). The role that one is prepared to assign to committee governance in EU policy-making seems to be partly related to the perceived purpose of deliberation: to reach consensus, to reach better substantiated decisions or to justify decisions? Public deliberation is supposed to guarantee all three at the same time while non-public deliberation is unable to do so.

The committee deliberation studied here is a type of elite or expert deliberation which hardly fulfils all the requirements of deliberative democratic theory. Yet, this type of deliberation can have other qualities and improve policy-making in other respects than by itself granting democratic legitimacy. For instance, in the case of the committees in the policy-formulation stage studied here, allowing a wider circle of views can ensure a more complete picture of various policy options. Decisions become better founded if many points of view are considered, something which the OMC permits for. However, this merit has not yet been fully exploited. Elster (1998) lists a number of advantages to the deliberative ideal, one being that deliberation can be creative. Policy-making is not just about deciding between available options but about developing alternatives. Moreover, in our case, it is clear that committee deliberation has been important in building confidence and provisional consensus between the national officials and the EU representatives in the sensitive OMC areas. Confidence-building and the stepwise acceptance of criticism may start processes of self-reflection, which in turn make actors prepared to rethink positions.

Yet this is not democracy. A distinction between deliberation as a mode of interaction and action coordination and deliberative democracy must be made. An important question, which we cannot address fully in this chapter, is to what extent deliberative exchanges in closed forums contribute to *democratic* governance. Democracy is not conceivable without a public sphere and, for the OMC to improve the democratic character of EU governance, its relationship with the public sphere, nationally and supranationally, must be strengthened. Today, the process is too closed, not only in relation to many stakeholders, but also in relation to the European Parliament, national parliaments and publics (see also de la Porte and Nanz 2004). Thus, there is no guarantee or mechanism ensuring that the interests of all affected will be considered. The question of accountability becomes urgent when national policy is settled in non-transparent trans-bureaucratic processes, even if these build on a culture of cooperative *inter-administrative partnership* (cp. Joerges and Neyer 1997b). In order to be legitimate, committee deliberation must be coupled with public discourses. In the case of the OMC, it must be so also in order to be effective. Since no binding decisions are taken at supranational level, implementation will not take place unless learning reaches down to lower levels of governance and is developed in public reasoning there. A *working agreement*, a provisional consensus as is – not always but quite often – reached in the committees is far from the standard of a rational consensus, and yet it is the product of reasoned argument. As such, it can lay the base for further cooperation.

Committee deliberation and polity development

Finally, what is the consequence of committee deliberation for the development of the EU as a polity in its own right?

The OMC, as a form of soft governance, has allowed a *functional expansion* of cooperation into new – and sensitive – welfare areas (Borrás and Jacobsson 2004). While hardly able in itself to balance the constitutionally Europeanized economic integration, this soft coordination at least serves to complement it by raising other types of concerns and priorities and institutionalizing a cooperation around them. While the division of tasks between the member states and the EU remains unchanged in formal terms, the task of defining collective goals has in practice been uploaded to the EU arena. As our study of committee interaction indicates, the EU level has been made an arena for policy development in these areas.

The OMC can be considered as a formula for *accommodating diversity* in terms of welfare institutions and traditions yet within a *single political project*. The OMC has contributed to the development of common action norms across particular welfare regimes. Instrumental here has been the *confidence-building function* of committee interaction, allowing a gradual opening up for criticism and self-reflection.

The coordination procedures ensure that national administrations are occupied with the same type of tasks and discussions, which include thinking and writing about employment policy in the light of common European challenges that have been defined and agreed upon. The committees, serving as central nodes of administrative networking, provide policy-makers with contacts and forums for exchanging experiences, and for sharing and increasing knowledge and awareness of policy options, also contributing to creativity and policy development. The networking and confidence-building taking place within and around the committees have contributed to the gradual development of common understandings and notions of common challenges and problems (ageing populations, the need to increase employment rates, problems of social exclusion, etc.). Whether this will be conducive to 'hard law' measures in these areas or not, at least it has made the EU's social dimension more salient.

We could speak of a *normative integration* to the extent that common frames of reference and norms for appropriate policy response are developed. The concrete results of the cooperation are, however, more difficult to predict since the means of reaching the goals remain at national level. That is to say that the concrete implementation is quite another issue.

Nevertheless, the OMC has contributed to *consensus formation* and thus the consensual underpinning necessary for the EU to develop as a legitimate polity in its own right. While it would be premature to speak of a postnational perspective being developed, the OMC has fostered a *Europeanization of outlooks* and perspectives in the new areas. However, while we can see a gradual legitimacy for the EU as a policy-maker in this area, at least at the level of political elites, it is still a very long way to full supranational competencies in these areas. It is also clear that if the OMC is to contribute to European normative and political integration – for which the OMC bears a potential with its fostering of policy learning and mutual understanding – it is important that this European perspective be spread to a wider public than is the case today.

Notes

1 See e.g. Christiansen and Kirchner 2000; Egeberg 1999; Joerges and Neyer 1997a, 1997b; Joerges and Vos 1999; Pedler and Schaefer 1996; Trondal and Veggeland 2000; van Schendelen 1998.
2 Some issues, such as the country-specific recommendations, pass through

COREPER and/or a Council working group, but this is for the most part a formality. Discussion of the proposals only occurs in the case of very sensitive issues.

3 Our findings have largely been confirmed by a study based on a questionnaire to the EMCO members with questions designed to test our findings (Vestergaard and Ørnsholt 2003) and by another interview-based study (Tucker 2003).

10 Widening or reconstituting the EU?

Erik O. Eriksen, John Erik Fossum and Helene Sjursen

Introduction

In this chapter we examine how the enlargement of the European Union (EU) feeds into the ongoing process of reforming its institutional and constitutional structure. So far, most of the literature on EU enlargement has paid little attention to its constitutional and polity implications. Rather, the focus has been on explaining the decisions to enlarge, as well as on the impact of membership on applicant states.[1] To a state, enlargement would be a question of major constitutional importance. The question is whether the same applies to the EU, which is not a state. The EU is based on a unique type of constitutional treaty, albeit its status as political entity is contested. The process of enlargement might increase contestation and generate more uncertainty as to the nature of the enlarged EU in polity and constitutional terms. One source of contestation is a clear standards–practice gap. That is, the entity's institutional and constitutional make-up deviates from the democratic standards that the EU embraces, which mirror that of the democratic constitutional state. The current process of constitution-making is an attempt to narrow this gap but it is likely to be influenced by enlargement. As the Nice Treaty and the Laeken Declaration confirm, the two processes are closely intertwined (European Council 2001a, 2001b). The main question we address here is: does enlargement further contribute to such a narrowing of the gap?

This question must be seen in light of the possibility that the problems associated with enlargement could make the EU revert back to a mere intergovernmental, *problem-solving organization*, hence further widening the standards–practice gap. In such a model of political organization, the onus would be on *efficient regulation*, as prescribed by management philosophies and as endorsed by technocrats and 'nationalists'. Such a result may appropriately be labelled as *widening*, to denote its non-constitutional outcome. Given the increased diversity that will come with the large number of new member states, enlargement could lead to a looser form of cooperation. Indeed, this is what many observers consider to be the most likely result of the enlargement process.

238 Eriksen, Fossum and Sjursen

But the EU might be able to narrow the gap through developing into a *rights-based, constitutionally entrenched union,* premised on full-fledged citizenship rights, a development which is consistent with the vision propounded by democrats and federalists. The EU holds traits that can support a process of constitutionalization; and enlargement might give impetus to such a development. The EU does not only demand that applicant states live up to certain economic and regulatory requirements; it also sets particular standards for fundamental rights protection; and it expects applicants to have a democratic system of government, hence reflecting the Union's embrace of democratic standards.

We expect that the stronger the discrepancy between the EU's externally projected standards and its internal practice, the stronger the pressure to reduce the standards–practice gap will be. This would produce a movement towards a rights-based, constitutionally entrenched Union. In its strongest form this would compel the EU to establish a democratic constitution *prior to* enlarging, and then *reconstitute* itself through the inclusion of new members.

The expectation that enlargement might stimulate constitutionalization is based on the assumption that, under given conditions, normative commitments affect political behaviour. The deliberative perspective that we draw on here is premised on the force of reason-giving in collective decision-making processes. Verbal statements raise expectations of consistency between claims and their correctness and between words and actions. In certain situations double standards and cognitive dissonance will be problematic. Under certain conditions, deliberation compels actors to explain and justify their preferences to critical interlocutors and revise them when criticized. This perspective is relevant to the study of the EU because some of the conditions are in place: the EU is an organization with democratic standards and deliberative sites for reason-giving and reciprocal justification.

In order to investigate the likely outcome of the current processes, we then develop our explanatory scheme based on three of the polity models outlined in Chapter 1. The first model – regulatory governance – corresponds to the widening possibility and would leave intact (or increase) the standards–practice gap, while the third model – a constitutionally based union – would narrow the gap. Later, we seek to demonstrate that the Union's decision to enlarge when seen in light of the conditions for accession (the EU's externally projected standards) reaffirms the EU as a liberal democratic order. In the following part, we examine the current reform processes of the EU in light of the enlargement criteria. When seen in combination, do these processes contribute to a reconstitution or merely to a widening of the European order? The final part holds the conclusion.

Legitimation through what?

In the post-Maastricht period the EU became increasingly concerned with democracy and legitimacy. In the Maastricht, Amsterdam and Nice Treaties, and in numerous speeches, policy papers and other documents the EU has professed a deep concern with its democratic legitimacy. This is also reflected in the criteria set out in the Copenhagen Declaration of 1993 for the selection of candidate states for membership in the EU. Not only a functioning market economy is required but so are institutions that guarantee democracy and human rights.

Given the sheer number of states knocking at the EU's door, the coherence and consistency of the future enlarged EU *qua polity* is at stake. What is more, the dynamic character of the EU on its own alerts us to the prospect that the integration process in Europe may take different directions: it may become more tightly integrated; it may become more complex and multifaceted; or the integration may unravel. The EU is a supranational polity that could, in principle, become a *regulatory agency*, a *value-based entity* or a *rights-based polity*. These modes respond to different normative criteria. The *regulatory* mode is based on epistemic regulation of common affairs, of social and political risks. It designates efficiency, knowledge and institutional capacity as assessment standards. The *value-based* mode is premised on collective identity, namely, on common socio-cultural values defining who the Europeans are. The third one is the *rights-based* mode which designates procedures, rights and respect for deontological principles as assessment standards.

These conceptions of the political order of the EU are underpinned by three notions of discursive justification, namely justification through outcomes, through collective values and through principles. The relevant criteria refer to *efficiency, values* and *rights*. 'Efficiency' refers to the ability to produce substantive results, in particular economic ones, with the minimum use of resources. The two latter criteria, values and rights, explicitly refer to normative justifiability. 'Value' refers to something which is seen to be precious, or ethically salient, and which is important to a group's, or community's sense of identity and conception of the good society. 'Right' is a legal entity, which presupposes mutual recognition and respect that every rights-holder is compelled to offer and essentially entitled to receive from other rights-holders according to principles of justice. In a modern democracy, rights ensure individual protection and participation and foster community-based allegiance and consent – and they can also foster critical opposition to deficient political systems. Different categories of arguments underpin the different conceptions of political order: pragmatic arguments pertaining to the output that it is expected to produce; ethical-political arguments referring to common values and traditions; and moral arguments speaking to principles of fairness and legal rights. The typology in Table 10.1 illustrates these connections.

Table 10.1 Categories of governance/government

Type of entity	Type of discourse	Validating criteria
Regulatory	Pragmatic-economic	Efficiency
Value-based	Ethical-political	Cultural values
Rights-based	Moral-judicial	Principles of justice

In contrast to so-called 'constructivist' approaches in International Relations, this theoretical scheme builds on a *conceptual distinction between values and moral norms*, where the latter refer to higher-order principles and claim universal validity.[2] Values are understood as collective representations of the goods that vary according to cultural and social context, and which are therefore relative and particular (Habermas 1996: 259). To establish what is good for us is logically different from establishing what is just or fair – all interests and values considered. The question of *justice* does not refer to an axiological value, but to a moral norm – a deontological principle. It is concerned with what we are obligated to do when our actions have consequences for others. The ability to reach consensus on such matters is then due to the obligation to provide *reasons*, which are imposed upon every participant in open discussion, i.e., a deliberative process. When reasons are scrutinized according to publicly endorsed norms of equality and impartiality, incoherence and inconsistency are discovered. Inconsistency or unequal treatment can only prevail at the pain of contradiction, i.e. it becomes evident that *double standards* are in use. Reason-giving and critical scrutiny are promoted through such mechanisms as public debate, institutionalized deliberation, peer and judicial review and complaint procedures. They are expected to have behavioural consequences. The explanatory power of deliberation is based on the motivational force of reasons, namely, that the insights into good reasons have 'real-world effects'. Further, according to the standards espoused by deliberative democracy, only those norms that are consented to by all in an inclusive discursive process are legitimate.

But it is well known that actors do not always adhere to the better argument as morality prescribes. Actors may very well continue to live by double standards, hence we should also include in this explanatory scheme that there is support for the idea of a more democratic union. Some of the actors within the Union have a preference for democracy. There is however a lack of compliance-ensuring mechanisms as the basis for law-based sanctions as well as for voting is weak. This relates to an inadequacy of 'non-majoritarian sources of legitimacy' in the Union, such as a collective identity. Deliberation and consensus-seeking compensate for this defect. Extended deliberation constitutes, so to say, a functional equivalent to voting and bargaining.

Which one of these conceptions of political order do the conditions for

Union membership speak to? By examining this we should acquire important information about the direction of the future European order. This is because, in order for an organization to find criteria for including (or excluding) members, one would expect it to have, or be forced to form, an idea of its own identity or legitimacy basis.

Setting conditions for enlargement

In order to become a member of the EU a state must be able to fulfil the following three conditions, set out at the Copenhagen European Council (1993):

- it must have a functioning market economy with the capacity to cope with competitive pressures and market forces within the EU;
- it must have achieved stability of institutions guaranteeing democracy, the rule of law and human rights;
- it must be able to take on the obligations of EU membership, including adherence to the aims of economic and political union.

An additional condition specifies that the EU must be able to absorb new members and maintain the momentum of integration (European Council 1993: 13). By setting such conditions for membership, the EU challenges the principle of external sovereignty at the core of the Westphalian order.[3] The setting of such standards is thus also suggestive of the emergence of a new order in Europe, one beyond intergovernmentalism. However, there may be degrees of interference in the domestic sphere of applicant states and there may be different types and degrees of acceptance of such interference. A closer look at the conditions of membership and how they have evolved over time might say something about this and also about the salience of a regulatory versus a democratic mode of government for the EU.

A new political landscape?

Interestingly, from a historical perspective, the emphasis on respect for democratic principles as a fundamental condition for membership has been present since the early days of the European Community, together with the value- and efficiency-based criteria. The basic condition for accession to the present Union was set out in the 1958 Rome Treaty (Article 237) – 'Any European state may apply to become a member of the Community.' Yet, as early as 1962 the then European Assembly stated that democratic rule was a condition for membership (European Parliamentary Assembly 1962). This was later confirmed by the Declaration on Democracy in April 1978, stating that 'respect for and maintenance of representative democracy and human rights in each Member State are essential elements of membership in the

European Communities' (European Council 1978: 5–6). This was a clear signal to Greece, Portugal and Spain that they could only become Community members if they proceeded with democratization. Specific membership conditions for the three countries were not spelt out, but certainly included respect for principles such as genuine free elections (Pridham 1994: 24). The Commission's opinions on the three applications, however, only mention briefly the transition to democracy. Much more attention was given to consideration of the applicant's economic and administrative capacities, and implications of enlargement for the Community.[4] Nonetheless, the importance of democracy as a basis for membership at this stage of the Community's history was an important signal that it was not just an economic integration project. Neither was it merely a regulatory project, as the pragmatic-administrative considerations failed to outweigh the moral ones.

This remained the situation on membership eligibility until the end of the Cold War, which dramatically increased the number of states wanting to join the Community. In the context of an ever-growing queue of membership applicants, including members of the European Free Trade Association (EFTA) as well as the Central and East European countries and several Mediterranean countries, the Community set out additional membership requirements.

In a report to the June 1992 Lisbon European Council, the Commission re-stated that there were certain fundamental conditions for membership: only European states could become members of the EU; candidate states must have a democratic constitution and must respect the principles of human rights. But it suggested several additional criteria. Perhaps most importantly, applicants had to accept the entire Community system, the *acquis communautaire*, and be able to implement it. This included the Single European Market and the Maastricht provisions on Economic and Monetary Union. Applicant states also had to accept and be able to implement the common foreign and security policy. This was implicitly aimed at the neutral applicants (Austria, Finland and Sweden), and due to concerns that they might impede development of a common defence policy, which was an important Maastricht Treaty objective. The possibility of 'variable geometry' or 'multi-speed Europe' – implied in the Maastricht Treaty opt-outs for Britain and Denmark – was to stop with the current member states (Sjursen and Smith 2001). Finally, applicant states had to have a functioning and competitive market economy; if not, it was argued, 'membership would be more likely to harm than to benefit the economy of such a country, and would disrupt the working of the Community' (European Commission 1992: 11).

What the Commission signalled was that 'widening must not be at the expense of deepening'. The Community, thus, was concerned about efficiency: enlargement could not be permitted to damage the progress made in implementing a single European market, a single currency or the objective of a common defence policy. Thus we see the relevance of regulatory considerations. But rights were also important. The key principles of democracy and human rights were to be protected and promoted. In the standards applied, there is a strong onus on values and principles designating the EU as *something more* than a mere regulatory agency. It is conceived of as an entity loaded with substantive content and with an obligation to bring about a new political landscape in Europe. As such, it is not enough to be a *European* state, i.e., to embrace an identity that relies on a set of culture-specific European values. Neither is it enough to have a proven record of economic performance and adequate institutional and administrative capacity. Applicant states must also adhere to universal standards of justice and legally guarantee the rights of the individual. This has been taken a step further in the context of the last round of enlargement. Here, the political criteria have also been reinforced and further specified.

Bringing in 'the East'

The Copenhagen conditions are by and large similar to the conditions set out in the Commission's 1992 report, with one important addition: respect for and protection of minorities. The Copenhagen conditions referred only to Europe (association) Agreement signatories: Bulgaria, Czech Republic, Estonia, Hungary, Latvia, Lithuania, Poland, Romania, Slovakia and Slovenia. They were not specifically intended for Cyprus, Malta or Turkey, which had applied for membership in 1990, 1990 and 1987, respectively. But since then, these conditions have been understood to form the basic conditions for all applicants.

A further condition introduced was that of good-neighbourliness. This implies a willingness to cooperate with neighbours, but also, more concretely, to agree on borders. It was first introduced in the EU's Pact for Stability, the conference held in 1994–5 to encourage the Central and East European applicants to reach bilateral and multilateral agreements guaranteeing minority rights and borders (Nello and Smith 1998). Subsequently, the European Commission (1997: 51) stated, in its Agenda 2000 report on enlargement that it 'considers that, before accession, applicants should make every effort to resolve any outstanding border dispute among themselves or involving third countries. Failing this they should agree that the dispute be referred to the International Court of Justice.' The Helsinki European Council reiterated this condition in December 1999: it stressed the principle of peaceful settlement of disputes in accordance with the United Nations Charter and urged candidate states to make every effort to resolve any outstanding border disputes and other related issues. The European Council would review the situation relating to any outstanding disputes, in particular concerning the repercussions on the accession process and in order to promote their settlement through the International Court of Justice, at the latest by the end of 2004 (European

Council 1999c: paragraph 4). Although not directly constitutional in nature, these conditions say something about the value base of the Union as well as the principles upon which it seeks to organize its relations with its neighbouring states.

The current political conditions for membership go far in interfering with the governing systems of individual states. The EU does not only demand that applicant states ensure a democratic system of government. It also sets specific standards for individual rights, and thus reaches far into the particular structure of each domestic political system. As such, enlargement seems to confirm that a new type of order is emerging in Europe: an order in which an authority above the states can itself legitimately 'lay down the law' and legitimately set standards for appropriate government. This order depicts a situation where the legitimacy of laws stems not solely from democracy conceived of as a community of fate that autonomously governs itself, but also from democracy conceived of as compliance with human-rights principles, hence is universal and cosmopolitan in nature. However, these are still only standards imposed on the applicant states. To what extent have these standards reflected back on the EU itself? If the EU decided to apply for membership, would it be accepted?

Towards a democratic EU?

The EU may be seen to represent a democratic surplus as it empowers the citizens and the states in times of denationalization and economic globalization but is nevertheless deficient in relation to the standards it endorses, in other words, there is a clear standards–practice gap.

Democratic discrepancies

The three most important deficiencies that are discussed in the literature are:

1   The EU is inadequate with regard to its rights basis. This applies to the range of rights, as well as to the still ambivalent legal status of EU rights. Further, the fact that Union citizenship is still derived from national citizenship precludes the EU from adopting a uniform citizenship. It also means that third-country nationals (denizens) are excluded. The pillar-structure of the treaties, with most of pillars two and three formally outside the reach of the ECJ, also constitutes a constraint on rights development.

2   The process of constitution-making has up to now been closed, executive-driven and technocratic. Citizens have had no assured way of knowing precisely which institutional practices the EU officials will adopt and how well these would correspond with the fundamental principles that the citizens embrace.

3 The EP and the national parliaments are weak and inadequate, as means of ensuring popular input, and as means of holding the executive accountable. Although the EP has obtained the power of co-decision in the EU law-making process, its role in treaty-making is marginal, which greatly limits popular inputs into the process. The weakness of the EP is compounded by the underdeveloped nature of intermediary bodies, such as European parties, and by the weakness of a European public sphere.

This list helps demonstrate that there is an important legitimacy gap and that the EU itself would not be accepted as a candidate for membership. However, in policy documents and speeches by central EU officials, there is a strong endorsement of a set of standards of legitimate government. These are essentially the same as those associated with the *democratic Rechtsstaat*. The standards set for enlargement also reflect this endorsement of constitutional principles and thus speak to the EU as a rights-based, constitutionally entrenched supranational entity – with far-reaching consequences for national sovereignty and international relations. The criteria for enlargement suggest that the reform process in the EU will move beyond the aim of efficient regulation. In this sense it contributes to move international relations in Europe beyond the Westphalian order.

Moreover, if the EU were a colonial power, it would be possible for it to impose standards of individual rights and democratic government, without being expected to live up to requirements of consistency. In other words, the requirement of the EU to live up to the same standards would not exist. Given the declared nature of the EU as an entity based on democratic principles, an expectation of consistency arises. Both public and judicial discourses are sensitive to contradictions. In general they work to reduce inconsistencies and incoherence in legislation and policy-making, as double talk and double standards threaten the very basis for cooperation. They lend credibility to the very notion that others are not performing their tasks – they are free-riding and rent-seeking actors – hence are undermining the very preconditions for trust and solidarity. Some indicators of such feedback processes can be found.

Normative feedback

Events in the aftermath of the sanctions imposed on Austria in 2000 by the 14 other member states for letting a right-wing, 'racist' party into government suggest that there is a willingness to turn the EU into an instrument for upholding democratic principles and respect for fundamental rights. While it was the member states that decided to impose sanctions against Austria, the EU itself has now established procedures to ensure that breaches of fundamental principles incur sanctions.[5] The Treaty of Nice includes an amendment of Article 7 TEU that further specifies the concrete procedures to follow in case of a 'clear risk of a serious breach' on the side of one member state. Moreover, when the Treaty of Nice comes into force, a qualified majority vote will be enough to take action against the recalcitrant member state.

Another strong indication of heightened consistency between externally projected and internally applied standards is revealed in the establishment of a Charter of Fundamental Rights of the European Union (2000), which was solemnly proclaimed at the Nice European Council meeting in December 2000. We return to this later.

Consistency in basic human-rights standards does not directly translate to the area of protection of minorities. The EU has made protection of minorities an important condition for the Central and East European countries (most notably, in the Copenhagen conditions). This is a case where the EU has been criticized for setting conditions for outsiders, which it could not set internally. The TEU does not have explicit provisions for the protection of minorities, although since 1990, state conduct towards minorities has increasingly been the subject of standard-setting at both European (Organization for Security and Cooperation in Europe, Council of Europe) and international (United Nations) levels (Jackson Preece 1997). The issue of minority rights has been controversial in the EU, with the member states divided over this question. France, for one, is more inclined to emphasize individual rights and has not ratified the Council of Europe's Framework Convention on National Minorities. Belgium signed (31 July 2001) but has not yet ratified the Convention. The same goes for Luxembourg, Greece and the Netherlands, but all other states have now signed the Convention.[6] Hence, although this issue has not yet been resolved, there is a case for arguing that the pressure to reduce the standard– practice gap in this case has been at work and led to some changes.

In overall terms, these examples suggest that the relevance and salience of rights-based standards have been amplified through the process of enlargement. They bolster the hypothesis of the European polity as an emerging rights-based, post-national union, albeit one still ridden with conflicts as to the range of rights and the depth of rights protection. The conditions for EU membership project an image and a vision to the accession states of an order based on human rights and democracy. But to fulfil this image, rights entrenchment becomes a *requirement* for the EU itself, and not only for the applicant countries. However, the most important issue is to what extent human rights and democracy are reflected in the general reform processes within the EU. Here it is important to take into consideration the White Paper on European Governance (European Commission 2001a), which proposed a set of actions to reform the Commission in preparation for the Intergovernmental Conference that started in the fall of 2003.

Regulating or reconstituting the EU?

The White Paper does not say much on enlargement. Presumably this could be because the Commission was so preoccupied with the process of forging a constitution as a vital step *in the preparation for* enlargement. The White Paper does, however, present various proposals for improving the functioning of the EU's system of decision-making and implementation. Key ideas are the Open Method of Coordination, working with key networks, and the simplification of Community law. Through better involvement of the citizens and through more efficient decision-making and enforcement policies, the authors of the policy paper hope to increase information and knowledge within the system and the loyalty and responsibility of the actors. The White Paper aims at more relevant and effective governance.

Governance constitutes the structure of rules and processes affecting the exercise of power, particularly with regard to openness, participation, accountability, effectiveness and coherence. These are the basic principles of good governance that are embraced. The standards – in particular their explication – differ from those that designate political rule through responsible institutions, such as parliament and executive. The latter amounts to *government*. Governance, on its part, is designative of innovative practices of networks or horizontal forms of interaction beyond the reach of public law. It is a method for dealing with political controversies in which actors, political and non-political, arrive at mutually acceptable decisions by deliberating and negotiating with each other. This is much in line with recent scholarship in its efforts to conceptualize the EU. The EU is conceived of as a *system of multilevel governance*, which consists of multi-tiered, geographically overlapping structures of governmental and non-governmental elites.[7] Some analysts term this the *new governance agenda*, which means that governing is no longer exclusively statal, that the relationship between state and non-state actors is non-hierarchical and that 'the key governance function is "regulation" of social and political risk, instead of resource "redistribution"' (Hix 1998: 39). The White Paper underscores the view of European cooperation as merely pragmatic and regulatory by accentuating the role of *agencies* in conducting public affairs. A range of regulatory agencies already exists in the member states, some of which apply Community law. However, the White Paper suggests, much in line with Giandomenico Majone (1996a), who opts for the *regulatory state*, that more independent agencies should be created. Even though the White Paper produces many suggestions with regard to improving efficiency and transparency, these suggestions do not cohere with the polity assumptions that inhere in the accession criteria. The White Paper was barred from considering any treaty amendments. This constraint has reduced its value as an input to the Commission's thinking on constitutionalization. Nevertheless, the Commission issued the White Paper and also noted that: 'There is much that can be done to change the way the Union works under the existing Treaties' (European Commission 2001a: 11). The proposals presented in the White Paper are not well connected to the actual ongoing process of making law equally binding for every part of the Community, hence raising the suspicion of inconsistency between externally projected and internally applied standards.

Chartering the EU

The decision to forge a Charter and to launch a comprehensive post-Nice debate, are both evocative of a commitment to reduce the standard–practice gap. The agenda for the IGC 2003, 2004, as set out in the Laeken Declaration (European Council 2001b) included:

- the inclusion of the Charter of Fundamental Rights into the EU treaties;
- the simplification of the EU treaties;
- the ordering of competencies between vertical and horizontal layers of governance;
- the weighting of power relations between member states and the EU institutions, and between the Council, the commission and the EP;
- and the future role of national parliaments in the governmental system of Europe.

This process of making a constitution was taken a vital step further with the proclamation of the Charter. The decision to frame a Charter was taken at the Cologne European Council (1999a) and at the Tampere European Council (1999b), where it was decided to establish a 62-member Convention to draft such a Charter.[8] This was a unique event in that it was the first time that the EP was represented in the same manner as the member-state governments and the national parliaments in a decision of a constitutional nature. The Charter contains provisions on civil, political, social and economic rights that we generally associate with constitutional provisions. Put together, these are intended to ensure the dignity of the person; to safeguard essential freedoms; to provide a European citizenship; to ensure equality; to foster solidarity; and to provide for justice. The number and range of rights that are listed are comprehensive. In addition to provisions, which most charters and bills of rights hold and which pertain to such clauses as the right to life, security and dignity, there are numerous articles that seek to respond directly to contemporary issues and challenges.

Together with the conditions for EU membership, this document clearly has the potential of shifting the focus from the EU as a mere regulatory regime to a *union of citizens* built upon shared values and binding universal norms. Furthermore, the Charter can be read as one of the most explicit statements of the Union's commitment to direct legitimacy that has ever been produced in the EU. Direct legitimacy implies that the institutions and the rights provided to the citizens by the EU shall, in themselves, provide the necessary basis for legitimate government. The text of the Charter is evocative of the EU as a full-blown polity although the citizenship provisions in the Charter are too weak to satisfy this condition (cp. Eriksen *et al.* 2003a).

The Charter was also a unique event in that its drafting took place in an open and inclusive manner, in contrast to the IGC 2000 process, and all other IGCs that have been conducted in an intergovernmental and secretive manner, the key executive officials of the member states *striking bargains behind closed doors.* The self-proclaimed Convention conducted the drafting process, which was of a deliberative kind (Schönlau 2003). A majority of the members were parliamentarians; 16 members from the EP and two members from each of the member-state parliaments participated and lent legitimacy to the process (46 out of 62 members were parliamentarians). The Convention consulted with other organizations and conducted open hearings with representatives from civil society; and it received numerous written submissions.

The Charter is still, in formal terms, a political declaration, but with a more ambiguous actual legal status (Menéndez 2002). It was written *as if* it was binding and is based on existing law (cp. Eckhout 2000). The Charter draws heavily on the system of rights entrenched in the European Convention of Human Rights (ECHR), and on the principles and practices from the common constitutional traditions of the member states. Thus, in so far as these developments can be deemed as part of a 'constitutionalization process', this is driven forward by the challenge of enlargement, as well as spurred on by a mutually reinforcing process of norm development – from 'above' and 'below' – which reinforces the conception of the EU as subject to basic democratic standards and requirements.

Reconstituting the EU?

The Charter Convention also served as model for the Convention on the Future of Europe (2002–3) which was established to prepare one, or several, proposals for the next round of reforms. This started with the Laeken Declaration in December 2001; and the Convention succeeded in forging a *Draft Treaty establishing a Constitution for Europe* (2003d). The IGC initially failed to obtain agreement on the Convention's draft, and only prolonged negotiations during spring 2004 secured an agreement that now awaits national ratifications. The Charter is incorporated in full in the *Treaty establishing a Constitution for Europe* (European Council 2004c: Part II). The question is what these developments entail with regard to the constitutional options listed above. Two items stand out. The first is the constitutional status of the text and the second is the Union's relation to the applicant countries.

On the constitutional status of the text, it is noteworthy that this is framed as a Constitutional Treaty and not a full-fledged constitution. The elimination of the pillars, the endowing of the EU with legal personality, the incorporation of the Charter, the strengthened role of the EP and the generalization of co-decision and qualified majority voting as general principles, all point in a constitutional direction. However, the member states remain key players. Among other things, they would retain control of the Union's sources of funds; the Council structure would be strengthened; and they would still control constitutional amendment. But the constitution, if ratified, would clearly move the EU closer to the constitutional than to the regulatory end of the continuum. The question remains as to what will come out of this.

As we have noted, the normative logic built into the enlargement process serves as a strong inducement for the EU to forge a constitution prior to enlargement. This is problematic in democratic terms, as the applicant states are already affected parties and thus should be represented in the Convention. However, given the nature of the enlargement criteria, not forging one would be even more problematic.

The Convention's status as preparatory body and with applicant members present as *observers* suggests that the EU sought to deal with the challenge of forging a constitution *prior to* enlargement and without properly including the applicants in the process. However, the Convention's working methods (the absence of voting, the organizing of the work to include all, the openness of its deliberations and the presence of a representative from the applicant states in the Praesidium) have given the applicants actual status on a par with the member states. The Convention's deliberative style helped them to propound their arguments and convey their concerns in the same manner as those from the member states. The remarkable *inclusiveness* that was shown here entails that the EU adopted the spirit of constitutionalization in connection with enlargement but followed the procedure for establishing a proper constitution *before* the next round of enlargement. The latter procedure in principle entails two sets of constitutional change: first the development of a constitution prior to enlargement, and then a *reconstitution* once enlargement has taken place. Instead, what the EU has done is to shift the burden of uncertainty onto the present member states – that leaves the fate of the new constitution in the hands of states that were not yet formal members. As is well known, Poland was one of the states that most ferociously rejected the Draft Treaty at the Brussels summit in December 2003.

The Convention's inclusiveness has thus helped foreclose the second aspect of reconstituting the EU after enlargement, which would anyway be ambiguous, given the very timing of the different processes involved. The applicants were full-fledged members of the IGC which started in the fall of 2003, and the constitution will have to be ratified in *all* the 25 member states. The EU thus far appears to have ended up with a hybrid mixture of two different constitution-making procedures.

The forging of a constitution is a contested endeavour, and it may yet be rejected. The above analysis of the White Paper is but one example to show that such a commitment may not be wholly integrated in all the various processes of change taking place in the EU. This analysis should not be construed as Commission reluctance to constitutionalize – rather it goes to show that even the most integration and constitution-friendly bodies in the EU may face strong constraints from reluctant member states. This further suggests that, even if the process does result in a ratified Constitutional Treaty, not distinctly different from the one proposed by the Convention, it may not meet with the requisite standards of a democratic constitution.

Conclusion

Presently the EU's system of representation and decision-making is in the process of being reformed to accommodate enlargement. However, different reform processes of the Union point in different directions. The White Paper on governance reflects the regulatory notion of the Union, whereas the Charter of Fundamental Rights and the Treaty establishing a Constitution for Europe reflect a rights-based notion. The embrace of a mere regulatory notion that implies only widening the present system would simply mean including new members without altering the legitimacy basis for the structure in place, hence violating the consistency requirement and abrogating democratic responsibility.

By setting standards of rights, the rule of law and democracy in the process of enlargement, and not only economic and administrative ones and by gaining acceptance for these standards, the EU not only confirms that it has moved beyond the principles laid down in the Treaty of Westphalia. It also shows that this transformation is conducted according to criteria of legitimate government. Enlargement is a process that contributes to the setting of new standards for the governing of Europe across national borders. Consequently, not only in nation states is enlargement a constitutional question. It is of major constitutional importance for the EU also.

It is generally accepted that democratic principles and human rights are important conditions for enlargement. This in itself is indicative of the EU's self-perception as a community constituted by liberal democratic norms. However, it is only by combining this knowledge with a closer examination of the reform processes within the EU that we can make a proper assessment of the extent to which such a claim is plausible. Taking the gap between the democratic standards that the EU embraces and the entity's constitutional and institutional make-up as our starting point, we have drawn attention to the steps taken by the EU to further the process of democratization and to reduce double standards. Hence this chapter fits with what existing research on enlargement has already implied, yet takes the analysis a step further by highlighting how enlargement feeds into the ongoing reform process. This is difficult to understand from a realist perspective. Reforms are not forged for functional reasons alone.

The process of enlargement is compatible with communicative processes relating to standards of equal treatment and expectations of consistency in the application of principles. The EU is an organization with democratic standards and deliberative sites for the forging of agreements, which makes living by double standards both a legal and a democratic problem. The reduction in the standards–practice gap cannot, thus, be properly explained without reference to the consistency requirement of public deliberation. As the above analysis has shown, the EU has faced up to the requirements of consistency between externally projected and internally applied standards to the extent that it left the fate of the new constitution in the hands of states that were still not formally members.

Notes

1 On this see Zielonka and Mair 2002; Sjursen 2002; Zielonka and Pravda 2001; Schimmelfennig 2001; Sedelmeier 2000; Fierke and Wiener 1999. To the extent that the impact on the EU is discussed the onus is on consequences for efficiency, not on democratic constitutionalization (Schimmelfennig and Sedelmeier 2002). But see further Sadurski 2002; de Witte 2003; Walker 2003.
2 On this consult literature referred to in note 1.
3 It asserts that states are entitled to conduct their affairs in a manner that they are free to decide by themselves (Osiander 1994).
4 See the EC Commission's opinions: 'Opinion on Greek Application for Membership', *EC Bulletin* 2/76; 'Opinion on Portuguese Application for Membership', *EC Bulletin* 5/78; 'Opinion on Spain's Application for Membership', *EC Bulletin* 9/78.
5 Article 6 TEU, Section 1, as amended by the Treaty of Amsterdam, declares that: 'the Union is founded on the principles of liberty, democracy, respect for human rights and fundamental freedoms, and the rule of law, principles which are common to the Member states'. Article 7 TEU, also inserted by an amendment included in the Treaty of Amsterdam, states that any member state that breaches the aforementioned founding principles of EU law may see its membership rights suspended. For a nuanced discussion on the Austrian case, see Merlingen *et al.* 2001.
6 See the Council of Europe's homepage: <http://conventions.coe.int/Treaty/ Commun/ChercheSig.asp?NT=157&CM=8&DF=30/09/04&CL=ENG>
7 As mentioned in Chapter 1, there is a large body of literature on this; see, for example, Marks 1993; Jachtenfuchs and Kohler-Koch 1996; Marks *et al.* 1996; Kohler-Koch and Eising 1999.
8 The Convention consisted of (a) representatives of the Heads of State or Government of the member states; (b) one representative of the President of the European Commission; (c) 16 members of the EP; and (d) 30 members of the national parliaments (two from each of the member states). It was led by a Praesidium of five.

11 Conclusion

From reflexive integration to deliberative supranationalism?

Erik O. Eriksen

In the preceding chapters we have, in addition to discussing alternative understandings of a reflexive approach to post-national integration, assessed the steps towards a common foreign and security policy, a common tax policy with redistributive purposes, the constitutional implications of enlargement and of the reform process of the EU. In this concluding chapter, I will address the findings in relation to the three ideal type models of the EU in order to identify the nature of the creature – save its *finalité politique*. The EU has moved beyond intergovernmentalism but in what direction is it developing? Is it developing into (a) *a regulatory entity* based on transnational structures of governance, (b) *a value-based polity* premised on a common European identity or (c) *a rights-based post-national union* of a federal type?

The salience of these models varies across levels and policy fields. We find that the EU is, above all, a political system that extensively makes use of law to create order and purpose, but law-making and law enforcement take place within a structure that combines hierarchical and horizontal procedures. Whereas a central body with a wide revenue basis is clearly absent, the system has developed a well-established legal hierarchy and consented authority relations buttressed by deliberative processes. Hence the concept of deliberative supranationalism, which depicts the painstaking quest for consensus within a binding legal structure.

Regulatory governance?

James Bohman conceives, in Chapter 2, of the EU as a poly-centric system of transnational governance and subscribes to the perspective of a *directly-deliberative polyarchy* as Cohen and Sabel (1997) have framed it. This means a model of direct participation and public deliberation in structures of governance in which the decision-makers are connected to larger strata of civil society through direct links. Transnational civil society, networks and committees, NGOs and public forums, all serve as arenas where EU actors and EU citizens from different contexts – national, organizational and professional – come together to solve various types of issues and where different points of access ensure democratic legitimacy. Three basic aspects of this order make it conducive to democratic governance: local problem-solving, institutionalization of links between units, and agencies to monitor decision-making within and between units.

Studies of 'comitology', which in fact has been described as a new stage in the integration process, are the main source of support for this perspective. Comitology denotes a system where the Commission's implementation of legislative acts is assisted by hundreds of expert committees mainly made up of representatives from the member states. The composition and interaction in committees as well as their outputs bear the burden of legitimation, not established hierarchies of one sort or the other. As comitology contributes to the finding of 'correct' answers to questions of risk as well as other cognitively demanding issues, it possesses normative quality. For the proponents of deliberative polyarchy the same goes for the *Open Method of Coordination* (OMC), which works through 'soft law' – through benchmarking, blaming and shaming, peer review – to establish common standards. This method was formalized as a form of governance at the Lisbon European Council (2000) and illustrates how cooperation within the field of social and economic policies may be enhanced. The OMC relies on a process of mutual adjustment and learning conducive to consensus on common standards. The OMC allows for divergences to be spelled out, and for member states to develop their own responses within a common framework of reference, but without formal sanctions. It is consensus formation pertaining to 'common assessment of the economic situation; agreement on the appropriate economic policy responses; and acceptance of peer pressure and, when necessary, adjustment of the policies being pursued' (Hodson and Maher 2001: 723).

In Chapter 9 Kerstin Jacobsson and Åsa Vifell examined the strengths and weaknesses of the OMC. It has made the social dimension more visible and, although deficient in democratic terms due to exclusion and opacity, it has fostered trust and a Europeanization of outlooks. It has expanded the size of, and the scope for, deliberation within the institutional nexus of the EU. On the basis of the White Paper on governance we pointed, in Chapter 10, to the prevalence of good governance measures in the reform processes of the EU pertaining to a more efficient and transparent Union. Several chapters underscore the salience of governance within the EU and deliberative circles of interaction conducive to reflexive integration. Deliberation is a fact-finding device that increases the possibilities for rational problem-solving. Many observations support the notion of the EU as a non-coercive deliberative system, but one that has re-regulative and market-redressing effects. In knowledge-based systems there is an incentive to identify positive-sum solutions. The system of comitology has managed to combine market integration with social measures, such as protection of health and safety; it has raised the standards of environmental protection; and has fostered consent and integration.

Positive integration has also been made possible, as solutions have been found that transcend the politics of the lowest common denominator. Deliberation in committees has, thus, facilitated Pareto-improvements – it has demonstrated both *epistemic and transformative value*. This is because such interaction facilitates the pooling of competencies and knowledge to such a degree that there is no basis for collective decisions other than those that leave all better or at least as well off as before.[1]

The EU is a comprehensive system of deliberation with significant problem-solving effects. It is held to be superior to the US regulatory system (Cohen and Sabel 2003). The directly-deliberative polyarchy perspective has merits but does not fully capture the present state of affairs in European integration. Union transactions are not merely functional problem-solving – they have turned 'political'. As we have seen, the EU is involved in a constitutionalizing process. Further, as integration is increasingly more about constitutional principles, as deepened integration affects the interests and identities of the citizens, questions of justice and democratic legitimacy are brought to the fore. Hence, deliberation in the *moral sense* is required. This is not covered by the directly-deliberative polyarchy perspective, which sees deliberation as primarily a cooperative activity for intelligent problem-solving in relation to a cognitive standard, and not as an argument about what is correct in the sense that it can be accepted by all those potentially affected. In the former case publicity is seen as needed only for detecting and solving social problems. This is the reason why Rainer Schmalz-Bruns finds, in Chapter 3, this proposal wanting in democratic terms. It cannot rule out the dangers of *epistocracy*. It is governance without democracy, because there is no chance of equal access and public accountability. What is needed is an epistemic account of the moral merit of democratic procedures. I will come back to this.

A value-based polity?

The EU seems to be more than a transnational system of governance as redistribution takes place, through for example the structural funds – the European Social Fund, the European Regional Development Fund, and parts of the European Agricultural Guidance and Guarantee Fund. Some 0.8 per cent of the aggregate EU GDP is allocated to agriculture and to the Cohesion Fund; and there are special programs supporting applicant countries. The EU exerts influence on the member states' power to tax and has certain taxing capabilities of its own, although possessing very limited control over resources. As Agustín Menéndez makes clear in Chapter 8, the Union has tax-collecting powers over customs, including a portion of the Value Added Tax collected in the whole Union and agricultural duties, in addition to having established a framework within which national tax administrations must act. The upshot is that the EU is able to facilitate collective decision-making at least with a minimum of distributional costs and differential advantages. This underscores the relevance of a concept of the EU as more than a transnational regime – a regulatory entity, but can it draw on a well-developed we-feeling – a common identity – in forging these kinds of policies?

The integration of a political order requires that allegiance to the polity on certain matters override competing group loyalties. A collective identity is held to provide the *non-majoritarian source of legitimacy* necessary for decision-making through majority vote. This is particularly pertinent to the problem of *redistribution*, as the latter requires a deeper sense of allegiance and collective we-feeling. A collective identity is needed to facilitate polity-building as well as welfare-state provisions. Such efforts require the *transformation* of a collection of disjunct actors (and groups) into a collective capable of common action – a solidaristic union. What are the prospects for such in the EU?

Chapters 4 and 5 inquire into the question of a common value base and the prospects for a European identity. In Western Europe, national identities are strongly influenced by profound common experiences and shared cultural histories that will not easily be superseded by a European Union identity, according to Bernhard Peters. Integration through deliberation is difficult when even a minimal collective identity is lacking. In the near future Peters does not foresee a common European public sphere because communication flows within the borders of the Union are not denser than communication flows outside. However, the essence of political allegiance in Europe is, as Gerard Delanty points to, reflecting a blending of a European identity and national identities. They are embroiled in and mirror collective learning processes and the major cultural changes in recent times (cp. Eder 1999). Post-national and cosmopolitan currents are dimensions of national identities and exhibit new European repertoires of evaluation. Bernhard Giesen (2004b) has pointed out that, in opposition to the heroic revolutionary tradition of modernity, there is a new European culture of apologies, mourning and collective guilt for national crimes (even though it is unevenly rooted in the member states). However, such an identity, which is formed through the distancing of oneself from the past, is thin and 'negative', and cannot form the basis of a stable political order for collective goal attainment and redistribution. There are, in other words, no strong indicators of a 'symbolized we' in the making. Chris Lord maintains, nevertheless, on the basis of survey data that, at the present level of integration: 'It is highly questionable that the Union lacks sufficient identity to support public acceptance of its decisions' (Lord 2004b: 44).

But the new tasks of the Union pertaining to recent and future enlargements, the establishment of a common foreign and security policy and, not least, the question of social-policy measures at the EU level, require a clearer understanding of what it is and what it aspires to. Such tasks require a notion of the collective enterprise, i.e. a conception of the entity's foundation, mission and value base beyond that of a free market. From the study of the enlargement negations we found, in Chapter 10, a strong onus on values and principles designating the EU as *something more* than a mere regulatory entity. The key principles of democracy and human rights were to be protected and promoted. The EU is, in this way, loaded with substantive content and with an obligation to bring about a new political landscape in Europe. It has moved beyond the principle characteristics of the Westphalian order as the autonomy of the states – their will power – is constrained by a supranational polity based on a common and supreme law. But whether all are really equal, or some are more equal than others, remains to be seen.

There is a distinct difference between how the EU addressed the former Communist countries of Eastern Europe in the accession negotiations compared to its attitude towards Turkey. The former groups were held to be 'one of us' while, with regard to Turkey, the questions were limited to compliance with the criteria of democracy and human rights. But even though there is no 'kinship' feeling with Turkey, the EU has committed itself to enlarge to it – as the latest communication from the Commission to the Council and the EP proves (European Commission 2004). Hence the European identity does not seem to be contingent on pre-political categories, but rather is malleable and shaped by public discourses (Sjursen 2002: 509). Identities should not be conceived of in essentialistic terms, but on the other hand, a demos – a people – does not automatically result from the constraints of a supranational order. The social preconditions for democratic government at the EU level – conducive to the formation of the public autonomy of a common European will – are not in place. Many of the intermediate associations and organizations of civil society, including a public sphere that could perform catalytic functions for identity formation, are to a large degree missing. It is also open to question whether the ongoing constitutional process will make a contribution in this regard.

A polity in its own right?

A constitution is the most important indicator of a full-fledged polity as it assigns rights, responsibilities and duties, legitimizes power and establishes authority structures singling out accountability lines and areas of competence. It establishes the collective identity of a community in a legal sense. Accordingly, several of the chapters have dealt with the Constitutional Treaty of the European Union, which contains the following basic revisions and developments of treaty law:

- incorporation of the Charter of Fundamental Rights into the Constitution (Part II, Articles 61-114);
- recognition of the Union's legal personality (Part I, Article 7);

- partial abolition of the pillar structure;[2]
- recognition of the primacy of Union law (Part I, Article 6);
- reduction and simplification of the legislative instruments and decision-making procedures, as well as the introduction of a hierarchy of legal acts (Part I, Articles 33-9);
- clearer division of competencies between the Union and the member states (Part I, Articles 12-15);
- decision-making by qualified majority as the main principle in the Council of Ministers (Part I, Article 25). Decisions to be adopted jointly by the Council of Ministers and the European Parliament on the basis of proposals from the Commission (Part I, Article 34-1, with reference to Part III, Article 396, though with important exceptions);
- the election of a President of the European Council for a term of two and a half years (Part I, Article 22);
- a Union Minister for Foreign Affairs (Part I, Article 28);
- a citizens' right initiative (Part I, Article 47-4);
- voluntary withdrawal from the Union (Part I, Article 60).

The Constitutional Treaty reduces the poly-centricity of the Union. The founding treaties recognized three different organizations – the three Communities – with different legal personalities, to which the Treaty of Maastricht added the European Union as a kind of umbrella. The Union and the Communities have now merged into a single organization. John Erik Fossum, in Chapter 6, finds that the Convention's draft (if ratified), through the formal abolition of the pillars, the instituting of a legal personality and numerous other unifying and simplifying provisions, will move the EU from a poly-centric to a *bi-cephalous entity*. The point is that the draft will not produce a uni-centric hierarchical structure for the Union but a 'two-headed' (bi-cephalous) structure framed on top of one common legal body. This is due to the preservation of a Council-led law-making system, where many issue areas are still subject to unanimity and amendment provisions warranting national veto. The Constitutional Treaty is a hybrid between a federal state constitution and an international treaty. Hence the title: *a constitutional treaty*, where the first paragraph refers to the 'will of citizens and states'. The Union has a double source of legitimacy: one springing from the will of the member states, and another from the will of the European citizens. The EU is both for the states and the citizens of Europe even though the states have the upper hand through the power of the Council.

Many observers of the process of drafting the Constitutional Treaty through the Constitutional Convention found that it had deliberative qualities. Chapter 6 documents the learning process and changes of position that testify to the transformative value of deliberation. This process has made clear that the EU, if not earlier, has now unequivocally entered the constitutional terrain. More stakeholders, in particular parliamentarians have been directly included in the process. The deliberations were conducted in public, exposing the political tensions and the divergent constitutional traditions. With regard to legitimacy, it is important to note that the EU Constitutional Treaty is not written from scratch, *ex nihilo*, but is clearly based on the existing primary law of the Union and international law, and is grounded in the constitutional traditions common to the member states. In fact, an important part of the process of European constitution-making since the very beginning has been the slow but steady convergence and fusion of national constitutional traditions. But democratic constitution-making implies the *appropriation* of the constitution by its citizens, bound by reasons, not by the past, namely, not bound by tradition but by the self-reflexive will of the people(s). It is thus only through a democratic ratification process that it can achieve popular legitimacy and normative validity.

The new Constitutional Treaty endows the EU with a stronger base for foreign and security policy, as the legal personality of the Union is now entrenched, and as a Foreign Minister is foreseen. Helene Sjursen in Chapter 7 questions the explanatory power of the intergovernmental model with regard to foreign and security policy. Although formally it may be depicted as such, the institutional nexus of policy-making and the many actors involved in the field of foreign and security policy depart from a simple intergovernmental organizing model. The Commission's activities affect traditional foreign-policy issues and it is difficult to distinguish between its competence domain (external relations) and that belonging to the member states (foreign, security and defence). Further, the frequency of meetings amongst national representatives in the various institutional settings organized under the Council and located in Brussels, the time spent on their preparation as well as their duration, are conducive to reflexive policy-making on this field.

The EU has obtained legal personality and can act within the international legal system. It has its own resources and enjoys *legal supremacy* based on a normative order whose authority has been accepted by member states. In this sense, it can be said that the Constitutional Treaty has moved the EU towards statehood based on entrenched hierarchical principles of law. This implies a shift from a poly-centric organization and a regulatory regime, towards a polity in its own right equipped with the authority to decide in larger fields of competence on the basis of majority vote. The Union as it is constituted does not comply with the requirement of unity of law based on the conception of a sovereign people. The text speaks to the notion of the EU as supranational polity which lacks proper egalitarian procedures of law-making. It is for example found wanting with regard to parliamentarian standards of democracy. It is still the Commission that has the right of initiative and the Parliament is excluded from law-making power in commercial policy, economic-policy coordination and monetary policy, as well as from all domains in which the OMC operates – social policy, employment and economic coordination. This is why some argue that the Constitutional Treaty falls way short of assuring the citizens the last word in the legislative procedure (Menéndez 2005; cp. Peters 2004; and Kokott and Rüth 2003).

Moreover, a polity in its own right cannot only be so in a formal sense – it also has to have material competence – the capability to act. The EU pools sovereignties, it compounds different modes of representation and shares competencies with the member states. It depends on the national administrations for implementation. The EU has no military capability but is aspiring to be more than a civilian power. It shares the competence to tax with the member states, but the tax base is very limited. Its financial means are capped at 1.27 per cent of the EU GNP. Hence, it is a polity not equipped with a fully organized capacity to act. How, then, can the Union be conceptualized?

We do not find that the EU mirrors any of the three ideal typical polity models. Even though regulation is a conspicuous feature of the EU, the integration process has moved cooperation beyond intergovernmentalism and pragmatic problem-solving. Cooperation has turned more political and constitutional, but there is no strong evidence of a common European identity of the kind presupposed by the value-based model. There is no unified people – 'Staatsvolk' – upon which statehood and political institutions can be built. But as the European citizens have obtained more rights, and as the competencies have been amended, one may say that there is a movement in the direction of a rights-based Union. However, much more needs to be done for the citizens to be able to see themselves as the authors of the law they have to obey. The EU is a law-based supranational polity lacking the identity of a people as well as the coercive means of a state a lack it seeks to compensate for through extensive processes of reflexive integration. We have tried to explicate the rationale of such processes from the vantage point of deliberative theory. This theory sets out to explain why the actors of the Union can reach a common position on what to do when there is no clear-cut win-win situation, when side-payments are excluded, when there are no sanction-based rules – no Leviathan. In the rest of this chapter I will explore the added value of this theoretical perspective to the integration process. What does its analytical potential consist in and what does it contribute to in conceiving of the EU?

Integration through deliberation

Integration has to do with the building of communities and with the widening of the boundaries of loyalty and solidarity, i.e. with the transformation of a collection of actors into a group with a distinct identity. It is a process where actors shift their loyalties and activities towards a new centre with the authoritative right to regulate interests and allocate resources. Deliberative theory is brought to the fore due to its aptitude in explaining integration – the ability of concerted action – in the absence of a European demos and a collective identity and when the EU is a very 'incomplete' constitutional arrangement. According to deliberative theory, agreements are based on the obligation to provide *reasons*, which are forced upon every participant in rational discourses. When reasons are scrutinized according to publicly endorsed norms of impartiality, inconsistencies are exposed. Inconsistency and double standards can only prevail at the pain of performative contradictions. But what gives arguments power – why can the actors come to obey by the force of the better argument, and not by passion and interest?

This is a problem for the theory of communicative action because speech acts do not directly coordinate action. Their coordinating power depends not merely on the rational content of what is said, but rather on the implicit *warrant* that the speaker takes upon herself to redeem the validity claim raised, if required. This brings trust and confidence to the fore as intermediate resources for the coordinative power of communicative action.[3] Trust as well as a collective identity are required to enter the deliberative circle as mentioned in Chapter 1. From a deliberative point of view, the question is not merely how much of such commonality exists, but also how it can be brought about in trust-fostering institutions, that is, in inclusive publics of different kinds. European integration provides an *experimentarium* for testing the modicum of trust and commonality required for communicative action.

While the theory of communicative action explicates the ability of actors to obey by the better argument, this does not warrant *collective action* or delegation of sovereignty. There may be reasons to oppose even a rational agreement; and nobody is obliged to comply with social norms unless all others also comply. There is always weakness of will and, as long as citizens are not reassured that the violation of norms will not be left unpenalized, general and spontaneous compliance is endangered. This is why the role of the law is such a conspicuous medium of governance in modern societies. It makes agreements into rights, laws or contracts, which make them equally binding on all the members of a political community. Furthermore, the medium of law stabilizes behavioural expectations as it is a way to solve *coordination problems* (Luhmann 1995: 136). It alleviates the information problem by signalling which rule to follow in practical situations – for example, on which side of the road you should drive. It is a stand-in for trust which cannot tell what one should do in particular contexts: even angels need 'a system of laws in order to know the right thing to do' (Honoré 1992: 3).

> Legal arrangements which lend special assurance to particular expectations, and make them sanctionable, are an indispensable basis for any long-term considerations of this nature; thus, they lessen the risk of conferring trust.
>
> (Luhmann 1979: 34)

In addition to its trust-grounding properties, the legal medium is a supplementary mechanism to deliberation as it removes the incentives for strategic action and 'solves' the problem of collective action. Because law imposes sanctions on non-compliance and defecting, it makes it less risky for actors to act in a communicative or morally adequate manner. Although law and trust are needed for deliberation to work, they do not offload deliberation as they are – in modern political contexts – futile unless formulated in intersubjectively convincing categories. Trust, as well as law, is supposed to be rationally defensible. Deliberation reaches deeper than both of these as it refers to the most fundamental human competence, namely, that of being language-users. Language constitutes the basic medium for common understanding and action coordination (cp. Brandom 1994: 229ff) and trust and law must continuously be re-appropriated through communicative means.

At the level of constitutional politics, the connection between deliberation and law is reflected in the fact that the latter is not just a system of sanctions but one of presumably rational principles claiming to be legitimate, and also one that makes clear the legitimate sources of a polity. In modern democracies the authority of the law stems from the fact that it is made by the people or their representatives through open deliberative processes of opinion formation and will formation. As the *pouvoir constituant* is always with the people, a constitution refers to the constituting will of the people. Because the people are the sovereign legislator, popular sovereignty requires, according to constitutionalists, the unity of the law that reflects the 'true will' of the people (Grimm 2004; Maus 1994). The legitimacy of the law stems from the fact that it is made by the people and is made binding on every part to the same degree and amount. But what about the EU then, which is constituted by *demoi* – several peoples – rather than a unified and sovereign *demos* – a single people? This question directs us to the problem of the exact sources of democratic legitimacy.

Throughput legitimation

Democratic legitimacy cannot just stem from direct popular participation in collective law-making as the people are never present to make choices in modern complex states.[4] It is hard to see how democratic legitimacy can be based merely on votes even in a nation state, as voting procedures are loaded with aggregation problems – majority vote does not guarantee full political equality (Estlund 1993). On the other hand, thanks to the new role of the media and more public criticism, politicians have to define and refine their mandate continuously and drum up support in the general public sphere. The mandate is unbound, it is not just transmitted via elections but has to be struggled for by communicative means. This links in with the epistemic value of deliberation.

[T]he democratic procedure no longer draws its legitimizing force only, indeed not even predominantly, from political participation and the expression of political will, but rather from the general accessibility of a deliberative process whose structure grounds an expectation of rationally acceptable results.

(Habermas 2001a: 110)

The epistemic interpretation of deliberative democracy holds that deliberation is a cognitive process for the assessment of reasons in order to reach just decisions and establish conceptions of the common good. Increased participation may not help in finding correct answers to intractable queries, neither does bargaining and voting. One cannot hold a vote on whether the sea is polluted or strike a bargain with regard to whether criteria for democracy and human rights have been complied with. This underscores the rationality presupposition, and not merely the institutional or participatory presupposition in conceiving of democratic legitimacy. In other words, democratic legitimacy is not merely a matter of congruence between addressees and authors of the law but is a matter of the presumed rationality of the decisions reached – that *the reasons* for political decisions are accepted by the ones affected by them. Only decisions that have been critically examined by qualified and entrusted members of the community through a reason-giving practice can claim to be legitimate. In the epistemic variant of deliberative democracy it is the 'institutionalised opportunities for discursive challenge' (Warren 1996: 55) which warrant the presumption of acceptable results. It is the *throughput procedures* of the political system that generate democratic legitimacy and which can lend support for the claim of democratic quality in post-national orders.

Procedurally regulated deliberation makes sure that viewpoints and interests receive due consideration. Thus decision-makers may maintain that they solve problems efficiently, that their solutions are fair and in everybody's interest, as far as they have managed to talk themselves into consensus and as far as the results endure a public, critical scrutiny. But how can we make sense of the epistemic account of the moral value of democratic procedures without egalitarian systems of law-making through which the citizens can influence the laws that affect them, and effectively determine whether the reasons provided are good enough? The question is whether the burden of legitimation is borne by the quality of the debate – the rationality and fairness of the outcome – or by the fact that the process of decision-making is based on equal rights, universal suffrage, elections, representation, etc.

Reflexive cooperation

The debate on post-national democracy within the camp of deliberative theory oscillates between seeing *society* as the normative source of integration (transnational networks and civil society) and the *state* (the law-based form of government) as the ultimate source of legitimacy for political integration. The state form depicts a hierarchical order based on the monopoly of violence within a territory, but also an order defining a legitimate and responsible government building on one source of authority – the people. Despite diversity, federations too, which are composite states, reflect unity as there is one single line of authority.[5] New governance structures and deliberation in a transnational civil society provide an alternative to the state model, an alternative to a government above the nation state, as sovereignty resides with the problem-solving units themselves. Intrinsic to this mode of legitimation have been dense transnational networks and administrative systems of coordination, amounting to *transnational constitutionalism* (cp. Joerges *et al.* 2004; Slaughter 2004). They are based upon the private-law framework of legal institutions 'that claim legitimacy beyond their own will or self-interest' (Möllers 2004: 329). Such problem-solving structures of governance, termed *heterarchy* in Chapter 1, may constitute a distinct mode of legitimation and it is of interest to know under what conditions and in what issue areas they can be deemed to be acceptable.

These structures emerge transnationally, in between societies and beyond the state, and reestablish the link between *input* and *output* congruence. Communicative spaces are created that put decision-makers to a test as soft power pushes hard power (Habermas 2001a: 71). Transnational deliberative bodies, which exert *communicative pressure*, also raise the information level and contribute to rational problem-solving because they include different parties that adhere to arguing as a decision-making procedure. Such bodies inject the logic of impartial justification and reason-giving unto the participants. They have epistemic value even if ideal communication requirements have not been met, because deliberative interaction forces participants to justify their standpoints and decisions in an impartial and neutral manner. Such a perspective sits very well in descriptive terms with a poly-centric polity based on multiple demoi and jurisdictions.

However, reflexive cooperation premised on democratic experimentalism in Dewey's version cannot ensure that the laws that all have to obey are consented to in a free, open and rational debate by all the affected parties. Such cooperative regimes represent an unstable solution not complying with the firmly egalitarian principle of participation. Even if the legitimizing force of the democratic procedure draws on the public acceptability of reasons, and not on direct participation of the citizens, transnational governance structures cannot replace institutionalized forms of control (including veto positions) and participation that are equally open to all. Such control forms function to hinder technocracy and paternalism. They are to block the potential danger that rationality puts aside all other concerns. This is important as even an intellectual instrumentalization is an instrumentalization after all. Deliberative governance cannot be sustained in normative terms as democracy entails that the reasons for binding norms should be generally and reciprocally justifiable (Forst 2001: 362). Only the possibility of revising and repealing norms through egalitarian structures of law-making can (fully) redeem these democratic procedures' claim to moral value. Hence the need for *legal formalism* and the coercive means for guaranteeing legal equality (Brunkhorst 2004: 98).

The net upshot is that heterarchy cannot substitute government, but merely ground a certain degree of *non-majoritarian sources of legitimacy* of the EU. Heterarchical structures may increase trust and lead to Pareto-improvements and may thus prepare the way for the surrender of sovereignty and post-national integration via hard law. Hence, they perform two important functions:

1 They enhance learning, trust and solidarity, and change loyalties and identifications that over time are conducive to ordinary law-making and constitutional reform.
2 They supplement the 'ordinary' channel of political decision-making. The existing institutional plurality of a multilevel system of governance suggests that a mix of processes and procedures are relevant for the assessment of its democratic quality today.

Rights-based integration

The net upshot of this is that, while the Deweyian perspective on polity-building as problem-solving and experimental deliberation sits very well with the actual trajectory of European integration – starting with rather piecemeal processes of addressing common problems, triggering reflexive processes of institution-building as common problems require common solutions, ending up in a supranational polity capable of collective action – it is found wanting from a normative point of view. It needs to be supplemented with a constitutional perspective, reflecting the need for an authoritative structure of law-making, guaranteeing equal rights to citizens, and hence becoming conducive to collective goal attainment and impartial conflict resolution on democratic terms. A certain hierarchical element is involved in the deliberative reconstruction of modern democracy, basically because deliberation itself cannot limit deliberation and hence participation. Then why the deliberative perspective? Why the focus on the public use of reason when votes including majority vote, and particular institutions such as parliament, government and courts are inevitable for redeeming the claim to democracy?

Some attributes of statehood are necessary in order to make the basic democratic requirements effective. However, the discourse-theoretical variant of the deliberative perspective digs deeper, beyond the equation of democracy with its institutional manifestations – as, for example, a parliamentarian or presidential democracy. It embodies the basic principles of self-government and conceives of rights as instruments for *ensuring equality*

and freedom in the realization of the idea of the sovereignty of the people. Through
its idealization of reflexive constitutionalism, seeing democracy as a legitimation principle more than identical with a particular organizational
form, discourse theory makes us aware of the many possible forms of institutionalization of the democratic principle, and why it has historically
come in many different forms and shapes. In the wording of Rainer
Schmalz-Bruns (Chapter 3), this kind of *epistemic proceduralism* can be
translated into different institutional forms of democracy.

While democracy and citizenship historically have been merged with
collective identity – with city-ethos and nationality – they have been
increasingly separated in modern times. Nationality and citizenship have
been conceptually disconnected in modern, Western societies (Habermas
1998a: 105ff; Eder and Giesen 2001: 262f). This is a development that the
EU seems to carry on as it pursues the liberal idea of statehood divorced
from nationhood, namely, of a polity not bound by pre-political features,
and hence the idea of a rights-based reflexive integration process.

Liberal states are based on entitlements entrenched in constitutions as
individual rights. This onus on basic equal rights reflects the fact that citizenship can take a cognitive turn. That is, when compatriots are to regulate their common affairs by law, they must, at the pain of performative
contradictions, acknowledge equal rights to each other. Political rights
turn human beings into a unified body of citizens capable of making the
very laws they are to obey. It is not necessary for citizens to be each
other's brother or sister, friend or neighbour, or to be a native inhabi-
tant, for political integration to come about. As *citizenship* implies the
ability to rule over one's equals and to be ruled in turn, it follows that the
collective must be made up of equals and further, that only the democratic process, governed by certain procedures, can lend legitimacy to
outcomes. Justice becomes a question of establishing the terms for *mutual
recognition* so that everybody's interests and values are taken into account.
In this perspective, deliberation becomes the medium for the political
execution of power: only public deliberation can get political results *right*,
as it entails the justification of norms to the people who are bound by
them.

The normative content of this perspective implies that reason is preserved, not as insight into universal truths and the excellence of modern
institutional forms. Rather it is conserved as the insight into the fallibility
of knowledge, into the contextuality of justice and the sensibility towards
difference and ambivalence. Thus, reason is preserved in the critical
standards for assessing irrationality at the level of meta-theoretical reflection – as a device for revealing unreason and the reflexive search for truth
and rightness. It is no longer substantial or personified but has retreated
into the very procedures of deliberation and collective decision-making.
Reason is conserved as trust in the institutions, procedures and processes
that guide the fallible search for valid solutions to common problems.

Among these are constitutional barriers which, by guaranteeing 'perpetual' discourse and contestation, are to prevent relapse into ethnocentrism and the camouflage of political power as rationality. When constitutions are reflexively institutionalized, they make democracy and the basic order of society itself open to deliberative decision-making (cp. Chapter 2).

Constitutions assign competencies, positions and powers and contain horizontal and vertical separation of powers, overrepresentation of small jurisdictions, vetoes, judicial review and delegation clauses, etc. In a deliberative perspective these are not seen just as constraining and prohibitive factors but as enabling conditions for rationality and democratic politics. Together with principles of representation, they are preconditions for political rationality as they secure institutional forums in which the members of constituencies through deliberation and *multiperspectival inquiry* can enlarge their horizons and solve problems on a broader basis. Together they make up an institutional nexus that subjects law-making to discursive challenge and reflexive processes of change.

Deliberative supranationalism

In this book we have pursued the idea that deliberation can provide a solution to the puzzle of how post-national integration is possible when the threat of sanctions and brute force is lacking, namely, when the polity does not possess the required means, such as monopoly of violence and taxation, a common identity and the majority vote to enforce its will. As the bargaining resources are rather slim, the implementation of EU policies and further integration works efficiently only if the enforcement mechanisms resonate with a readiness on the part of the member states to accept their disciplining role. The many veto points, the lack of forceful compliance mechanisms, representation and problem-solving through committees and networks underscore the deliberative mode of decision-making. The infrequent use of majority vote – most decisions in the Council are unanimous – makes the EU into a kind of *consensus democracy*.[6] Small countries are systematically overcompensated in the voting formula of the Council of Ministers and unanimity is required on a whole range of issues, which in fact gives member states veto power and thus puts them on an equal footing (akin to the principle of equality of states). Vetoes are held to be a main barrier to supranationalism but represent a constraint on interaction that induces reason-giving: when parties can block outcomes, actors have an incentive to convince all the others. They cannot solely apply arguments that convince some of the participants – a majority – but have to pick arguments convincing to all. Reason-giving and critical scrutiny are further promoted through such mechanisms as public debate, institutionalized meeting places, peer and judicial review and complaint procedures. In such a non-majoritarian system as the EU, there are many reflexive mechanisms that establish critical opposition and induce communicative interaction conducive to transformation of opinions and preference formation.

The chapters in Part II of the book have documented the increase in EU competencies and capabilities in recent years. Even though it is not a federation and the member states control the most powerful body of the Union, the Council, the EU is a supranational polity. It has got a legally binding (even if formally not incorporated) Charter of Fundamental Rights, a (not yet fully developed) competence catalogue delimiting the powers of the various branches and levels of government, a two-chamber system of legislation; as well as authoritative dispute-resolution mechanisms particularly embodied in the authority of the Court of Justice. The Constitutional Treaty moves the EU towards becoming a quasi-federal, supranational legal system based on the precepts of higher-law constitutionalism. This system of representation and accountability gives the citizens at least a minimal input into the process of framing and concretizing their rights. The EU has also organized mechanisms to obtain and implement collective goals, which have market-redressing and redistributive effects.

Notwithstanding these hierarchical elements, the EU is not a state-federation as it possesses shared sovereignty within an unfixed territory; the unity of law is lacking; and there is no established agreement about the demos – on the criteria for inclusion/exclusion. The EU is more varied in organizational terms than the most diverse federal state. As long as it is not clear who are the legitimate subjects of the polity, who the people is, observance of the principle of sovereignty – according to which all political authority emanates from the law laid down in the name of the people – is not ensured. However, the social preconditions for a full-blown parliamentarian system at the EU level are not in place (yet) as a distinct European collective identity is lacking, as are many of the intermediate associations and organizations of civil society, including a unifying public sphere conducive to identity formation on the basis of the public autonomy of the European citizens. Where then to look for explanations of the viability of the integration project?

The protracted 'constitutionalization' processes, that can be seen to have been going on since the very inception of European integration – from the Paris Treaty of 1951 and onwards, culminating with the signature of the Constitutional Treaty in 2004 – point to the fact that the EU is a system in transition and that the legitimacy of this project depends to a large degree on the open-ended and long-lasting discussion of its *finalité politique*. Constitutional reflexivity has increased by every round of treaty revision. Moreover, the Convention method, which is the most reflexive of all, seems now to be accepted as the proper procedure for constitutional amendment. Through the entrenchment of this method, there is consolidation of a model for 'constitutional politics' differing from 'normal politics', and from treaty changes conducted through turf battles at Intergovernmental Conferences.

This links in with the contention that the quality and direction of the integration process itself is crucial for the legitimacy of the Union. As it is easier to agree on procedures and norms for how to proceed than on common purposes and *finalité*, the EU is very much an organization in motion. It is the manner in which the changes are conducted, the quality of procedures and processes, which lend legitimacy to the whole experiment. The EU is work-in-progress, hence the hypothesis of a *working agreement* as the description of the present state of affairs. Several contributors to this book have addressed this notion of something in between bargained compromises and a rational consensus. A working agreement rests on reasonable reasons, but ones that do not convince all. It is modelled on the idea that, even though democratic legitimacy results from an open, public deliberative process, the reasons that convince many need not convince all, but despite that, may still be widely recognized and respected. Working agreements have a preliminary status, which makes it clear that they are not the end product but something that may work while we wait for an overall consensus – that may never come. It is this open-endedness, the preliminary character of the whole project that makes it viable. As there will be a next choice because everyone is guaranteed a place in the process and can withdraw their support at every stage, they do agree *for the time being*, and as long as they are not convinced to the opposite by better arguments.

*   *   *

The EU is neither a value-based polity nor a full-blown rights-based polity premised on the unity of law, but it is more than a regime of transnational governance. It is a polity with no sole apex of authority, but with an (limited) organized capacity to act. The EU is not a single and sovereign demos, but is involved in reflexive processes of constitutionalizing itself. It is a polity-in-motion based on a thin kind of statehood – a supranational polity with a deliberative imprint.

Notes

1 See Joerges and Neyer 1997a; Neyer 2003, 2004; Cohen and Sabel 1997; Gerstenberg 2002a, 2002b; Joerges and Vos 1999; Egeberg 1999; Wessels 1998. See also Stone Sweet 2004 for the role of the ECJ with regard to positive integration.
2 Meaning the structure of three categories of cooperation with different areas of competence: the economic community (pillar I); the common foreign and security policy (pillar II); and the cooperation in the fields of justice and home affairs (pillar III). This is evident from the following articles: Part I, Article 7 on the legal personality of the Union; Article 34 on legislative acts, with reference to Part III, Article 396 on decision-making procedures; and Part I, Article 25 on qualified majority.
3 The proclivity to let oneself be bound by reasons '...rests on specific kinds of trust that are supposedly rationally motivated' (Habermas 1987: 182).
4 'Wer würde es merken, wenn es gar kein Volk gäbe?' (Luhmann 2000: 366).

5 In Chapter 2 Bohman, however, opts for the possibility of *multination federalism* as an alternative to integrated federalism (cp. Kymlicka 2001).
6 '...even where QMV is available, Member States prefer to decide by consensus, and to legislate against the wishes of one of their number less frequently than the rules permit' (Lord 2004b: 106).

Bibliography

Abromeit, H. (1998) *Democracy in Europe: Legitimising Politics in a Non-state Polity*, New York: Berghahn Books.
—— (2002) *Wozu braucht man Demokratie?*, Opladen: Leske & Budrich.
Ackerman, B. (1980) *Social Justice and the Liberal State*, New Haven, CT: Yale University Press.
—— (1991) *We the People: Foundations*, Cambridge, MA: Harvard University Press.
—— (1997) 'The Rise of World Constitutionalism', *Virginia Law Review*, 83: 770–97.
—— (1998) *We the People: Transformations*, Cambridge, MA: Harvard University Press.
Ackerman, B. and Fishkin, J. (2004) *Deliberation Day*, New Haven, CT: Yale University Press.
Aggestam, L. (2000) 'Europe Puissance: French Influence and European Independence', in H. Sjursen (ed.) *Redefining Security? Redefining the Role of the European Union in European Security Structures*, ARENA Report 7/00, Oslo: ARENA.
—— (2004): 'A European Foreign Policy? Role Conceptions and the Politics of Identity in Britain, France and Germany', Doctoral Dissertation, Stockholm University, Department of Political Science.
Alexy, R. (2002) *A Theory of Constitutional Rights*, Oxford: Oxford University Press.
Allen, D. (1998) '"Who Speaks for Europe?" The Search for an Effective and Coherent External Policy', in J. Peterson and H. Sjursen (eds) *A Common Foreign Policy for Europe?*, London: Routledge.
Alonso, W. (1995) 'Citizenship, Nationality and Other Identities', *Journal of International Affairs*, 48(2): 585–99.
Archibugi, D. (1998) 'Principles of Cosmopolitan Democracy', in D. Archibugi, D. Held and M. Köhler (eds) *Re-imagining Political Community*, Cambridge: Polity Press.
Archibugi, D., Held, D. and Köhler, M. (eds) (1998) *Re-imagining Political Community*, Cambridge: Polity Press.
Asad, T. (2002) 'Muslims and European Identity: Can Europe Represent Islam?', in A. Pagden (ed.) *The Idea of Europe: From Antiquity to the European Union*, Cambridge: Cambridge University Press.
Balibar, E. (2004) *We, the People of Europe? Reflections on Transnational Citizenship*, trans. J. Swenson, Princeton, NJ: Princeton University Press.
Banchoff, T. and Smith, M. (eds) (1999) *Legitimacy and the European Union*, London: Routledge.

Banús, E. (2002) 'Cultural Policy in the EU and the European Identity', in M. Farell, S. Fella and M. Newman (eds) *European Integration in the 21st Century: Unity in Diversity?*, London: Sage.

Barnett, C. (2001) 'Culture, Policy, and Subsidiarity in the European Union: From Symbolic Identity to the Governmentalisation of Culture', *Political Geography*, 20(4): 405–26.

Barry, B. (1989) *Theories of Justice*, London: Harvester-Wheatsheaf.

Bauman, Z. (2001) *Liquid Modernity*, Cambridge: Polity Press.

Beach, D. (2003) 'Towards a New Method of Constitutional Bargaining?', Online Paper 13/03, London: The Federal Trust. <http://www.fedtrust.co.uk/Media/Beach.pdf>

Beck, U. (1986) *Risikogesellschaft. Auf dem Weg in eine andere Moderne*, Frankfurt: Suhrkamp.

Beetham, D. and Lord, C. (1998) *Legitimacy and the EU*, London: Longman.

Bellah, R. N., Madsen, R., Sullivan, W. M., Swidler, A. and Tipton, S. M. (1985) *Habits of the Heart: Individualism and Commitment in American Life*, Berkeley: University of California Press.

Bellamy, R. and Castiglione, D. (2000) 'The Uses of Democracy: Reflections on the European Democratic Deficit', in E. O. Eriksen and J. E. Fossum (eds) *Democracy in the European Union: Integration through Deliberation?*, London: Routledge.

Benda, J. (1993) *Discours à la nation européenne*, Paris: Gallimard.

Beyers, J. and Dierickx, G. (1998) 'The Working Groups of the Council of the European Union: Supranational or Intergovernmental Negotiations', *Journal of Common Market Studies*, 36(3): 289–317.

Bogdandy, A. von and Nettesheim, M. (1996) 'Ex Pluribus Unum: Fusion of the European Communities into European Union', *European Law Journal* 2(3): 267–89.

Bohman, J. (1996) *Public Deliberation: Pluralism, Complexity, and Democracy*, Cambridge, MA: MIT Press.

—— (1999) 'International Regimes and Democratic Governance: Political Equality and Influence in Global Institutions', *International Affairs*, 75(3): 499–513.

—— (2001) 'Cosmopolitan Republicanism', *The Monist*, 84(1): 3–22.

Bohman, J. and Rehg, W. (1996) 'Survey Article: Discourse and Democracy: The Formal and Informal Bases of Legitimacy in Habermas' "Faktizität und Geltung"', *Journal of Political Philosophy*, 4(1): 79–99.

—— (eds) (1997) *Deliberative Democracy: Essays on Reason and Politics*, Cambridge, MA: MIT Press.

Boltanski, L. and Thévenot, L. (1991) *De la justification: Les Économies de la grandeur*, Paris: Gallimard.

Borneman, J. and Fowler, N. (1997) 'Europeanization', *Annual Review of Anthropology*, 26: 487–514.

Borrás, S. and Jacobsson, K. (2004) 'The Open Method of Co-ordination and New Governance Patterns in the EU', *Journal of European Public Policy*, 11(2): 185–208.

Brague, R. (2002) *Eccentric Culture: A Theory of Western Civilization*, trans. S. Lester, South Bend, IN: St Augustine's Press.

Brandom, R. B. (1994) *Making It Explicit: Reasoning, Representing, and Discursive Commitment*, Cambridge, MA: Harvard University Press.

Breckenridge, C. A., Pollock, S., Bhabha, H. K. and Chakrabarty, D. (eds) (2002) *Cosmopolitanism*, Durham, NC: Duke University Press.

Brubaker, R. and Cooper, F. (2000) 'Beyond "Identity"', *Theory and Society*, 29(1): 1–47.

Brunkhorst, H. (1998) *Demokratischer Experimentalismus*, Frankfurt: Suhrkamp.

—— (1999) 'Heterarchie und Demokratie', in H. Brunkhorst and P. Niesen (eds) *Das Recht der Republik*, Frankfurt: Suhrkamp.

—— (2004) 'A Polity without a State? European Constitutionalism between Evolution and Revolution', in E. O. Eriksen, J. E. Fossum and A. J. Menéndez (eds) *Developing a Constitution for Europe*, London: Routledge.

Brunkhorst, H. and Kettner, M. (eds) (2000) *Globalisierung und Demokratie*, Frankfurt: Suhrkamp.

Buchanan, A. (2002) 'Political Legitimacy and Democracy', *Ethics*, 112: 689–719.

Calhoun, C. (ed.) (1994) *Social Theory and the Politics of Identity*, Oxford: Blackwell.

Calliess, G.-P. (2002) 'Reflexive Transnational Law: The Privatisation of Civil Law and the Civilisation of Private Law', *Zeitschrift für Rechtssoziologie*, 23(2): 185–216.

Caporaso, J. (1996) 'The European Union and Forms of State: Westphalian, Regulatory or Post-modern?', *Journal of Common Market Studies*, 34(1): 29–52.

Castano, E. (2004) 'European Identity: A Socio-psychological Perspective', in R. K. Herrmann, T. Risse and M. B. Brewer (eds) *Transnational Identities*, New York: Rowman & Littlefield.

Castles, S. and Miller, M. J. (1999) *The Age of Migration*, London: St Martin's Press.

Cederman, L.-E. (ed.) (2001) *Constructing Europe's Identity: The External Dimension*, London: L. Rienner.

Cerutti, F. (1992) 'Can There Be a Supranational Identity?', *Philosophy and Social Criticism*, 18(2): 147–62.

—— (2003) 'A Political Identity of the Europeans?', *Thesis Eleven*, 72: 26–45.

Chalmers, D. (2003) 'The Reconstitution of European Public Spheres', *European Law Journal*, 9(2): 127–89.

Chambers, S. (1996) *Reasonable Democracy: Jürgen Habermas and the Politics of Discourse*, Ithaca, NY: Cornell University Press.

—— (1998) 'Contract or Conversation? Theoretical Lessons from the Canadian Constitutional Crisis', *Politics and Society*, 26(1): 143–72.

Cheah, P. and Robbins, B. (eds) (1998) *Cosmopolitics: Thinking and Feeling beyond the Nation*, Minneapolis: Minnesota University Press.

Christiansen, T. and Kirchner, E. (eds) (2000) *Committee Governance in the European Union*, Manchester: Manchester University Press.

Christin, T. and Trechsel, A. H. (2002) 'Joining the EU? Explaining Public Opinion in Switzerland', *European Union Politics*, 3(4): 415–43.

Citrin, J. and Sides, J. (2004) 'More than Nationals: How Identity Choice Matters in the New Europe', in R. K. Herrmann, T. Risse and M. B. Brewer (eds) *Transnational Identities*, New York: Rowman & Littlefield.

Closa, C. (2003) 'Improving EU Constitutional Politics? A Preliminary Assessment of the Convention', ConWEB Paper 1/2003. <http://les1.man.ac.uk/conweb/>

—— (2004) 'The Convention Method and the Transformation of EU Constitutional Politics', in E. O. Eriksen, J. E. Fossum and A. J. Menéndez (eds) *Developing a Constitution for Europe*, London: Routledge.

Cohen, J. (1989) 'Deliberation and Democratic Legitimacy', in A. Hamlin and P. Pettit (eds) *The Good Polity: Normative Analysis of the State*, Oxford: Blackwell.

Cohen, J. and Sabel, C. (1997) 'Directly-Deliberative Polyarchy', *European Law Journal*, 3(4): 313–42.

—— (2003) 'Sovereignty and Solidarity: EU and US', in J. Zeitlin and D. M. Trubek (eds) *Governing Work and Welfare in the New Economy: European and American Experiments*, Oxford: Oxford University Press.

Collignon, S. (2004) *Vive la République européenne*, Paris: Éditions de la Martinière.

Craig, P. (2003) 'What Constitution Does Europe Need? The House That Giscard Built: Constitutional Rooms with a View', Online Paper 26/03, London: The Federal Trust. <http://www.fedtrust.co.uk/uploads/constitution/26_03.pdf>

Curtin, D. (1993) 'The Constitutional Structure of the Union: A Europe of Bits and Pieces', *Common Market Law Review*, 30(1): 17–69.

Dahl, R. (1989) *Democracy and Its Critics*, New Haven, CT: Yale University Press.

—— (1999) 'Can International Organizations Be Democratic? A Skeptic's View', in I. Shapiro and C. Hacker-Cordón (eds) *Democracy's Edges*, Cambridge: Cambridge University Press.

Dassesse, M. (2004) 'The EU Directive "On Taxation of Savings": The Provisional End of a Long Journey', *EC Tax Review*, 13(2): 41–6.

De Búrca, G. (2003) 'The European Court of Justice and the Evolution of EU Law', in T. Börzel and R. Cichowski (eds) *The State of the European Union*, Oxford: Oxford University Press.

De la Porte, C. and Nanz, P. (2004) 'The OMC – A Deliberative-democratic Mode of Governance? The Cases of Employment and Pensions', *Journal of European Public Policy*, 11(2): 267–88.

De Swaan, A. (2001) *Words of the World*, Cambridge: Polity Press.

De Witte, B. (2003) 'The Impact of Enlargement on the Constitution of the European Union', in M. Cremona (ed.) *The Enlargement of the European Union*, Oxford: Oxford University Press.

Delanty, G. (1995) *Inventing Europe: Idea, Identity, Reality*, London: Macmillan.

Derrida, J. (1994) *The Other Heading: Reflections on Today's Europe*, Bloomington: Indiana University Press.

Deutsch, K. W. (1956) 'Shifts in the Balance of Communication Flows: A Problem of Measurement in International Relations', *Public Opinion Quarterly*, 20(1): 143–60.

Deutsch, K. W. and Markovits, A. S. (1980) *Fear of Science – Trust in science: Conditions for Change in the Climate of Opinion*, Cambridge: Oelgeschlager, Gunn & Hain.

Dewey, J. (1927) *The Public and Its Problems*, reprint, Chicago, IL: Swallow Press, 1954.

Dorf, M. and Sabel, C. (1998) 'The Constitution of Democratic Experimentalism', *Columbia Law Review*, 98(2): 267–473.

Drèze, J. and Malinvaud, E. (1994) 'Growth and Employment: The Scope of a European Initiative', *European Economic Review*, 38(3–4): 489–504.

Dryzek, J. S. (1990) *Discursive Democracy: Politics, Policy, and Political Science*, Cambridge: Cambridge University Press.

—— (2000) *Deliberative Democracy and Beyond*, Oxford: Oxford University Press.

Easton, D. (1953) *The Political System: An Inquiry into the State of Political Science*, New York: Alfred A. Knopf.

Eckhout, P. (2000) 'The Proposed EU Charter of Fundamental Rights: Some Reflections of Its Effects in the Legal Systems of the EU and of Its Member States', in K. Feus (ed.) *The EU Charter of Fundamental Rights*, London: Kogan Page.

Eder, K. (1999) 'Societies Learn and yet the World Is Hard to Change', *European Journal of Social Theory*, 2: 195–215.

—— (2000) 'Zur Transformation nationalstaatlicher Öffentlichkeit in Europa', *Berliner Journal für Soziologie*, 2: 167–84.

—— (2001) 'Integration through Culture? The Paradox of the Search for a European Identity', in K. Eder and B. Giesen (eds) *European Citizenship between National Legacies and Postnational Projects*, Oxford: Oxford University Press.

Eder, K. and Giesen, B. (eds) (2001) *European Citizenship between National Legacies and Postnational Projects*, Oxford: Oxford University Press.

Eder, K. and Kantner, C. (2000) 'Transnationale Resonanzstrukturen in Europa: Ein Kritik der Rede vom Öffentlichkeitsdefizit in Europa', in M. Bach (ed.) *Die Europäisierung nationaler Gesellschaften: Sonderheft 40 Kölner Zeitschrift für Soziologie und Sozialpsychologie*, Opladen: Westdeutscher Verlag.

Eder, K., Giesen, B., Schmidtke, O. and Tambini, D. (2002) *Collective Identities in Action: A Sociological Approach to Ethnicity*, Aldershot: Ashgate.

Egeberg, M. (1999) 'Transcending Intergovernmentalism? Identity and Role Perceptions of National Officials in EU Decision-making', *Journal of European Public Policy*, 6(3): 456–74.

Egeberg, M., Schaeffer, G. and Trondal, J. (2003) 'The Many Faces of EU Committee Governance', *West European Politics*, 26(3): 19–40.

Eisenstadt, S. N. and Giesen, B. (1995) 'The Construction of Collective Identity', *European Journal of Sociology*, 36(1): 72–102.

Elster, J. (1992) 'Arguing and Bargaining in the Federal Convention and the Assemblée Constituante', in R. Malnes and A. Underdal (eds) *Rationality and Institutions*, Oslo: Universitetsforlaget.

—— (ed.) (1998) *Deliberative Democracy*, Cambridge: Cambridge University Press.

Eriksen, E. O. (2003) 'Integration and the Quest for Consensus: On the Micro-foundation of Supranationalism', in E. O. Eriksen, C. Joerges and J. Neyer (eds) *European Governance, Deliberation and the Quest for Democratisation*, ARENA Report 2/03, Oslo: ARENA.

—— (2004) 'A Cosmopolitan Europe in the Making?', Working Paper 2/04, Madrid: Instituto Universitario de Investigación Ortega y Gasset.

Eriksen, E. O. and Fossum, J. E. (eds) (2000) *Democracy in the European Union: Integration through Deliberation?*, London: Routledge.

—— (2002) 'Democracy through Strong Publics in the European Union?', *Journal of Common Market Studies*, 40(3): 401–24.

—— (2004) 'Europe in Search of Legitimacy: Strategies of Legitimation Assessed', *International Political Science Review*, 25(4): 435–59.

Eriksen, E. O. and Weigård, J. (1997) 'Conceptualising Politics: Strategic or Communicative Action?', *Scandinavian Political Studies*, 20(3): 219–41.

—— (2003) *Understanding Habermas*, London: Continuum.

Eriksen, E. O., Fossum, J. E. and Menéndez, A. J. (eds) (2003a) *The Chartering of Europe: The Charter of Fundamental Rights and Its Constitutional Implications*, Baden-Baden: Nomos.

Eriksen, E. O., Joerges, C. and Neyer, J. (eds) (2003b) *European Governance, Deliberation and the Quest for Democratisation*, ARENA Report 2/03, Oslo: ARENA.

Estlund, D. (1993) 'Making Truth Safe for Democracy', in D. Copp, J. Hampton and J. Roemer (eds) *The Idea of Democracy*, Cambridge: Cambridge University Press.

—— (2000a) 'The Insularity of the Reasonable: Why Political Liberalism Must Admit the Truth', *Ethics*, 108(2): 252–75.

—— (2000b) 'Democratic Authority: Toward a Philosophical Framework', paper presented at the conference 'Deliberating about Deliberative Democracy', University of Austin, Texas, 4–6 February. <http://www.la.utexas.edu/research/delpol/conf2000/papers/DemocraticAuthority.pdf>

Farmer, P. (2003) 'The Court's Case Law on Taxation: A Castle Built on Shifting Sands?', *EC Tax Review*, 12(2): 75–81.

Fierke, K. and Wiener, A. (1999) 'Constructing Institutional Interest: EU and NATO Enlargement', *Journal of European Public Policy*, 6(3): 721–42.

Fine, R. and Smith, W. (2003) 'Jürgen Habermas's Theory of Cosmopolitanism', *Constellations*, 10(4): 469–87.

Fishkin, J. and Laslett, P. (eds) (2003) *Debating Deliberative Democracy*, Oxford: Blackwell.

Fiss, O. M. (1979) 'Foreword: The Forms of Justice', *Harvard Law Review*, 93(1): 1–58.

Foden, D. and Magnusson, L. (eds) (2002) *Trade Unions and the Cardiff Process: Economic Reform in Europe*, Brussels: ETUI.

Forst, R. (2001) 'The Rule of Reasons: Three Models of Deliberative Democracy', *Ratio Juris*, 14(4): 345–78.

Fossum, J. E. (2000) 'Constitution-making in the European Union', in E. O. Eriksen and J. E. Fossum (eds) *Democracy in the European Union: Integration through Deliberation?*, London: Routledge.

—— (2003) 'The European Union in Search of an Identity', *European Journal of Political Theory*, 2(3): 319–40.

—— (2004) 'Still a Union of Deep Diversity? The Convention and the Constitution for Europe', in E. O. Eriksen, J. E. Fossum and A. J. Menéndez (eds) *Developing a Constitution for Europe*, London: Routledge.

Fossum, J. E. and Menéndez, A. J. (2005) 'The Constitution's Gift? A Deliberative Democratic Analysis of Constitution-making in the European Union', *European Law Journal*, 11(4): 382–412.

Frankenberg, G. (2003) *Autorität und Integration*, Frankfurt: Suhrkamp.

Fraser, N. (1992) 'Rethinking the Public Sphere. A Contribution to the Critique of Actually Existing Democracy', in C. Calhoun (ed.) *Habermas and the Public Sphere*, Cambridge, MA: MIT Press.

Friese, H. and Wagner, P. (2002) 'Survey Article: The Nascent Political Philosophy of the European Polity', *Journal of Political Philosophy*, 10(3): 342–64.

Fuchs, D. and Klingemann, H.-D. (2002) 'Eastward Enlargement of the European Union and the Identity of Europe', *West European Politics*, 25(2): 19–54.

Fung, A. (2003) 'Survey Article: Recipes for Public Spheres: Eight Institutional Design Choices and Their Consequences', *Journal of Political Philosophy*, 11(3): 338–67.

García, S. (ed.) (1993) *European Identity and the Search for Legitimacy*, London: Pinter.

Gauthier, D. (1986) *Morals by Agreement*, Oxford: Oxford University Press.

Gerbet, P. (1983) *La construction de l'Europe*, Paris: Imperie Nationale.

Gerhards, J., Neidhardt, F. and Rucht, D. (1998) *Zwischen Palaver und Diskurs*, Opladen: Westdeutscher Verlag.

Gerstenberg, O. (1997) 'Law's Polyarchy: A Comment on Cohen and Sabel', *European Law Journal*, 3(4): 343–58.

—— (2002a) 'The New Europe: Part of the Problem – or Part of the Solution to the Problem?', *Oxford Journal of Legal Studies*, 22(3): 563–71.

—— (2002b) 'Expanding the Constitution beyond the Court: The Case of Euro-constitutionalism', *European Law Journal*, 8(1): 172–92.

Gerstenberg, O. and Sabel, C. (2002) 'Directly-Deliberative Polyarchy: An Institutional Ideal for Europe?', in C. Joerges and R. Dehousse (eds) *Good Governance in Europe's Integrated Market*, Oxford: Oxford University Press.

Giddens, A. (1991) *Modernity and Self-Identity: Self and Society in the Late Modern Age*, Cambridge: Polity Press.

Giesen, B. (2003) 'The Collective Identity of Europe: Constitutional Practice of Community of Memory', in W. Spohn and A. Triandafyllidou (eds) *Europeaniza-tion, National Identities and Migration*, London: Routledge.

—— (2004a) 'The Trauma of Perpetrators: The Holocaust as the Traumatic Reference of German National Identity', in J. C. Alexander, R. Eyerman, B. Giesen, N. J. Smelser and P. Sztompka (eds) *Cultural Trauma and Collective Identity*, Cambridge: Cambridge University Press.

—— (2004b) *Triumph and Trauma*, Cambridge: Cambridge University Press.

Goody, J. (2004) *Islam in Europe*, Cambridge: Polity Press.

Grimm, D. (1995a) 'Does Europe Need a Constitution?', *European Law Journal*, 1(3): 282–302.

—— (1995b) *Braucht Europa eine Verfassung?*, Munich: Carl Friedrich von Siemens Stiftung.

—— (2004) 'Treaty or Constitution? The Legal Basis of the European Union after Maastricht', in E. O. Eriksen, J. E. Fossum and A. J. Menéndez (eds) *Developing a Constitution for Europe*, London: Routledge.

Guéhenno, J.-M. (1996) 'Europas Demokratie erneuern', in W. Weidenfeld (ed.) *Demokratie am Wendepunkt*, Berlin: Siedler.

Haas, E. B. (1958) *The Uniting of Europe*, Stanford, CA: Stanford University Press.

—— (1961) 'International Integration: The European and the Universal Process', *International Organization*, 15(3): 366–92.

Haas, P. (1992) 'Introduction: Epistemic Communities and International Policy Coordination', *International Organization*, 46(1): 1–35.

Habermas, J. (1973) *Legitimationsprobleme im Spätkapitalismus*, Frankfurt: Suhrkamp.

—— (1981) *Theorie des kommunikativen Handelns*, Frankfurt: Suhrkamp.

—— (1987) *The Theory of Communicative Action, Vol. II*, trans. T. McCarthy, Boston, MA: Beacon Press.

—— (1989a) *The Structural Transformation of the Public Sphere*, Cambridge, MA: MIT Press.

—— (1989b) 'Towards a Communication Concept of Rational Collective Will-Formation', *Ratio Juris*, 2(2): 144–54.

—— (1992) *Faktizität und Geltung*, Frankfurt: Suhrkamp.

—— (1993) *Justification and Application: Remarks on Discourse Ethics*, trans. C. Cronin, Cambridge, MA: MIT Press.

—— (1994) 'Struggles for Recognition in the Democratic Constitutional State', in A. Gutmann and C. Taylor (eds) *Multiculturalism*, Princeton, NJ: Princeton University Press.

—— (1996) *Between Facts and Norms: Contributions to a Discourse Theory of Law and Democracy*, Cambridge, MA: MIT Press.

—— (1998a) *The Inclusion of the Other: Studies in Political Theory*, Cambridge, MA: MIT Press.

—— (1998b) 'Jenseits des Nationalstaats? Bemerkungen zu Folgeproblemen der wirtschaftlichen Globalisierung', in U. Beck (ed.) *Politik der Globalisierung*, Frankfurt: Suhrkamp.

—— (2001a) *The Postnational Constellation*, Cambridge, MA: MIT Press.

—— (2001b) 'Constitutional Democracy: A Paradoxical Union of Contradictory Principles', *Political Theory*, 29(6): 766–81.

—— (2003) 'Interpreting the Fall of a Monument', *Constellations*, 10(3): 364–70.

—— (2004a) 'Why Europe Needs a Constitution', in E. O. Eriksen, J. E. Fossum and A. J. Menéndez (eds) *Developing a Constitution for Europe*, London: Routledge.

—— (2004b) 'Hat die Konstitutionalisierung des Völkerrechts noch eine Chance?', in J. Habermas (ed.) *Der gespaltene Westen*, Frankfurt: Suhrkamp.

Habermas, J. and Derrida, J. (2003) 'February 15, or What Binds Europeans Together: A Plea for a Common Foreign Policy, Beginning in the Core of Europe', *Constellations*, 10(3): 291–7.

Hanny, B. and Wessels, W. (1998) 'The Monetary Committee: A Significant though Not Typical Case', in M. van Schendelen (ed.) (1998) *EU Committees as Influential Policymakers*, Aldershot: Ashgate.

Hasselgård, M. (2003) *Playing Games with Values of Higher Importance? Dealing with 'Risk Issues' in the Standing Committee on Foodstuff*, ARENA Report 1/03, Oslo: ARENA.

Hayashi, C. (1998) 'The Quantitative Study of National Character: Interchronological and International Perspectives', *International Journal of Comparative Sociology*, 39(1): 91–114.

Heath, J. (2001) *Communicative Action and Rational Choice*, Cambridge, MA: MIT Press.

Hedetoft, U. (1999) 'The Nation-state Meets the World: National Identities in the Context of Transnationality and Cultural Globalization', *European Journal of Social Theory*, 2(1): 71–94.

Held, D. (1995) *Democracy and the Global Order: From the Modern State to Cosmopolitan Governance*, Stanford, CA: Stanford University Press.

Herrmann, R. K., Risse, T. and Brewer, M. B. (eds) (2004) *Transnational Identities: Becoming European in the EU*, New York: Rowman & Littlefield.

Hill, C. (1993) 'The Capabilities–Expectations Gap, or Conceptualising Europe's International Role', *Journal of Common Market Studies*, 31(3): 305–28.

Hitzel-Cassagnes, T. (forthcoming) 'Discursive Processes in the European Institutional System', in J.E. Fossum, P. Schlesinger and G.O. Kvaerk (eds) *A European Public and Civil Society?*, ARENA Report, Oslo: ARENA.

Hix, S. (1998) 'The Study of the European Union II: The "New Governance" Agenda and Its Rival', *Journal of European Public Policy*, 5(1): 38–65.

Hodson, D. (2004) 'Macroeconomic Coordination in the Euro Area: Scope and Limits of the Open Method', *Journal of European Public Policy*, 11(2): 231–48.

Hodson, D. and Maher, I. (2001) 'The Open Method as a New Mode of Governance: The Case of Soft Economic Policy Co-ordination', *Journal of Common Market Studies*, 39(4): 719–46.

Hofstede, G. (1998) 'A Case for Comparing Apples with Oranges: International Differences in Values', *International Journal of Comparative Sociology*, 39(1): 16–31.

Holmes, S. and Sunstein, C. R. (1999) *The Costs of Rights: Why Liberty Depends on Taxes*, New York: Norton.

Holzinger, K. (2003) 'Tax Competition and Tax Co-operation in the EU: The Case of Savings Taxation', EUI-RSCAS Working Papers 2003/7, Florence: European University Institute.

Honneth, A. (1991) 'Pluralisierung und Anerkennung: Zum Selbstmissverständnis postmoderner Sozialtheorien', *Merkur*, 508: 624–8.

—— (1998) 'Democracy as Reflexive Cooperation: John Dewey and the Theory of Democracy Today', *Political Theory*, 26(6): 763–83.

Honoré, T. (1992) 'The Dependence of Morality of Law', *Oxford Journal of Legal Studies*, 13: 1–17.

Howorth, J. (2000) 'European Defence and the Changing Politics of the European Union: Hanging Together or Hanging Separately', *Journal of Common Market Studies*, 39(4): 765–89.

Inkeles, A. (1998) *One World Emerging? Convergence and Divergence in Industrial Societies*, Boulder, CO: Westview Press.

Ipsen, H. P. (1972) *Europäisches Gemeinschaftsrecht*, Tübingen: Mohr.

Jachtenfuchs, M. (1996) 'Regieren im dynamischen Mehrebenensystem', in M. Jachtenfuchs and B. Kohler-Koch (eds) *Europäische Integration*, Opladen: Leske & Budrich.

—— (2002) *Die Konstruktion Europas*, Baden-Baden: Nomos.

Jachtenfuchs, M. and Kohler-Koch, B. (eds) (1996) *Europäische Integration*, Opladen: Leske & Budrich.

Jackson Preece, J. (1997) 'National Minority Rights vs. State Sovereignty in Europe: Changing Norms in International Relations?', *Nations and Nationalism*, 3(3): 345–64.

Jacobsson, K. (1997) 'Discursive Will Formation and the Question of Legitimacy in European Politics', *Scandinavian Political Studies*, 20(1): 69–90.

—— (2004) 'Soft Regulation and the Subtle Transformation of States: The Case of EU Employment Policy', *Journal of European Social Policy*, 14(4): 355–70.

Jacobsson, K. and Schmid, H. (2002) 'Real Integration or Just Formal Adaptation? On the Implementation of the National Action Plans for Employment', in C. de la Porte and P. Pochet (eds) *Building Social Europe through the Open Method of Coordination*, Brussels: PIE Peter Lang.

—— (2003) 'The European Employment Strategy at the Crossroads: Contribution to the Evaluation', in D. Foden and L. Magnusson (eds) *Five Years' Experience of the Luxembourg Employment Strategy*, Brussels: ETUI.

Jacobsson, K. and Vifell, Å. (forthcoming) 'New Governance Structures in Employment Policy Making?', in I. Linsenmann, C. Meyer and W. Wessels (eds) *Economic Government of the EU*, Basingstoke: Palgrave Macmillan.

Jenkins, R. (1996) *Social Identity*, London: Routledge.

Jiménez, A. M. (1999) *Towards Corporate Tax Harmonization in the European Community*, Dordrecht: Kluwer.

Joas, H. (1996) *The Creativity of Action*, Cambridge: Polity Press.

Joerges, C. (2000) 'Transnationale deliberative Demokratie oder deliberativer Supranationalismus?', *Zeitschrift für Internationale Beziehungen*, 7(1): 145–61.

—— (2003) '"Comitology and the European Model?" Towards a *Recht–Fertigungs–Recht* in the Europeanisation Process', in E. O. Eriksen, C. Joerges and

J. Neyer (eds) *European Governance, Deliberation and the Quest for Democratization*, ARENA Report 2/03, Oslo: ARENA.

Joerges, C. and Neyer, J. (1997a) 'From Intergovernmental Bargaining to Deliberative Political Processes: The Constitutionalisation of Comitology', *European Law Journal*, 3(3): 273–99.

—— (1997b) 'Transforming Strategic Interaction into Deliberative Problem-solving: European Comitology in the Foodstuffs Sector', *Journal of European Public Policy*, 4(4): 609–25.

Joerges, C. and Vos, E. (eds) (1999) *EU Committees: Social Regulation, Law and Politics*, Oxford: Hart Publishing.

Joerges, C., Sand, I.-J. and Teubner, G. (eds) (2004) *Transnational Governance and Constitutionalism*, Oxford: Hart.

Kagan, R. (2003) *Paradise and Power: America and Europe in the New World Order*, London: Atlantic Books.

Kant, I. (1797) [1991] 'Theory and Practice', in I. Kant [ed. H. Reiss] *Political Writings*, Cambridge: Cambridge University Press.

Kantner, C. (2004) *Kein modernes Babel: Kommunikative Voraussetzungen europäischer Öffentlichkeit*, Wiesbaden: Verlag für Sozialwissenschaften.

Kettner, M. (1998) 'John Deweys demokratische Experimentiergemeinschaft', in H. Brunkhorst (ed.) *Demokratischer Experimentalismus*, Frankfurt: Suhrkamp.

Kielmansegg, P. G. (1994) 'Lässt sich die Europäische Gemeinschaft demokratisch verfassen?', *Europäische Rundschau*, 22(2): 23–33.

King, A. (2003) *The European Ritual: Football in the New Europe*, Aldershot: Ashgate.

Knight, J. and Johnson, J. (1994) 'Aggregation and Deliberation: On the Possibility of Democratic Legitimacy', *Political Theory*, 22(2): 277–96.

Kohler-Koch, B. and Eising, R. (eds) (1999) *The Transformation of Governance in the European Union*, London: Routledge.

Kohli, M. (2000) 'The Battlegrounds of European Identity', *European Societies*, 2(2): 113–37.

Kokott, J. and Rüth, A. (2003) 'The European Convention and Its Draft Treaty Establishing a Constitution for Europe: Appropriate Answers to the Laeken Questions?', *Common Market Law Review*, 40(6): 1315–45.

Kristeva, J. (2000) *The Crisis of the European Subject*, trans. S. Fairfield, New York: The Other Press.

Kymlicka, W. (2001) *Politics in the Vernacular: Nationalism, Multiculturalism and Citizenship*, Oxford: Oxford University Press.

Ladeur, K. H. (1999) 'Towards a Legal Concept of the Network in European Standard-setting', in C. Joerges and E. Vos (eds) *EU Committees: Social Regulation, Law and Politics*, Oxford: Hart Publishing.

Laffan, B. (2004) 'The European Union and Its Institutions as "Identity Builders"', in R. K. Herrmann, T. Risse and M. B. Brewer (eds) *Transnational Identities*, New York: Rowman & Littlefield.

Laitin, D. D. (2002) 'Culture and National Identity: "The East" and European Integration', *West European Politics*, 25(2): 55–80.

Larking, B. (2001) 'Another Go at the Savings Directive – Third Time Lucky?', *EC Tax Review*, 10(4): 220–34.

Lenaerts, K. and Desomer, M. (2002) 'New Models of Constitution-making in Europe: The Quest for Legitimacy', *Common Market Law Review*, 39(6): 1217–53.

Lepsius, R. M. (1997) 'Bildet sich eine kulturelle Identität in der Europäischen Union?', *Blätter für deutsche und internationale Politik*, 42(8): 948–55.

Levy, D. and Sznaider, N. (2002) 'Memory Unbound: The Holocaust and the Formation of Cosmopolitan Memory', *European Journal of Social Theory*, 5(1): 87–106.

Lindberg, L. N. (1970) 'Political Integration as a Multidimensional Phenomenon Requiring Multivariate Measurement', *International Organization*, 24(4): 649–731.

Linklater, A. (1996) 'Citizenship and Sovereignty in the Post-Westphalian State', *European Journal of International Relations*, 2(1): 77–103.

Linsenmann, I. and Meyer, C. (2003) 'Eurogruppe und Wirtschafts- und Finanzausschuss', in W. Weidenfeld and W. Wessels (eds) *Jahrbuch der Europäischen Integration 2002/2003*, Bonn: Europa-Union Verlag.

Lord, C. (2004a) 'New Governance and Post-Parliamentarism', POLIS Working Paper 5, Leeds: POLIS.

—— (2004b) *A Democratic Audit of the European Union*, Basingstoke: Palgrave Macmillan.

Lose, L. (2001) 'Communicative Action and the World of Diplomacy', in K. Fierke and K. E. Jørgensen (eds) *Constructing International Relations*, New York: Sharpe.

Luhmann, N. (1979) *Trust and Power: Two Works of Niklas Luhmann*, Chichester: John Wiley & Sons.

—— (1987) *Soziale Systeme*, Frankfurt: Suhrkamp.

—— (1991) *Soziologie des Risikos*, Frankfurt: Suhrkamp.

—— (1995) *Das Recht der Gesellschaft*, Frankfurt: Suhrkamp.

—— (1997) *Die Gesellschaft der Gesellschaft*, Frankfurt: Suhrkamp.

—— (2000) *Die Politik der Gesellschaft*, Frankfurt: Suhrkamp.

Lyal, R. (2003) 'Non-discrimination and Direct Tax in Community Law', *EC Tax Review*, 12(2): 68–74.

MacCormick, N. (1997) 'Democracy, Subsidiarity, and Citizenship in the "European Commonwealth"', *Law and Philosophy*, 16(4): 331–56.

—— (2003) 'Foreword', in E. O. Eriksen, J. E. Fossum and A. J. Menéndez (eds) *The Chartering of Europe*, Baden-Baden: Nomos.

Macedo, S. (ed.) (1999) *Deliberative Politics: Essays on Democracy and Disagreement*, New York: Oxford University Press.

Magnette, P. (2004a) 'Deliberation or Bargaining? Coping with the Constitutional Conflicts in the Convention on the Future of Europe', in E. O. Eriksen, J. E. Fossum and A. J. Menéndez (eds) *Developing a Constitution for Europe*, London: Routledge.

—— (2004b) 'When Does Deliberation Matter? Constitutional Rhetoric in the Convention on the Future of Europe', in C. Closa and J. E. Fossum (eds) *Deliberative Constitutional Politics in the EU*, ARENA Report 5/04, Oslo: ARENA.

Majone, G. (1993) 'The European Community between Social Policy and Social Regulation', *Journal of Common Market Studies*, 31(2): 153–70.

—— (1996a) *Regulating Europe*, London: Routledge.

—— (1996b) 'Redistributive und sozialregulative Politik', in M. Jachtenfuchs and B. Kohler-Koch (eds) *Europäische Integration*, Opladen: Westdeutscher Verlag.

—— (1998) 'Europe's "Democratic Deficit": The Question of Standards', *European Law Journal*, 4(1): 5–28.

—— (1999) 'The Regulatory State and Its Legitimacy Problems', *West European Politics*, 22(1): 1–24.

Malmborg, M. and Stråth, B. (eds) (2002) *The Meaning of Europe: Variety and Contention Within and Among Nations*, Oxford: Berg.

Mancini, G. F. (1998) 'Europe: The Case for Statehood', *European Law Journal*, 4(1): 29–43.

Manin, B. (1987) 'On Legitimacy and Political Deliberation', *Political Theory*, 15: 338–68.

Manners, I. (2002) 'Normative Power Europe: A Contradiction in Terms?', *Journal of Common Market Studies*, 40(2): 235–58.

March, J. G. and Olsen, J. P. (1989) *Rediscovering Institutions: The Organizational Basis of Politics*, New York: Free Press.

March, J. G. and Simon, H. (1958) *Organizations*, New York: John Wiley.

Margalit, A. (2002) *The Ethics of Memory*, Cambridge, MA: Harvard University Press.

Marks, G. (1993) 'Structural Policy and Multilevel Governance in the EC', in A. W. Cafruny and G. G. Rosenthal (eds) *The State of the European Community, Vol. 2: The Maastricht Debates and Beyond*, London: Longman.

Marks, G., Hooghe, L. and Blank, K. (1996) 'European Integration from the 1980s: State-centric v. Multi-level Governance', *Journal of Common Market Studies* 34(3): 341–78.

Maull, H. W. (2000) 'Germany and the Use of Force: Still a Civilian Power?', *Survival*, 42(2): 56–80.

Maurer, A. (2003) 'Schliesst sich der Kreis? Der Konvent, nationale Vorbehalte und die Regierungskonferenz. Teil II – Datenbasis und Detailanalyse', CONVEU-30 Working Paper, Berlin: SWP.

Maus, I. (1986) 'Perspectiven "reflexiven Rects" im Kontext gegenwärtigeer Deregulierungstendenzen', *Kritische Justiz*, 19: 390–405.

—— (1994) ' "Volk" und "Nation" im Denken der Aufklärung', *Blätter für deutsche und internationale Politik*, 39(5): 602–12.

McKim, R. and McMahan, J. (eds) (1997) *The Morality of Nationalism*, Oxford: Oxford University Press.

Mead, G. H. (1934) *Mind, Self, and Society from the Standpoint of a Social Behaviorist*, reprint, Chicago, IL: University of Chicago Press, 1962.

Mearsheimer, J. J. (2001) *The Tragedy of Great Power Politics*, New York: Norton.

Melucci, A. (1996) *Challenging Codes: Collective Action in the Information Age*, Cambridge: Cambridge University Press.

Menéndez, A. J. (2001) *Justifying Taxes*, Dordrecht: Kluwer.

—— (2002) 'Chartering Europe: Legal Status and Policy Implications of the Charter of Fundamental Rights of the European Union', *Journal of Common Market Studies*, 40(3): 471–90.

—— (2004a) 'Human Rights: The European Charter of Fundamental Rights', in W. Carlsnaes, H. Sjursen and B. White (eds) *Contemporary European Foreign Policy*, London: Sage.

—— (2004b) 'Three Conceptions of the European Constitution', in E. O. Eriksen, J. E. Fossum and A. J. Menéndez (eds) *Developing a Constitution for Europe*, London: Routledge.

—— (2004c) 'Taxing Europe: Two Cases for a European Power to Tax', *Columbia Journal of European Law*, 10: 297–338.

—— (2005) 'Between Laeken and the Deep Blue Sea: An Assessment of the Draft Constitutional Treaty from a Deliberative-democratic Standpoint', *European Public Law*, 11(1): 105–44.

Merlingen, M., Mudde, C. and Sedelmeier, U. (2001) 'The Right and the Righteous? European Norms, Domestic Politics and the Sanctions against Austria', *Journal of Common Market Studies*, 39(1): 59–77.

Mestmäcker, E.-J. (1994) 'On the Legitimacy of European Law', *RabelsZ*, 58: 615–36.

Meyer, C. (2002) 'The Soft Side of Hard Coordination: Analysing Discourses on Fiscal Policy Publicised in Germany and Ireland', paper presented at the ECPR conference in Bordeaux, 26–28 September.

Meyer, C. and Kunstein, T. (forthcoming) 'A "Grand Débat Européen" on Economic Governance?', in I. Linsenmann, C. Meyer and W. Wessels (eds) *Economic Government of the EU*, Basingstoke: Palgrave Macmillan.

Michelman, F. I. (1999) *Brennan and Democracy*, Princeton, NJ: Princeton University Press.

—— (2001) 'Morality, Identity and "Constitutional Patriotism"', *Ratio Juris*, 14(3): 253–71.

Mikkeli, H. (1998) *Europe as an Idea and as an Identity*, London: Palgrave.

Miller, D. (1995) *On Nationality*, Oxford: Oxford University Press.

Miller, G. (1992) *Managerial Dilemmas: The Political Economy of Hierarchy*, Cambridge: Cambridge University Press.

Möllers, C. (2004) 'Transnational Governance without a Public Law?', in C. Joerges, L.-J. Sand and G. Teubner (eds) *Transnational Governance and Constitutionalism*, Oxford: Hart.

Monnet, J. (1978) *Memoirs*, New York: Doubleday.

Moravcsik, A. (1991) 'Negotiating the Single European Act: National Interests and Conventional Statecraft in the European Community', *International Organisation*, 45(1): 19–56.

—— (1993) 'Preferences and Power in the European Community: A Liberal Intergovernmentalist Approach', *Journal of Common Market Studies*, 31(4): 473–524.

—— (1998) *The Choice for Europe: Social Purpose and State Power from Messina to Maastricht*, London: UCL Press.

—— (2003) 'In Defence of the "Democratic Deficit": Reassessing Legitimacy in the European Union', in J. H. H. Weiler, I. Begg and J. Peterson (eds) *Integration in an Expanding European Union: Reassessing the Fundamentals*, Oxford: Blackwell.

Müller, H. (2001) 'International Relations as Communicative Action', in K. Fierke and K. E. Jørgensen (eds) *Constructing International Relations*, New York: Sharpe.

Mummendey, A. and Simon, B. (eds) (1997) *Identität und Verschiedenheit*, Bern: Hans Huber.

Murphy, L. and Nagel, T. (2002) *The Myth of Ownership: Taxes and Justice*, New York: Oxford University Press.

Musgrave, R. A. (1965) *Essays in Fiscal Federalism*, Washington: Brookings Institution.

—— (1969) 'Theories of Fiscal Federalism', *Public Finance*, 24(4): 521–32.

Nanetti, F. and Mameli, G. (2002) 'The Creeping Normative Role of the EC Commission in the Twin-track Struggle against State Aids and Harmful Tax Competition', *EC Tax Review*, 11(4): 185–91.

Nassehi, A. (2003) 'Der Begriff des Politischen und die doppelte Normativität der "soziologischen" Moderne', in A. Nassehi and M. Schroer (eds) *Der Begriff des Politischen*, Baden-Baden: Nomos.

Nello, S. and Smith, K. E. (1998) *The European Union and Central and Eastern Europe: The Implications of Enlargement in Stages*, Aldershot: Ashgate.

Neyer, J. (2003) 'Discourse and Order in the EU', *Journal of Common Market Studies*, 41(4): 687–706.

—— (2004) *Postnationale politische Herrschaft*, Baden-Baden: Nomos.

Niethammer, L. (2000) *Kollektive Identität: Heimliche Quellen einer unheimlichen Kultur*, Hamburg: Rowohlt.

Nino, C. S. (1996) *The Constitution of Deliberative Democracy*, New Haven, CT: Yale University Press.

O'Donnell, G. (1999) 'Horizontal Accountability in the New Democracies', in A. Schedler, L. Diamond and M. Plattner (eds) *The Self Restraining State*, Boulder, CO: L. Rienner.

Offe, C. (1984) 'Korporatismus als System nichtstaatlicher Makrosteuerung? Notizen über seine Voraussetzungen und demokratischen Gehalte', *Geschichte und Gesellschaft*, 10(2): 234–56.

—— (1998) ' "Homogeneity" and Constitutional Democracy: Coping with Identity Conflicts through Group Rights', *Journal of Political Philosophy*, 6(2): 113–41.

—— (1999) 'How Can We Trust Our Fellow Citizens?', in M. E. Warren (ed.) *Democracy and Trust*, Cambridge: Cambridge University Press.

Offe, C. and Preuss, U. K. (2003) 'Democratic Institutions and Moral Resources', in C. Offe (ed.) *Herausforderungen der Demokratie: Zur Integrations- und Leistungsfähigkeit politischer Insitutionen*, Frankfurt: Campus.

Olsen, J. P. (2004) 'Survey Article: Unity, Diversity and Democratic Institutions: Lessons from the European Union', *Journal of Political Philosophy*, 12(4): 461–95.

Orchard, V. (2002) 'Culture as Opposed to What? Cultural Belonging in the Context of National and European Identity', *European Journal of Social Theory*, 5(4): 419–33.

Osiander, A. (1994) *The States System of Europe, 1640–1990: Peacemaking and the Conditions of International Stability*, Oxford: Clarendon Press.

Padgen, A. (1996) *Lords of All the World: Ideologies of Empire in Spain, Britain and France c. 1500–c. 1800*, New Haven, CT: Yale University Press.

Pantel, M. (1999) 'Unity-in-diversity: Cultural Policy and EU Legitimacy', in T. Banchoff and M. P. Smith (eds) *Legitimacy and the European Union: The Contested Polity*, London: Routledge.

Parsons, T. (1951) *The Social System*, London: Routledge & Kegan Paul.

Pedler, R. H. and Schaefer, G. F. (eds) (1996) *Shaping European Law and Policy: The Role of Committees and Comitology in the Political Process*, Maastricht: European Institute for Public Administration.

Peters, A. (2004) 'European democracy after the 2003 Convention', *Common Market Law Review*, 41(1): 37–85.

Peters, B. (1991) *Rationalität, Recht und Gesellschaft*, Frankfurt: Suhrkamp.

—— (2002) 'A New Look at "National Identity"', *European Journal of Sociology*, 43(1): 3–32.

Petersson, O., Mørth, U., Olsen, J. P. and Tallberg, J. (2003) *Demokrati i EU – Demokratirådets rapport 2003*, Stockholm: SNS.

Pettit, P. (2001) 'Deliberative Democracy and the Discursive Dilemma', *Philosophical Issues* (supplement to *Nous*), 11: 268–99.

—— (2004) 'Depoliticizing Democracy', *Ratio Juris*, 17(1): 52–65.

Pijpers, A. (1996) 'The Netherlands: The Weakening Pull of Atlanticism', in C. Hill (ed.) *The Actors in Europe's Foreign Policy*, London: Routledge.

Pires, M. (2002) 'The Wrong Path of the European Union or Do the Stork and the Fox Have the Same Possibilities?', *EC Tax Review*, 11(3): 160–1.

Pistone, P. (2002) 'An EU Model Tax Convention', *EC Tax Review*, 11(3): 129–36.

Pogge, T. W. (1997) 'Creating Supra-national Institutions Democratically: Reflections on the European Union's "Democratic Deficit"', *Journal of Political Philosophy*, 5(2): 163–82.

Pollack, M. A. (2003) 'Control Mechanism or Deliberative Democracy? Two Images of Comitology', *Comparative Political Studies*, 36(1–2): 125–55.

Pridham, G. (1994) 'The International Dimension of Democratisation: Theory, Practice and Inter-Regional Comparisons', in G. Pridham, E. Herring and G. Sanford (eds) *Building Democracy?*, London: Leicester University Press.

Putnam, H. (1991) 'A Reconsideration of Deweyan Democracy', in M. Brint and W. Weaver (eds) *Pragmatism in Law and Society*, Boulder, CO: Westview Press.

Radaelli, C. (2003) 'The Code of Conduct against Harmful Tax Competition: Open Method of Coordination in Disguise?', *Public Administration*, 81(3): 513–31.

Ratner, S. (1967) *Taxation and Democracy in America*, New York: Wiley.

Rawls, J. (1971) *A Theory of Justice*, Oxford: Oxford University Press.

—— (1993) *Political Liberalism*, New York: Columbia University Press.

Regul, R. and Renner, W. (1966) *Finances and Taxes in European Integration*, Amsterdam: International Bureau of Fiscal Documentation.

Ricoeur, P. (1995) 'Reflections on a New Ethos for Europe', *Philosophy and Social Criticism*, 21(5): 3–13.

Rifkin, J. (2004) *The European Dream: How Europe's Vision of the Future Is Quietly Eclipsing the American Dream*, New York: Tarcher.

Risse, T. (2000) '"Let's Argue!": Communicative Action in World Politics', *International Organization*, 54(1): 1–39.

—— (2004) 'European Institutions and Identity Change: What Have We Learned?', in R. K. Herrmann, T. Risse and M. B. Brewer (eds) *Transnational Identities*, New York: Rowman & Littlefield.

Risse-Kappen, T. (1995) *Co-operation Among Democracies*, Princeton, NJ: Princeton University Press.

Roche, M. (2001) 'Citizenship, Popular Culture and Europe', in N. Stevenson (ed.) *Culture and Citizenship*, London: Sage.

Rokkan, S. (1966) 'Norway: Numerical Democracy and Corporate Pluralism', in R. A. Dahl (ed.) *Political Oppositions in Western Democracy*, New Haven, CT: Yale University Press.

Rosecrance, R. (1998) 'The European Union: A New Type of International Actor', in J. Zielonka (ed.) *Paradoxes of European Foreign Policy*, The Hague: Kluwer Law International.

Ruchet, O. (2004) 'European Integration, Representation, and Democracy: Andrew Moravcsik and the Legitimacy of the European Union', paper presented at the ECPR-SGEU Second Pan-European Conference on EU Politics, Bologna, Italy, 24–26 June. <http://www.jhubc.it/ecpr-bologna/docs/544.pdf>

Ruggie, J. G. (1996) *Constructing the World Polity: Essays on International Institutionalization*, London: Routledge.

Sabel, C. (1997) 'Constitutional Orders: Trust Building and Response to Change', in J. R. Hollingsworth and R. Boyer (eds) *Contemporary Capitalism: The Embeddedness of Institutions*, Cambridge: Cambridge University Press.

Sabel, C. and Zeitlin, J. (2003) 'Active Welfare, Experimental Government, Pragmatic Constitutionalism: The New Transformation of Europe', paper presented at the International Conference of the Hellenic Presidency of the European Union, 'The Modernization of the European Social Model and EU Policies and Instruments', Ioannina, Greece, 21–22 May.

Sadurski, W. (2002) 'Charter and Enlargement', *European Law Journal*, 8(3): 340–62.

Scanlon, T. M. (1998) *What We Owe to Each Other*, Cambridge, MA: Belknap Press of Harvard University Press.

Scharpf, F. W. (1975) *Demokratietheorie zwischen Utopie und Anpassung*, 2nd edn, Kronberg: Scriptor.

—— (1988) 'The Joint-decision Trap: Lessons from German Federalism and European Integration', *Public Administration*, 66(3): 239–78.

—— (1999a) *Governing in Europe: Effective and Democratic?*, Oxford: Oxford University Press.

—— (1999b) 'Demokratieprobleme in der europäischen Mehrebenenpolitik', in W. Merkel and A. Busch (eds) *Demokratie in Ost und West*, Frankfurt: Suhrkamp.

—— (2002a) 'The European Social Model', *Journal of Common Market Studies*, 40(4): 645–70.

—— (2002b) 'Regieren im europäischen Mehrebenensystem: Ansätze zu einer Theorie', *Leviathan*, 30(1): 65–92.

—— (2003a) 'Problem-Solving Effectiveness and Democratic Accountability in the EU', MPIfG Working Paper 03/1, Köln: MPIfG.

—— (2003b) 'Was man von einer europäischen Verfassung erwarten und nicht erwarten sollte', *Blätter für deutsche und internationale Politik*, 48(1): 49–59.

Schauer, H. (1997) 'Nationale und europäische Identität: Die unterschiedlichen Auffassungen in Deutschland, Frankreich und Grossbritannien', *Aus Politik und Zeitgeschichte*, 10: 3–13.

Schimmelfennig, F. (2001) 'The Community Trap: Liberal Norms, Rhetorical Action, and the Eastern Enlargement of the European Union', *International Organization*, 55(1): 47–80.

Schimmelfennig, F. and Sedelmeier, U. (eds) (2002) 'European Union Enlargement: Theoretical and Comparative Approaches', Special issue of the *Journal of European Public Policy*, 9(4).

Schlesinger, P. (2001) 'From Cultural Protection to Political Culture? Media Policy and the EU', in L.-E. Cederman (ed.) *Constructing Europe's Identity: The External Dimension*, London: L. Rienner.

Schmalz-Bruns, R. (1995) *Reflexive Demokratie: Die demokratische Transformation moderner Politik*, Baden-Baden: Nomos.

—— (1999) 'Deliberativer Supranationalismus: Demokratisches Regieren jenseits des Nationalstaats', *Zeitschrift für Internationale Beziehungen*, 6(2): 185–242.

—— (2002) 'The Normative Desirability of Participatory Governance', in H. Heinelt, P. Getimis and G. Kafkalas (eds) *Participatory Governance in Multi-level Context*, Opladen: Leske & Budrich.

Schmitter, P. C. (1969) 'Three Neofunctional Hypotheses about International Integration', *International Organization*, 23: 161–6.

—— (1998) 'Is It Really Possible to Democratize the Euro-Polity?', in A. Føllesdal and P. Koslowski (eds) *Democracy and the European Union*, Berlin: Springer.

—— (2003) 'Neo-neo-functionalism: Déjà vu All Over Again?', in A. Wiener and T. Diez (eds) *European Integration Theory*, Oxford: Oxford University Press.

Schön, W. (1999) 'Taxation and State Aid Law in the European Union', *Common Market Law Review*, 36(5): 911–36.

Schönlau, J. (2003) 'New Values for Europe? Deliberation, Compromise, and Coercion in Drafting the Preamble to the EU Charter of Fundamental Rights', in E. O. Eriksen, J. E. Fossum and A. J. Menéndez (eds) *The Chartering of Europe*, Baden-Baden: Nomos.

—— (2004) 'Time Was of the Essence: Timing and Framing Europe's Constitutional Convention', in C. Closa and J. E. Fossum (eds) *Deliberative Constitutional Politics in the EU*, ARENA Report 5/04, Oslo: ARENA.

Schuppert, G. F. (2003) *Staatswissenschaft*, Baden-Baden: Nomos.

Scott, J. and Trubek, D. (2002) 'Mind the Gap: Law and New Approaches to Governance in the European Union', *European Law Journal*, 8(1): 1–18.

Sedelmeier, U. (2000) 'Eastern Enlargement: Risk, Rationality and Role-compliance', in M. Green Cowles and M. Smith (eds) *The State of the European Union: Risks, Reform, Resistance, and Revival, Vol. 5*, Oxford: Oxford University Press.

Shaw, J. (1998) 'The Interpretation of European Citizenship', *The Modern Law Review*, 61(3): 293–317.

—— (2003) 'Process, Responsibility and Inclusion in EU Constitutionalism', *European Law Journal*, 9(1): 45–68.

Shore, C. (2000) *Building Europe: The Cultural Politics of European Integration*, London: Routledge.

—— (2004) 'Whither European Citizenship? Eros and Civilization Revisited', *European Journal of Social Theory*, 7(1): 27–44.

Siedentop, L. (2000) *Democracy in Europe*, London: Penguin.

Sjursen, H. (2002) 'Why Expand? The Question of Legitimacy and Justification in the EU's Enlargement Policy', *Journal of Common Market Studies*, 40(3): 491–513.

—— (2003) 'Understanding the Common Foreign and Security Policy: Analytical Building Blocks', in M. Knodt and S. Princen (eds) *Understanding the European Union's External Relations*, London: Routledge.

—— (2004) 'Changes to European Security in a Communicative Perspective', *Cooperation and Conflict*, 39(2): 107–28.

Sjursen, H. and Smith, K. (2001) 'Justifying EU Foreign Policy: The Logics Underpinning EU Enlargement', ARENA Working Paper 1/01, Oslo: ARENA.

Slaughter, A. M. (2004) *A New World Order*, Princeton, NJ: Princeton University Press.

Smith, A. (1992) 'National Identity and the Idea of Europe', *International Affairs*, 68(1): 129–35.

Smith, K. E. (2003) *European Union Foreign Policy in a Changing World*, Cambridge: Polity Press.

Smith, M. (1998) 'Does the Flag Follow Trade? "Politicisation" and the Emergence of European Foreign Policy', in J. Peterson and H. Sjursen (eds) *A Common Foreign Policy for Europe? Competing Perspectives on the CFSP*, London: Routledge.

Smith, R. M. (2003) *Stories of Peoplehood: The Politics and Morals of Political Membership*, Cambridge: Cambridge University Press.

Smith, S. (2000) 'The Increasing Insecurity of Security Studies: Conceptualising Security in the Last Twenty Years', in S. Croft and T. Terriff (eds) *Critical Reflections on Security and Change*, Portland, OR: Frank Cass.

Somers, M. (1994) 'The Narrative Constitution of Identity: A Relational and Network Approach', *Theory and Society*, 23(5): 605–49.

Soysal, Y. N. (2002) 'Locating Europe', *European Societies*, 4(3): 265–84.

Spinelli, A. (1966) *The Eurocrats – Conflict and Crisis in the European Community*, Baltimore, MD: Johns Hopkins University Press.

Stoker, G. (1998) 'Governance as Theory: Five Propositions', *International Social Science Journal*, 50(155): 17–28.

Stone Sweet, A. (2003) 'European Integration and the Legal System', in T. Börzel and R. Cichowski (eds) *The State of the European Union*, Oxford: Oxford University Press.

—— (2004) *The Judicial Construction of Europe*, Oxford: Oxford University Press.

Strauss-Kahn, D. (2004) *Construire l'Europe Politique*, report to the European Commission.

Taylor, C. (1985) *Human Agency and Language*, Cambridge: Cambridge University Press.

TEPSA (Trans European Policy Studies Association) (2003) 'The Broad Economic Policy Guidelines 2003', Study for the European Parliament. Draft Final Report. Available at <http://eucenter.wisc.edu/OMC/Papers/EconPolCoord/Tepsa draft2003.pdf>

Teubner, G. (2003) 'Globale Zivilverfassungen: Alternativen zur staatszentrierten Verfassungstheorie', *Zeitschrift für ausländisches öffentliches Recht und Völkerrecht*, 63(1): 1–27.

Thedvall, R. (2004) 'Transparency at Work: Transnational Co-operation and Cultural Dynamics in the Construction of a European Labour Market', mimeo, Stockholm: SCORE.

Tonra, B. (2001) *The Europeanisation of National Foreign Policy: Dutch, Danish and Irish Foreign Policy in the European Union*, Aldershot: Ashgate.

Trenz, H.-J. (2002) *Zur Konstitution politischer Öffentlichkeit in der Europäischen Union*, Baden-Baden: Nomos.

Trondal, J. and Veggeland, F. (2000) 'Access, Voice and Loyalty: The Representation of Domestic Civil Servants in the EU Committees', ARENA Working Paper 8/00, Oslo: ARENA.

Tsoukalis, L. (2003) *What Kind of Europe?*, Oxford: Oxford University Press.

Tucker, C. (2003) 'The Lisbon Strategy and the Open Method of Coordination: A New Vision and the Revolutionary Potential of Soft Governance in the European Union', paper presented at the Annual Meeting of the American Political Science Association, 28–31 August.

Tully, J. (2001) 'Introduction', in A.-G. Gagnon and J. Tully (eds) *Multinational Democracies*, Cambridge: Cambridge University Press.

—— (2002) 'The Unfreedom of the Moderns in Comparison to Their Ideals of Constitutional Democracy', *The Modern Law Review*, 65(2): 204–28.

Van de Steeg, M. (2002) 'Eine europäische Öffentlichkeit? Die Diskussion um die Osterweiterung der EU', *Berliner Debatte Initial*, 13(5–6): 57–66.

Van den Hurk, H. and Theunissen, A. (2001) 'Several Institutional and Fiscal Aspects of the European Economic Area', *EC Tax Review*, 10(1): 26–38.

Van Schendelen, M. (ed.) (1998) *EU Committees as Influential Policymakers*, Aldershot: Ashgate.

Verdun, A. (2000) 'Governing by Committee: The Case of Monetary Policy', in T. Christiansen and E. Kirchner (eds) *Committee Governance in the European Union*, Manchester: Manchester University Press.

Vertovec, S. and Rogers, A. (eds) (1998) *Muslim European Youth: Reproducing Ethnicity, Religion, Culture*, Aldershot: Ashgate.

Vestergaard, T. and Ørnsholt, K. (2003) 'The Open Method of Coordination: A Deliberative Governance Project in the EU?', Master thesis, Århus University, Department of Political Science.

Viehoff, R. and Segers, R. T. (eds) (1999) *Kultur, Identität, Europa: über die Schwierigkeiten und Möglichkeiten einer Konstruktion*, Frankfurt: Suhrkamp.

Villiers, T. (2001) *European Tax Harmonisation: The Impending Threat*, London: Centre for Policy Studies.

Waldron, J. (1999) *Law and Disagreement*, Oxford: Oxford University Press.

Walker, N. (2003) 'Constitutionalising Enlargement, Enlarging Constitutionalism', *European Law Journal*, 9(3): 362–85.

Wallace, H. (1993) 'Deepening and Widening: Problems of Legitimacy for the EC', in S. Garcia (ed.) *European Identity and the Search for Legitimacy*, London: Pinter.

Warren, M. (1996) 'What Should We Expect from More Democracy?', *Political Theory*, 24(2): 241–70.

Weiler, J. H. H. (1995) 'Does Europe Need a Constitution? Reflections on Demos, Telos and the German Maastricht Decision', *European Law Journal*, 1(3): 219–58.

—— (1999) *The Constitution of Europe: 'Do the New Clothes Have an Emperor?' and Other Essays on European Integration*, Cambridge: Cambridge University Press.

—— (2001a) 'European Democracy and the Principle of Toleration: The Soul of Europe', in F. Cerutti and E. Rudolph (eds) *A Soul for Europe, Vol. 1*, Leuven: Peeters.

—— (2001b) 'Federalism without Constitutionalism: Europe's Sonderweg', in K. Nicolaidis and R. Howse (eds) *The Federal Vision*, Oxford: Oxford University Press.

—— (2002) 'A Constitution for Europe? Some Hard Choices', *Journal of Common Market Studies*, 40(4): 563–80.

—— (2003) *Un'Europa Cristiana*, Milan: Rizzoli.

Wendt, A. (2003) 'Why a World State is Inevitable', *European Journal of International Relations*, 9(4): 491–542.

Wessels, W. (1998) 'Comitology: Fusion in Action: Politico-administrative Trends in the EU System', *Journal of European Public Policy* 5(2): 209–34.

Wessler, H. (1999) *Öffentlichkeit als Prozess*, Opladen: Westdeutscher Verlag.

White, B. (2001) *Understanding European Foreign Policy*, Basingstoke: Palgrave.

Wintle, M. (ed.) (1996) *Culture and Identity in Europe: Perceptions of Divergence and Unity in Past and Present*, Aldershot: Ashgate.

Woods, N. (2000) 'Order, Globalization and Inequality in World Politics', in D. Held and A. McGrew (eds) *The Global Transformations Reader*, Cambridge: Polity Press.

Wright, Q. (1957) 'The Mode of Financing Unions of States as a Measure of Their Degree of Integration', *International Organization*, 11: 30–40.

Zaller, J. (1992) *The Nature and Origins of Mass Opinion*, Cambridge: Cambridge University Press.

Zanon, F. (2003) 'EU Constitutional Reform and the Convention Method', *The International Spectator*, 4: 75–90.

Zielonka, J. and Mair, P. (eds) (2002) *The Enlarged European Union: Diversity and Adaptation*, London: Frank Cass.

Zielonka, J. and Pravda, A. (eds) (2001) *Democratic Consolidation in Eastern Europe, Vol. 2: International and Transnational Factors*, Oxford: Oxford University Press.

Zürn, M. (1996) 'Über den Staat und die Demokratie im europäischen Mehrebenensystem', *Politische Vierteljahresschrift*, 37(1): 27–55.

Official documents

Charter of Fundamental Rights (2000) *Charter of Fundamental Rights of the European Union*, Official Journal of the European Communities 2000/C 364/01.

Convention on the Charter (2000) CHARTE 4105/00, *Record of the first meeting of the Body to draw up a draft Charter of Fundamental Rights of the European Union (held in Brussels, 17 December 1999)*, Brussels, 13 January.

Council of Ministers (1973) *Declaration on the European Identity*, EC Bulletin 12-1973, Copenhagen, 14 December.

European Commission (1975) COM 392 final, *Proposal for a Directive of the Council concerning the harmonisation of systems of company taxation and of with-holding taxes on dividends.*

—— (1992) *Europe and the Challenge of Enlargement* (Prepared for the European Council, Lisbon, 26 and 27 June 1992), EC Bulletin, Supplement 3/92.

—— (1996) COM 546 final, *Taxation in the European Union. Report on the development of tax systems*, Brussels, 22 October.

—— (1997) *Agenda 2000: For a Stronger and Wider Union*, EU Bulletin, Supplement 5/97.

—— (2001a) COM 428 final, *European Governance: A White Paper*, Brussels, 25 July.

—— (2001b) COM 582 final, *Towards an Internal Market without Tax Obstacles: A Strategy for providing companies with a consolidated corporate tax base for their EU-wide activities*, Brussels, 23 October.

—— (2003) COM 726 final, *An Internal Market without company tax obstacles: achievements, ongoing initiatives and remaining challenges*, Brussels, 24 November.

—— (2004) COM 656 final, *Communication from the Commission to the Council and the European Parliament, Recommendation of the European Commission on Turkey's progress towards accession*, Brussels, 6 October.

European Convention (2002a) SN 1565/02, *Introductory speech by President V. Giscard d'Estaing to the Convention on the Future of Europe*, Brussels, 28 February.

—— (2002b) CONV 40/02, *Note on the plenary meeting – Brussels, 15 and 16 April*, Brussels, 25 April.

—— (2002c) CONV 345/02, *Contribution by Mr. P. Hain, member of the Convention – Constitutional treaty of the European Union*, Brussels, 15 October.

—— (2002d) CONV 354/02, *Final Report of Working Group II*, Brussels, 22 October.

—— (2002e) CONV 369/02, *Preliminary draft Constitutional Treaty*, Brussels, 28 October.

—— (2003a) CONV 489/03, *Contribution submitted by Mr. Dominique de Villepin and Mr. Joschka Fischer, members of the Convention*, Brussels, 16 January.

—— (2003b) CONV 574/1/03 REV1, *Reactions to draft Articles 1 to 16 of the Constitutional Treaty – Analysis*, Brussels, 26 February.

—— (2003c) CONV 601/03, *Summary report on the plenary session Brussels 27 and 28 February 2003*, Brussels, 11 March.

—— (2003d) CONV 850/03, *Draft Treaty establishing a Constitution for Europe*, Brussels, 18 July.

European Council (1978) *Declaration on Democracy*, Copenhagen, 8 April. EC Bulletin, 3/78.

—— (1993) SN 180/93, *Presidency Conclusions*, European Council Meeting in Copenhagen, 21 and 22 June.

—— (1999a) SN 150/99, *Presidency Conclusions*, European Council Meeting in Cologne, 3 and 4 June.

—— (1999b) SN 200/99, *Presidency Conclusions*, European Council Meeting in Tampere, 15 and 16 October.

—— (1999c) SN 300/99, *Presidency Conclusions*, European Council Meeting in Helsinki, 10 and 11 December.

—— (2001a) *Declaration on the Future of the Union*, Annex to the Treaty of Nice, Official Journal of the European Communities C 80/01: 85–6.

—— (2001b) SN 273/01, *Laeken Declaration on the Future of the European Union*, Laeken, 15 December.

—— (2003a) CIG 50/03, *Draft Treaty establishing a Constitution for Europe (following editorial and legal adjustments by the Working Party of IGC Legal Experts)*, Brussels, 25 November.

—— (2003b) *A Secure Europe in a Better World: European Security Strategy*, Brussels, 12 December.

—— (2004a) CIG 81/04, *Meeting of Heads of State or Government*, Brussels, 16 June.

—— (2004b) CIG 85/04, *Meeting of Heads of State or Government*, Brussels, 18 June.

—— (2004c) CIG 87/2/04 REV2, *Treaty establishing a Constitution for Europe*, Brussels, 29 October.

European Parliament, Committee on Constitutional Affairs (2003) PROVISIONAL 2003/0902(CNS), Par 1, *Draft Report on the Draft Treaty on the European Constitution and EP Opinion on the Convocation of the Intergovernmental Conference (IGC)*, Brussels, 5 August.

European Parliamentary Assembly (1962) *Rapport de la Commission politique de l'Assemblée Parlementaire Européenne sur les aspects politiques et institutionnels*, Document 122, 15 January.

Index

accountability 14, 25, 40–1, 50–3, 58, 62, 71, 76, 120, 230, 234, 255, 268; democratic 179–80; line of 11; mechanism 116; mutual 49

agreement 16, 67–9, 104, 108, 122, 176, 218, 235, 252; on common rules 178

allegiance 99, 144, 179; to the polity 256

Amsterdam, Treaty of 14, 156, 197, 220, 239, 252

anarchical international system 77, 171–2, 180

anti-Americanism, European 135–6

applicant states 237, 239, 241, 243–4, 250; in the European Convention 165–6

argumentation 16, 60, 67, 87, 102, 107, 176–7, 216, 227, 232, 239, 261; force of 149

authority 11, 37, 42, 46, 54, 80, 129, 244, 262–4; delegation 50, 76; democratic 38, 44, 75; seat of 23, 27

autonomy 19, 38, 45, 76–8, 101, 116, 170, 185, 199, 257; of citizens 63

bargaining 1, 14–16, 148, 161, 175–6, 217–20, 227–8, 232–3, 240, 263, 267–9; strategic 227

beliefs 89, 91, 97, 121, 141; collective 93; typologies of 98

bicephalous structure 5, 161–3, 258

Britain 147, 152, 165, 242

budget 188, 203, 210; deficits 197; European 192, 195

Charter of Fundamental Rights of the European Union 6, 14, 27, 44, 51–2, 161, 194, 198, 246, 248, 251, 257, 268; Convention 148, 161, 249

Christianity 133, 164

citizens 27, 34, 92, 100, 146–8, 164, 244, 263–5, 268; autonomous 23, 63; equality among 71–2, 187–9; of the European Union 43, 49–50, 115, 118, 157–8, 193–4, 253, 258, 260; rights and obligations 20, 99, 110, 161–2, 180

citizenship 30, 55, 141, 249, 266; economic 167; of the European Union 30, 117, 162, 244; national 137; political 24, 167, 188; see also demos

collective goals 268; attainment 265

collective identities 85, 90–3, 109–14, 129–30, 134, 239, 256, 261, 266; competing 93–4; deficit of 84, 94–6; evaluation criteria 94–7; inclusive 97; manipulated 96; supra European 128–31, 137, 139, 141; transnational 94

collective memories 95; of trauma 136

comitology 26, 51, 217, 220, 232, 254

Commission see European Commission

common good 17, 19, 23, 69, 98, 111, 263

Common Market 32, 143–6, 191, 206, 208

communication 18, 106, 141, 176, 217, 261, 268; flows 89, 112–13, 252, 256; political 87; rational 20, 177–8; spaces 140, 264

communitarian concept of the EU 156, 191, 193, 205

community 92; of communities 38, 155; cultural 128, 137, 153, 167, 188, 193; epistemic 25, 50, 52, 61–71, 224, 233, 239, 255, 266; of fate 244; moral 63, 74; political 34, 84, 188, 193–5, 261;